Choosing *Single* MOTHERHOOD

The Thinking Woman's Guide

Mikki Morrissette

HOUGHTON MIFFLIN COMPANY
BOSTON · NEW YORK

For information about permission to reproduce selections from this
book, write to trade.permissions@hmhco.com or to Permissions, Houghton Mifflin
Harcourt Publishing Company, 3 Park Avenue, 19th Floor, New York, New York 10016

www.hmhco.com

Library of Congress Cataloging-in-Publication Data
Morrissette, Mikki.
Choosing single motherhood : the thinking woman's
guide / Mikki Morrissette.
p. cm.
"Originally published by Be-Mondo Publishing, 2005."
Includes bibliographical references.
ISBN 978-0-618-83332-0
1. Single mothers. I. Title.
HQ759.915.M673 2008 649'.1'0243 — dc22 2008009394

PRINTED IN THE UNITED STATES OF AMERICA

BOOK DESIGN BY VICTORIA HARTMAN
DOH 10 9 8 7 6 5 4
4500630638

Visit choosingsinglemotherhood.com for more about this book and
its author. Visit choicemoms.org for up-to-date information, resources,
and many innovative tools specially created for the Choice Mom
community. Note: At the request of certain interviewees, the following
names appearing in this book are pseudonyms: Vanessa, Dora,
Sara, Beth, Morgan, Max, Ted, and Greg.

Choosing Single Motherhood

Dedicated to
Sophia and Dylan
who make everything
possible

Contents

❧

Acknowledgments x

Introduction: About the Author, About the Book xii

STAGE 1: TYPICAL INNER CONFLICTS · 1

1. ## AM I SINGLE-MOTHER MATERIAL? 5

   Can I handle it? Do I have the proper motivation? Is it fair
   to the child? Do I have enough resources to be a good single
   parent? . . . transitioning to motherhood

2. ## CAN I AFFORD IT? 22

   Spending habits . . . childcare costs and tips . . . big-ticket
   expenses . . . long-term issues . . . the cost of conception

3. ## GRIEVING THE CHILDHOOD DREAM 43

   Living with grief . . . choosing to wait . . . getting to the
   roots . . . when you keep walking

4. ## WILL MY COMMUNITY ACCEPT US? 60

   "You are selfish" . . . why the opposition? . . . why do we
   care? . . . helping the child . . . . revisiting the *Murphy Brown*
   vs. Quayle debate

STAGE 2: IS IT FAIR TO THE CHILD? • 83

5. THE IMPACT OF A SINGLE-PARENT HOME   85

What the research says . . . portrait of a successful single
parent . . . how Choice Moms succeed . . . moral parenting

6. GROWING UP WITHOUT A FATHER   115

The skepticism . . . two loving parents . . . balance . . .
gender identification . . . self-control . . . kids' perceptions
of fathers

STAGE 3: CHOOSING THE METHOD • 139

7. KNOWN DONOR: PROS AND CONS   141

What can go wrong . . . what can go right: child's identity
and medical history . . . questions to ask and understand . . .
reflections on being a known donor

8. USING DONOR INSEMINATION   171

Alphabet soup . . . the ethics . . . open-identity option . . .
who are the donors? . . . choosing a donor . . . the process

9. CHOOSING ADOPTION   201

Thinking about age, race, special needs, contact with birth
family . . . expense . . . finding assistance . . . the home
study . . . transracial adoption

STAGE 4: DAY-TO-DAY PARENTING • 229

10. DEALING WITH THE STRESS   231

How to reduce stress . . . how do we handle it alone? . . .
the difference a partner makes . . . tips for the caregiver's
soul . . . having two

11. ANSWERING THE DADDY QUESTION   259

Answering what kids really want to know . . . basic dos and don'ts . . . age-appropriate expert advice . . . when kids meet donor dads

12. CONFRONTING IDENTITY ISSUES   282

Why it matters to the kids . . . typical ages and stages . . . the donor-conceived child . . . the adopted child . . . the transracial family

13. HOW TO RAISE A WELL-BALANCED CHILD   313

Meet the experts . . . the basics . . . understanding the child . . . community . . . mutual respect . . . authoritative parenting . . . the four-point game plan . . . raising a boy

STAGE 5: THE LEGACY OF CHOICE · 337

14. OF POLITICS AND POLICY   339

Who gets to try? . . . "I was turned away five times" . . . who can be a donor? . . . taking it to court . . . rights around the world . . . changes in adoption . . . where gays and lesbians need not apply . . . insurance . . . how marriage policy pertains

15. HOW ARE THE KIDS TURNING OUT?   365

Social development . . . effect of stigma . . . will Choice Kids marry? . . . the mothers' perspectives . . . strengths and weaknesses . . . conversations with Kyla, Greg, Cambra, Laurabeth, Ryan, Grace, Zac

Conclusion: Connecting the Dots   394
Notes   405
Resources   420

Acknowledgments

As with my two children, I am solely responsibly for creating, fine-tuning, and delivering this labor of love to the wider world — yet I could not have done it alone. There are so many people who enabled this book to happen, starting with my agent, Theresa Park, who encouraged me to pursue the idea over a year-long development process and then made sure it got into the hands of the editor Jane Rosenman at Houghton Mifflin . . . the designer Mary Leir, who has given a tremendous amount of invaluable time helping me create an online community for Choice Moms . . . my parents (and various child-care providers) for giving me the child-free time to write . . . Sophia and Dylan for finding ways to amuse themselves as I pressed forward.

In a book with so many different sources, covering so much territory, it is impossible to list every one of the resources that helped to educate me. But I would like to single out a few of the therapists, child experts, and social scientists who offered time for consultation and chapter reviews. I am particularly grateful to Richard Weissbourd for his thoughtful critiques, to Stephanie Coontz for her inspiration, to Kyle Pruett for his balanced advice, and to Michael Gurian for his spiritual wisdom. Elaine Gordon, Joann Paley Galst, Diana Greenwald, Carole Lieber Wilkins, Lois

Gilman, Amanda Baden, and Charlotte Patterson gave me helpful insight during the process. Andrew Vorzimer, Jody DeSmidt, and Ami Jaeger offered time for legal discussion. And the wonderful resources provided by the Donor Conception Network and Diane Allen of Infertility Network were invaluable.

Most of all, I am in debt to every single woman who shared her story with me — on the record, off the record, anonymously, or for attribution. Starting with Jane Mattes, the founder of Single Mothers by Choice . . . including Wendy Kramer, the cofounder, with her son, of the Donor Sibling Registry . . . and ending with the single women who offered to review chapters, in order to keep me focused on answering the right questions in an effective way. Especially Renai Gallagher, who was as generous with her feedback as a good friend.

Introduction

About the Author, About the Book

When I was a little girl, I spent more time playing tag and shooting baskets than taking care of dolls. In junior high school I was more interested in starting a school newspaper and doing "roots" research than in cooking and sewing classes; I consistently earned my lowest grades in home economics.

In high school I launched another school newspaper and worked as a sports reporter at the community paper. I did very little babysitting. My best friend was a gay male, and I generally spent my weekends four-wheeling and playing poker with seven guy pals. I had my share of swooning over dark-haired boys with slight builds, but I dated only two boys and had no desire to attend prom.

In college, I still had primarily platonic male friends. I became sports editor of the University of Minnesota newspaper, worked in the press box at Minnesota North Stars hockey games, sometimes wrote about the team for the Associated Press, and dabbled in sports broadcasting.

In sum, I tended to be a tomboy, with no daydreams of marriage and children and domestic life. My dream instead was to work in magazine journalism, so I moved to New York City when I was 22. I had one acquaintance there — someone I'd met when he was covering a swim meet for *Sports Illustrated* during my internship with U.S. Olympic Swimming. When I was 25, we married. Seven years later we divorced. At 36, after dabbling in dating and falling in love once, I met someone who would enable me to fulfill my new dream, the one that had started growing in me about becoming a single mom. My daughter, Sophie, was born in 1999.

A few years later I decided Sophie should have a sibling. The same donor was used. When I was five months pregnant I met Dave, my future husband. He and Sophie were in the delivery room when my son, Dylan, was born in 2004. Ten months later, Dave and I married.

Women You Will Meet in This Book

Maybe my story isn't typical, but one thing I've learned as a journalist is that no story is typical. I personally know the stories of more than 300 single women who have decided, generally in their thirties and forties, whether, when, and how to become a mother. I have largely met an incredible group of intelligent, professional, and emotionally together women.

Some of these women are "Thinkers" — the term used by Jane Mattes, founder of the Single Mothers by Choice organization, to describe women considering single motherhood. Some are "Tryers," and have taken steps to conceive or adopt. And many are "Choice Moms" — my term, used throughout this book, for women who consciously and responsibly choose single motherhood after asking serious questions about what the lifestyle means, for self and child.

> *I define a Choice Mom as someone who proactively seeks to become a nurturing mother on her own.*

In my case, ironically, I didn't give a lot of serious thought to Choice Motherhood before I jumped in. It simply seemed the logical next step for me. I had a high-paying job in magazine publishing. I owned my New York City apartment, debt-free thanks to some good early real estate investments. I'd done extensive travel and didn't feel that there was any interest I hadn't already pursued except one — the long-term commitment of motherhood.

At the time, although this was 1998, I didn't know anyone who had chosen single motherhood on purpose. The concept had vaguely been planted during the hoopla that surrounded the Dan Quayle/Murphy Brown social debate of the early 1990s. I simply knew that my independence and fairly recent divorce didn't make me marriage material anytime soon. Dating a divorced father of one had made me realize, in my midthirties, that I did (to my surprise) deeply want to be a parent. So, being goal-driven as I am, I set out to make it happen.

Like me, many of the women I have talked to have been passionate about professional goals and hobbies, but not about dating — and realize that the time is right to throw themselves into motherhood. Others are serial daters who have not yet found anyone they want to have a child with. Some are lesbians with no intention of marrying. Others are open to the idea of wedded bliss, someday — just not in time to satisfy their urge for a child. Some accidentally conceive, and realize maybe it had subconsciously been their goal. Others are simply taken by surprise when it happens, and then dedicate themselves to becoming the best parents they can be.

I've met women like Brooke, a former model and current television reporter. To be honest, I was stunned when I sat down with her. She is a tall, thin blond with poise and obvious intelligence, and I wondered, despite myself, why she wasn't married. She explained that she had held on to her dream of finding a husband until she approached her forties and hadn't yet found the man she wanted to settle down with. After being a "deep thinker" for a year, she organized a girls' night to vote on which of her five potential anonymous donors she should choose. A few weeks after we spoke, she confirmed that an insemination had worked. She is now a Choice Mom.

I've met Vanessa, who truthfully would prefer to raise a child with a long-time friend of hers. But his choice of a career in the military conflicts with her law career, and she has no interest in following him around until he completes his tour in six years. She was hoping to conceive with his sperm before he left for Afghanistan, but was unsuccessful and is waiting for his next leave.

I know women like Dona, the mother of a college-age son. She decided to keep her child, in a conservative Southern community, after an unplanned pregnancy with a man she did not want to marry. "My friends thought I'd lost my mind," she recalled. "Now they're all divorced with kids, and think I was the smartest one of them all. My attitude is that life is an adventure. Of course there's going to always be tough times. Some days I don't want my baby to grow up, other days he doesn't grow up fast enough. But you can let things drive you crazy or let it go. In the end, we've been lucky, being able to spend more time together than most parents and kids do. We've had it very special." Dona is an obviously strong-willed woman.

Janet, a university professor in the Southwest, told me with utmost confidence that her daughter "has a really great situation in her life. A mother, grandparents, aunt, and uncle who adore her. An amazing community around us. More than a hundred people came to her baby-naming ceremony. She has a great deal of security in her life. Maybe someday she'll mourn the absence of a father, and I'm here to support her if she does." To her surprise, years later she found the yin to her yang and is marrying.

I learned the amazing story of Diana, who adopted a 13-month-old neglected child. Years of Choice Motherhood later, her daughter had become a top student at an Ivy League college, and had parlayed curiosity about the differences between her adoptive mother's Jewish background and her own Puerto Rican roots into a passion for understanding other cultures. She was described by a former teacher as someone who is "open to the world, open to explore new, challenging ideas, and open to learn about life far from her milieu, while listening closely to her inner voice. She shows a maturity that is rare for most students her age and is not cowed by anyone."

My friend Shelly talked with a man about her desire to become a Choice Mom — then, to his surprise, became pregnant the first time she had unprotected sex with him. They share partial custody. She has since adopted an African-American son in an open domestic adoption, which includes regular contact with the teenage birth father (and, she hopes, with the birth mother too someday).

Why This Book?

As my conversations with women continued, I began to realize the universality of the concerns of these women — particularly those who were thinking about making this choice, who tend to be hungry for insight from experienced Choice Moms. All too often, as mothers yield to the busy schedules of school-age children, their collective wisdom disappears from online discussion groups and single-mom get-togethers. There are many pioneering Choice Moms who have guided their children from infancy through the budding awareness of childhood, through rebellious teenage years and into young adulthood. But their advice — as well as the perspectives of their children — has not been readily available to the growing audience.

This book intends to correct that absence.

It's impossible to get a good approximation of how many women contemplate this choice each year, since so many women decide not to pursue single motherhood. But I do suspect that tens of thousands of single, unpartnered women end up saying yes to motherhood each year, based on the following:

1. Roughly 185,000 single women ages 30–44 give birth each year, based on a 2004 U.S. Census report.[1] Another report revealed that 134,000 unmarried women between the ages of 35 and 50 gave birth in 2001, based particularly in New

York City, Chicago, Detroit, Los Angeles, Philadelphia, Boston, Miami, Dallas, Seattle, and San Francisco, in that order. One study indicates that roughly half of these women are living with a partner,[2] which could mean that 50,000 single, mature women who know about birth control give birth each year.

2. Many of these single women who conceive use donor insemination, as opposed to a known donor or former partner. Industry speculation (15 years old) is that there are 30,000 inseminations each year. Roughly one third of the clients are single women.*

3. This number does not include the many single women who adopt. Industry speculation is that there are roughly 125,000 adoptions each year, and an estimated one-third are by single parents.

No matter what the actual number, today's growing population of women considering single motherhood could benefit from comprehensive, up-to-date information about the implications of this choice, as well as the perspectives of experienced Choice Moms and Choice Kids.

As a journalist who made the decision to become a Choice Mom — twice — I wanted to get a closer look at this lifestyle and how it affects our children. I wanted to share what I was learning, first- and secondhand, about the realities, and myths, of Choice Motherhood. I wanted to talk to experts who had specialized insight into child development, identity issues, and legal concerns. I wanted to dig up and summarize some of the excellent resources already out there.

The result of my quest is this book. Among other things, we will look at the faces behind the trend — real women who are making this decision, and their concerns as they contemplate the

---

* Single women account for nearly half of the business at California Cryobank, one of the world's largest sperm banks, which ships about 2,500 ampules of sperm each month. Some places have more limited work with single clients, so one-third is a safer estimate.

choice. We will consider advice and wisdom on the common questions women struggle with: Can I afford to do this? Should I adopt, use anonymous donor insemination, or find a known donor? How do women handle the stress of solo parenting?

Although I wrote the book to answer typical questions before making the decision, women who have already become Choice Moms also will benefit from much of the advice. The chapters in Stage 5 walk through practical and emotional issues Choice Moms face with their growing children.

Although I kept my focus narrowed to issues of concern among single women — rather than the many lesbian couples and single men who are turning to this option — I could not ignore some of the political and policy issues that affect many of us (in particular, see chapter 14).

Although the material is written for a U.S. audience, I know from contact I have with Choice Moms in other countries that many of our concerns are universal.

How the Trend Began

During the 1980s and 1990s, as more women entered their thirties with financial and emotional security of their own creation, child rearing without a mate seemed like the logical step for many. Some of them accidentally became pregnant and felt empowered enough to decide against an abortion or adoption plan. Others felt their commitment to a career was cheating them out of a personal life, and opted to fill in the blanks by creating their own family. Still others, coming of age in a divorce culture, saw Choice Motherhood as a positive alternative to putting a child through the traumas of an unstable marriage.

In essence, the pioneers of Choice Motherhood grew up feeling better able to create their own destinies than previous generations of women did. Some women grew up learning that marrying young primarily to have children, without being particularly invested or balanced in their relationship with a partner, was a mistake. They held out for the right partner, and then felt educated, connected, and well paid enough to move into motherhood as planned, even before the partner came along.

"Twenty years ago middle-class women believed it took a man to have a child, but that's no longer true," said Rosanna Hertz, chair of the Women's Studies Department at Wellesley College, to a *Newsweek* reporter in 2001.[3] Hertz, author of a sociological look at the trend, *Single by Chance, Mothers by Choice* (Oxford, 2006), said it was hard to find women to interview when she started in the mid-1990s, but "now they're all over — next door, at the playground, in your kid's classroom. They've become a normal part of the terrain."

In previous lives, Hertz said, women would have settled by marrying Mr. Almost Right, but today settling can mean having the baby even if you can't find the husband.

As I talked with Mattes, the founder of Single Mothers by Choice, I could detect her surprise at the way things have changed since she became a single mother in the early 1980s. "Now nearly everyone I talk with knows of at least one person — a neighbor, a cousin, a coworker — who has become a single mother by choice."

When Mattes chose to become the unmarried mother to her son, the decision was a much lonelier one to make. It was more subject to disapproval and scorn than it is today. That's why she formed SMC organization (www.singlemothersbychoice.com), where Thinkers, Tryers, and Mothers find support groups.

Why the Trend Is Growing

When the TV character Murphy Brown decided to become an unmarried mother in 1992, the sitcom caused a national stir, thanks partly to public denunciation of the message by Vice President Dan Quayle. But ten years later, *Friends, Frasier, Will and Grace,*

Sex and the City, and other popular shows have embraced the lifestyle option with little fanfare. Today, television and theater roll out plot lines featuring single women, fertility clinics, and sperm donors without controversy.

One reason for the growth of the trend is that there are increasing numbers of single professional women working in large cities across the country. In Los Angeles, San Francisco, Boston, and New York in particular, untraditional households are simply more acceptable.

Yet even women I spoke with in Kansas and Florida and Arizona were turning to the option as a way to fulfill a traditional dream of having children. Family-oriented women in their early thirties were aware of biological deadlines, thanks partly to books and articles pointing out how quickly fertility can decline after the age of 35. For them it was simply too important to become a mother than to wait for an opportunity to start a family with a husband who might not show up.

Also, pioneers of Choice Motherhood have largely been successful in raising well-adjusted children, which has helped legitimize the option, sociologist Jane Bock pointed out to the *Boston Globe* in 2002. And the image of single motherhood expanded from that of welfare-dependent teenagers to include strong, empowered women such as Jodie Foster, Angelina Jolie, Meg Ryan, and Sheryl Crow.

High rates of divorce in the 1970s and 1980s made single parenthood common. A woman raised by a lone parent because of divorce can be less intimidated by the choice — and in some cases, not willing to risk that trauma with her own child. According to *Newsweek,* "For many women, the barrier to marriage may be that they care too much about it, not too little, and they want to get it right. If they can't find the perfect soul mate of their dreams, they'd rather stay single. So they're postponing that walk down the aisle until after college, graduate school or starting a career and putting a little money in the bank ... Some of these women are the adult children of divorce, who don't want to make their own offspring suffer the pain of watching a parent leave."[4]

National Public Radio commentator Lori Gottlieb wrote in the *Atlantic Monthly* about her own decision to become a Choice Mother.[5] "Unlike women a decade or two our seniors, we took it for granted that we could do anything we wanted," she said. "The way my generation sees it, if you're not forced to compromise, why should you? But sometimes we forget that if you don't choose anything, eventually you're left with nothing."

Every woman's story is different as to how they came to a point in their lives when Choice Motherhood seemed like the decision it was time to make. One single woman I talked to had been married eight years before divorcing. When she was growing up, her parents had a high-conflict marriage, made more difficult because of alcoholism. She hadn't had a relationship with her mother for ten years. Her sister had become pregnant at the age of 18, and her daughter, then 13, had a father who was an unhealthy influence in her life. This no-nonsense woman knew that she did not want to put a child through the same conflicts.

Yet she also realized her dating had gotten off track. "Every man I dated I was looking at as potential father material for my child, not as a partner for myself," she told me. "I pushed them away by wanting to be a mom so bad. I wanted to fast-forward everything to know if it was going to work."

Some women believe it is more responsible to have a child alone than to get married for the sake of having a child. Others feel that if they earn an income while being a good parent, the lack of partner should make no significant difference. And still others wonder what they can do to make up for the lack of a father in the home.

The Goals of This Book

America's sense of family identity continues to evolve so rapidly that we rarely take time to understand what it means for our children. Reproductive technologies, the overwhelming demand for international adoption, and the needs of foster-care agencies are making the "conventional" harder to define. Court battles are challenging the definition of "social" and "genetic" parent. Popular culture is portraying diverse families on TV and movie screens. Yet children today still pick up on the fact that large segments of society prefer the biological "mom, dad, and kids" model. What impact, really, can Choice Motherhood have on our children?

Some of the concerns we will explore in this book include:

- What research says about the influence of growing up with a single parent; how and when to answer a child's "daddy" questions; and the potential identity issues of transracially adopted and donor-conceived children
- The politics of choice, including the simmering debate about how children — and society, by extension — are affected by fatherless homes
- How grown children of pioneering Choice Mothers feel about the way they were raised and the impact it has had on their life

Whether you are a Choice Mom, contemplating single motherhood, or simply curious about the faces behind the trend, the intention of this book is to offer an in-depth look at the reasons women make this choice, as well as the obstacles, politics, and psychology they confront along the way.

Although I tend to be encouraging, my purpose is not to promote Choice Motherhood as a lifestyle for everyone — it is not the right decision for many to make. Rather, my goal is to offer an honest and realistic picture of what the lifestyle is and is not, so that all Choice Kids are raised by mothers who consciously, and continuously, prepare for the challenge.

— MIKKI MORRISSETTE
September 2007

STAGE 1

Typical Inner Conflicts

I was one of the lucky ones. Before I became a Choice Mom, I was oblivious to the issues that many Thinking Women face. I didn't worry about whether I could afford it, because I had a high-paying job. I didn't worry about whether I could handle the stress of solo parenting, because I assumed that I could handle anything. I didn't grieve the fact that I was embarking on motherhood without a lifetime partner, because I had never been a fan of convention. So I was lucky — at the start, anyway. Ignorance can be bliss.

Shortly after I became pregnant I started to freak out about whether I would actually like being a mother. Maybe I'd been foolish to think it was the logical next step of my life . . . maybe I was supposed to stay solo, traveling and writing and having experiences as a lone wanderer in the universe. Wouldn't my life stop if I was locked inside four walls changing diapers and, ohmigod, actually preparing three meals a day, and helping someone else turn into a person who had experiences? *Bump.*

After my daughter was born, in that first year of often lonesome, scary motherhood I discovered many moments of sadness that I wasn't sharing her development, and mine, with someone else. My local friends were single and child-less, with no real interest in being part of my motherhood journey. My family was literally a thousand miles away. I didn't have a childhood dream of "husband, wife, and kids" to grieve, but I found myself grieving something I couldn't even define. *Bump.*

After three months of unpaid leave, I was ready to return to my well-paid job — only to learn that I was being "elimi-nated." *CRASH!*

Talk about a rude awakening to the realities of life.

In hindsight, I'm happy I was oblivious beforehand to how much my life would change. After talking to more than 100 women about their struggles in reaching this decision — and their struggles after — I understand how lucky I was to avoid many of the typical concerns before Sophie was born.

Although I had no regrets about being a Choice Mom, my hard-won lessons about the bumps in the road made it more difficult to make a decision the second time. It took about two years of inner debate before I chose Choice Motherhood again, and Dylan was born.

Today's Choice Mothers feel less stigma about their deci-sion than did pioneers of the 1980s. But that doesn't mean it's an easy choice. Women today tend to focus less on whether having a child will be seen as "legitimate" for her and the child, and more on whether the decision itself is a le-gitimate one: Will I have the strength and energy to be a good mother? Do I have the financial, emotional, and support re-sources to pull it off? Should I wait a little longer to see if life turns a new corner?

If you're struggling with some of the typical "Should I?" conflicts, the next four chapters have been written to help you through.

"Am I Single-Mom Material?" looks at some of the most common reasons women hesitate as they contemplate this choice.

"Can I Afford It?" explores the number one issue of concern, finances, based on results of an informal survey I did in 2003.

"Grieving the Childhood Dream" includes personal stories of women who came to this decision reluctantly, having dreamed for years of raising children with a lifetime partner.

"Will My Community Accept Us?" examines the disapproval women have faced from family, friends, and other members of their local network. It also revisits the national conversation Vice President Dan Quayle launched in 1992 about Choice Motherhood when he decried the TV show *Murphy Brown* for mocking the importance of fathers.

NOTE: *These are very common concerns. While the material here is ultimately reassuring — so many women have addressed them and gone on to Choice Motherhood — there are many more women who have chosen not to become a single mother because of these questions. Listen closely to yourself.*

· 1 ·

Am I Single-Mother Material?

One morning when I was riding to work on the subway, visibly pregnant, I ran into an acquaintance who congratulated me on having the courage to become a single mother. She was a highly paid corporate lawyer in her early forties and had considered but rejected the idea of Choice Motherhood for herself. As she stood squeezed between the elbows of fellow commuters, she told me she was too "tightly wound" to take care of a child without a partner.

I confidently told her that I had always loved a challenge. But I didn't tell her about the night, a few weeks after my pregnancy test was positive, when I melted down in my small New York City living room, feeling isolated, panicked, and completely unsure about whether I had what it would take to be a good mother.

She would never know about the moment, a few days after returning from the hospital with my newborn girl, when I wearily watched my mother diaper Sophie yet again, after I'd finished nursing yet again, while my father prepared dinner yet again, and I wondered how I would ever manage alone.

She would never hear me internally disparage my parenting skills in comparison to others, as I saw the patience a friend had with the monotony of her preschooler's play, or as I admired the playful water-balloon-throwing spirit of another mom.

You could have the confidence of Joan of Arc, but no matter who you are there will be many moments spent wondering if you have what it takes to be a Good Mother. And you will have worries and fears no matter where you are in the process, whether you are thinking about the choice — should I wait? go ahead? or is remaining childless okay for me? — or whether you are in the middle of a pregnancy or adoption, or well into the realities of taking care of an infant, toddler, or teen.

Although only you can decide whether you have the temperament to handle the inevitable stresses of being a Choice Mother, remember that doubts about your strength, energy, and patience are natural. In this chapter we examine typical situations that may trigger these doubts, and how women have persevered in the face of sometimes overwhelming emotions about their ability to be a good parent.

The "Before" Time: Can I Handle It?

Some women have such a strong desire for motherhood that they wonder even in their twenties why they have to wait for a husband. Others, fortyish, wonder if they want a child simply because they feel they are supposed to. But most women I've talked to fall somewhere in between: I'd like a child, I'd like a husband, I'm in my thirties and not sure if I should wait and hope my situation changes. Or, I know I want to do this — the question is how?

The fears of any woman who considers motherhood are largely the same, whether she is married or not: Do I have the "right" personality to handle it? Am I too selfish to take care of someone else? Will I regret not having the time, money, or energy for spontaneous nights out? Am I ready to commit myself to nurturing a child for 18 years? Have I taken care of my baggage? If I've never had a burning desire to take care of a child before, can I trust my motives now?

These questions take on added significance for the single woman because of the lack of a backup parent who can help balance daily life and perceived character weaknesses. As one Thinker told me frankly: "I can be selfish and domineering. Best of all worlds would be to have a partner so my personality impact is diluted on the child, and he or she doesn't have to bear my moods alone."

For women who do hope to find a partner someday, it is daunting to consider that it tends to be more difficult to date after a child comes. It's not impossible (see chapter 3), and some women report that the shifting of priorities seems to make it easier to find someone, but odds are that parenting will replace partnering in the Choice Mother's future.

Many women (I was one) have very little experience taking care of young children and have no way of knowing if it's the right role for them. Some women have tested themselves with volunteer work with youth-oriented organizations and babysitting friends' kids.

One Choice Mom I know had an unusually difficult time deciding whether she had the inner resources to become a mother. She had been sexually abused as a child and never had been able to develop a trusting relationship with a man. She didn't think she would be comfortable having the physical exams necessary for insemination. "Even if I adopted, I was very concerned that my fear of men might be passed on to a daughter, or unintentionally taken out on a son," she told me. "Would my inability to be physically touched leave me unable to nurture my child?"

In the end, with the support of family and friends, she conceived a daughter through anonymous insemination and discovered that "all my fears were unfounded. I had no trouble bonding with my child." When we talked, she was considering having a second. "The one thing I have learned is that I do have a tendency to exaggerate the potential pitfalls," she said, "and that life does somehow manage to go on despite all the potholes in the road."

Do I have the proper motivation?
Many women wonder if the reasons they want to have a child are "good enough" to warrant going ahead. Some realize they wish to

replicate the loving relationship they had with a parent. Others understand they don't want to grow old alone — they see how happy their parents are to have kids and grandkids around them. Or they see the lonesome aunt and want to avoid a similar fate.

But being able to say out loud that you want to fulfill a human need for family and companionship isn't easy. Wanting to nurture a child in order to make yourself happy sounds selfish to some people. But it's generally the same reason a married person might give if asked. The difference is that most married people aren't asked why they want to be a parent.

> *Knowing they will need to justify to others their decision to have a child can make single women question whether they deserve it — can they convince others of their right to self-fulfillment?*

My conversations with Choice Moms reveal, however, that justifying your decision to others is much less important after you have a child. As long as your child is happy, that's the only person whose opinion matters. (We'll deal with your child's happiness with your decision in future chapters.)

Am I too selfish?

Not surprisingly, this is a big question for many single women who have become accustomed to doing things how they want to, when they want to. It was certainly one of my big questions before I gave birth. My social life had begun slowing down already because of my professional life, so I wasn't put off by the idea of being at home so much. But I wondered how I'd handle being at the mercy of a child when I hadn't had to mesh with anyone else's life since leaving my marriage six years earlier.

As soon as Sophie was born, however, I didn't want to be apart from her. She stayed with me every moment that we were in the hospital, and we were nearly inseparable until she started preschool. Which is not to say that I didn't covet my alone time. I felt liberated each time I walked the streets of New York City solo in that first year while Sophie was home with the babysitter: nothing but my backpack and a subway token . . . how free!

It does take a leap of faith to trust that the changes in your social life will seem worth it. When you're on the other side of motherhood, it can be daunting to think you'll be stuck inside four walls after the baby comes. As Amy told me when she was a Thinker, she was reluctant "to give up the life I have now. No more spur-of-the-moment weekends away, no more theater subscriptions, no more long dinners out, no more peace and quiet when I close my door."

After motherhood, there are solutions to break the monotony of a more sedentary life. Some mothers arrange for a scheduled night out every few weeks — any more can seem like a hassle for a busy mom, any less doesn't give her the mental break she might not realize she needs. Another advantage of the scheduled night is that babysitters can be lined up in advance.

As one woman said, before her daughter was born she went out about four times a week. "Since then, it's not so much that I can't go out, but I am so tired that I'm very happy reading a book, taking a long bath, or watching a movie. I go out about once a month now. This has been such a learning experience for me. I miss the freedom of jumping in my car and going wherever I please. Most of my friends don't come around as much now that the novelty of me having a baby has worn off. It's bittersweet, but I do feel I know what's truly important now."

In my case, with two kids and a husband I rarely see, I tend to have a scheduled "date night" each week. It's a great way to refresh and feel like an adult again.

You will miss your freedom, sometimes for months at a time while your child is going through a particular stage. And it's important to know that dating — and developing long-term relationships — likely will be more difficult. But parenting is a "transformative experience," one therapist told me, that typically triggers unanticipated changes in individual values and priorities. When I heard from Amy after she had been a Choice Mom for more than a year, she said, "Yes, I do occasionally miss the spontaneity, but I don't at all miss the solitude, and I never, ever doubt I did the right thing."

Is it fair to the child?

When I asked a group of women who were considering Choice Motherhood what their greatest hesitation was, many reported that they were concerned about the impact it would have on a child to grow up without a father.

This is a good reaction for any potential mother to have. Ultimately the greatest gift of motherhood is the grace that comes from thinking first and foremost about another human being. In the end, it is that kind of commitment and dedication to your child that will make the biggest difference in his or her life.

Carol consulted with everyone she could think of before becoming a mother. She discussed it with a priest, a rabbi, and a minister. "I thought they might say it wouldn't be appropriate or that every child needs a father, but they all basically said the same thing: that I was bringing a child into this world who would be loved and cared for by a mother who felt the most important thing was to love and to show others love." Even Carol's highly conservative brother approved of her decision to go ahead before her fertility declined. As she recalls, "That really shocked me."

She said she worried that she might hurt her child psychologically or emotionally by not providing him with a father, but an adopted male friend convinced her that continuous love and honesty would make her child feel blessed. "He said my child might wonder about his donor dad, but he'll know he was so wanted by his mom — and this is what will be most important."

Do I have enough resources to be a good single parent?

This is a very important question, and one we'll get into more as the book develops. We're not simply talking about finances — although that's a big enough question, especially in the early stages, that it's the topic of our next chapter.

We're also talking about emotional and community resources.

Choice Chat with a Typical Thinker

✦ I've been thinking for nearly 12 years. Something in me just seemed to "know" that I was going to end up going this route. I keep hoping that Mr. Right will come around. But I will be turning 35 soon, and the time seems to be ticking a bit faster these days. At some point fairly soon I know that I will have to stop thinking and hoping and just do it.

For the past few years I have been constantly trying everything I can think of to meet men: meeting new friends and networking, telling everyone I know that I want to meet someone, Match.com, Fast Dating, and so on. Along the way, I have met some wonderful men (and many, many duds!). But none that I felt I could be happy with for the rest of my life.

I'm not as concerned about finances as many others. I am fortunate to have an excellent job, home, and everything else. However, I also know that could change any day. I *am* concerned about being fair. I'm very concerned about how I will answer everyone's questions at work, neighbors' questions, and so forth. And I am concerned about how others will act toward my future child — and how my child will fare without a father.

My biggest concern, though, is not all these questions. I guess I know in my heart that we will just figure them out as we go along. My challenge is knowing when I have waited for Mr. Right long enough. I wish God would send me a sign — and a very obvious one!

Who will help you raise your child? You'll need a stronger network than you have now. Many of your single friends won't end up being there after you become a mom. You will need mentors and male role models for your child. You will need community ties to help you alleviate stress, to give your child wider experiences, to provide spiritual growth. You will need family or neighbors to help in emergency situations. You will need good child-care options that won't make you feel so guilty about working. You will need to connect with other single mothers for empathy. And you will need to expand your resources as soon as you can, so you know where to turn when you're too busy or tired to figure it out.

A therapist I consulted for this chapter suggested that any woman considering Choice Motherhood needs to ask herself these questions:

- Do I have stability in my life (financial, familial, emotional, supportive)?
- Do I have realistic expectations about motherhood?
- Have I considered health issues in becoming pregnant?
- Can I be flexible and roll with the punches?
- If something happened to me, who would take over?

Transitioning to Motherhood

It's one thing to contemplate your ability to parent when you're a single woman. It's quite another to be stabbed with fear when you're pregnant or on your way to pick up an adopted child. Yet it is extremely common for women to panic when their life is on the verge of changing. One woman I know had dreamed of having a child for more than ten years. In her midthirties, she decided to conceive, gave herself six months before inseminating, and became pregnant on her first attempt. Two months later, hormones were in full force, and she was "scared to death."

One woman's panic was triggered by certain events: making her first clinic appointment; during each insemination process; discovering she was pregnant; at various points in the pregnancy; even after her child was born, when she thought about the immense responsibility of being a parent. But she also reported profound confidence that her decision to become a mother was the right one.

In 2005, the Associated Press published a profile of Rep. Deborah Pryce, the highest-ranking Republican woman in Congress.[1] Pryce was a single, 53-year-old white woman who had gotten a call from an adoption agency that the 17-year-old black birth mother of a baby girl wanted to meet her. "I was terrified," Pryce told the AP reporter Malia Rulon. "I didn't want anything to stop this from happening, and she didn't know I was white . . . she didn't know how old I was, she didn't know that I was single."

Pryce and her ex-husband had tried for ten years to have a child, lost an adopted daughter to cancer at age 9, and were at odds over whether to adopt again when they divorced in 2002. As a busy Ohio Congresswoman, Pryce juggled a tough schedule. "I can't say it's easy," she told Rulon. "But you can make things work if you have enough love in your heart and the desire to see it happen."

The author Shari Thurer[2] wrote an excellent book about the myths of motherhood, and reminded us that there is no such thing as perfection. "The briefest glance at history will dispel any notion that there is one correct way to mother. Your grandmother may have bottle-fed your father on a rigid schedule and started his toilet training when he was the tender age of three months, practices generally regarded as ridiculous today. Yet he managed to grow up. Youngsters tend to survive their parents' bungled efforts. The nervousness parents feel about their adequacy will dissipate when decent people are encouraged to mother in their own decent way."

After You've Become a Mother

Motherhood is filled with intense moments. Sophie can sit in her room singing "Frosty the Snowman, was a tolly holly snow," earnestly sharing her muddled lyrics with her dolls, and it makes my heart burst with pride at how cute she is. Then I discover she's scrawled permanent red marker over the bedroom wall.

One Choice Mom talked about how astonished she was at the depth of love she felt for her child. But she also remembered going through an extremely painful time in her life, when she wanted to withdraw from the world and cry, yet the requirement of being Mom was to play and talk about nonsensical subjects. "You just do it," she says.

After 9/11, when I witnessed the devastation 20 blocks away and on the TV screen, it was astonishing to have a clueless 2-year-old dancing like normal in the living room. When I was in the middle of an emotional interview with a Muslim teenager who saw the tragedy from his school, Sophie loudly interrupted with an urgent message. "Come and look," she proclaimed. "I've gone poo-poo in the potty." She was so proud and insistent that I had to put my interviewee on hold while I dutifully followed her into the bathroom. Yet although the dichotomy of Sophie's world and my own during that emotional time was disconcerting, her child's perspective helped me cope much better than watching continuous news coverage ever could have.

The dark days

Any mother, single or not, needs to be prepared for the rough moments. Sometimes they come because the child is stressed. Sometimes they come because the mother is stressed.

One mother complained of more than a year of stubborn behavior she endured from her daughter — trying every trick she could to survive — until in the end the phase lifted. In hindsight, she realized there was nothing she could have done differently, except try to be patient that "this too shall pass."

Karyn used to be frustrated by her son's tantrums and defiant attitude. One particularly difficult weekend, she said, she locked herself in the bedroom several times. "He would scream, beg, plead, and say everything he thought I wanted to hear. Then I'd see his little fingers crawl under the door, desperately reaching for some sort of contact. I would go over to touch them, and that diffused things so that I would come back out — until ten minutes later, when the whole thing would repeat itself." As a coping mechanism, she sent e-mails to friends with older kids. "It turns out, we're normal."

> *"Sometimes it's boring to be a parent, sometimes frustrating. But never for a moment, even with the memory of that weekend, do I doubt this life is good."*

Every mother will have dark moments, sometimes for unbearably long stretches of time. And every mother will have moments of profound joy. The difficult thing for many Thinkers is having faith that she will be able to balance the bad with the good, that she won't snap hysterically, that it will all be worth it.

From the Author's Journal

✦ It's a Wednesday night and I've just snapped at Sophie, who didn't deserve it. She was jumping and hovering while I was trying to read the newspaper, and I was annoyed at not having my personal space. Rather than asking her to give me space — which she probably would have ignored out of 3-year-old incomprehension — I yelled at her to "leave me alone . . . can't you just leave me alone?" She takes these occasional outbursts in stride now, which makes me feel horrible. Her general cheeriness in contrast to my nighttime crabbiness makes me feel momentarily inadequate as a parent. Is this unusual short-temperedness of mine showing up now because I'm stressed and not aware . . . an inevitable result of being a single parent . . . or a byproduct of simply being a parent?

Thursday night. I yell at Sophie for not cleaning her room, despite at least six requests in the last few hours, and dramatically scoop up everything on her floor — dolls, ▶

toys, clothes, books, movies — and whisk them "away." I ignore her cries, commanding that if she can't take care of her things then she's not responsible enough to have them. Is this discipline that I've done? Or nasty-mother torture?

The next night, she and I make a special dessert for company. The next night . . . I'm teaching Sophie how to use chopsticks at a sushi bar after watching an Omnimax movie about chimps. The next day . . . we're exploring African art at a local museum. The next night . . . she's sitting with me at a reading of a Jon Hassler story, fidgety but doing her darnedest to follow this "grown-up" event. The next night . . . I get teary as I walk into Sophie's preschool with other parents, about to watch her first "dance" recital. The next night . . . she's excitedly bouncing to the beat on my lap as we watch professional skaters in an ice show. Of course, she nods off on the way home, and I carry her three flights up to bed, where she curls sweetly into a cherub ball. I sit and watch her sleep, unable to take my eyes off her face.

After my inadequate moments of motherhood, we've had a week of wonderful togetherness and joy as mother and child.

Final Thoughts

One of the things — honestly — that I got down about when I was pregnant was how much time I'd have to spend shopping. Yet now that I'm a mom, I love picking out new things for my kids. Of course, that's not the most rigorous test of my ability to be a good Choice Mom. But my point is, all mothers do find strength and joy in little — and big — things that may never have excited or interested them before.

Children interfere with your sleep, privacy, savings, career ambitions, errand running, love life, travel destinations. Yet there is no way to anticipate the rewards of being a mother until you are one, because so much of parenting transcends the simple tasks of taking care of another human being.

A capable woman can be a capable mother. All of us have faced obstacles, down periods, crabby times, and low moments. Yet we all find ways to persevere. We seek support from others, devise creative solutions, chill out behind closed doors, or treat ourselves to a much deserved night out or pampering session. Our children learn from our example about how to deal with frustrations they will inevitably feel.

Parenthood is always a juggling act, balancing time and energy and finances and emotions with your child's — and your own — natural good days and bad days. There are serious issues that you need to face if you decide to become a Choice Mom, which we will cover in upcoming chapters. But if you are motivated enough to continue reading this book, being a good mother is not likely to be one of your issues.

Choice Chat with Nicola

MOTHERHOOD IS NOT CONDITIONAL

✦ *There are profound joys of Choice Motherhood, but it is important to remember that no one can pick her child's temperament, skills, and attitude. When you say yes to parenthood, you say yes to everything, as this story reminds us.*

Although I strongly believe in the autonomy of women to make the choices that are right for them, I have been distressed to hear single women say, "I couldn't cope on my own with a child who has a disability."

Although some may be speaking from experience and a ▶

real sense of themselves, I want to ask: Will you be able to cope with a child who barely sleeps for the first two years? Will you be able to cope with a child with cerebral palsy or autism, or one of the other disabilities for which there is no prenatal testing and which may not be diagnosed for months or even years? Will you be able to cope with a child who is of a temperament you don't warm to (very timid, very loud, very sporty, very bookish, whatever)?

I believe that becoming a mother requires a degree of commitment to a child that is in no way provisional. I also know from experience that the fundamentals of parenting (offering love, security, boundaries, guidance, planning, teaching, and so forth) are the same for any child, of whatever ability. It is only the detail that is different.

I am the single mother by choice to two special needs children. My daughter, age 8, has Down syndrome. I didn't do any of the testing you can do when you're pregnant, partly because she was a much-wanted baby, conceived by donor insemination, and because I knew I would never terminate.

A few months after my daughter's birth, my father asked me if I would want her to take a magic drug to cure the Down syndrome, if the drug were to ever exist. We looked at each other and were both surprised to find ourselves saying, "No!" Her DS is part of who she is. She is a wonderful, funny, determined, warm little girl who loves to dance and ride and swim; plays her own CDs in her room; argues with (and loves) her brother; tells me to calm down when I get ratty; is cheeky, moody, interested in everything; loves to dress up for parties.

Last night she went to a party and scorned my advice that the other girls would be wearing jeans, insisting on a pink party dress and a sequined purse. I was right, but she was not fazed. When I asked her what the others thought about what she was wearing, she said firmly, "They loved ▶

it," and that was the end of that. Temperamentally, she's a lot like me! I can't imagine her being someone else, which is what she would be if she didn't have DS.

I look at my daughter's beautiful face and it hurts to know that one day she will realize that many people feel so strongly about who she is that they kill babies because they are like her. That sounds brutal, but I can't imagine how that knowledge will make her feel.

As someone who has valued intellectual activity above everything else, the irony of having a child with learning difficulties is not lost on me. If I were a religious person, I would be tempted to think it was a special test or blessing. I'm not, so I think that we've both been lucky. My daughter has a mom who really loves her and is interested in knowing how best to help her, and I have a daughter I adore and whose achievements make me just as proud as if she was top of her class.

When I tried to get pregnant a second time, the genetic counselor urged testing. I realized that for me it felt wrong to have some kind of checklist — this child would be acceptable, this one would not. If I was going to have another child, I would need to do so feeling that I would love and care for him or her no matter what.

After two miscarriages, when I was pushing 41, I decided, with some difficulty, that it was time to stop. A few years later I adopted my son — who was diagnosed with Noonan syndrome — when he was 3. He has learning and behavioral difficulties, heart problems, an extroverted and charming personality, short stature, and curly hair.

My son is the bravest little boy I know. At 3, he said goodbye to everyone he'd ever known (including the birth parents and brothers he was seeing weekly) and crossed the country to a new life. For months, he never cried. He tested me out a lot, wrecked the house, attacked his new sister, did unspeakable things — some of which were just that he's a ▶

BOY. It took my daughter and I a few months to recover from the maelstrom of male energy that hurtled into our little enclave.

Adoption of a toddler is hard at the beginning partly because you don't love them but you have to pretend to. With an older child you could talk about it, but with a 3-year-old you just have to pretend and wait for the feelings to grow. What is heartbreaking, of course, is that the child is doing just the same. It is wonderful when you can both relax because it has become real.

I would a million times rather be a mother to a child with special needs than not be a mother at all. If I had not become mother to my daughter, I'm sure I would not have gone on to adopt. I simply wouldn't have had the confidence to feel that I could persuade someone else that I could raise a child.

I love being a mom, and really enjoy my children. I feel as though I'm in a club that I never particularly wanted to join, but now I'm here it feels rather exclusive and special. I'm pretty sure my daughter feels the same way about having DS — that it's the other people (including me) who are outsiders, not her and her friends with DS. And that's the other thing you never know about unless it happens to you — the huge, warm community that people with disabilities share with parents, friends, groups, teachers, and others.

I would say that my two are in no way more difficult to raise than, say, a ferociously bright child who is demanding. And certainly I would find it harder to parent a child who had difficulty with affection.

My son needs a lot of help calming down and being the best person he can be, but he also soaks stuff up like a sponge. When he came, he had very little vocabulary (just "water" for a drink, a river, the sea, a pond). I think his foster parents had never read to him at night. A few weeks later, we were reading how the Gruffalo was in a "deep, ▶

dark wood" when he said, "That's not a wood, it's a forest!" There is so much pleasure in seeing little people develop and grow.

It isn't about what difficulties they have, it's about how they manage them. And if I'm going to get all philosophical, I guess I think that's what all of us are doing in life — trying to do the best with what we've got and what happens to us. I do think I've been lucky.

The one thing you can say for certain about becoming a mom is that nothing is certain. You don't know how you'll feel, how you'll react, what your child will be like, what life will be like a year, ten years, twenty years down the line. It's a big leap in the dark for anyone, and that may feel more frightening when you're taking it on your own. But of course, you're not on your own, and whatever happens, as a woman with the courage to take this step, you'll be able to find the resources you need, even if the outcome is very far from what you expected.

· 2 ·

Can I Afford It?

Ask 50 women — as I did — what their primary concern was before becoming a Choice Mom, and half of them will tell you it related to money. "Can I afford to do this?" is the logical question of many. ("Can I afford *not* to do this?" is the emotional counterpart of others.) "How much should I save before pursuing motherhood?" "What happens if I lose my job?"

Ask those same women how much money they need in order to feel secure and you'll get a different answer from each one.

Mary, in her late thirties, lives in a medium-sized city on the East Coast. She has some debt, is trying to get a down payment together for her own home, and says she needs to have $15,000 in the bank before she'll begin trying to become a mother. Another woman in the same area has a different yardstick. She won't think of becoming a mother until she has an annual income of $60,000. Still others intend to become mothers with only a few thousand in the bank, a salary in the midtwenties, and a modest level of debt. Their desire to parent is so great that they believe they'll find a way to make it work with what they have.

Everyone has a different comfort zone when it comes to money. It tends to drive my mother insane that I don't have a conventional job. She grew up poor, worked at the same place for more than 25 years, and believes there is no such thing as financial security. But I have largely been self-employed for 15 years, have never had credit card debt, don't spend beyond my means, and own a nice home that provides rental income and is my retirement investment. I'm comfortable living this way.

The last time I had a full-time job was the three years prior to my daughter's birth. The nearly six-figure salary is what enabled me to feel confident that I could afford to become a Choice Mom. But a few months after Sophie was born, my job was eliminated. So much for financial security.

Darla is another woman who thought she had her ducks in a row. She was in a low-paying, dead-end job when she started thinking about becoming a Choice Mom.

Over a five-year period before giving birth to her son, she took computer science classes and worked as a software developer. Things were going great — until her company closed down her unit. After eight months of fruitless searching in the IT field, her severance pay was gone and her unemployment compensation and savings were dwindling.

"I finally took an entry-level job at a big company located a couple miles from my house. Money is really tight, but we're making it. I'm hoping that I can eventually move into an IT job within the company," she told me. "My point is that I waited until I was in good shape financially to have my child, but now I'm not much better off than I was before. You just have to deal with what comes."

> *"Maybe those people who say that 'if you wait until you're financially well-off to have a child, you'll never have one' aren't as far off the mark as I always thought they were."*

Most Choice Mothers who responded to a survey I sent out to 100 women reported a salary of more than $60,000, generally related to their postgraduate education. But a growing number of women who are making this choice today are not as highly paid as the pioneers. Just as with two-income families, it can be difficult to stretch existing funds — whatever they might be — for childcare, recreation, education, and basic expenses.

Yes, you need to have money for health insurance, a safe home, and healthy food in order to be a responsible Choice Mom. However, there is no magical formula and no magical amount that will enable single motherhood to become a reality with no bumps on the road. You cannot plan for everything.

What you can do is assess — honestly — your current financial picture, and then determine if you can make things happen as a Choice Mom while maintaining your own comfort zone. Some women sit down with a financial adviser, who typically will ask you to determine your current net worth, track your income and expenses, estimate your future spending and saving, create a cash reserve, take care of debt, and set aside funds for emergencies. If you're the type that doesn't even balance your checkbook (that's me) you do need to make an assessment of your spending habits before you can go any further.

Once you have a realistic sense of who you are as consumer and breadwinner, you will be ready to understand what you can and should do in order to afford responsible Choice Motherhood.

Check Your Spending Habits

AnnaMarie got pregnant on her first insemination try. During one low night of panic she considered terminating the pregnancy because she hadn't had time to save the money she thought she needed.

"I was irrational and obsessive about the finances," she told me, five years after her child was born. "A very dear friend set me straight. He told me to look at my single life, with all the eating out, the movies, the expenses of socializing, traveling, entertaining myself. He reminded me about my parents, who raised twelve children on only one salary. I spent the next several months taking a good hard look at cutting my out-of-pocket expenses. I was amazed at how much money I had set aside in no time flat. It has been tight, but I've been able to make it without outside help."

Living on the same income while supporting a child does not have to be difficult. Often your money doesn't have to stretch further, it simply goes into different categories. Many women report that they spend less as a mother than they did as a single person — they have less interest in expensive travel, shopping, restaurants, and entertainment. A lazy afternoon becomes playtime with child rather than mall cruising. A wintry day is spent making snowmen instead of shushing down the slopes.

As AnnaMarie found, once she cut out happy hours with co-workers and other forms of avoiding loneliness and blowing off steam, she was saving at least $100 a week. "I also shopped my insurances — all of them. Many people don't do this," she said. "They take their company's insurance, or the insurance company their realtor recommends. I shopped my homeowners, health, dental, life, and car insurance, and did better in a couple areas. I called credit card companies and demanded they lower my interest rates or I'd close my accounts. I got a home equity line of credit to get a lower rate and moved some balances, stretching the payments out for a longer term.

"Mainly, for the first time in my life, I put myself on a strict budget for things like groceries, clothes, shoes, and so on. I went to Hair Cuttery for ten-dollar cuts, and began coloring my own hair after my daughter was born. It took some time and discipline, but it was worth it."

Like AnnaMarie, when I was a single New Yorker, I regularly spent $100 each week at restaurants and bars without blinking. I had five magazine subscriptions, paid for standard cable, rented at least one video each week, and went to the movie theater a few times a month. I easily dropped $200 each year at the bookstore.

After Sophie was born, I stopped reading magazines, dropped to basic cable (I do miss Comedy Central), started using Netflix, rarely saw movies in the theater, and made library visits. Because of my new lifestyle, I ended up saving about $800 a year on entertainment alone.

When I was single, I made it a point to visit a different country each year, and reached my goal of spending time in all 50 states. It was an expensive passion. Although I want both my kids to love travel — Sophie visited 4 countries and 20 states in her first five years — my travels have slowed down significantly now that I have two children and am working only part-time.

Do I miss travel? Yes, but I'll get back to it someday, with and without kids in tow. An inexpensive visit to friends and family in other states will do for now.

In the meantime, I live frugally. I don't spend much on clothing or shoes. I get my hair cut for $11. I notice which gas station is cheapest. I buy used music CDs. I invite friends over to drink a decent merlot for $6 per bottle. And life is perfectly happy.

Anticipate Your Baby-Shopping Habits

Some women find great satisfaction in being bargain shoppers: using coupons, buying and selling on eBay, seeking out consignment shops, flea markets, thrift stores, factory outlets, garage sales, and discount grocery stores like Sam's Club and Costco. As a mother of two on a limited budget, I find that I've become a much smarter consumer than I used to be.

When Sophie was born, work colleagues and friends chipped in on new big-ticket items: stroller, glider chair, Pack 'n Play. In fact, the portable playpen, with foam inserts, worked as her crib until she was ready for a bed. I used a hand-me-down highchair, bought all of her clothes at a consignment shop, and didn't have space for many toys — which was fine, since she preferred boxes, digging into drawers, dancing, trying on my clothes, and playground sandboxes during the first few years. Not anticipating then that I would have a second child, I sold what I could as soon as she outgrew it.

Although I wasn't extravagant in Sophie's early years, I am finding even greater resources for Dylan. I had no maternity leave pay, bigger medical bills because of weaker health insurance coverage, and no work colleagues to shower me with big gifts. His crib, bouncer chair, jumper, swing, Exersaucer, and bassinet were free hand-me-downs, most of them from one generous Choice Mother. The baby monitor, breast pump, bottles, and most of his first-year clothes were gifts. His stroller came from a thrift shop. I didn't use a changing table or fancy high chair. My only significant purchase for his first year was an infant car seat, and then a convertible one after he outgrew the first one at 9 months.

I tended to buy generic diapers and formula. Instead of buying Gerber's baby food, I made my own. When he was an infant, a day's worth of Gerber's pears cost nearly $2. Instead, I bought pears in bulk, boiled them, pureed them, froze them, and fed him for two weeks for about $6. I'm no earth mother, and I don't like cooking. But even I managed to save money that way.

If money is an issue, you'll learn how to shop differently. And you'll discover that the $100 crib meets the same federal safety guidelines as the $600 one. That your infant doesn't notice if something is old or new. That a non-brand-name diaper works too. That your baby eats just as well from a $15 portable seat as from a pricey highchair that tilts, swivels, and adjusts. That your toddler doesn't know the difference between a $3 toy and a $30 one. That your preschooler thinks a cousin's hand-me-down bicycle is just as cool as a store-bought one.

Honestly, my infant son preferred a piece of crinkly paper to the $4 wrist bands I bought him. And my daughter spent far more time drawing and coloring than using her $50 LeapFrog device.

Up until the age of 15, I wore hand-me-downs that my parents

— both decently paid and loving — got from friends. When I was older, I rejected most of them because of the conservative styling, but there were usually one or two items in the bag that were funky enough for my tastes. I never resented my parents for bringing the bag home.

Having money to spend on your child doesn't mean you need to. If money is tight but you're prepared to bargain shop for daily essentials, your child won't suffer. It's cliché but true: What they want most is your time, not what you can buy them.

Determine Child-Care Costs

Daily essentials are one thing, but childcare is something else entirely. Any working mother without a retired relative to depend on will report that her primary expense is childcare. And this is a non-negotiable item in which bargain-basement pricing is not the goal. No one should enter into motherhood until they know they can afford reliable childcare.

The average annual cost for childcare, according to the Nation's Network for Child Care Resources and Referral, is $6,750 for infants, $4,750 for preschoolers, and $3,500 for school-age children.

When I was living in New York City with Sophie, I spent one-third of my income for her babysitter. When work was slow I used the $10-per-hour sitter three days a week, for a minimum of 25 hours. When work was flowing I used the sitter more.

Primarily to save on child-care expenses, we moved to Minnesota, where I cut the babysitter cost in favor of free family and friends for the odd nights out, and enrolled her in tax-deductible preschool three days a week at roughly $4,500 per year. The average daycare center would have cost me about $225 per week. The average home-based care would have cost about $150 per week. For the last two years, I have found someone to live in our house for free or reduced rent in exchange for 15 to 20 hours of childcare per week.

Tips: Finding Childcare

✦ Type in "childcare referral" to launch an online search and you'll find good resources. An excellent starting place is the Nation's Network of Child Care Resources and Referral (www.naccrra.net), which represents more than 850 resource centers throughout the United States. One of its goals is to help families find affordable, quality childcare by offering lists of licensed daycares in every region, tips about choosing a provider, funding options, and much more. To find the CCR&R in your community, call Child Care Aware at 1-800-424-2246 or look it up online at www.child careaware.org.

Another great resource is referrals from other moms. I found Sophie's babysitter simply by mentioning my need to a mother I didn't know, who was using her only two days a week. It was an invaluable referral, as she turned out to be Sophie's second mother for three years — and they maintain contact still, years after we've left New York. Consider researching early and getting on waiting lists — although, be aware that most centers won't put your name on a list until the child is physically present.

It's easy to assess personality and philosophy in a simple phone conversation.

Typical questions to consider:
• How long have the kids been with the same provider?
• What is the maximum number of kids cared for?
• How old are the current kids?
• How are meals offered, and what do they consist of?
• Is this a job, or does the provider seem to love kids?
• How much communication does the provider generally have with parents?
• What is the provider's parenting and disciplining philosophy?

▶

- How often is the TV used as a babysitter? (Consider pop-in visits.)
- Are there regular art projects and preschool learning programs?
- How up-to-date are the baby furniture and toys?
- Does the price include food, formula, and diapers?
- What are the hours? Vacation and holiday schedules?
- What are backup plans for provider illness and vacation?
- Are you expected to pay for certain provider holidays, or weeks that care is not actually offered?
- What is the policy for sick kids?
- How flexible will the provider be in emergency situations?
- Are fees charged for late pickups?
- If it's home-based, are there pets?
- Is there a fenced-in outdoor play area?
- Is outdoor play a daily occurrence?
- What is the policy during rainy and winter months?

Ask the provider to describe a typical day. Is the provider someone you feel comfortable with as a "second parent"? When you visit with your child, be sure to notice how well-behaved and enthusiastic the kids are. What is hanging up on the walls? What kinds of toys and games are around?

If the provider has no space, ask for recommendations and critiques of others in the area. Verify the license with the county and check into any complaints that have been lodged. Above all, Choice Moms and daycare providers recommend "going with your gut" on whether the place is the right fit for your child. If something doesn't seem right to you, pay attention to that.

Always identify a backup babysitter if you are using home daycare. Unlike child-care centers, the home provider usually requests paid holiday and vacation days regardless of your schedule.

In my case, I consider it easier and more fulfilling mom-wise to work part-time from home and make ends meet rather than pay for full-time care. My parents are willing caretakers in the summer months (six months of the year, they live in Arizona), but I don't ask them to step in more than a few days a week.

Many moms don't have the luxury of working flexible hours with family sitters. One woman I know spent $8,000 annually for full-time care for her preschooler (more in the infant year). After her child entered the free public school, she was still spending $4,000 for summer care, after-school programs, and camps.

The only way to estimate this expense is to make calls in your area, since costs differ significantly by region. Check the range of costs with nanny agencies, want-ad listings, daycare centers, church and school sitting services, preschools, and home-care listings. And call many sources. Daycare prices in particular can vary considerably from place to place, and might be significantly more expensive than licensed home care. And don't forget to ask if the programs are closed for long holidays and in the summer, if they shut down for school breaks that your employer doesn't recognize, if they only allow toddlers to attend a few days a week for part-time hours — anything that will affect your schedule or expenses.

Many mothers end up switching child-care providers for various reasons — their child is unhappy, the provider is quitting, their job site moves — so don't assume you'll stick with one option until kindergarten begins. That's why fully exploring your options and determining price ranges is important, before you need it.

If the dollars are more than you can afford, ask yourself these questions:

- Are you willing to move in order to use cheaper (or free) family and friends?
- Are you able to launch a babysitting co-op with neighborhood families?

- Can you convince your company to open an inexpensive care center?
- Can you work flexible hours at home and hire a "mother's helper"?
- If you love kids and are open to a career change, could you run your own daycare, or work at a preschool for reduced or free tuition for a few years?
- Can you share an in-home nanny with another mom?
- Can you offer room and board to a college student in exchange for babysitting?
- Are you willing to change jobs to allow for more flexible or part-time status?
- Can you earn income by taking in a renter or doing a home-based craft?
- Can you move to a less expensive area to reduce your housing costs?
- Can you find a better-paying job?

Reduce Debt

Many women report that the most important thing they should have done before having a child was to get credit-card debt under control. I've managed to be a freelance writer and homeowner with an up-and-down income, whereas single friends with no children struggle to make down payments on property or live paycheck to paycheck, simply because of mounting credit problems.

If you are drowning in debt, take care of that first. Pay attention to the interest rates, as AnnaMarie did, and switch to a less costly credit card company. Or open a home equity line of credit, if that's an option for you, and get a lower rate to pay off those cards. (And while you're at it, make sure you're with a bank that doesn't nickel-and-dime you with monthly fees.)

Choice Chat About Money

✦ *I surveyed Choice Moms about how money issues affect their daily lives. Here's a sampling of what they said:*

"If I had enough of it I would stay home with my daughter and not have to deal with DAYCARE!"

"Finances have some impact, because of course we have little of it. But I never had much to begin with and am not materialistic, so it doesn't have a huge impact."

"It took a tremendous amount of money during the Trying Phase (between $600 to $1,000 per month). I was able to come up with that money . . . and now that money goes to daycare."

"If my income were higher I would go out and adopt a second child tomorrow! To pay for the full-time daycare expenses, I had to live partially out of savings until my daughter entered kindergarten. I congratulate myself that I haven't had to tap into savings since last summer. But I also haven't saved an additional dime for either retirement or college, I need to buy a car in two years, and I'm finding that summer childcare seems to run about double what daycare costs."

"Now that my children are getting older, financing all of their extracurricular activities (piano lessons, gymnastics, swim team, preschool, etc.) is a juggling act."

Calculate Taxes, Insurance, and House Costs

I won't pretend that by the time you're reading this anything I write about finances and taxes will be current. But children aren't simply a financial debit — you win some decent tax deductions as well. As head of a household with a dependent, you qualify for a few tax breaks, including a child-care credit and a child tax credit.

Based on 2004 data from the U.S. Department of Agriculture, the typical family spends $134,000 to $270,000 to raise their child from birth to age 17, depending on income level. Housing is the single biggest expense, followed by food, transportation, clothing, health care, childcare and education (not including college), and miscellaneous. MSN Money's website has a very helpful article about these typical expenditures, strategies for cutting costs, and tax tips for the average family. (Search for "Raising Your Quarter-Million Dollar Baby" at moneycentral.msn.com.)

Note: The USDA survey is helpful, but no substitute for doing your own research. The child-care number in that survey alone is the average price paid by families — the highs and lows divided in half — including those who have free help. Remember that your circumstances will vary considerably based on geographic location, child-care arrangement, and health insurance variables.

Geography makes a big difference in many ways. Where you live usually is more important than the size of your house. As one Choice Mom told me, her small house in a good school district costs the same as a large house in other areas of her city.

If you lived somewhere else, would you be paying less in utilities, real estate taxes, homeowners insurance, mortgage or rent — or more? These are the big-ticket monthly expenses that are hard to trim. If a move might be in your future — so your child can attend better schools or you can find a better-paying job — check county records, documents at open houses, and your friendly insurance broker for numbers.

Other questions to explore, preferably with a financial adviser:

• How much more will you be paying for health insurance with a dependent, including premiums, deductibles, and copays? If you got laid off, or became self-employed, do you know what this insurance would cost you?

- Does your employer offer a pretax dependent care benefit? (If so, take it.)
- Will your out-of-pocket medical expenses add up to 7.5 percent of your income? This is especially important if you are considering clinic insemination. (Doctor fees, prescribed drugs, hospital fees . . . some people have even deducted the cost of sperm.) If you meet the requirement for itemized deductions, you can realize additional tax savings.
- What would it cost, based on your income, to get disability insurance?

Consider Long-Term Issues

If you intend to invest in real estate before becoming a mother — as several women I talked to did — make sure to get a good house inspector before you buy any property. The furnace, plumbing, and other maintenance can be damaging, especially for houses that are more than 40 years old.

As one Choice Mom discovered after her house of 15 months sprung a leak, the repair was not, as she hoped, a $250 fix but a whopping $10,000 overhaul. When she read the fine print on her inspector's report — the inspector who said her roof would be fine for years — she learned that he disavowed any reliable knowledge of roofing matters.

A friend bought quickly, and paid for it later with costly plumbing repairs. She took the previous owners to court for failure to disclose, and lost that battle as well.

Before beginning her quest to become a mom, Teresa put together a plan with a financial adviser to reduce her debt and buy a house. "So I had a pretty solid grip on my financial situation and goals," she told me. "I did not have substantial savings, but I knew that if I waited until I could afford a child, I would never have one. Instead I decided to look at how I would afford it if I was a mother. I created a pre- and post-baby budget, started saving as aggressively as possible, refinanced my house, and set up a home equity line of credit. I made a list of other potential income sources I could consider if needed. I bought additional life insurance.

> *"I know my financial situation is not ideal, but neither was the one I grew up in, and I know my son and I will be just fine. The greatest financial burden will be daycare, and that's a short-term financial obligation, not unlike taking on a mortgage or grad school tuition, which I have done in the past."*

In my case, when Sophie was conceived I thought I was financially set. I had a high-paying job at a strong company, was well-respected by my clients, colleagues, and most of management. I contributed to a 401(k), had great benefits, was able to pay off my mortgage (thanks to the sale of property bought in my 20s), and intended to set aside money every year.

Of course, it was extremely unnerving to lose my job just as I was preparing to return to full-time work, a few months after my paid maternity benefits had ended. Although I eventually worked out a good severance package with my employer, I no longer had a long-term plan, and for five months pre-package I was very nervous about money.

But I returned to the mantra that had carried me through many prior years of freelance struggles: The universe will provide. And it has.

In hindsight, losing that job was the best thing that could have happened to me. Instead of being locked into a job with long hours and a boss that didn't want me to return, I was free to relocate to Minnesota, sell my 700-square-foot New York apartment, and buy a seven-bedroom house (which provides me with rental income) for the same money. The move enabled me to publish a novel, write this book, have the space for a second child, spend quality preschool years with Sophie and Dylan, and meet the man who would become my husband — who is himself not much better off financially than I am.

The Cost of Conception

✦ Many Choice Mothers choose to inseminate with an anonymous donor. This sometimes costs less than adoption, but the numbers add up. If you are considering this route, investigate your insurance coverage and create a game plan for covering the expense. Barring fertility issues, there are three primary methods: vaginal, with a syringe; intracervical (ICI); and intrauterine insemination (IUI), which involves a catheter. The least expensive method, using a needleless syringe, can be performed at home. Intracervical and intrauterine inseminations, which can only be performed in a safe, sterile manner by a doctor, are more expensive but tend to have a higher success rate. Here are a few ballpark numbers:

• Intrauterine insemination generally costs $300 to $700 per cycle. This does not include fertility drugs, sperm storage, consultations, bloodwork, and physical exams. The success rate is roughly 15 percent using frozen sperm. Often these expenses are not covered by insurance. One Midwest clinic charges $200–$300 for initial consult, $37–$90 for nurse practitioner visits, $160 for follicular ultrasounds, $38 for a pregnancy test, $69 for an estradiol lab test, and $138 for each insemination (two per cycle).

• Sperm generally costs between $300 and $600 per vial. Some doctors suggest you will need two vials per cycle. On average, it takes about six cycles to get pregnant. Many insurance companies won't cover this expense — although one woman I know used her company's healthcare spending account to pay for sperm, using a simple, unitemized lab receipt. Other typical fees, using the costs of one sperm bank as an example, include: registration ($100), long profile ($11), audiotaped interview ($25), storage ($300 for a year), and delivery ($100 overnight). ▶

- Expenses increase significantly for women requiring assistance in fertility. The combination of the fertility-enhancing drug Clomid (roughly $50/month), ultrasound monitoring, a trigger shot, and sperm, cost one woman $900 per month in out-of-pocket expenses — and that's with insurance covering another $900 per month. Insurance is more likely to cover if infertility is proven.
- In vitro fertilization involves removing eggs from your ovaries, fertilizing them with sperm in a laboratory, and putting the resulting embryos in your uterus. Roughly 30 percent of these attempts succeed. The procedure usually costs between $8,000 and $15,000. One clinic reports an average cost of $9,000 for IVF, including office visits, injections, bloodwork, monitoring, embryo freezing, lab fertilization, hospital costs, and physician time, with average medication costs at $2,700 per cycle. Another clinic offers women under 35, who meet weight requirements, three fresh sperm cycles and three frozen sperm cycles for $15,000, with cycle monitoring at $3,000 to $5,000. This does not include consult, drugs, or infertility workup fees.
- One woman reported that it cost her about $1,100 per cycle to try to conceive. Her silver lining? She felt confident that if she could afford that, she could eventually afford childcare.

I may have sacrificed five easy retirement years down the road, but in my mind these early years with my kids are more important than the years I'll have after they leave home. I do have a large real estate investment in my home, which I expect to tap into when it's needed. And I intend for my kids to earn scholarships or financial aid to help pay for college.

I realize that many of you — perhaps the majority of you — cannot live in such a precarious way. That's why every woman needs to determine her comfort zone and respect it. If it's im-

portant that you take advantage of earning years so you can retire comfortably, or that you offer your child summer camp and
costly music programs as well as a top-quality education, then you
should acknowledge that and figure out how to make it happen.

And that's why the answer to "Can I Afford It?" depends entirely on you, not the advice and numbers that worked for someone else. Your standard of living and ability to handle financial
stress are uniquely yours. Assess your personality honestly as you
consider these questions:

- How long could you survive financially if the economy took a
  downturn and you lost your job? Are there family and friends
  you could turn to?
- After you've covered the fixed costs of basic necessities —
  home, car, food, clothing, household, childcare — what else
  is in your budget? How much are you paying for cable, subscriptions, cell phone, Internet connection, entertainment?
  Would you be willing to trim them if it meant being able to afford to have a child?
- Do you find that you feel more energetic and happy when you
  have money, or does money have very little to do with your
  times of inspiration and joy?
- Are you confident about your ability to earn money and be resourceful about spending it? Do you tend to do whatever it
  takes to make ends meet?
- Can you save for emergencies and have the strength to not
  touch it?
- Are your financial concerns related to trying to offer what you
  never had as a child, or to provide at least as much as you
  were given?

It comes down to priorities and values. Know what yours are.

Ultimately, living and working in high-paying New York City,
my home for 18 years, was less important to me than being able to
enjoy community living near family in Minnesota. I would never

have believed it possible before I had Sophie, but after she was in my life, moving was the logical next step and it didn't hurt a bit. Many Choice Moms I've talked to, in fact, have made similar big moves in order to make a better life for their child.

How Does Your Income Compare?

✦ According to a 2004 Current Population Report, based on U.S. Census Bureau data, the median income of men who worked full-time, year-round, was $40,668 in 2003. The median income of the comparable group of women was $30,724. "Median" means half make above that amount, half below.

Golden Rules

If having a child is important to you, you will make it work and your child will love you for the commitment you bring to parenting. But:

1. Make sure you know what you're prepared to do if a drastic change is required. Even though I'm optimistic about money matters, I have had years of training as a poor, self-employed writer — and always had a modest security blanket in the bank.
2. Understand what things cost in your neighborhood. Make educated choices about how you will save and how you will spend.
3. Determine whether you can create a loving environment while making ends meet. If you need to sacrifice a responsive environment because of career goals, then maybe it's not the right time to become a parent.

Said one woman, "I had two working parents. But there were years when my father was unemployed and my mother's secretarial salary, our savings, and the kindness of extended family supported us. And those years were just as good because what was important was not whether we took vacations or had new clothes, but that we loved and supported each other in all ways."

Said another woman, "I grew up without a computer, cell phone, cable TV, microwave, TV in my bedroom, VCR, designer clothes. I went to school, dressed like most other kids, and joined extracurricular activities. What I would have liked more of as a child was my parents' attention and love."

And yet another woman indicated that her pursuit of "enough" money cost her years in fertility. In hindsight, she said, she wishes she hadn't waited so long to try to conceive as it ended up costing her the ability to give birth.

Rae, a new mother, told me she thinks the real question women need to ask is "Can I afford to wait?" Because of the cost of fertility drugs and procedures many "older" women have to take, she decided to conceive in her midthirties. She also decided to move ahead because her mother was healthy and available for childcare, and she didn't know if that would be the case if she waited.

Final Thoughts

If the affordability of parenthood seriously concerns you after reading this chapter, be sure you understand why. Maybe there is a threshold income or savings that you require in order to feel comfortable, and flirting with poverty is not an option. Figure out what it is, preferably with the help of a financial adviser, and see if you can make it happen.

Maybe you believe that a few years of paying off debt, or saving for a down payment on a home, or building that cushion, or finding what you need for fertility treatments or adoption, is worth waiting for. Your child will benefit from your excellent planning skills.

But also consider whether there is something else holding you back. Do you think it's vital that other things happen first: getting the house you never had, the house you did have, a husband, a higher-paying job? Is the absence of the "perfect" picture bothering you? Don't let money be the excuse if the ailment is elsewhere. People can spend a long time in pursuit of the "right" amount of money simply because they aren't taking steps to accomplish what actually will make them happy.

Have you ever known someone who made a list of goals and methodically reached them, only to end up still feeling discontented? Someone who got the right job, found the spouse, moved into a nice house, had kids, but still woke up with a major midlife crisis . . . or plunged into an affair . . . or dreamed eternally about "someday." People with lots of money still get divorced and still raise unhappy kids. If something is off balance in your life, money won't cure it. And neither will kids. Or a second wage earner.

Examine your core and what you require to maintain it. Then and only then will you be able to determine whether you can afford to be a Choice Mom.

· 3 ·

Grieving the Childhood Dream

For anyone who grew up imagining herself raising a family with a loving partner by her side, giving up the traditional childhood dream of a glorious wedding followed by babies can be very difficult. Single motherhood can feel like a decision of "no other choice" rather than of choice: if I can't find a man in time, I have to do this on my own or miss my opportunity to become a mother.

Many women become serial daters, wading through men quickly and methodically in order to find someone "in time." Some become hopeful daters, confusing any potential relationship with the urgency that this be The One. Still others tell themselves the dream doesn't matter after all — men are generally pigs and relationships usually fail.

Some women have the benefit of perspective, having been married and divorced — perhaps because they married primarily in order to have kids, without having a deeper foundation. They don't intend to make the same mistake again.

Others find themselves in love with a man who doesn't want children, often because he has older ones of his own from a previous marriage. These women are faced with having to decide if they can give up their dream of having a child of their own, or give up their life partner.

And still others are in relationships with men who are ambivalent about having children. It becomes a question of "How much longer should I wait for him before I do something else?"

Many women report that their criteria for finding Mr. Right has changed dramatically. A man who likes kids suddenly seems to have everything a woman needs — for a while.

Even if we think we've given up the dream, it still can be hard to retain equilibrium as men come into our lives while we're considering Choice Motherhood. Should I not date at all to avoid confusion? What if I go out with this guy and we hit it off?

Should I tell him I'm thinking of becoming a single mom? Would this put a strain on the relationship and end it? Should I postpone my plans without telling him anything? Or would I regret it if the relationship didn't work out? Is it wrong to let him get involved without telling him what my hopes are? But when is it too soon? And when is it too late?

In the end, there are no right answers to any of these questions. This is a highly emotional place to be. The only solution is to buckle up and take the ride — letting your gut be your guide — and not jump off prematurely. If you're not sure whether to become a Choice Mom, take the time to waffle and don't rush to resolve your discomfort. Don't shut yourself off from dating if it interests you. There is no script for how you're supposed to do anything, and there is no reason to stop walking toward any of your goals. When the situation is right, you'll know what to say or do.

Most women, accustomed to success and being able to make things happen, never imagine themselves to be in this position. Revising the fairy tale can be a difficult process. But as the stories of the women featured in this chapter reveal, if you remain honest with yourself, the passages through grief, anger, sorrow, and acceptance can lead you to many different resting places.

Case #1: Living with Grief

Judy admitted that she was "insane" in her twenties, involved in "not great" relationships. She entered therapy in her thirties. For five years she chose not to date. She eventually emerged as emotionally healthy and centered. She never became a serial dater, and never dated to find a father, but only if she legitimately wanted to be with a certain person. Once she unexpectedly got pregnant with a man who was "not the right man, and on his way out." She never regretted the fact that the pregnancy didn't lead to a birth. Some of her friends who once thought she was too picky ended up divorced. Others lamented being "stuck raising my kids with this jerk who has the morals of a flea."

When Judy was 40, she had no partner. Childlessness was not an option for her — that much was clear. She visited her doctor for fertility testing, got involved with the Single Mothers by Choice (SMC) network, and knew she was taking steps she needed to realize her dream of having a child. But emotionally she was in pain, having a difficult time letting go of her longing to have a child with a partner, and struggling to embrace what felt like the overwhelming challenges of Choice Motherhood. She wavered between sadness and anger, and was concerned that she would never end up in another relationship if she became a mother.

She considered the choice for years. "I thought the reason I was stuck was because of my fear of affording it and being able to manage it all on my own. But in therapy it became clear that the real reason was that I couldn't let go of the dream. I'm becoming a single mother by default, not by choice. I'm blessed to have the choice and all that crap, but it's been a big struggle. I want the total package. I'm afraid that if I choose this path I'll never find the time to date. I don't like the fact that I won't have someone going through the challenges and excitement of pregnancy with me. And I keep asking myself, 'Who's going to want me?'"

Through it all, she fought with her emotions. "How did I get here? At 40, this isn't where I wanted to be." The fantasy of the right man coming along "in time" was gone. "I was grief stricken."

Judy also was angry. "If I'd come from a healthier family, I wouldn't have had to spend the first 35 years of my life getting my act together. Once I got to a good place, I wondered where all the men in a good place were. And I was ticked off at the biology of it all. Men didn't want women who were approaching 40. They wanted women under the age of 34. I was automatically knocked out of the vision of any man who wanted biological children. It's a frustrating system."

She recognized that if she waited to completely let go of the grief she would never be a mother. "There would never be a day for me when I had peace and total acceptance of the road ahead." She didn't want to stay stuck, so she decided to allow herself to continue to feel the grief and become a Choice Mom anyway. She took the leap into Trying.

Case #2: Choosing to Wait

Dev too was weary of the emotional pendulum: I should become a single mother; I should not become a single mother. For months she was comfortable with her decision to go ahead, but then she was strongly confronted by doubt, thinking it was too difficult to raise a child alone. Only the model of two parents worked for her.

She attended meetings of the local SMC network, did journaling, went through fertility tests, and planned everything but the donor she would use. Then, at the age of 38, she met a guy and felt enormous relief. "Now I don't have to do that," she thought.

The relationship didn't last, but she never felt inspired to pursue Choice Motherhood again. When we first talked, it had been two years since she'd gotten off the path. "I feel that a man will come eventually. I want to let life unfold. Two years ago I was taking control of my life, my business, my spiritual journey. I was planning and pushing so hard. Now I think I'm more realistic about what single motherhood would mean. It would be a lot of work, emotionally, financially, physically. I think the biggest factor is that the process would be overwhelming and lonely, and I wouldn't have anyone to share that with me."

Childlessness was an option for her. So she decided to wait for a better situation.

Case #3: Getting Focus

Cheri is from a conservative state where Choice Motherhood is rare. She wanted the traditional family, met someone she thought might be The One while in her thirties, and cried every night after it ended. When she recovered, she started dating "fast and furious," including time with some "real flakes."

When she refocused, she could see that the dream that she would have it all — husband, home, and kids — was putting a timer on her relationships, and derailing many of them in the process. Her priority, she realized, was to be a mother. So she developed a plan to do that first. She continued dating, was upfront about her plans for Choice Motherhood when it seemed appropriate, and felt good about herself. "I knew where I was going."

The process was difficult, however. A few months before her plans for insemination were to start, she began dating someone she liked. She wondered if she should put her plans on hold. But when her next cycle started, she was in the doctor's office getting bloodwork done — and she kept going. "I'm glad I decided not to wait."

If she had approached Choice Motherhood intellectually, Cheri believes she never would have moved forward, primarily for financial reasons. But the emotions of the first painful breakup helped her realize what she wanted in life — motherhood — and she listened and acted. When we talked, she was 25 weeks pregnant.

Having time gives us a chance to see what our motivations are — to get clarity on our priorities — just as it's easier to see the truth in someone else's life than in our own. Of course, if we had time on our hands, many women wouldn't be making this decision in the first place.

Desire for a Partner

Eventually the regret and remorse about timing can be confronted, learned from, and used as a launch pad to action. But women whose childhood dream is based on a deep desire for a partner, as opposed to a vision of how life should play itself out, seem to have fewer options for controlling their destiny. There is great power in making your priorities known to yourself, but sometimes the universe doesn't bless us how or when we think it should.

It's important to recognize and respect what your true values are. If having a partner is important to you, don't pretend it's not. It is often a defense mechanism to consider ourselves lucky to be without a partner, as if all men are unworthy and all relationships are doomed.

I used to be that woman. Once upon a time I insisted to a therapist that I could never be in a real, full-time relationship because it forces you to compromise and lose your identity. And not long ago, I sat in a friend's kitchen and proudly declared that I was such an independent spirit that I didn't want a man in my life, even if it would make it easier to raise two children.

But after I took care of my needs, dealt with baggage, made choices, and grew into my independent skin more fully, I met someone who had recently done the same.

I strongly believe that a relationship can add to our existing life. But only when we have met our own needs first. The question for all of us to answer is: Do we need the man before having the child, or not?

Getting to the Roots

It's hard to hear the inner voice when you have such a life-changing choice to make. The wrong man can look "good enough." The decision can seem impossible to make. In talking with many women who are grappling with the childhood dream, it seems the ones who have trouble reaching a decision about whether to become a Choice Mother are stuck for one of three reasons.

1. **Timing.** They know they want to be a mother, wish there was a father, and ultimately are stuck emotionally — with anger, sadness, depression — because of the unfairness of timing. "Why can't I meet the right man before it's too late?" "I know I can adopt, but it's not fair that I have to do this alone." "What if the right man is around the corner and if I wait a little longer I'll be able to do this the 'right' way?"
2. **Desire for a partner.** They want to be a mother, but they deeply want to share the experience with a life partner. For logistical, emotional, or financial reasons, they want to have the husband and father in the picture and aren't sure if being a mother alone is enough. Some fear that becoming a Choice Mom will limit their options for finding a mate in the future.
3. **Wanting to offer a father.** They want to be a mother, but worry that it is selfish to deny their child a father. This type of guilt is common and normal, said one Los Angeles–based therapist who frequently counsels single women.

It sounds obvious, but only when you know what your true goals are can you decide what to do. As I mentioned in the previous chapter, I had no idea when Sophie was born that it would lead me to eventually leave New York City, where I had loved living for 18 years. But I knew I didn't want to work simply to make ends meet, that it would be good for both of us to be near extended family, and that I could never afford a second child unless I moved. It became an unexpectedly simple decision to move to Minnesota once I really examined my priorities.

Question yourself

If you're struggling with the childhood dream, ask yourself these questions to get a deeper understanding of what your issues really are.

Is it more important to you to have a parenting partner for your sake, or for the sake of your child? If your conflict about proceeding without Mr. Right has more to do with providing a father for your child, see chapter 6.

Are you dating men in order to find a partner, or to find a father? If you are dating primarily to have a child, then maybe you need to take a step back and try an alternate route. As one therapist told me, "Choosing a man for the purpose of having a father for a child will not sustain a marriage."

What is it about the childhood dream that you want the most? Is it the intimacy of an adult relationship, the support of a parenting partner, the legitimacy of a socially acceptable family life, or the seed to create life? Think deeply about what ranks number one for you.

Is having a child an attempt to combat loneliness? A child can add richness to our life, but does not make us feel "whole." That needs to come from within.

What is it that appeals to you the most about the two-parent model? Was your family life great with a dad so you'd hate to have a child miss that? Or was your childhood lousy and you're not sure you want to single-handedly be responsible for forming someone else's childhood? Determine what you think you lose emotionally in a one-parent family structure. For example, will you miss combining genes with a beloved partner?

If you could magically have the child without a partner — and no financial, moral, logistical, or emotional burdens — would you? If you truly don't see a family life being complete without a man in it — or you being happy as a mother without also being a mate — pay attention to that. On the other hand, if your concerns are primarily about handling parenthood alone, then maybe it would help to widen your perspective and look to others for support. Talk to them: maybe the man can come later, after you've built a support network and established logistical solutions. (See chapter 10.)

Once you specifically know what it is that you are grieving, it will be easier to confront it and move on to whatever decision is right for you.

Controlling the clock

When it feels like the biological clock is ruling our lives, it can make anyone feel angry or depressed that something so important seems to be out of our control.

Some women find it easy to regain that sense of control in their lives by moving toward Choice Motherhood. They have a confidence that, whatever the timing, they will eventually find the right man, without deadline pressure. There might be many temporary relationships before we find the permanent one, but only a dwindling amount of time to have that permanent child.

The philosophy that carries other women is that there are lessons to be learned from every step of the journey and that as long as you are honoring your needs, the "package" you want will follow, maybe in a form you hadn't expected. My story is an illustration of this.

Case #4: My Story

Much to my surprise, when I was five months pregnant with my second child, I met the man I would marry. The man who unexpectedly changed the complexion of the family life I had set up for myself.

Psychologically I was "ready" to meet him. I had made my own decisions about having kids, was happy about my choices, was making ends meet in an okay fashion, and had a solid support network around me. I had created a warm home environment with a good friend, who had moved into my house with her son — my daughter's best friend since the moment they met on a playground.

Although I rarely dated after Sophie was born (and was a reluctant dater before), I knew I would marry again someday. I didn't care when it happened. I presumed it would be after my kids were grown and I had the time and interest to look.

I was on a boat cruise, enjoying a beach bonfire, when I met Dave. Although we didn't talk long, I knew there was something about him that I liked (and I knew from our host that he was single). After discovering his last name and finding his address in the phone book, I wrote him a letter. I laid all the cards on the table: I was pregnant (it wasn't noticeable yet) with a young daughter, looking for male role-model material and friendship. Was he interested in becoming better acquainted? He laid his cards on the table in an e-mail response: He was a widower with a teenage son and a special needs daughter with aggression issues who required a lot of his energy. Yes, he needed more time being with an adult to balance out all the time he spent being dad.

We met over drinks. Two days later, he invited Sophie and me over for a family dinner. Everything clicked and within days, it seemed, we were in love. Six months later he proposed after a hot-air balloon ride. *Bing, bang, boom.*

In hindsight, do I wish I had waited to conceive again so that Dave and I might have had a child together?

Not at all. I was just shy of my 42nd birthday when Dylan was born, which for me was plenty late enough in life to be undergoing the last trimester of pregnancy and tending to an infant again. Dave's vasectomy years earlier made it unlikely for us to conceive. Ultimately we both felt satisfied that I have my kids and he has his kids. Our challenge has been to attempt to share a life together — for various reasons, in two separate homes — and squeeze in as much alone time as we can.

When we are on the present-day side of timing, we have no idea what's in store for us on the future side. If I had been childless when I met Dave, not only would I have missed the wonderfully "exclusive" four years that Sophie and I shared, but I likely would have been stepmom only, because of his vasectomy and teenage children.

If we had met even six months earlier, when I was trying to conceive, I likely would have put those plans on hold — and precious Dylan wouldn't be in my life. Or I would have brought an urgency and confusion to our dynamic that would have derailed the relationship. Or been so focused on my goal that I wouldn't have noticed Dave. He and I met when the timing was just right.

> *The moral of my story: I believe things happen when they do for a reason. We can't foresee any of it.*

It's important to deal with grief about timing, but don't get stuck thinking there is only one way to end up with what you want. It might not happen the way you envisioned it, but the door doesn't shut on having relationships.

On the other hand, most women I talked to for this book remained single while raising their children, without regrets. In fact, none of the Choice pioneers told me they wished they'd had a partner, although a few said they wished they'd had a second child.

There are lots of doors to choose from if you keep walking. Some of them include a partner. Some do not.

Setting Goals

Dr. Joann Paley Galst, a New York City–based therapist who reviewed several chapters in this book, counsels many single women who are contemplating motherhood. She knows that many of them are not ready. As she shared with me, "Parenthood, whether single or within the context of a couple relationship, is not for everyone. For a single woman, if she is actively grieving the loss of the dream of a partner along with parenthood, and if a child might be a reminder of this loss, rather than embraced as a gain to one's life, the woman may not yet be ready for single motherhood."

Forget, for a moment, the deadline pressure of age. If it's the connection with a mate that feels most important to you in your gut, then keep focused on finding Mr. Right. If as a result you don't end up having a child, yes, there will be regret — but like everything in life, there are options (adoption, foster care, travel, hobbies, volunteerism, activism). There is no one path to fulfillment.

If that feels hollow to you — if you want the mate but also want the child — then keep giving serious thought to having the child now and finding the partner later. Do the work you need — emotionally, financially, logistically — to reach this goal.

If you become a Choice Mother, you might not have time and energy and inclination to date for a few years, or you might meet men who don't click with your child and vice versa, or you might decide you don't want to spoil the family dynamic you've built by adding a new person to the mix. But if you're open to meeting a man, being a mother won't make you off-limits.

Ellen is one Choice Mom who met her husband while in the process of adopting her second child. "It took a lot of dating to meet a good guy," she told me. "It was hard to fall in love with him. I was so involved with my son, I just wanted things to be perfect for him." One thing that helped a lot, she said, was that her future husband brought a present for her son on their first date.

And here's another interesting turn-of-events story to share with you that makes the point that life happens in mysterious ways . . .

Case #5: When You Keep Walking

After the breakup of a 13-year relationship, Paley moved to another state and bought a house with land in a more rural area where she could tend to the misfit collection of dogs she loved. She was happily single when she met a recent divorcé, fell in love, and made plans to marry. Eventually he realized he wasn't ready to commit to having another child and a brood of animals, and called off the wedding.

Despite a lifetime of loving relationships, Paley discovered, like Cheri, that it wasn't the dream of being married that she missed, but the dream of being a mother. After months of soul-searching, Paley realized that she could have the child without the man, and felt a sense of empowerment by separating the baby dream from the relationship dream. She began to pursue Choice Motherhood.

Sounds simple in summary, but it was a gut-wrenching process.

"It took me a number of months to recognize the damage and pain that the relationship actually caused me," she said. "I'm pretty tough and smart and independent and capable, even about emotional stuff, and I thought I was okay. But I was wrong. A part of me died. That part of me was The Dream. I don't know how I'll ever believe again. With him, for the first time, I had let myself believe that the dream was possible. The wedding was planned, the invitations sent, I had my gown — now boxed up in the closet."

Over time, however, Paley began to feel liberated. She shared these thoughts with me: "From here on in, I can evaluate future relationships with men for who they are and what they can offer my child and myself, not based on whether he can fulfill my dream of marriage and a baby. Maybe I'll still dream of marriage after my baby is born. Maybe I'll just want a solid relationship with someone. Maybe I'll still be too hurt and jaded to believe again for a really long time. But the one thing I will have believed in will have been myself, my life, and my ability to bring a beautiful child into this world who I can raise in a stable, loving home and with whom I can share my knowledge, my experiences, and the magic that life shows us."

The interesting twist to this story is that, after an emotional miscarriage with a child conceived with an anonymous donor, Paley married her ex-fiancé a few months after we talked, and became pregnant with their child.

"None of this invalidates what I felt or the direction my life was likely to take," she said. "I would still be an SMC in an instant, without any reservation. Both are uniquely wonderful life choices that would have made me happy and complete. Things just changed, and he and I were able to work things out. Some would say I got lucky. I know I am blessed, but not because I have a husband and have recaptured that elusive dream. I feel I am blessed because I have found a life, whatever it may be, that works, that is fulfilling — and I get a baby, too!"

Finding Your Path

A cataclysmic event like a breakup can awaken the senses to what we want. If you've had the benefit of being dumped just when you thought you were about to reach the childhood dream, ask yourself what you miss about the man. Maybe he made you feel warm and loved. Maybe the sex was great. Maybe he made you laugh. Maybe he took you to great restaurants. Maybe it was great to snuggle and listen to music together.

Someone else can come along to provide those things again someday. Keep looking for that next door to open.

But if what you miss most is the dream of sharing the joys of motherhood with someone, then ask yourself if the sharing is as important as the having. Would it be okay to have a close friend massage your shoulders through the last months of pregnancy, or a parent travel with you to China to bring home your baby girl? Could family members share the first gurgles and smiles and steps with you? Can that too-bad-he's-gay buddy help you paint the nursery?

If you don't have that kind of support network, with or without a partner you must develop them before you have a child. As we discuss in many chapters of this book, a support network helps immeasurably — more than one partner ever could. I have had a few good friends, one tremendous babysitter, supportive parents, and a baby-loving sister-in-law to help in spurts over the years, and can't imagine succeeding as well as I have without any of them.

*As Galst said, "A woman who is isolated, without a solid
support network for herself, may be too insular to offer
her child an adequate sense of security in the world outside of the nuclear family. And it may be just too tough
for her to go it alone."*

To be honest, it does feel good to have Dave along for the ride
with my second child — at least part-time, as it is — starting with
Dylan's first major kicks in the womb. He was by my side, holding
my hand and taking pictures like a proud papa, when Dylan was
born. I'll always remember how sweet it was to share my second
night in the hospital with him, when he arrived with chocolate and
champagne and we snuggled until 2:00 A.M. to the murmur of the
hospital's "nature sounds" loop on the television. I couldn't have
picked a more thoughtful man to share with me the last trimester
of pregnancy, the pain and fear and excitement when contractions
began, the blurriness of late-night feedings.

But it meant as much to me to hear Sophie squeal with delight
when Dylan poked his head out. (I had taken drugs this time, so I
was oblivious to pain and was not screeching irrationally.)

The incredible four-plus years of one-on-one bonding with
Sophie had started in those first moments alone in the hospital after she was born, when I was tired and a little lonely, but mainly
fascinated with this new being I had created and was now responsible for. I didn't need sleep — or snuggling or chocolate or champagne — so much as to have her always by my side so I could look
at her nonstop.

The experiences of both births were extremely different, yet
both were wonderful. And certainly the experience of being Sophie's
mother has been no less powerful because of the absence of a mate
in the first years — quite the opposite.

There are times when I feel sad about the way my relationship
with Sophie is changing. One night, shortly before her brother's
five-month birthday, she asked if she and I could do something together, just the two of us, not Dave, not Dylan. It was a sweet mo-

ment. Of course, I was disappointed in myself that she'd had to ask, although I was happy she was able to articulate that she was missing something.

But change is constant. With or without Dave and an extended family, when she watched her brother Dylan come into the world our bond was permanently affected. And before I know it, her increasing circle of friends soon will mean even less mother-daughter intensity.

My point is, a partner — a sibling, a job — makes a huge difference in the level of interaction you have with your child. There is a positive and a negative, a yin and a yang, to everything. A partner can be a tremendous plus to having a child, but there will be negatives as well. Just as adding a child to your life will have regular ups and downs. (In one day I can spill over with love for the child that is Sophie, and be infuriated with the child that is Sophie.)

Don't think that having a partner is the one ingredient that would make motherhood complete, because life can be simpler in many ways without one. Parenting skills, disciplining methods, communication patterns, and energy levels, to name a few, differ greatly between adults, causing friction no matter how much they love each other. As one married friend told me, she finds motherhood much easier when her husband is traveling on business.

A Choice Mom of three sometimes fantasizes about how nice it would be to have an extra income and a father in the home for her children, but she knows that the compromise involved in bringing another adult into the family would be a tough one for her to make. Only five years into Choice Motherhood, she said, "I've outgrown the desire to be married."

Logistically, many women decide they can do without a partner. Emotionally, embarking on parenthood without a partner is a different matter.

It can be difficult (or less desirous) to find a partner after children. And it is sometimes impossible to have children after finding a partner. Analyzing which possibility would make you feel worse — and how you think your child will fare with or without a father — is sometimes the only way single women can move on.

Final Thoughts

Staying in a bad marriage to have children, or remaining childless, are legitimate choices — as is becoming a Choice Mom when what you wanted was a partner first. But don't "settle" because you're afraid that half the dream is the best you can do.

Don't use your grief as a crutch either, because no one gives you back the time you spend waiting. Every setback, every disappointment, and every emotion ultimately can be used as a way to assess your priorities.

Judy, the woman we met earlier who decided to become a Choice Mom despite her grief, kept walking — and became pregnant on her seventh insemination attempt.

Dev, the woman who decided not to become a Choice Mom, kept walking too. A few years later, when I talked to her a second time, she was engaged to a man with two children, and they were talking about having a child together. "It was really helpful for me to speak with you, as it reaffirmed my desire to parent with a partner," she said. "I believe that setting my intention very clearly and directly helped to bring this dream into reality."

I couldn't have planned a better way to make the major point of this chapter:

> *Life reveals itself in ways you cannot control or predict, so allow yourself to mourn that plans are not going according to schedule, but don't let it stop you from moving. Life has surprises in store for you if you just keep walking.*

Will My Community Accept Us?

> "Good mother" came to have a precise meaning. You know
> her well, for she has lingered all these years in the background
> of our domestic values. She is most assuredly not Murphy
> Brown or Mia Farrow or Hillary Rodham Clinton. She is,
> rather, properly married, faithful, subservient, modest, a
> woman who puts aside her own desires to rear and inspire her
> children. She is part of our mental furniture: the doormat.
>
> — Shari Thurer, *The Myths of Motherhood* (1994)

Today there is much greater acceptance of Choice Motherhood
than there was 20 years ago. Yet many women thinking of becoming a Choice Mom still feel the bite from those who feel they are
wrong to bring a child into a fatherless world, and that children
who are raised in this environment are less likely to learn proper
values and more likely to grow up as behaviorally troubled members of society.

All of us have our own definition of which circles of community
mean something to us. For some, it includes only the inner sanc-
tum of friends and family. Others would include in that list neighbors, co-workers, fellow churchgoers, playground parents, clients,
or customers. Sometimes the opinions of social acquaintances,
people in the doctor's office, and distant relatives affect us. Or the
wider network of people in our hometown, strangers on the street,
society in general. Maybe even the viewpoints of people in the
news.

If you become a Choice Mom, you must be prepared to expect everything from strong, vocal criticism of your choice to a low level of disapproval. No matter how tight and supportive your circle, it can still rattle you the first time you hear the disparaging comments of those who believe it is immoral to raise a child without a father. Or see the upraised eyebrow of a client or boss who clearly disapproves, and who you fear might now look at you in a different light. Or listen to your mother tell you that if you lost weight it would be easier to find a husband.

Many women get full support from loved ones and colleagues who understand their strengths and self-sufficiency. Many do not.

As Jody astutely told me, "Lack of community acceptance can really hurt, because it can be a painful mirror for a woman's feelings of loss."

Most of us have trouble — at least initially — dealing with even that one person who doesn't understand why you would consider this choice. Sometimes the criticism can come out as shrill opposition; other times as a disappointed murmur.

AnnaMarie is from a Catholic family of 12 kids. "It was hard for my mother and father to accept this decision. They felt I should play the cards I was dealt. Not having a mate was my hand. But I could see the sad example of my maiden aunt, who never married and never had kids, although I know she loves children.

"My mother actually asked me if I had had a psychological evaluation before I was inseminated. I asked her if she had one before she got married and pregnant at age 19. I mean, come on! Who gets to decide if I'm fit to be a good parent but me? At age 37 I felt I was bound to be a better parent than lots of people."

> *"Although they love my daughter [now 5] and support me, I know deep down they feel my decision was not the best. My father still thinks my daughter has gotten a raw deal. I don't think he can see her or our family as whole."*

"I tell him I see couples arguing about who is right and which way to go with parenting issues and styles. My married sisters are always complaining about how little their husbands contribute to the household beyond finances. For me, it's easier and less stressful, and easier and less stressful for my child."

When Ellen announced her pregnancy, her mother said, "That's the worst news I've heard in a long time." Her father, on the other hand, was supportive. And her sister, who was in the process of divorcing, said, "It's better not to have any partner than to have the wrong one."

Another woman told me that a close friend — also single, childless, and in her forties — tried to talk her out of Choice Motherhood. "I think her view is due to her being conservative, a little stubborn, and generally averse to risks. She worries about everything going wrong. She lives near her family and shares an office with her dad. Closeness to family is a good thing, but she's not very independent."

One woman said her sister didn't talk to her for six months because she didn't approve of the decision to become a single mother. But after her sister's son was diagnosed with cancer, the two reopened communication, except "about this hugely important thing in my life. It is a great sadness for me."

Another woman told me her Jewish background emphasized that "family is the most important thing in your life," and that having children fulfills the command to "be fruitful and multiply" rather than to satisfy a "man-woman dynamic." Initially her grandmother was opposed, but after she realized the child would be her first great-grandchild, she softened.

Many women find that there is less opposition after the child is on its way — say, in the second trimester of pregnancy or after a green light on adoption — rather than when the idea is a concept some might see as preventable.

One woman, who grew up Catholic on a family farm, had nine supportive siblings living in the area. Only her father expressed concern about her pursuit of single motherhood, right up to the day she left for the airport to pick up her daughter in China. When she returned home there was a message from her father saying he would like to see his granddaughter. "From that time on, he'll call, see how she's doing — he's been wonderful! He's been probably more support for me in a lot of ways than anyone since we've gotten home."

Others recognize that sometimes loved ones simply need time to accept and embrace what for them seems to be a decision out of the blue. But many women recognize that their decision will be criticized no matter what.

Dora is an elementary school teacher in a conservative town. "My principal told me that I could not bring my baby into the building when I came in for my check while on maternity leave. I had two colleagues say to my face something about being 'immoral' and 'your scandal.' Another colleague spread a rumor that a parent requested not to have her child in my class."

Dora's mother was equally as unsupportive. When she met her grandchild for the first time, her comment was, "How do you know he doesn't have AIDS?"

Others in her community have been more encouraging. Such as the aunt who said, "Most people are supportive of another person's good fortune." And the student's parent who said, "You finally have one that you don't have to send home at 3:15!"

Although many women will be faced with a stray friend or relative who opposes Choice Motherhood, for women in conservative communities, or who adhere to religions that disapprove, the challenge is far greater.

As Cindy told me, "I have been very concerned about what the Christian community and my church will think. I have read that Christians are against anonymous donor insemination, even for married couples, and I have been told that it is wrong for me to even consider being a single parent. I also have been told that being pregnant and single will affect my ability to be witness to other Christians because others will assume I am having sex outside of marriage. I worry that my child and I won't be able to find a supportive church, and I wonder how other Christian parents will treat him or her."

Some women report that criticism of their decision leaves them re-questioning their choice, such as the woman who told me of the nurse who said no doctor in their small town would help her get pregnant by insemination because it is morally wrong for a single woman to bring a child into the world.

"I felt I had come to a crisis," she recalled. "Was it fair to bring a child into a community that was so close-minded?"

She talked to people she respected but didn't know in a close way, such as a 70-year-old co-worker and "an old male friend that I rarely see anymore, but who I knew would tell me the truth even if I didn't want to hear it. Basically they all felt that if I went into this responsibly and thoughtfully, I and any child would be okay."

"You Are Selfish"

Several months before my daughter was conceived, I told a good friend of my interest in becoming a Choice Mom. He surprised me with his very vocal opposition to the idea. "How can you purposely bring children into the world knowing they won't have a dad? That's selfish. You're thinking only of yourself, not the child."

As our impassioned debate unfolded over dinner, he went on to say that adopting was morally better than purposely making a life, but even then I'd be putting the child into a disadvantaged situation.

His reaction is a common one among those who are opposed to Choice Motherhood. The roots of this argument are based on the idea that a child's right to have two parents is more important than a woman's desire to parent, and that by purposely depriving a child of a father, the mother has made a selfish choice that should not have been hers to make. Some of these critics believe that it is less selfish to choose an already existing child — preferably one from a foreign orphanage — whose prospects for a good life are already weakened.

A male acquaintance of mine — a divorced father of two — also thinks it's selfish for a woman to choose this lifestyle for her child. It's a difficult way to raise kids, he said, and shortchanges everyone involved. He too is against the idea of a single woman giving birth, finding it more redeeming to at least adopt a needy child.

While I understand that some people think of it that way, many Choice Mothers agree that giving up time, money, freedom, and an independent lifestyle to raise another human being is not a selfish act. Any good parent, married or not, enters into the task with the "selfish" desire to experience the highs that come from unconditional love for a child — knowing the lows that come with it. The world needs more kids who are raised by a loving person who actively chooses parenthood.

That is, in fact, why I refer to it as Choice Motherhood. Those who make this choice are actively choosing to parent (and reading this book, among others, because they want to make a responsible decision and effort). It is not a choice that is made lightly. As one Choice Mother pointed out, it is more selfish — and harmful — to marry a man you don't love in order to build a family.

Another woman suggested, "With the divorce rate over 50 percent, your odds of becoming a single mother are greater than your odds of staying married. So is it selfish to have children in a marriage knowing that statistically you are likely to divorce, thereby destroying the family that your child has come to know? Aren't children better off, or at least as well off, with only one parent than starting off with two parents and having that family ripped apart?"

Why the Opposition?

What can be seen as an almost natural next step for a woman accustomed to being on her own can be a terrifying prospect for anyone else. Often the strongest opposition comes from married people who find child rearing to be a difficult process. Many of them entered into it without as much thought as Choice Mothers tend to give, and cannot imagine taking it on single-handedly.

Sometimes these parents are full-time caregivers, and cannot understand why or how anyone could juggle motherhood and a job. Or they expected their spouse to share child-rearing duties, rather than considering it "babysitting," and are angrily entrenched in thinking that no one should handle the responsibility alone. Or they have very supportive mates who are engaged with the kids, and cannot relate to approaching parenthood any other way.

Others run headfirst into a person's religious beliefs. This opposition tends to see Choice Motherhood as an immoral act that goes against God's plan. I expected my strongly Catholic grandmother and great-aunt to hold this view, but was pleasantly surprised to learn that both considered children to be gifts from God, irrespective of the method by which they arrive.

One of the first (among few) social scientists to study Choice Motherhood is Jane Bock, who in 2000 published a journal article titled, "Doing the Right Thing: Single Mothers by Choice and the Struggle for Legitimacy."[1]

She wrote that Choice Mothers interviewed over a two-year period often made significant changes in their lives for the benefit of their child — arranging their careers so they could spend more time at home, or moving to an ethnically diverse neighborhood so their adopted child wouldn't stand out.

The mother generally feels her choice is morally acceptable if she can answer yes to questions such as: Can I afford a child? Do I have the skills to be a competent parent? Do I have the kind of job that will permit me to handle motherhood and work? But religious grounds often played a large role in deciding whether others would consider their choice to be morally acceptable.

One interesting similarity Bock noticed among the women she interviewed who were comfortable with their choice was that the majority of them were Jewish. Among Reform Jews, the discussion tends to be focused not on the legitimacy of the child, but on the motive for having the child. Said one, "We are very traditional women . . . the idea of not having children is not okay."

A single Orthodox Jewish mother of three, quoted in *Hadassah Magazine,*[2] said, "It's precisely because religious women are steeped in family values that they want children and seek ways to have them. By 35, I realized I had dragged out relationships that were not appropriate because of my desire to have children."

Another woman quoted in the article, who was a Holocaust survivor, became a pioneering Choice Mother when she was in her forties. "My whole family was destroyed in the Holocaust and I felt there must be continuity for our family."

Liberal Protestantism also tends not to concern itself with questions of legitimacy, Bock reported. "Instead, it focuses on the moral or ethical components of decision making."

On the other hand, a Catholic woman she spoke with said her priest refused to baptize her baby with others during Mass, insisting instead that a private ceremony would be more appropriate. Since Catholicism defines any child conceived out of wedlock as illegitimate, and anything that replaces marital intercourse as a method of conception as "morally illicit," one single woman did not tell her Catholic parents of her pregnancy until the eighth month.

One woman Bock met had a clever comeback for those who opposed her decision on moral grounds: "Jesus was the product of donor insemination!"

Bock reported that most of the women she talked to sought guidance from friends, relatives, therapists, and religious leaders before making their decision about whether or not it was "right" to become a Choice Mom. "With the exception of those exposed to Roman Catholic doctrine, little concern focused on the legitimacy of the child. Instead, concern was more focused on whether living in a single-parent household would affect the child's psychological or emotional well-being."

What can you do?

Whatever the reason for nonacceptance of the decision to pursue Choice Motherhood, it is usually rooted in the person's own deep-seated experiences and values — and biases. It generally isn't productive to try to convert him or her to your perspective on the subject. Often the best you can do is agree to disagree and move forward.

As an extreme example of this, who among us would expend the time or energy trying to change the viewpoint of the following letter writer to *Newsweek,* who complained in 2001 about the Choice Motherhood trend? He wrote that this was a selfish choice that would intentionally disadvantage the next generation, with only the goal of pleasuring the mother. Trying to change biology "threatens the very fabric of our society," he wrote. He blamed feminism for instilling "in the mainstream American woman" an idea that is "disgusting, immoral and unethical." He urged that it was time to stop supporting all types of family structures.

Although most people around us are not as acidic, even the less passionate naysayers generally are speaking from their own in-grained perspective. Just as many Choice Mothers have strong opinions about whether a donor should be called "daddy," for example, or whether a 66-year-old Romanian woman should have been allowed to give birth, there are lines drawn for some who believe that Choice Motherhood should never be an option.

In the end, there are only a handful of approaches you can take to deal with those who disagree with you (about anything):

1. Arm yourself with facts (some of which appear in later chapters of this book) and attempt to address their concerns logically;
2. Listen to their concerns, let them know you hear them, and move on respectfully without engaging in battle (returning with emotionally based fire makes people think they've hit a nerve and are therefore "right");
3. Come to a mutual agreement that you'll never share the

same viewpoint, but that you have the right to make your
own choices for your life, just as they do for theirs;

4. Fight endlessly about the issue;
5. Take flight and surround yourself with supportive allies.

Nicola, the Choice Mother of two, offers this advice: "Often
you have to let other people know how to behave towards you and
yours. About becoming a single mom, I would always get the
words in first and say, 'I know not everyone would think it was the
right thing to do, but it has been right for me.' There's really not
much that someone can say to that. I've acknowledged their possible disapproval and declared that it's not relevant to me. Very few
people make negative comments after that, but since I've already
said it's okay if they do, it doesn't seem to matter."

It might not seem satisfying to accept that some people don't
approve of you — and it often can be more stressful with silent
dissenters, as opposed to the vocal ones who get it out in the open
— but focus instead on those who do approve of you.

And always keep in mind that moral values vary with time,
place, and person. Remember the story of Amina, the woman in
Nigeria sentenced in 2002 to be stoned because she had a child out
of wedlock? Was that decision more "right" than that of those
who eventually overturned the sentence? Rules change because
they aren't based on absolutes. Choice Motherhood is not morally
"wrong" unless you think it is, no matter who disagrees with you.

A look back in history

My ancestor Hannah Duston was kidnapped by Indians with her
newborn and her midwife (coincidentally, an ancestor of my ex-
husband). This was seventeenth-century Haverhill, Massachusetts,
when tribes were rewarded by Canadian settlers for bringing them
white slaves.

Early in the journey north, one of the Indians horrifically killed
Hannah's baby girl to stop the crying. Days later, Hannah organized other kidnapping victims for the late-night killing of their

captors, and returned home with the scalps as proof. In a ceremony on the Boston Common, her husband was awarded bounty money for his wife's heroism — values being what they were — and Hannah returned to the simpler life of mother and wife. She eventually was lauded in history books, and a statue with her likeness was erected as the first memorial to an American woman.

Ironically, also on the Boston Common, Hannah's younger sister Elizabeth was hanged for bearing twins out of wedlock. Cotton Mather, the fundamentalist preacher of his day, shamed her publicly as an example of someone who "consorted with the devil." The babies' father denied the charges and went on to father other twins in town — values being what they were.

Although unmarried mothers are no longer hanged — and men are less blatantly rewarded for the courage of women in their lives — much of the basis for rejecting Choice Motherhood has its roots in values that are based on economic worth.

As Mary Ann Mason wrote in her book *From Father's Property to Children's Rights:*[3] "For most of our history, well into the twentieth century, the worth of children was seen primarily in terms of economic, not emotional, value. Fathers, recognized as the economic heads of the household and the supervisors of their children's labor, were granted paramount rights to custody and control of their children. Mothers, who had no economic power or responsibility, had no right to custody as long as the father was alive. Custody disputes, which usually occurred only if the father died, were often determined practically by considering who could support the child (mothers often could not) or which relative needed the child's labor."

In fact, she wrote, only if the birth occurred within the legal institution of marriage was parenthood of consequence. "Children born out of wedlock were considered *filius nullius* — or child of no family — allowing neither the mother nor the father custodial rights. Such children were usually put out as apprentices to another family."

Orphanages and foster homes weren't yet available, so even if the mother was alive, courts would apprentice the children to masters, who had similar rights and obligations as biological fathers. Only after children's labor was replaced by the use of new immigrant labor, and motherhood became more important, did children become emotional assets rather than economic ones. Parents were encouraged to have fewer children and to put more effort into nurturing and educating them, instead of having many children who served as workers. Parenting increasingly became a sentimental role, rather than an economic task.

It wasn't until the late 1800s that most states passed legislation declaring that a "bastard child" was a member of his mother's family (not his father's). However, even through the Progressive era, unwed mothers were considered unworthy mothers and were given little help in supporting their children.

Why Do We Care What People Say?

Jody was thinking about becoming a Choice Mom when she shared with me some interesting comments about why it matters what other people think about this choice. "Many women spend a good number of years truly believing and trying to get the childhood dream to come true for them," she suggested. "Being a single mother is not how most of us were raised, and is not what society tells us is 'right.' First you are a failure for not getting married, then you are a failure for bringing a child into the world in what some see as a 'disadvantaged' position. Or you are a cautionary tale about the price women pay for being 'too' successful."

> *"Since most of us tend to be independent women who have been successful at what we do, as time goes by and we fail to have a family in the traditional sense, it's hard to accept that we're not viewed as a 'successful achiever' anymore."*

The reflection of others tends to push the self-esteem button that is already within us. If we're confident in our choice, we don't usually care whether others agree. But when there is a nagging voice in our head — placed there, or of our own making — telling us we aren't as 'perfect' as we should be, the sound of everyone who echoes that notion, whether in a shout or a whisper, can affect us deeply.

As Jody put it, "Society tends to be more comfortable with women as victims, of divorce or whatever, rather than assertively making their way in the world or doing it their own way. They are viewed by some as being selfish, having too much fun to settle down, not accepting that they can't have it all, being too picky to marry, being too successful."

Community disapproval can be even harder for women who are considering Choice Motherhood as the only remaining option for having children. It can be hard to defend your choice if it is not something you're particularly happy about doing.

On the other hand, as Diane told me, "I think it's best for me to simply ignore any naysayers. There's no point in absorbing the negativity of others. I am an emotionally strong person and most likely wouldn't be considering this as an option if I wasn't. I truly, truly believe that it is not the number of parents, or the type of family that contributes to a healthy child. I truly believe that it is the care, love, honesty, and respect that children receive while growing up that sculpts who they will be as an adult. Choice Mothers understand that they are a universe within themselves, and by using whatever resources they can put their hands on they will be able to provide their children what they need to grow up healthy."

Helping the Child

Although acceptance of Choice Motherhood grows every year, largely because of the success stories and the inevitable trends in women's lives, sharp criticism from any corner can still do damage — if not to the woman, then to her child, at any age.

Anyone who decides to become a Choice Mother must be prepared to develop skills to help her child cope with anyone who disapproves of the family structure, such as:

- Keeping the lines of communication open so he or she feels free to share with you something that was said at school;
- Showing the pride and confidence you feel as a loving parent;
- Not apologizing for choices you have made while acknowledging that life might not always be perfect;
- Making an effort to bring other role models and single parents into your network.

Remember too that many of the most inquisitive and blunt questions will likely come from other children — your child's young cousins, schoolmates, and neighborhood kids.

Although the harsh community reaction to Dora and her son, now a second grader, subsided with time ("I guess I'm 'old news'"), she does talk about it with him when needed. "He and I have a wonderful rapport and talk things through when they come up." After his music teacher made an inappropriate comment, she wrote a letter of complaint — rather than letting it slide — and pointed out to him that some people have trouble accepting families that are not "traditional," then explained what that meant.

She has protected him by cutting off contact with her disapproving mother. "So far, so good. He is delightful and hasn't seemed to have any problems. He's successful at school, popular, well-behaved — and the joy of my life. He's been worth everything!"

Dora recently added to their family by adopting. Her son went with her to Russia and was involved in the adoption process. "He's very proud of this and feels a special protectiveness of his sister."

Final Thoughts

As you consider this choice, and how support — or lack of it — affects your resolve, consider taking these steps:

1. Define who in your community means the most to you.
2. One by one, ask yourself if the rejection of this person or that group would derail your intent to have a child.
3. Consider how you react when these people have a different viewpoint than yours.
4. Reflect on why this person's or that group's disapproval would affect you. What self-esteem button would it push?

Answering these questions won't make the disapproval go away, if it ends up being there in the first place (and quite often we are surprised by who understands and who does not), but it can help you sort out feelings logically before the emotions of a particular dynamic kick in.

And remember: Typically a Choice Mother doesn't encounter as much resistance when the product of her "selfish" or "immoral" act grows into a happy and well-adjusted child. The Choice Mom who is proud and positive usually disarms even the most judgmental critics.

Although the friend who criticized my choice has never disparaged my daughter's existence in my life, I've never forgotten his words. Or the pointed comment from a family friend that "every child wants two parents." Or the shock from a traditional couple that couldn't believe I'd do something so crazy. Or the accusations of an acquaintance who belittled the Choice lifestyle as a dangerous trend that Hollywood celebrities were ushering in "as if it was a good thing."

So yes, down deep under my determined nature, I might have cared a little about what other people thought of my choice. But I don't today — and in fact I haven't heard disapproval from anyone for having a second child, perhaps because my daughter is obviously happy, smart, and well-behaved.

Every day that I spend with my children, I am happily secure that my conservative but open-minded brother was right when, after he learned I was pregnant with Sophie,

> *he said in his thick Minnesota drawl, "The kid's going to*
> *have an interesting life."*

And security, after all, is what enables us to have a thick skin with our detractors.

✦ BONUS SECTION ✦

Revisiting the *Murphy Brown* Debate

When loved ones and members of a community raise eyebrows at the choice to raise a child in a single-parent home, the concern is sometimes rooted in a basic philosophical debate about what children need in order to grow up strong and whole. A central aspect of that debate is whether having both biological parents married and living in the same household will resolve problems that affect society.

On the one hand, as Barbara Dafoe Whitehead wrote in a powerful *Atlantic Monthly* article in 1993:[4]

> If we fail to come to terms with the relationship between family structure and declining child well-being, then it will be increasingly difficult to improve children's life prospects, no matter how many new programs the federal government funds. Nor will we be able to make progress in bettering school performance or reducing crime or improving the quality of the nation's future work force — all domestic problems closely connected to family breakup. Worse, we may contribute to the problem by pursuing policies that actually increase family instability and breakup.

But if raising strong children is the goal, Stephanie Coontz wrote in a 2002 *American Prospect* article, "Nostalgia as Ideology," the method should be to support parents on a global scale.[5]

> The most constructive way to support modern marriages is to improve work-life policies so that couples can spend more

time with each other and their kids, to increase social-support systems for children, and to provide counseling for all couples who seek it. But many in the center-right marriage movement resist such reforms, complaining that single parents and unmarried couples — whether heterosexual or of the same sex — could "take advantage" of them.

In the next few chapters, we will start to examine single parenthood as seen from the perspective of sociologists, policymakers, and child development experts. But before we do, let's take a walk through recent history to examine the roots of many of the "moral values" arguments against Choice Motherhood. Although most criticism of the lifestyle is based on research with divorced or abandoned households, it is useful to understand where many of the objections come from.

The Quayle Controversy

An estimated 34 million Americans tuned in — 35 percent of the TV audience — on the night in 1992 that the TV character Murphy Brown became an unwed mother. The plot line itself might not have attracted as much notoriety were it not for comments that then–Vice President Dan Quayle made during a 45-minute speech.[6] His intention at a San Francisco talk was to discuss a recent trip to Japan, but Quayle decided to talk about values instead, since riots in Los Angeles had recently erupted after white police officers were acquitted on abuse charges in the beating of the black motorist Rodney King.

The infamous passage was: "Bearing babies irresponsibly is, simply, wrong. Failing to support children one has fathered is wrong. We must be unequivocal about this. It doesn't help matters when prime-time TV has Murphy Brown, a character who supposedly symbolizes today's intelligent, highly paid professional woman, mocking the importance of fathers by bearing a child alone and calling it just another lifestyle choice."

As Quayle explained later, his criticism was not against single mothers, but against the attitude that fathers are not important anymore.

On the ten-year anniversary of his infamous speech, Quayle spoke to an audience at the National Press Club.[7] "I believe it even more now," he said about the need for fathers to be directly involved with their children. "I never criticized single mothers. What I was trying to do was point out the reality of their struggle, particularly a single mother who doesn't have financial wealth." He said one of his complaints with the show's premise was that the father was going to be completely uninvolved.

Coincidentally, on the same night Quayle gave his anniversary speech, the unmarried character of Rachel on the popular TV show *Friends* was scheduled to give birth. "We've made some progress," Quayle said. "The father is apparently going to get involved with that child."

Social commentary

Whatever Quayle's initial intent, commentators who agreed with his premise took it another step. Some of them began compiling evidence to indicate the "wrongness" of single motherhood — that a family without a father produces children who are a burden to society.

The sociologist David Popenoe, for example, published a book called *Life Without Father: Compelling New Evidence That Fatherhood and Marriage Are Indispensable for the Good of Children and Society.*[8] Although he indicated that few studies had examined the effects of fatherlessness, independent of all other variables, on children, he pointed out that "almost anything bad that can happen to a child occurs with much greater frequency to the children of divorce and those who live in single-parent families."

In Whitehead's *Atlantic Monthly* article, she wrote that she understood why some people choose an alternative path. But she worried that what might make a parent happy might detract from a child's need for stability, continuity, harmony, and permanence in family life. She implied that it was a mistake for society not to frown upon anything but the two-parent model, and that pop culture was awakening a fantasy of individuality.

She largely used the 1986 book *Single Mothers and Their Children*, written by Sara McLanahan and Irwin Garfinkel,[9] for proof that even single mothers who are not poor are not financially secure. She indicated that single mothers move much more frequently than two-parent families, which can lead to different friends, schools, and neighbors. Whitehead also was concerned that boyfriends and babysitters would be moving in and out of a child's life.

Whitehead made the point that the proliferation of diverse family structures had led to greater poverty, rising crime rates, and declining school performance. She indicated that if everyone came from a stable two-parent household, these social issues could be more easily avoided.

She pointed out that more than 70 percent of all juveniles in state reform institutions came from fatherless homes. Controlling for income, many studies had indicated that boys from single-mother homes were significantly more likely than others to commit crimes. She said that schools across the country were reporting more aggressive, acting-out behavior, especially among boys living in single-parent families.

Author commentary

Critics of single parenthood tend to (1) focus on the less successful stories as the norm, and (2) group divorced and Choice households together — even though in Choice homes there is no disruption, no trauma of separation and conflict, and no breakdown of family structure. Those are very good reasons why the statistics of single parenthood do not generally apply to Choice Mothers.

I have no doubt that stable, loving two-parent homes — where both mother and father have a healthy emotional investment in their children — offer tremendous benefits. And I have no doubt that an unstable, unhealthy single-parent home does not offer children the emotional security they need to grow up strong. But as Whitehead herself recognized, not every two-parent home is "good," and not every single-parent home is "bad."

Discouraging one common family structure because some don't do it as well as others is akin to not allowing people in their twenties to marry because statistics show these are the couples most likely to divorce.

Some parents are buried by financial problems, self-destructive behavior, and emotional instability. And these tend to be the ones who don't parent well, whether they are married or not.

A single woman who is unable to provide a secure environment — who cannot earn an income, find quality childcare, maintain relationships with a healthy network of supportive people, and offer authoritative parenting — is not Choice Mother material. Period. Married couples who cannot provide the same have no business becoming parents either.

In fact, the instability of single-parent families that Whitehead was concerned about in 1993 is not a factor for most Choice households. Most Choice Mothers I have interviewed have moved at least once, but the end result was to improve the lives of their children by moving to a better neighborhood, a better school district, a bigger home, or closer to family.

Most Choice Mothers and Thinkers I have talked to earn more than $40,000 a year and have completed college. In fact, 34 of 64 respondents in a survey I randomly sent out earned more than $60,000 (55 above $40,000), and 42 had postgraduate degrees.

As Whitehead pointed out in her essay, a stable environment is important to any child. But I also do not equate security and stability with "lack of change." Every childhood and every life involves change. I'm not one who thinks that is preventable, whether you are married or not, wealthy or not. Nor do I think it is bad. Nor do I think it affects people in the same way, no matter how they are raised.

One or two variables — growing up poor, moving a lot as a kid, even losing a parent — does not take precedent over every other variable in life. We all grow up with influences and adjustments that help make us who we are. A sibling is added to the household and suddenly a firstborn doesn't feel as special. A move is made to a nicer house in a different community and a child must cope with the loneliness and self-consciousness of being the new kid. A beloved grandparent dies and no one can protect a child from experiencing the pain of loss.

As we'll discuss in the next section, growing up in a single-parent home and growing up without a father will have an impact on a child. But it doesn't have to be a destructive impact. There are things to be learned from every change, every loss, every difference. The trick is to help our children navigate as best as we can, so that they will grow from every experience in their own individual, healthy way.

In short, change and diversity are not negative influences when the Choice Mother gives her child the tools — required for any successful adult life — to deal with challenges. (We'll look at how to develop those tools in chapter 13.)

> *A theme we'll return to several times in this book: Being a good parent is more important than being a married parent.*

Final Thoughts

In 2001, Quayle published an essay in *Newsweek* entitled "Why I Think I'm Still Right,"[10] in which he wrote that his primary issue with the *Murphy Brown* story line was that fathers came across as irrelevant to a child's life.

He wrote that time pressure, for one, is leading to turmoil in families today. "Time formerly spent in family activities is now spent on the computer, in front of the television, on the phone, in the car and at the mall. We are a harried society."

He pointed out that the strains of economic pressure means that more parents need to work. The tendency for mobility means that more families live far apart, which reduces the natural support network. Pop culture often tends to tear down institutions that offer a sense of stability.

I applaud Quayle for putting his name to one of the more rational and well-stated formulas for raising a healthy child. As his essay said:

> Children must have hope. Hope comes from a good education, good values, self-respect and living in a society that values every person, expects the best from each of us and does not tolerate abhorrent behavior.

Quayle indicated that odds are, a two-parent household is still the best place to raise a child. But, "Since the support system of extended families . . . in most cases does not exist today, we need to expand the idea of extended family to include neighbors, friends and community. We each need to look around our community and see who needs nurturing. Is there a child who needs a grandparent figure, a father figure, a mother figure or a doting aunt or uncle? Fill that void for them. The sense of belonging, of being a part of a greater whole, is what is sorely needed by so many."

The historical writers Stephanie Coontz and Steven Mintz have written wonderful books that point out how dramatically our communities have changed. (See Resources section.) Once upon a time, people did believe in using the village or urban community to raise children. In the 1950s we started to shift child-rearing responsibility solely to "nuclear" family units — and I think that's when many children started to get shortchanged.

As Quayle aptly pointed out, it is connection to others that makes such a dramatic difference in the life of every child.

The History of Private Life
by Steven Mintz[11]

✦ We hear a great deal these days about traditional family values. But precisely when did traditional family values reign supreme? Certainly not in the world of the Old Testament or classical antiquity . . .

In colonial America . . . ministers described romantic love as a form of madness and urged young men to choose their mates on the basis of rational consideration of property and family . . . In colonial Virginia, an average marriage lasted . . . seven years. Till death do us part meant something quite different than it does today.

Families were . . . too large to allow parents to give much attention to each child. The average woman bore between 8 and 10 children. Fathers . . . were the primary parent . . . Children of six or seven were sent to work as servants or apprentices . . .

It was not until the mid-19th century that the family patterns that we call traditional begin to emerge . . . And yet, we must be careful about assuming that the 19th century was an era of traditional family values . . . Our best guess is that between 5 and 10 percent of young urban women practiced prostitution . . . The major method of birth control was abortion . . . The proportion of single-parent, female-headed families was almost as high as it is today because of the higher death rate.

Today, we tend to assume that families are weaker and more fragile than those in the past. But I think this view is wrong. From a historical perspective . . . we invest much more emotional and psychological significance in family life than did our ancestors. We regard family ties and intimacy as the key to our personal happiness . . . Our high divorce rate doesn't reflect a low valuation on marriage; it reflects our overly high hopes and expectations.

STAGE 2

Is It Fair to the Child?

Although the politics of Choice Motherhood doesn't usually inhibit single women who desire to become mothers, the psychological impact of their decision often does. Nearly half of the women I polled in an informal survey spontaneously brought up as a major concern how a child's development, behavior, and attitude toward her might be influenced by growing up without a father.

My conversations with Choice Mothers reveal that most of their kids — who tended to be under the age of 10 — had no strong issues related to growing up in an "unconventional" family. Many children were curious about the absence of a father, but, in general, had no particular feeling of "lack." In fact, more of them tell me they wish they had a sibling, rather than expressing a wish for a dad. However, as we also will discuss in future chapters, some related issues that are important to be mindful of can evolve when children enter adolescence, around the age of 12.

In this section we begin to explore the myths and realities of Choice Motherhood as influences on a child's development and well-being.

Two methods of single motherhood not by choice — divorce and young, accidental pregnancy — have largely influenced the understanding of how children can be affected growing up with one parent. In "The Impact of a Single-Parent Home" we examine more closely the statistics about troubled teens to find out how family structure does and does not matter.

In "Growing Up Without a Father" we will candidly assess what a child can miss without a father's influence, according to child experts, and what Choice Moms can do to help.

· 5 ·

The Impact of a Single-Parent Home

There are few studies that examine the impact it has on a child to grow up in a single-parent home with a Choice Mother. My ongoing interviews with mature Choice Kids — some featured in chapter 15 — are the only extended reportage of their viewpoints that I know of.

The hundreds of studies that have been done about the impact of single parenthood on children primarily have looked at how divorced or "disrupted" households compare to two-parent homes. Few have effectively looked at the impact on children of growing up in a one-parent home that was not affected by disruption. Although some critics of single parenthood like to lump Choice Mothers in the same category, with the same host of problems that can occur in divorced households, the many emotional traumas of divorce on kids is a variable too powerful to make most of these studies reliable to the woman considering Choice Motherhood.

In this chapter, we will explore research findings that provide valuable perspective for Choice households, including a great deal of anecdotal evidence that offers insight into the "right" way to be a single parent.

The "Right" Kind of Single Parent

Vanessa is not a Choice Mom yet. But she wants to be. She has a known donor, currently stationed in Afghanistan, who is interested in helping her have a child. She has a law degree and a master's in political science. She has studied in Cairo and Istanbul. She is hoping to move into a career in international trade, specializing in energy resources or working for the Department of Commerce.

When Vanessa was 3, her 32-year-old father died suddenly of a brain aneurysm. Eventually her mother, who had been widowed at the age of 24, went to college, leaving Vanessa and her two siblings largely in the care of their great-grandmother.

Although Vanessa's mother would prefer to see her start a family as someone's wife, she is supportive of Vanessa's intent to become a Choice Mom. She even suggested having a party of friends to help her pick out an anonymous donor option, if her known donor doesn't work out. "That's okay, Mom," Vanessa replied. "It's not like I'm buying Tupperware here."

Vanessa is an effervescent, youthful 31-year-old woman who has lived and made close friends in many places. Her most recent relocation was to help her mother through a bout of cancer. She is honest, direct, and openhearted. She recognizes, from a child's perspective, the difficulties of growing up with a single parent. But she didn't fall to the maladies typically attributed by some to a single-parent household: teenage pregnancy, drug or alcohol abuse, dropping out of school.

So what was it that Vanessa's single mother did right?

Choice Chat: Vanessa's Story

✦ I don't feel that being raised by a single mother did any damage to me. My self-esteem is intact, I don't have a poor self image, and I never had an identity crisis. I tell people all the time I've known who and what I was about since I was 5. I largely attribute this to the fact that my mother was, and is, a remarkably resourceful woman.

I think the one thing I struggle with the most in my own choice in becoming a single parent is, will I have the ability to juggle having a career and being a mom? But I don't know one working mother, married or single, who does not have this fear. Mine stems from growing up with a mother who was totally driven. When I was a child it bothered me that there were field trips missed, times where she was late picking us up from school, and things like that. I don't re-call her ever attending a parent-teacher conference.

But I was also blessed to know my great-grandmother as a primary caregiver. She taught me and my cousins about her Cherokee tribe's ways. She taught me how to ride a bike.

While my mother went through medical school, I learned Latin and French. It was my first exposure to being a lin-guist. (I now know several languages.) My brother and sis-ter and I would help her make flash cards and study. We all did our homework at the same time.

As we got older, we attended formal hospital functions with her. I bet we wouldn't have been exposed to those grown-up social functions if my father had been alive. In fact, if my father had been alive, I don't know that she would have even put herself through medical school in the first place, and served as the role model that she did in that way.

My mom, and my best friend's mom (also single), taught us how to rebuild an engine, change oil, and replace an al-ternator one long summer.

▶

My best friend's dad (who I happen to still call Dad), was one of the only fathers in my peer group growing up. I think altogether there might have been five full-time dads. All the other kids were raised by their mothers, who were either divorced, widowed, or not married to their child's birth father. I had one friend who was raised by her single father. She was always over, because she was the youngest girl with three brothers and no mom. So it was like having another sister around.

Obviously we all made it work somehow. Just because there is an imbalance does not mean it's imperfect.

I learned the art of negotiating with my mom. Very key. Since she was only one person, and could be spread only so thin, being able to ask for what you want and compromise in getting it was a big influence on me. You also have no one else to run to when you're angry with a single parent. It teaches you to talk it out and get some resolution quick. Face it: with a single parent, the only thing you can do is hash it out. Maybe that's why I'm trained as a lawyer today.

My bond with my mother is probably one hundred times stronger than I think it would have been if I'd grown up with my father as well. Maybe that's because she didn't also have to be responsible for my dad, but only for us kids. Maybe it's because we couldn't run elsewhere. Or hide behind the good cop–bad cop system, since she had to be both, and we had to just deal with that.

Absolutely the most important and coolest thing I learned from my single mom was my self-reliance. I wouldn't be who I am today without it.

Succeeding in a Single-Parent Home

There are three obvious strengths from Vanessa's single-parent upbringing that contributed to her being the strongly connected woman she is today.

First, her mother found the support and sense of community that she and her children needed, in the form of extended family and friends who played essential roles in providing (and receiving in return) nurturing and growth. This was not a mother who felt she had to sacrifice everything for her children. She took care of herself as well — investing in her own education and career while also including her children in that environment — and sought out the camaraderie of other families in the neighborhood.

Second, Vanessa's mother did not play the role of a victim. Suddenly widowed at 24, she certainly would have felt overwhelmed at how life had taken a turn for her, but rather than retreating into a state of despair, bitterness, or self-pity that would be difficult to emerge from, she focused on creating the best life she could for her and her children.

Third, Vanessa herself was imbued with a temperament that helped her to find the positives and personal strengths in her life, rather than to dwell on the negative and personal weaknesses. Our society tends to focus on the failings of parents when children suffer lapses of judgment — which is understandable — but we need to also recognize that children have innate characteristics as well. Two children growing up in the same household can grow up into very different people. Some kids learn lessons in their own way, not easily controlled even by loving hands.

A dynamic divorced mother that I've known since childhood has three wonderfully bright and active teenagers. But the middle child feels a greater sense of loss about their father's absence and aloofness, and has attached to friends involved early in drinking and illegal driving. Now that her mother has imposed curfews, sets the security alarm at night so no one can leave the house, and tries to restrict involvement with certain friends, I've heard the teen argue bitterly that her mother doesn't let her have any fun.

Will this young woman eventually regain her balance? Probably. She has a strong family around her, and is herself as strong-willed and bright as her mother. But it seems that she's working out issues in her own way, that for now involve alcohol and irresponsible behavior, despite the very different background and values of her family.

One expert in single-parent families who I consulted for this book is Dr. Mavis Hetheringon, a psychologist and the author of the excellent book, *For Better or For Worse: Divorce Reconsidered*.[1] She offers wonderful insight into what the parenting style and personality of the successful single parent looks like, as well as the potential pitfalls facing anyone who is parenting without a partner.

What I especially like about Hetherington's qualifications is that she interviewed 1,400 families — including 2,500 children — at regular intervals over a period of 30 years, rather than focusing on families only during the relatively short few years after divorce. In this way she was able to note the experiences of children who suffered long-term repercussions from the trauma of divorce, compared to those who did not, as well as the quality of the parenting they received along the way.

In order to understand issues common to all families, she included a comparison group of married couples, which corrected another inadequacy of several studies.

Hetherington's ambitious research offered deeper, specific answers about why some kids (and parents) in single-parent homes do well and others do not, which tells us much more than statistical and anecdotal information can. Although her families were married, separated, or divorced, I found many of her observations to be relevant to Choice households.

Two paths: overwhelmed, or in control

Hetherington indicates that a mother who is involved, supportive, and firm often can counter the effects of both the lack of a father and poverty. But as she and Richard Weissbourd, another expert I respect, have pointed out, some single parents don't have enough time or energy to invest in their children, to enforce adequate limits, or to offer the affection required. Some are so depressed or self-involved that they neglect their children's needs.

It might be easy for the Choice Mom to feel confident that the child she wants to raise so badly will always have the attention he or she deserves. But it won't always happen that way. It doesn't happen that easily for married parents either.

Stress sets in, for example, when your child wants to play while you're cooking dinner, and you might scold her away instead of calmly explaining that "Mom needs to do this right now." Or when the house is a mess, again, and you are tired of being the only one to clean, so you berate your child for not helping you out. Or when your kids are picking up energy at the end of the day and squabbling over a plastic toy when all you want to do is collapse into bed and catch up on sleep.

Short-lived as they sometimes are, these are the times when I feel inadequate as a mother. These are the times I wonder if my daughter will resent me as a teen because of the way I talk to her when I am tired. These are the times when I wonder whether having my husband living with us would soften the impact — or add to it, since he doesn't have unlimited tolerance either.

We all get irritated, worn down, hormonal, impatient, angry. Without a second parent, our children are always with us when, frankly, we'd rather take a nap or disappear into a book or work it off at the gym. Our kids inevitably see us at our worst, as well as when we feel the most giving. In our children's eyes, we can be erratic in our attention and in our discipline.

It requires both logistical planning, as well as the development of certain personal traits, in order to be the supportive, loving, and consistent adult they can trust.

Getting on the "controlled single parent" track

As one child development expert I talked to told me, the basic needs of kids are the same in every home:

- Infants need warmth, protection, and sensitivity to their signals.
- Children need control and limit setting.

• Teens need help negotiating greater independence while remaining connected.

"One person trying to provide all these things for a child, without backup of help from another involved adult, can feel overloaded and overwhelmed at times," she said. "It's harder for single than coupled parents to do all this, but it can be done."

The ones who don't pass the stress of running a household, a job, and a family on to their children are not superheroes. They tend to do things in a way that minimizes the feelings of being overwhelmed, such as

1. feeling comfortable and confident about the childcare and schooling they have consciously selected for their child;
2. having support networks in place to help when illness and emergencies throw off the regular routine;
3. having stress-relief outlets so that they are emotionally present and involved when they are with their child.

We'll talk more about these logistical issues later. In the meantime, let's look at the Good, the Bad, and the Ugly of single parenting.

The Good: Single-Parent Strengths

The happiest Choice households I know, that are formed deliberately and with foresight, can be stronger in many ways than households with a parent who had no intention of raising a family without a partner. But even single mothers "by chance," as they are sometimes called, often find their balance if the strengths they bring to a child's life are developed to outweigh the weaknesses.

The parent-child dynamic
One researcher who set out to identify the strengths of single-parent homes, in order to build on them, reported her findings in *Ad-*

vances in Nursing Science.[2] She found that single-parent families tend to have a more cooperative and egalitarian parent-child relationship. In contrast to the typical focus on lack of discipline and control in a single-parent household, she wrote that the egalitarian approach "has been linked to [a child's] higher levels of autonomy, responsibility, self-esteem and personal aspirations."

I see this firsthand, in my part-time marriage with Dave. When he is with me and my children, he and I usually decide what family activities we will pursue. I spend more time talking exclusively to him, and not as much with the kids. I don't spend as much time asking them questions. It becomes more of a "two adults with two children" scenario.

In comparison, when he is not around, which is the majority of the time, typically Sophie and I discuss our options for the day and agree on what we'll do. We have more parent-child time together. We spend more time negotiating, rather than me telling Sophie and Dylan what to do. As a threesome, we are a unit.

The drawbacks from my kids' perspective? They would probably tell you that when Dave is not around, I try to squeeze in more hours of work at night and on weekends. (I hope that will change when I have five days per week to work.) They also would say that I don't play nearly enough to suit them, being the Serious Mom with chores and work that I tend to be. And they might tell you that I yell at them more frequently when he's not here, especially when trying to get them out the door on time, or into bed.

Gender roles

Another study examined whether individuals reared in one-parent families hold different gender-role beliefs than individuals reared in intact two-parent families, as reported in *Sex Roles: A Journal of Research.*[3]

Michael Slavkin and his associates determined, based on answers to survey questions, that kids of both sexes raised by a single mother were more likely than those in two-parent families to describe themselves in traditionally masculine terms, such as "independent," "assertive," "self-sufficient." In a similar vein, a small sample of kids raised in a father-headed one-parent family described themselves using traditionally feminine characteristics, such as "affectionate," "gentle," "understanding," "sensitive."

Anecdotally, I'd concur that the bulk of the kids growing up in my local Choice Mom community — I know about 30 families well — have fairly independent daughters (who still like dolls and pop singers) and fairly sensitive boys (who still like to smash swords and cars). I think the difference might be that without the "traditional" role playing in the home, it might be okay for girls to define themselves as self-sufficient and for boys to be affectionate for a longer period of time.

In other words, without a mother-father structure in the home, kids have no particular reason to think some traits are more "manly" or "feminine" than others.

The teenagers I've interviewed tend to be comfortable without particular boundaries to conform to. Undoubtedly this tends to be related to the strength of their mothers, who do things in their own way.

Others raised by single women have talked about admiring the strength of their mother to persevere despite the odds.

Attention

Small but growing research, specifically with Choice households, is finding that the attentiveness of Choice Moms might be giving young children advantages when compared to children in some two-parent homes. Some special needs children are specifically placed in single-parent homes for this reason.

A London-based study looked at 21 Choice Mothers and 46 married couples who had 2-year-old children conceived by donor insemination.[4] The published report revealed that Choice Moms "showed greater pleasure in their child and lower levels of anger," along with a perception of their child as less "clingy." These young children were also exhibiting fewer emotional and behavioral difficulties than those of married couples.

Another group of researchers interviewed 30 lesbian mother families, 42 single heterosexual mother families, and 41 two-parent heterosexual families with 6-year-old children.[5] At that age, mothers in fatherless families reportedly showed greater warmth toward their children and interacted with them more than mothers in father-present families. Disputes between mothers and children were found to be more serious, but no more frequent, in fatherless families, although the children did not show increased levels of emotional and behavioral problems.

Many of these families were interviewed again when the children were 12. Children in fatherless homes perceived their mothers as interacting more with them and being more dependable. Mothers in father-absent homes reported more irritability and loss of temper related to discipline. They also reported, like Slavkin and others, that boys raised without a father showed more feminine characteristics, although no less masculine ones.

Are single mothers better for boys?

One interesting theory, posed by Cornell University psychology professor Peggy Drexler, based on studies of 60 fatherless boys over a ten-year period, suggested that boys raised without a father are often better off than those with a father in the home. Her controversial book, *Raising Boys Without Men: How Maverick Moms Are Creating the Next Generation of Exceptional Men,*[6] pointed out that many single mothers go out of their way to find male role models for their sons, such as grandfathers, godfathers, uncles, friends, teachers. These "collected families" sometimes give boys a wider network of positive influences than a child in a traditional home.

She also argues that many boys in mother-led homes are taught to deal with their normal aggressive impulses in more empathetic ways than those in coupled homes. She believes they have an advantage in having a wider range of interests and friendships, in dealing with conflict, and in taking a more sophisticated approach to many situations.

The Bad: Survey Says . . .

So much attention is paid to children who "go bad" in single-parent households, that the more statistically significant stories of the children who "go right" are often seen as the anomaly, rather than the other way around.

Yet unquestionably, it is more difficult to parent as one person rather than two. Couples who work together well as parents might be rare, but do logistically make it easier. Since single parenting can be overwhelming, and since not all kids bounce back as well from the errs of the shaping (or lack thereof) of their parents, it's important to understand the statistics behind the concerns about single-parent homes.

Widely cited numbers about single-parent households come from work that Princeton University sociology professor Sara McLanahan published in the 1980s and 1990s.[7] She and partners analyzed statistics from several national surveys to determine whether children who grow up with both of their biological parents are better off than those who grow up with only one.

In the 1994 book *Growing Up with a Single Parent*,[8] McLanahan and her coauthor Gary Sandefur examined a pool of single mothers who were divorced, widowed, abandoned by a partner, or otherwise alone. Although they did not study Choice households, we'll re-examine some of the findings here as a measure of what can happen when single women don't have the economic and community resources needed to raise a child.

The disclaimers

Critics of Choice Motherhood frequently use McLanahan's numbers as evidence that a child in a one-parent home is more likely to drop out of high school, become sexually promiscuous, or turn to crime. However, they don't usually connect the dots to explain when this tends to happen, or why. For the single woman who faces this criticism with some concern, first let's point out several important differences between Choice households and disrupted households, so it is apparent what is applicable and what is not.

Anger and resentment

McLanahan and Sandefur review existing research to point out the persistence of anger in most disrupted homes. Fathers tend to withdraw from their children in the pain following separation. Children are angry about the separation, and tend to feel betrayed and abandoned. Parents often communicate anger about the other to or through the child. Even in amicable separations, there is a great deal of stress and loss of trust felt by the children. Yet as they write:

> Children who never lived with their fathers or never knew their fathers do not feel the same kind of anger as children who experience their parents' separation directly.

Loss of resources

Perhaps the most important point made in the book is that family disruption often leads to a loss of economic, parental, and community resources. When one household separates into two, expenses for housing, food, and utilities double. The father usually takes most of the family's income with him. Often the children end up moving to communities with fewer resources, including schools in poorer districts. The researchers found that a full 34 percent of single-parent families moved because they were evicted or could no longer afford the rent, compared to 15 percent of moves in two-parent homes.

This change in living conditions, the book details, is the *primary reason* that a child's school performance, ambition, and promiscuity are affected in disrupted households. As they write, "Income and residential mobility together account for all of the educational disadvantages of children living in single-parent families!"

Some of the reasons for this, according to the authors:

- Downwardly mobile children are more likely to attend schools with high dropout rates.
- Their schools tend to have a higher percentage of minority students and minority teachers, which on average have less money to spend per child and higher teacher/student ratios.
- Mobility leads to weaker connections to friends and neighbors.

Hetherington's research confirmed this tendency for mobility. On average, she found, women moved four times in the first six years after a divorce, and poor women moved seven times.

A Choice household, however, generally does not suffer from this tendency for downward mobility.

In 2005, I sent a brief survey to 100 single women who were thinking about making this choice, or who had already done it. Of the 64 women who responded, more than half had moved once since becoming mothers; three had moved twice; three had moved more than twice (one because of her law career). Sixteen had not moved at all, and had no intention of moving, as they were happy with their child-friendly community. Most women moved into homes they purchased; 53 were homeowners.

Nearly everyone who moved listed reasons such as getting into a more family-oriented neighborhood; finding better schools, more space, or a less urban setting; or to be nearer to family.

Three had moved in with their mothers. One was considering relocation to get more space. One moved to be closer to doctors for her special needs child. Another moved closer to parents and new work after being laid off. Others were not yet mothers, but were open to moving in order to provide a more child-friendly environment, or a more diverse neighborhood for an adopted child. None of them said they moved to live in a less expensive area.

Mother's education

A mother's education is generally regarded as the best predictor of a child's school achievement. So McLanahan and Sandefur tested the numbers and confirmed, "Having a mother with less than a high school degree doubles the risk of dropping out of school."

Many unmarried or divorced single mothers in their test samples were young and not well-educated. This not only helps explain some of the high-school dropout rate, but clearly differs from most Choice Mothers. Of the women who responded to my survey, 42 had postgraduate degrees, 16 more were college graduates, 4 had attended some college, 2 had not gone beyond high school.

Parents' age and income

Most single parents are younger than married parents, the authors reported. In 1992, the median income for all families with children was about $43,000, and about $13,500 for all single-parent families.

The authors' research found that the lower income of young parents accounted for about half of the difference in high-school dropout rates, teen birth rates, and idleness. Choice Mothers, however, tend to be older women who earn significantly more than the poverty threshold. Most women in my survey became single mothers in their thirties; eleven of them were in their forties. On average, the women who were thinking about this choice were in their midthirties.

None of the women who responded to my question about income earned less than $25,000. Six earned between $25,000 and $40,000; 21 earned between $40,000 and $60,000; 34 earned more than $60,000; and several voluntarily reported earning more than $100,000, including two lawyers who earned more than $200,000.

On the other hand

There are several points made in the book that could be applicable to a Choice Mother. Even controlling for education level of the

parents and race, there were statistical differences between children of two-parent homes and one-parent homes that should not
be ignored. McLanahan and Sandefur found that 16 percent of
white children in one-parent homes, whose parents *both* had some
college education, dropped out of high school (compared to 5 percent in two-parent households), and 5 percent became pregnant as
teenagers (compared to 1 percent).

One theory offered by the authors for the lower performance
standards of children in disrupted households — besides economic insecurity and greater mobility — is that a single parent is
more likely to spend less time helping a child with homework, listening to them, attending school activities, and monitoring their
leisure time.

> *The stress of the single-parent lifestyle, McLanahan and
> Sandefur write, can lead to higher levels of anxiety, de-
> pression, and inadequate parenting, as well as reduce the
> likelihood that the parent is providing the affectionate
> and disciplined approach that is best for children.*

In my work with my daughter's school, and as a PTA member, I
have worked on closing a gap between parents who get involved
with their child's school, and those who don't. There are cultural
issues (and language barriers) that can give the message to some
children that school is simply something they are required to attend by the government, rather than a valuable part of a family's
community network. In our very diverse city district we're looking
into reasons and solutions.

The Choice Mom does not fit the typical profile of the parent
who avoids her child's school environment, but the potential is
there for being too overworked to participate fully, as Vanessa recalled from her childhood. Most of the active members of our
PTA, for example, are one half of a married couple, even though
many of our kids are being raised by single parents (or even grandparents).

McLanahan's data also indicated that a child in a single-parent home is likely to have 26 fewer meals each year with Mom than a child in a two-parent home. However, "Divorced mothers appear to compensate for this deficit at mealtime by spending more time reading to their children."

Most mothers of all family structures tended to know the child's whereabouts, have a curfew, and have an established bedtime. But the never-married mother was slightly less likely to have TV rules or chores for her child.

I also can attest to this. Although some Choice Moms are much stronger at this than I am, I do tend to be lax in my discipline about TV, computer, and chores. Some of this is my personality — I want my children to take responsibility themselves (which doesn't always work) — but I know an element of it is my own discomfort with routine and structure.

If Dave were living with us, we'd undoubtedly jointly carve out greater expectations of, and rules for, the kids, partly so that the household would run more smoothly. My daughter and I have established a "star" system, which gives her points toward particular goals (such as a ski outing, or sleepover with a friend, or purchase of a coveted prize), but often I am too distracted to keep us both focused on it. And frankly, I tend to decide I'd rather do the chores quickly myself rather than nag for it. It's an instinct I'm trying to adjust.

In sum

McLanahan and Sandefur concluded that children in single-mother households tend to be deprived of needed resources because of low incomes, inadequate attention and guidance, and a lack of community resources, all due to living in disadvantaged neighborhoods with shady peers and frequent moves.

In particular, low incomes and sudden drops in income are the most important reasons that children in single-parent families have a lower high-school graduation rate than other children. A parent's time doing homework, reading, listening, and supervising activities outside of school is also vital.

The Moral for Choice Moms
Make sure you have the financial resources and network you need so your children have the time, security, and attention they deserve.

The Ugly: Potential Pitfalls

There are several major pitfalls any parent can struggle with, but especially the single parent. Choice Moms need to be aware of these if she is to create the "right" single-parent environment for her child.

Stress can lead to "bitchy" parenting
The goal we have as parents is to explain rationally why behavior is bad, and nudge our children toward the right choices and action. But as Hetherington found, there is a tendency for "the tired, pre-occupied woman [to bark] out a command. If the command is ignored, the woman nags or explodes or both, and if the child still ignores her, she usually gives up or blows up."

To get relief, a stressed or emotional parent will often give in or reward the child for bad behavior — such as giving the child a snack and putting him or her in front of the TV — which further erodes the dynamic between parent and child.

Added pressure comes from not having a back-up parent
In a related vein, when there is only one parent in the home, the quality of that person's parenting skills needs to be solid. Even with dedicated grandparents and role models, that one parent is the person each child wants to turn to as a safe, protective constant.

As Hetherington wrote: "Rejection, irritability, or neglect floods directly onto the child, with no second parent able to deflect or lessen the impact. The bad news is that because of the many stresses in their lives, divorced women were on average less competent parents than women in nondivorced families. This is in part because authoritative parenting, which requires a great deal of energy and focus, is harder to do when there is no assistance and cooperation available from another partner."

Mother-daughter relationships can be too close

In her research, McLanahan found that children reported "talking with parents" more often in single-parent families (44 percent compared to 40 percent in two-parent homes). For some reason not made clear, the authors gave this a negative connotation, attributing this to "the argument that single mothers rely on their children as confidants."

Hetherington also raised this issue, indicating that many divorced women describe their 10-year-old daughter as being like a close friend or sister. They indicated they felt they could discuss anything with their girls, including problems in personal relationships, fears, depression, finances, dating, and loneliness.

I do certainly talk seriously with my daughter a great deal, as I undoubtedly will do with Dylan when he's ready. But since I feel quite healthy about my choices in life, I do not at all consider our conversations to cross a line that blurs the parent-child boundaries. Our conversations, I hope, will lead to greater openness as she matures and we need to discuss sex, drugs, and other important matters of judgment.

But I do know what it looks like when mothers rely on their daughters as friends, and strongly believe it happens when women feel isolated and disconnected from the wider world. A woman who has built a life around her partner, for example, and then feels the rug has been pulled out from under her in a divorce, will not always have the best judgment about whom she talks to, especially if she has focused almost exclusively on the mothering role and lost touch with solid friendships.

In a similar vein, any single woman who feels depressed about a "lack" in her life, and turns to her child for comfort, certainly needs to seek an adult therapist instead. As social scientists have learned, children who are confronted with adult problems often become apprehensive or resentful. In Hetherington's study, children who felt responsible for problems they could not solve began to develop a sense of helplessness, which often bloomed into depression and low self-esteem by the time the girls were interviewed at 15.

There is a harm done when children grow up too fast

If a child's responsibilities and independence interferes too much with play, sports, homework, and other normal activities, Hetherington found that it often leads to depression in girls and rebelliousness in boys.

Respect must be earned over the long term

This might seem obvious, but Hetherington, for one, found that many parents assume their child should obey them because they are the parents, imbued with the wisdom, experience, and power of age and position. Yet it is trust and admiration that builds respect.

I think that is why so many Choice Kids I talk to speak in good terms about their mother. Ultimately, most of them feel they have been respected along the way, perhaps because the mother herself is aware of the blessings that come from knowing your own path in life and being able to make choices based on independent thought and goal setting.

Teenagers aren't going to have this level of respect for parents if they don't feel they were listened to in childhood, or if they feel their parents have imposed their values on them, rather than welcoming and discussing differences of opinion.

Being an authoritative parent requires energy

As we've discussed, the stressed parent is more likely to yell and scold without taking the time to explain or impose predictable rewards and punishments. Earning respect as a parent requires a history of firm discipline, caring, and nurturing.

The parenting styles to avoid include:

• permissive parents, who usually end up with children lagging behind in emotional self-control;
• the rigid authoritarian, who tends to produce rebellious, defiant, and confrontational children;
• the disengaged and withdrawn parent, who, according to many child experts I've talked to, is the most harmful parent. This tends to happen with the narcissistic, overwhelmed, or depressed parent.

In Hetherington's study, in fact, it was the children of disengaged parents who were the most troubled: wild, unhappy, and prone to problems with work, marriage, crime, drugs, and alcohol.

We'll talk more about how to be an authoritative parent in chapter 13.

Which kids "stay on track"?

Two years after divorce, most boys and girls in Hetherington's study — all of whom tended to have the support of at least one caring adult — were beginning to function reasonably well again. But some, by age 10, were clearly headed for trouble: 10 percent from nondivorced households, and 20 percent from divorced households.

By age 15, this group was antisocial, depressed, or anxious. These kids were sullen, oppositional, angry, and tense. In adolescence, they commonly turned to drugs, alcohol, and delinquency. Its members had the highest pregnancy rate and highest attempted-suicide rate in the study.

Experts indicate that any child can begin to disengage from the family as early as 10, especially if they live in high-conflict homes. An adult mentor outside of the household can serve as an important adviser in these more awkward, confusing years. At my Unitarian Universalist church, in fact, all children in ninth-grade religious education are paired with a mentor from the community, regardless of their family structure. I've worked as a mentor with an eager, proactive young woman whose parents are married and very supportive of her interest in the UU philosophy, which she was introduced to by friends.

We all know kids from that 80 percent of divorced households in Hetherington's study who grow up to be strong adults. They tend to be aided by their own personal characteristics — intelligence, independence, confidence — as well as from having outlets where they can achieve, in school, sports, arts, or community involvement. Hetherington found that physical appearance and lessons in self-control also had a great deal to do with their ability to find the support they need.

The strong teenagers I've talked to from Choice households not only have many of these attributes — likely a combination of mom's example and genetics — but they also don't see their single-parent lifestyle as a big deal. Many seemed almost confused when I asked the question. Perhaps some of them were unconsciously defensive about their upbringing, or hadn't yet found a voice in pinpointing things to complain about to a virtual stranger. But, quite honestly, I've talked to a very strong-minded group of teens who weren't rebellious enough to trash Mom or life without a father, even when they were invited to.

And contrary to the concern of those who see kids from contentious home environments grow up without the skills of partnership — and without the ability to negotiate, compromise, exert self-control, and interact with respect — most of the Choice Kids I've talked to say that their model for relationships is the one they've learned directly from mom.

Of course, some do privately harbor anger and resentment, or suffer from low self-esteem. It has been especially difficult to find teenage boys willing to talk to me. I presume more of that is awkwardness about talking about something as uncool as how they have been raised.

In a one-on-one household, that kind of distance can be very isolating. One Choice Mom described the late teenage years as the most difficult challenge she'd faced in parenting yet.

Without a buffer parent, or an outside mediator, that child could certainly turn to the wrong influences to bury emotions or unresolved conflict. To avoid that path, the goal is to establish a respectful, well-connected environment for parent and child that has healthy outlets for stress relief. Friends, family, church, school, volunteerism, gym. Resolving life problems without playing the role of "victim" is also important.

Again, some parents are able to do that better than others. Married or single, the parent who is isolated from other activities and networks is going to have more trouble over time.

On being a moral parent

Richard Weissbourd, a child psychologist, lecturer at Harvard's Graduate School of Education and the Kennedy School of Government, and author of *The Vulnerable Child: What Really Hurts America's Children and What We Can Do About It,* published an essay about parenting in *The American Prospect* that caught my attention.[9]

The crux of his essay was that family structure matters less to a child's moral development than the quality of parenting. As Hetherington and McLanahan also reported, Weissbourd pointed out that after divorce children tend to be greatly affected by downward mobility, as well as abandonment by their fathers. "This is not the soil out of which a sense of responsibility for others can easily grow," he said.

He pointed out that studies indicate that high rates of behavioral troubles among children can show up before a divorce. Parents during that time are less likely to provide models of consistency, attentiveness, and encouragement, which can harm a child's sense of trust. And emotions felt by parents can greatly inhibit their ability to be a model of fairness, respect, and compassion.

Yet as he too reminded us, "the reality is that most children in single-parent families are not morally defective. They are growing up to be quite good people."

He noted that good parenting doesn't tend to get the support it needs, and that adults don't often get the opportunity to cultivate crucial moral qualities that are critical to our children.

> The focus on the structure of families has ignored what is most important to any child's ethical development: an on-going, trusting relationship with at least one adult who is ethical and mature, and who listens and encourages without shying away from his or her moral authority. A mountain of research now shows that it is the content of adult/child interactions, not the structure of families, that most strongly determines the shape of children's ethical development.

We'll explore some of Weissbourd's recommendations later in this book, but one of the points he makes — an echo of Hetherington's in-depth research — is that parental depression can have great implications for the health of our children. As he has written: "As many as 25 percent of children will grow up with a depressed parent, and parental depression undermines almost every key aspect of parenting. Depressed parents are far more likely to be moody, to lash out unexpectedly, and to criticize unfairly."

Many depressed adults can still provide good parenting, he has told me, but it is a widespread issue that deserves more attention.

In sum
Although 80 percent of children from divorced homes in Hetherington's study eventually became reasonably well adjusted or better, it is the 20 percent of troubled youth in this group who make the statistical headlines. Largely the product of neglectful, narcissistic, or depressed single parents, they had the highest dropout rate and the highest divorce rate of the kids in the study. They were more likely to be earning a low income. Girls in this category were more likely to have left home early and to have experienced at least one out-of-wedlock pregnancy.

Hetherington noted that 10 percent of youth in nondivorced families had this same level of trouble. "Most of our troubled young men and women came from families where conflict was frequent and authoritative parenting rare."

The author Stephanie Coontz has frequently expressed this same point.[10] "Living with two cooperating parents is better than living with a single parent. But high conflict in a marriage, or even silent withdrawal coupled with contempt, is often more damaging to children than divorce or growing up in a single-parent family," she wrote. "According to the National Center on Addiction and Substance Abuse at Columbia University, teens who live in two-parent households are less likely, on average, to abuse drugs and alcohol than teens in one-parent families; but teens in two-parent families who have a fair to poor relationship with their father are more likely to do so than teens who live with a single mother."

Tying together the Good, the Bad, and the Ugly of single parenting, there are two points that stand out:

1. Single parenthood is not inherently damaging unless the parent is too overwhelmed to provide the affectionate and disciplined style of parenting that is required.
2. Since a single parent needs to be the foundation of ethics, trust, and happiness for her child, the toughest job is to maintain emotional and financial resources in order to be the authoritative parent every child needs.

The Moral for Choice Moms
A conflicted, disrespectful, neglectful, or victimized parent tends to be at the root of most of our troubled youth. Don't embark on parenting unless you are prepared to find appropriate ways to deal with the inevitable stress (and loneliness) of running a household and career on your own. Many single parents are able to do this. Be sure you are one of them.

Choice Moms Discuss Their Biggest Issues

Talking with child development experts and social scientists is one thing. But it's also important to learn from the direct sources: Choice Moms themselves.

I have asked many experienced Choice Moms to pass along advice and wisdom about the biggest issues for them as single parents. Here is a sampling of what I hear:

Energy. "The biggest issues now are sickness, time, and energy. I had a major back injury 18 months after having my son. I had to really reach out to the village during that time. You learn that you can't do everything on your own, and definitely not when you're sick. Having a child demands lots of energy. I now go to bed at 9:00 P.M. Whenever I have extra time, I either take a nap, go have a massage, or go have a facial . . . something that's soothing and relaxing."

Time. "Five years in, time is definitely the worst issue. I started living well below my means a long time ago, so the financial issues aren't a hassle. But my well-paying job is what kills my time, especially the commute. Fairness, for me, was never an issue. It wasn't fair that I was raised by a man who was so depressed he couldn't see beyond his own nose — and whose depression hampered my mother's ability to parent. It wasn't fair that I might have had a child by my ex-husband, who valued boys over girls. Why would having a single parent be less fair than these options? Other than time, I can't think of any issues. There are days I'm emotionally drained, but I have great friends to rely on."

Said another: "My biggest issue is not having enough time with my child. What with schoolwork, her homework, meal preparation, and general chores, the hour or so we spend together in the morning and the maybe three hours we spend together in the evening on weekdays just don't feel like enough. I find that by the time we get to Friday, I really miss her, even though neither of us has gone anywhere. This is one place my decision to eat out one night a week has made a big difference. That night I don't have to cook or clean up. We can sit and eat together, at the same time, face to face, and we talk. It's become a special time that both of us look forward to."

Money. "Finances have remained the major issue. It's tough. When he was really little there was childcare. Once full-time childcare wasn't an issue anymore, there was after-school care and after-school activities. And now that he doesn't have any after-school care, his other activities are often costly. It's no longer cool to take lunch to school, so he is buying it. And then I needed to leave my stable job (something I hadn't counted on) and I took a major cut in salary. So money is definitely an issue."

Childcare. "The worst time I ever had was because it was torture for me, when she was an infant, and I had to go back to full-time work. I didn't want to leave her. I cried all the way to work. A few months later, I quit my job and used all my retirement savings to stay at home with her another seven months. Eventually I took a live-in job taking care of a younger retarded woman and deaf woman so I could stay home another year. I never would have predicted that of myself. But I never regretted it for a second, and have always cherished that time I had with her."

Fairness. "Before I got pregnant, I didn't worry as much about fairness. I was pretty sure that I'd be a good mother. I chose a known donor so that I could enable my son to know his father. In the early years, I think most of us are too busy with daily life to get hung up worrying about fairness. It stops being a question — it just is. And our kids tend to reinforce this, because overwhelmingly they do really well in their single mom households. We struggled to make a decision to become a single parent, but that was never their struggle. It's just their life. But things change. Our life wasn't very different from others until my son hit middle school.

Our experience was that kids were often cruel, my son wanted to fit in, and being different was like having the plague. Hormones were beginning to rise, and rebellion was in the air. Sarcasm became the major form of communication.

"I think at this point in his life, my son would tell you that this lifestyle choice is not fair to children. It makes our family different, and although most of his friends don't know that I am a single mother by choice, he knows, and that makes it tough on him. I honestly believe that with time this will change. I think he appreciates that our family is loving and supportive, and that if I hadn't made the decisions I made, it wouldn't exist. Maybe I'm deluding myself, but I think that he will forgive my decision with time."

"Daddy" issue. "My daughter is 3 years old. The daddy issue is coming up more. She talks about her daddy all the time and almost always has a daddy in her play themes. I worry about it a little more now, from the perspective that she has to deal with being different than her peers. I don't worry that she is missing out on anything. She has a lot of male influences, including an uncle and grandfather. I read books that have different types of families, and I reassure her that our family is okay. I make sure that my child knows that not everyone is the same. I don't usually see this kind of focus from 'traditional' families. It should be there, but I don't see it."

Hindsight. "If I knew then what I know now I would have tried a little sooner. There is a significant financial cost to waiting. Using a reproductive endocrinologist (RE) and more advanced methods of conception starts adding up in increments of $1,000 rather than $100."

Support. "Raising a baby is very hard, especially for women used to being in control and succeeding at everything — which, in my experience, describes myself and many women who consider Choice Motherhood. You lose control of your body, your life, and suddenly become the loving slave of a tiny little being. You fail at small things like staying awake or big things like learning how to breastfeed. Worst of all, you have to learn to let other people help you. My advice is this: Don't have a baby if you don't have a support system in place. You will need parents, family, and friends to help out when you get sick, haven't slept in days, need emotional support, or are just having a difficult time. You really can't do it all by yourself, and you shouldn't. Your baby will benefit from getting love and care from other people, and so will you. Work it out so you can pay back these people in other ways, if it makes you feel better."

Overall philosophy. "I never saw it that I had to be two parents, just one very good one. The most important thing is, don't do this unless you decide to put that child first, to give him or her the time and energy required. I wouldn't trade my twenty-plus years of being a mother for anything. How many times I've been just so happy to be with her, to see what she does. I worked hard to do things as well as I could, letting her know she's loved, letting her know she's a great human being. Not to make light of the responsibility it is, but I was ready for it — and it was so very worth it."

Taking the Nontraditional Route

One relatively new Choice Mom who contacted me as I was writing this book was Carol, who discovered when she was 32 that she was showing signs of perimenopause — a genetic tendency in her family. She had been dating someone who wasn't ready to settle down, so they broke up, and, after consulting with friends and getting unexpected encouragement from her conservative brother, she decided to have a child on her own through donor insemination.

"My greatest concern when I was thinking about bringing my son into the world was that I might hurt him psychologically or emotionally by not having a father in contact with him on a daily basis," she told me. "One of my very good male friends reassured me that my son would always know that his mother had so much love that she wanted to share with him. What really helped me decide, though, was that I stopped thinking so much and listened to my heart. It just felt right to me.

"Now, as I look at my son beginning to reach his first levels of independence as a toddler, I realize that bringing him here was a blessing from God. The ability to show my son love and affection, and to guide him to become the wonderful young man I know he will be one day, gives me faith that there is the divine in all of us, and in all of our actions of love and goodness."

· 6 ·

Growing Up Without a Father

Paternal neglect is causing the ruin of many families.

— New England pastor, 1842

It's not a new phenomenon that observers of families have been concerned about the changing role of fathers. Once upon a time fathers were the center of moral education for their children. Throughout the eighteenth century, child-rearing books were directed to men, not women. Until the 1960s, according to the surveyor Daniel Yankelovich, "being a real man meant being a good provider for the family."

By 2004, however, 23 percent of children were living without a father in the home, compared to 11 percent in 1970, according to a Child Trends report.[1] And authors such as David Blankenhorn were publishing books such as *Fatherless America: Confronting Our Most Urgent Social Problem* (1996).[2]

Blankenhorn writes that fatherlessness is the "underlying source of our most important social problems." He adds that single mothers cannot provide "a father's distinctive capacity to contribute to the identity, character, and competence of his children."

When I surveyed members of the Single Mothers by Choice network in 2003, almost equal to the number of women citing "Can I afford it?" as their single greatest concern was the number of women who brought up an issue that purposely was not on my list: "Is it fair to the child to be raised without a father?"

The single women who wrote me, without prompting, to explain their concerns about this issue indicated to me that Thinking Women understand that fathers do matter. Some women reported grappling with this issue for years before deciding whether or not to go forward with Choice Motherhood.

As Tina told me, "My relationship with my dad is a good one for the most part. We never have been super close, but I have always known he loves me and cares about me. When I think back to my childhood, he was always tired; he came home from work usually too tired to be much involved in my life. It left me always feeling awkward around him, like I didn't want to burden him with anything. It wasn't until he was retired and had energy, when I was an adult, that we got to know each other."

Even without a strong relationship with her father growing up, she said, "My main concern is not knowing how best to handle or navigate the effect on the child of not knowing the daddy. I know there are 'answers' to the daddy question that sound good when I read them. But I guess the answers leave me wondering how really this satisfies the child's question."

The concerns raised throughout this book are all important. But this "fairness to the child" issue, I believe, is the most complex.

This chapter will focus on the most important differences between children raised by a Choice Mother and children raised with a father in the home. I make no claims that raising children without a father does not have an impact on their development. Rather, we will explore what the literature says, hear from child experts I interviewed, and learn how best to navigate as your child grows.

First, the Skepticism

As William Pollack, author of *Real Boys: Rescuing Our Sons from the Myths of Boyhood*, has said, single mothers "get the worst rap imaginable. They are blamed for everything from hangnails to violence. [Yet] women are not only very important role models for their sons, but they are often their son's heroes."[3]

Indeed, there are plenty of theories about the impact of fatherlessness that are exaggerated or based on outdated ideas. Blankenhorn, for example, has expressed dismay that the absence of a father means a child won't have someone to help him or her buy a car, make a down payment on a house, buy furniture for an apartment, go to college, or cosign a bank loan.

He probably didn't realize that most Choice Mothers are highly self-sufficient, and consider that to be a positive trait that they pass along to their children.

For example, I very much grew up believing that I am responsible for making my own way. Although my parents always have been supportive, I worked my way through college and the purchase of my first home, furniture, and car without expecting handouts — and got a great deal of satisfaction from that.

Blankenhorn probably also didn't realize that a substantial number of Choice Mothers have postgraduate degrees and are comfortably middle class — with plenty of highly paid doctors, lawyers, and psychologists in the mix.

Access to someone else's money is one thing. But the most serious theme he raised is this: boys without fathers get guns; girls without fathers get babies.

Boys and guns
Blankenhorn wrote that there is a rite of passage boys need to undergo in order to separate from their mothers and mature into healthy, whole individuals. Fathers are invaluable to this process, Blankenhorn argued, as they guide their sons into the community of men and the meaning of maleness.

Many child development experts agree with Blankenhorn, and his theory is borne out in both clinical and anthropological studies. But Blankenhorn had his own unique perspective on what happens when a boy doesn't have his father around to teach him how to be a man.

"When this process of male identity does not succeed — when the boy cannot separate from the mother, cannot become the son of his father — one main result, in clinical terms, is rage," Blankenhorn continued. "Rage against the mother, against women, against society. It is a deeply misogynistic rage, vividly expressed, for example, in contemporary rap music with titles such as 'Beat That Bitch with a Bat.'"

Hypermasculinity is a common result of growing up without a father, he wrote — "the aggression and swagger of boys who must prove their manhood by themselves."

Others have different theories about the roots of male violence. Pollack believes that it is disconnection from loved ones and fear of shame that lead some boys to violence. He wrote, "Violence is the most visible and disturbing end result of the process that begins when a boy is pushed into the adult world too early and without sufficient love and support. He becomes seriously disconnected, retreats behind the mask, and expresses the only 'acceptable' male emotion — anger. When a boy's anger grows too great, it may erupt as violence."

Ironically, he added, violence against others can be part of an attempt to reconnect with others and boost self-esteem; these boys "bond" through violent acts in a way that other boys do through sports activities.

Some point out that aggression usually springs from deep-seated pain, and that boys who haven't been neglected or abused tend to have a greater capacity for avoiding violent behavior.

Myriam Miedzian, author of *Boys Will Be Boys,* said the problem, to a certain extent, is fathers who teach traditional masculinity — the values of toughness, dominance, repression of empathy, and competitiveness.[4]

Michael Gurian, a male development specialist who consulted with me on several chapters of this book, believes basic neuroscience accounts for many differences between the sexes.[5] "Boys have dramatically different brains than girls, making it logical for them to be more impulsive, and as a result in need of more concentrated training by family, elders and other members of the community to teach them the moral codes of society," he said.

Girls and babies

Some also believe that girls without fathers are vulnerable to turning to men to fill a void in their life. As Blankenhorn wrote, "Women who have had good relationships with their fathers are less likely to engage in an anxious quest for male approval or to seek male affection through promiscuous behavior."

He cited research by Judith Musick to indicate that girls who do not have a stable relationship with a nonexploitative, loving adult male remain developmentally stuck and struggle with issues of security and trust. As Musick reported, these girls focus on one question through adolescence: "What do I need to do, and who do I need to be, to find a man who won't abandon me, as the men in my life and my mother's life have done?"[6]

Musick, however, doesn't place the blame solely on the lack of a father, but regards it as part of a more complex equation that includes the presence of many abusive men in a mother's life.

Blankenhorn's book expresses the view that daughters who don't have a loving father never get over it. "When a girl cannot trust and love the first man in her life — her father — what she is missing cannot be replaced by money, friends, teachers, social workers, or well-designed public policies aimed at helping her. She simply loses."

In 1995, he was no more forgiving of Choice households than he was of divorced or abandoned households.

> "A society of Sperm Fathers is a society of fourteen-year-old girls with babies and fourteen-year-old boys with guns."

Author comment

I mention Blankenhorn's views not simply to rile readers of this book, but because he has been a prominent critic of single parenthood. A mission of the institute that Blankenhorn founded in 1987 is to "change the views of U.S. policy makers on the importance to children of the two-parent home" and to expose the "cost of unwed child-bearing." He was not available when I requested an interview with him, but presumably he continues to believe that even an educated and professional single woman who chooses to dedicate herself to motherhood cannot do a good job raising her child without a father — and his voice speaks for many.

Real-world experience, of course, tells us that crime and other social ills are caused by many factors that often have nothing to do with fatherlessness. In the small, white, middle-class town where I grew up, I knew of several boys who ended up attempted rapists, shoplifters, drug users, school dropouts, and drunk drivers. One, who I knew personally in high school, was convicted of killing his wife. All of them had a decent, law-abiding father in the home. In fact, most of them had siblings who had no such issues. How do you explain that? In brief, there is no simple explanation.

Children all have the potential to make bad choices with their lives — big and small — and it's a combination of genetics, environment, and individual emotional and mental health that plays into the end result, as well as values imparted by important role models.

Nurturing and interactive fathers can do amazing things in bringing up their children. I applaud efforts to train men to be fathers (and husbands), and deplore policies that are designed to promote marriage as the only "right" way to live.

While there does seem to be research to support the view that women turn to skewed relationships with men to fill a "father void" in their life, when you look closely at the lives of a wide segment of women, there are persuasive arguments supporting the idea that any girl, whether from a one- or two-parent home, can grow up with relationship issues.

One of my close friends grew up with a nurturing mother and a withdrawn father. Into her forties, she had never married (or had children), and tended to fall into relationships with men who did not offer enough of themselves to be committed to a future.

Another friend, with a highly accomplished father and a lonely childhood because of frequent moves, was a "daddy's girl," but very mistrustful of developing a close relationship with anyone.

Another friend emulated her strong-minded father, and grew up equally as strong-minded — making it difficult for her to sustain a loving relationship with any man.

Another friend grew up in a small town with narrow-minded parents; to this day she bristles from their example and is finding her own way in a rather rootless fashion.

An old friend who was attached to her at-home father was one of the most promiscuous girls I knew.

And yes, I also know many people, from different backgrounds, who have committed themselves to adult relationships, with all the ups and downs they entail.

It does make sense that a girl who grows up with a father who leaves the family might approach commitment with a fear of abandonment or betrayal that could lead to short-lived sexual relationships, inhibitions, or overboard reactions to male attention. And with the numbers of families without fathers in the home, this would lead researchers to find many examples of this tendency.

But look around and listen and you'll find many women who grew up with a father in the home yet still developed their own commitment issues. Typically, around the age of 30, they turn to therapists to try to confront these patterns. Ideally they work through their issues — after all, kids are responsible for moving past whatever weaknesses they grew up with.

This said, however, it does have an effect on a child to grow up without a father, as we'll explore next.

Two Loving Parents

Although many of the concerns about fatherless homes can be remedied with quality parenting from one attentive mother and solid role models that every child should have, there are some things a Choice Mom cannot provide for her child no matter how great she is as a parent. The most important of these, in my view, is the absence of a second person who is actively involved and emotionally present.

The bond between Choice Mom and Choice Kid is intense — often more so than what children experience with parents who also have a partnership to maintain. Grandparents and attentive uncles and male role models provide invaluable love, nurturing, and education. And many children in two-parent homes do not have the kind of interaction with one or both parents that we're talking about here. Yet in a different world, a loving, interactive father would be a second person the child could have a meaningful relationship with.

When I married Dave in 2004, my children automatically "acquired" a stepfather. He's a loving, responsible, fun-loving man with strong values. His family-oriented siblings and parents are inclusive and warm. My daughter is the right age to revel in our extended family get-togethers. But that doesn't change the fact that Dave is not a second "me."

Especially because we don't live together, Sophie generally considers him to be the man married to Mom. We do not push her or Dylan (who is only now starting to realize there are fathers in the world) to call him "Dad," unless it is the term of endearment they prefer (which happens occasionally).

If my kids had two of me — two who consider their needs first; two who spend lazy summer evenings enjoying simple moments at the lake on a consistent, reliable basis; two who help them grow day-by-day — how great that would be for them.

But I decided to be a Choice Mom, and these two beautiful kids were the result. My marriage doesn't change that. Having a known biological father doesn't change that. Having loving grandparents and caring family and friends doesn't change that. They have one bond to a deeply committed parent.

However, I do not consider that to be a "bad" thing. It simply is the unique structure our family was founded on. Perhaps because of our dynamic, Sophie and Dylan might be exposed to a wider network of loving relationships and diverse experiences than other kids will. Theirs will be an upbringing that I believe will bless them with unique gifts.

Influence

Another benefit of having two parents in the home is the fact that there are two adults serving as active role models. Two sets of good (and bad) traits and mannerisms to emulate (and reject).

From a young age, I did not like the way my parents handled disagreements. Their marriage is conflicted, but they have persevered, giving me a chance — especially after I moved out and had the distance required — to appreciate their individual strengths. For example, my mother is personal-growth oriented: she returned to college when I was in junior high school, introduced me to a Holocaust survivor who was my first interview subject at age 12, and was always eager to travel. She exposed me to new experiences, which is a gift I value highly and regard as something I can do for my children.

My father was the one who helped me feel like I could make my own decisions. Although I often make decisions that would not be his choices, he has rarely been critical of the way I live my life. My hope as a parent is to give my kids the same ability to recognize that life is theirs to create, in whatever way they feel they need to.

Obviously I would have grown up without either of these influences, but differently. Just as, without my friend Troy in high school, I might not have gotten comfortable living outside the box (which included picking him as a friend in the first place). Without my first job at the community newspaper I might not have developed a strong identity as a journalist at an early age. Without being the victim of date rape in college, I might not have had such difficult issues to work through during my twenties.

In addition to the basic genetic coding that impacts the person each of us turns into, there are any number of pivot points and people who come into our lives and dramatically affect our direction. Having two influential role models in the home allows a child an alternative way of seeing how to approach life. Ultimately it gives the child yet another way of choosing his or her own set of values.

Balance

In his book *Life Without Father*,[7] David Popenoe made some good points about the balance that can be struck in a home with both a maternal and paternal influence. As he wrote: "In attitude and behavior, mothers tend to be responsive and fathers firm; mothers stress emotional security and relationships, and fathers stress competition and risk taking; mothers typically express more concern for the child's immediate well-being, while fathers express more concern for the child's long-run autonomy and independence. The importance of these different approaches for the growing child should not be underestimated.

"All children have the need for affiliation with others but also the drive to go off on their own, to be independent. They need both the personal security brought by strong social ties ('roots') and the push away from the group toward autonomy ('wings'). They need a parent who says 'strive, do better, challenge yourself,' along with one who comforts them when they fall short."

Although it might seem stereotypical, since a parent generally is capable of striking a balance between two extremes, it is useful to consider the ways men and women tend to differ.

Communication style

Dr. Kyle Pruett, author of *Fatherneed: Why Father Care Is as Essential as Mother Care for Your Child,*[8] talked to me about how mothers and fathers parent differently, as he discusses at great length in his book.

For one, he says, men and women not only have distinctive-sounding voices, but have different verbal styles, which can provide infants with an important source of stimulation and learning. Mothers tend to simplify their words in order to help the child understand quickly. Fathers, on the other hand, make the child work harder in order to be understood, which challenges them linguistically. His theory, he told me, was that there is more opportunity and need for infants to work harder to get understood by men than by women. And that when they succeed, often something new and stimulating is the reward — such as being picked up and thrown gently into the air.[9]

An excellent handout provided by Head Start[10] states: "Father's talk tends to be more brief, directive and to the point. It also makes greater use of facial expressions and subtle body language. Mothers tend to be more descriptive, personal, and verbally encouraging."

Although both of my kids developed excellent motor skills at a young age, both of them were late talkers. I suspect Pruett's theory might be part of the reason for that.

Playtime

One of the noticeable differences between Dave and me is the way we "play." When Dylan was an infant, I was more comfortable putting him into his jumping apparatus, or taking Sophie to classes and cultural events, than getting on the floor with them. Dave calls me the "intellectual one." He, on the other hand, tosses my son in the air, teaches canoeing to my daughter, takes his daughter to amusement parks, hikes and skydives with his son, and, in general, pushes for physical activity.

This difference is largely a result of our temperaments. My Choice Mom friend Shelly is also more likely to teach my kids how to ride a bike, ski, and skate than I am. But, in general, there is a tendency for men to be more active as "doers" and women to be "nurturers." The type of play men engage in seems to offer kids some unique skills.

> *Fathers tend to be louder, rougher, and more competitive than mothers. Experts believe the rough-housing form of play typical of men is helpful in teaching a child self-control.*

"The male play style helps develop spatial-mechanical centers of the brain, which are good for all kids, teaches a different way to handle emotion than talking, and teaches healthy competition and aggression," Gurian told me. "It is especially resonant for more male children, and for 'bridge brain girls' who are more tomboy, because the brains of these kids already format toward more gross motor activity and more spatial-mechanical-aggression stimulation."

Gurian points out that aggression is an essential and nurturing part of human nature. This is in contrast to violence, which is a learned behavior (sometimes genetic) that is destructive.

Risk taking

I didn't think it possible before I had kids, but there also tend to be differences between the sexes in the willingness to allow for risk. I cannot believe how often I heard the word *careful* coming out of my mouth. Go to any playground and, in comparison to mothers, you'll generally see fathers pushing the swing higher, encouraging kids to climb farther, and spinning the merry-go-round faster. Even for the woman who might take her own risks, it can be instinctive to err on the side of caution when your child is involved.

Of course, pushing the limits without considering the dangers isn't healthy. And avoiding risk can limit a child's sense of independence and confidence. But together the two can help a child feel safe and secure while building new skills. This also can help a child learn tolerance for frustration, which is part of the self-control instruction.

After my daughter had taken three ski lessons from my friend Shelly, she almost overconfidently tackled a hill, then got scared because she'd come down it faster than she should have. Sophie berated herself for making a mistake by not remembering part of her lesson, and vowed never to ski again.

Two weeks later, we had her back on skis. Within ten minutes, Shelly had Sophie on the chairlift for the first time. If it had been purely up to me, she never would have left the safety of the smaller training hill. But I trusted someone else — and importantly, so did Sophie — to know what she was capable of, and to push her to that next step. After that, it was hard to get Sophie to take a break.

I've seen the same thing with Sophie in sliding, swimming, and other endeavors. When she and I trust someone else to do the pushing, Sophie accomplishes a great deal more than I would have expected. This is the kind of balance that mothers and fathers can often find with each other.

Discipline

Studies tend to point out that fathers are keepers of the "justice, fairness, and rule-bound duty" lessons, while mothers are the relationship-oriented ones who point out the importance of sympathy, flexibility, and understanding.

Pruett draws the interesting example of a mother whose toddler has thrown food. She might talk to the child about how much work it is for her to clean up the mess, or how disappointed she is personally in the behavior. A father, on the other hand, is less likely to employ shame and more likely to emphasize the consequences of misbehavior in the wider universe, such as pointing out in a fight over a toy that the child isn't going to have any friends by being selfish. When fathers draw a line, they tend to appear to be less easily manipulated; the rule being taught is less personal and more clear-cut.

In general, the idea is that fathers help children prepare to be part of the world, and mothers tend to emphasize how behavior affects others. Pruett, for one, says both approaches are needed: "The value to children of experiencing both a maternal and a paternal approach to discipline, blended into the foundation of their conscience, can't be overestimated."

Gender Identification

We obviously need to find male role models to acquaint our kids with the general traits and appearance of our opposite sex, since it makes up roughly half of the world's population. Our children need to feel familiar and secure in the world of men.

Studies tend to indicate that healthy relationships with fathers can help daughters have more confident relationships with boys and men, ideally giving them a chance to see the respectful way men should act toward women. They also are less likely to be curious about experiencing the "differentness" of boys and men before they are able to be a better judge of character.

The prevailing wisdom for boys is that if they grow up with a solid father figure in the home, they can more easily learn how to channel their masculinity and strength in positive ways.

Most research on gender identification, however, is a comparison between children who grow up with healthy, involved fathers and children who grow up with less-involved fathers. Having an emotionally distant father is the culprit in many studies. There is little research to reveal what happens when you have one very involved (female) parent and no male parent at all.

The research is clear, however, that children need strong "non-mother" influences in their lives in order to provide balance and enhance the child's autonomy. A man's warmth, masculinity, and "differentness" influence a child in ways that even highly dedicated mothers cannot replace.

Self-Control

Statistics do show a correlation between fatherlessness and juvenile delinquency. As we read earlier in this chapter, there are many theories about why this might be. And, as we learned in chapter 5, variables including drops in income, charged emotions, and withdrawn parenting are important factors. However, there are lessons in the self-control research that Choice Mothers need to pay attention to.

As Pruett has said, "Fatherlessness in any social class seems to catalyze a kind of obsessive hypermasculinity. The classic study by Beatrice and John Whiting found that the most violent cultures had the least paternal involvement. In gang and fraternity violence, males without fathers are the most rabid disparagers of everything female — it's as though they think this is the one true path to a masculine identity.

> *"Can such probabilities be overcome by any single mother? Of course. They're overcome all the time — but not without help, thought, and a plan."*

We'll get into the plan in more detail in chapter 13. For now, let's explore what children need in order to develop self-control.

As we alluded to earlier, some believe it is the style of play that men engage in with children, and their tendency to push children through their natural frustration level, that gives the best instruction in self-control. Fathering expert John Snarey has said that "children who rough-house with their fathers usually quickly learn that biting, kicking, and other forms of physical violence are not acceptable."[11]

A committee of the National Research Council's Board on Children and Families concluded, "Children learn critical lessons about how to recognize and deal with highly charged emotions in the context of playing with their fathers. Fathers, in effect, give children practice in regulating their own emotions and recognizing others' emotional clues."[12]

Pruett told me that especially in the toddler years, children begin to feel uncomfortable about their own impulsiveness and power. Children with involved fathers tend to learn more easily that controlling these impulses is an internal task, rather than something that is out of their control.

According to Richard Weissbourd, another helpful consultant for this chapter,[13] a child whose long-term frustration is not noticed or remedied by a parent will begin to lose a sense of hope and fairness. "I have spoken with many children who lose their way, who become dangerously passive or dangerously destructive, because they simply do not believe that their good intentions and hard work will be rewarded," he has written, "or because they are convinced that they will never get a fair shot, that they are not playing on a level playing field because of their race, gender, ethnicity, or some other immutable characteristic."

As a regular reader at my daughter's elementary school, I can see that for every 20 children, there are usually one or two kids in the classroom who do not participate as readily as the others. I've been startled to see the anger or distance at such a young age. These are the kids who particularly need to be reached by mentors who can help them channel their emotions in positive ways. Teachers who have the role of helping kids learn cannot solve the problems that likely are brewing at home. That's why children need the positive role models that an entire community has to offer, not simply the one or two or three adults they're likely to come in regular contact with. Otherwise the bad role models can just as easily become the mentors, rather than the good ones.

Kids who have access to weapons, violent older siblings, and ineffective lessons in resolving conflict are likely to make bad choices. I don't believe that fathers can cure these inadequacies unless they themselves have been taught by positive role models. In

Weissbourd's newest research, he told me, he is finding poor moral guidance in suburban settings, as well as in inner cities. What we need, his work implies, is more people who can teach kids how to be good people, rather than simply "the best."

There are other factors that demoralize our children as well. Research indicates that early childhood experiences of shame and humiliation, poor communication skills, inadequate schooling, and difficulty reading social cues also contribute to violent behavior over time.[14]

Kids' Perceptions of Fathers

It's not only what fathers can provide for children that we need to consider, but what it means to children to be without a loving relationship with a male parent.

A dissertation we will explore in detail in chapter 12 reported on the impressions young children of Choice Mothers had about their nonpresent donor fathers.[15] The reactions of children are quite varied, from disinterest to embarrassment to intense curiosity and, in some cases, to expressed yearning to have a dad. One young child often pretended that his biological father was a superhero (Batman). A 7-year-old boy occasionally indicated he wanted a dad so his mother could stay home with him "but wants a dog more."

> *Wanting a father in order to have more time with mom is a common reaction of young children, as is desiring a dad who can do activities that mom doesn't.*

One 5-year-old boy in the study said if he had a dad, "He could be in the front driving, and my mom sitting in back with me. It would be fun. We could play together and wrestle."

The dissertation included a review of a study published in 1992 that compared thirty-five 6-year-old children born to Choice Mothers via a known donor.[16] The kids had varying degrees of contact with their biological fathers. Some never saw their fathers and had been given little information about them ("ghost fathers"), some had sporadic contact ("visitors"), and some saw their fathers with the same frequency as a noncustodial parent ("auxiliary fathers"). They were compared to children with married parents.

More than three-fourths (77 percent) of the children with ghost fathers or erratic visitors felt their fathers viewed them negatively, compared to less than half (37 percent) of the group with married parents. Children with auxiliary fathers, or those who were close to a grandfather, were less likely to feel their fathers viewed them negatively.

In other words, having an important male figure in a child's life can help them feel more secure.

Reality Check

As we have been discussing, studies indicate that if a child has a loving relationship with dad, the child might become:

- more confident in unfamiliar situations;
- better able to deal with frustration (because fathers don't step in as quickly as mothers to alleviate the stress);
- more patient, curious, and confident as students.

Although these studies[17] tend to be well-meaning in their attempt to point out the value of having an active father, it should not be assumed that the opposite result is true when the home has no father — which is the conclusion many people leap to.

For example, one study surveyed nearly 400 people over a 26-year period and determined that fathers who spend time alone with their kids doing routine childcare at least two times a week raised children who were the most compassionate.[18] Does this mean that a child who grows up without a nurturing father in the home will be a bully? No. It simply indicates that if you take out all the other variables, children with an engaged father tend to be more sensitive than children with an unengaged father. Makes sense.

Another point: Henry Biller, a long-time researcher in fathering, has said that the average daily amount of one-to-one father-child contact in the United States is less than 30 minutes. He found that fewer than 25 percent of young boys and girls in two-parent households experience an average of at least an hour a day of individualized contact with their fathers.[19]

In a national study of students in grades six through twelve, almost 20 percent of the children reported not having had a good conversation (lasting at least ten minutes) with their mom or dad within the last month.[20]

Double Standards

In *Reviving Ophelia*,[21] Mary Pipher wrote about the double standard that tends to exist in America about parenting. Namely, that mistakes made by mothers are considered to have great power to do harm, while the attention paid by fathers is considered to have great power to do good. Strong daughters, for example, are often credited to having strong fathers, while the strength of their mothers often can be overlooked.

Pipher interviewed high school girls in the 1970s for research about father-daughter relationships. One-fourth of the girls had fathers who had died, one-fourth had parents who were divorced, and one-half had parents who were together. The focus of her research was how daughters' relationships to fathers affected their self-esteem, sense of well-being, and reactions to males.

As Pipher wrote: "I quickly found that the physical presence of the father had little to do with the quality of the relationship. Some girls whose fathers lived in the home rarely spoke to them, while other girls who never saw their fathers were sustained by memories of warmth and acceptance. Emotional availability, not physical presence, was the critical variable."

The presence of supportive fathers, who were described as fun and deeply involved, led to daughters with high self-esteem, a sense of well-being, and confidence with the opposite sex.

But there were two other types of relationships that also exist, with less positive outcomes.

Abusive relationships involved fathers who were emotionally, physically, or sexually abusive. "These were the fathers who called their daughters names, who ridiculed and shamed them for mistakes, and who physically hurt or molested their daughters."

A majority of fathers in Pipher's study fell into the distant-relationship category. "They may have wanted relationships, but they didn't have the skills," Pipher wrote. For these daughters, the income their fathers brought home was appreciated, but little else.

What Thinking Women Say

Talk to ten different women about how growing up without a father in the home might impact their child and you'll get ten different reactions. While many women do have concerns about this impact, and do their own reading of literature I've summarized here, the conclusions weigh differently on their minds.

As one woman told me, "I wouldn't be pursuing single motherhood if I thought 'no dad' was a deal breaker. I do believe, however, that a two-parent household is 'best' for a child. Despite the studies that show it's quality of parenting that counts, rather than two parents or one, I believe there is an inherent difference for a child living with two loving adults who strive to honor their relationship. I'm counting out bad couples here, as well as bad single moms and bad single dads. That said, I think it's extremely valuable for a child to witness two parents solving their issues. I think it's the best role model for a child to see their parents experience differences and still remain bonded, to learn how women and men may think and behave in different ways but still respect one another and compromise.

"I firmly believe our kids can turn out great, otherwise I would not be pursuing this," she continued. "And I do not think any of us are wrong for pursuing single motherhood. But I do believe it's a different reality. Do our kids gain from having a single mom? Yes. Do our kids lose by not having a dad? Yes. But if we all waited for perfection that child might never be."

Others believe that a good father figure is not necessarily a father, and that kids benefit from having a diverse set of role models. Many women (myself included) know Choice Moms who seek a wide network of mentors for their children, perhaps more so than a child in a traditional family structure, where mom and dad are expected to provide most of the lessons.

Some women, admittedly, operate from almost a base of fear. They recognize that children face tremendous stress and loss of trust and security when their family life is disrupted by divorce. They believe that losing a parent is more damaging than growing up without a second parent.

Still others believe that every child would benefit from having many things the universe doesn't always provide: paid leave for both parents for the first year of an infant's life, schools filled with quality teachers and resources for all, no discrimination or prejudice, crime-free neighborhoods, funding for arts and sports education, access to good medical care and nutrition, and so on. Growing up with one parent rather than two is part of the way life sometimes works out.

In exchange for what the universe does not provide, these women point out, they are utilizing the tools available to them to help their child grow up into a responsible and happy adult.

The Moral for Choice Moms
There are unmistakable natural differences between men and women, and anyone contemplating this choice must be sure that there are strong male role models available throughout the child's life. (See chapter 13 for suggestions about how to ensure this, and when.)

Final Thoughts

Most of the hundreds of single women I know would not hesitate to marry a loving man who will treat them as an equal partner in love and child rearing, be a nurturing and interactive parent, and serve as a model of commitment and responsibility. The problem has been in finding him. As one woman told me, she was angry to discover at age 35 that after she had worked through her childhood issues (from a two-parent family) and was finally ready for a healthy relationship, she couldn't find any available man who had done the same and was looking for someone approaching 40 with whom to start a family.

When I started writing this chapter, my intention was to give everyone a chance to hear both sides of the issue and make their own judgment. That is still the goal of the entire book. No woman with grave concerns about any of these issues should proceed. If you think you will do your child a disservice by raising him or her without a father in the home, you should not put yourself through that moral quandary.

But as I dug into the research, I recognized that the lives of people I know all have been affected from every variety of family background — divorced, abandoned, happily together, unhappily together. Every family can be dysfunctional if we let it. And every child will grow up with "issues," whether we like it or not.

Children should grow up valuing life, responsibility, and succeeding at his or her goals. When the home doesn't teach those values, kids do turn elsewhere, and might end up on a destructive path. Yes, many single parents have to work entirely too hard to feed, clothe, and shelter their kids. In some cases, supervision and time and nurturing go out the window as a result. So it makes sense that a fatherless home can have serious troubles.

But a home without a father is not the same as a home without values — this is an important distinction that some forget to make.

Where Blankenhorn, Popenoe, and others diverge from child experts such as Pruett, Gurian, and Pollack is when they claim that only biological fathers can provide the balance in the home that mothers need to raise well-adjusted kids. The latter group believe the support of extended family and friends can — and should — play an important role in raising kids. Gurian, in fact, has written a great deal about how even two-parent homes need to actively build an extended network.

Although we were specifically talking about mothers and sons, Gurian offered me this advice useful for any Choice Mother: "I think it is human nature to try to share child raising, and I sympathize with single parents who can't do that. If a single mother is going to raise a great son, though, she is going to have to get help — a female community to support her, male mentors for the boy once he becomes prepubescent, sports or the arts or something both expressive and physical that he can immerse himself in. She is going to have to fight to curtail his immersion in unhealthy influences, including bad diet — which messes with hormones — and obsessive computer and video game use. She is going to have to find him some kind of religion or spiritual or identity-developing community larger than his narcissistic adolescent world. This is a lot for her to do, but to decrease the probability of having troubles with her son, or raising one who underperforms, she finds herself compelled to do a lot of these things."

In large part I believe the best thing we can do for our children is to instill them with a sense of responsibility — for taking control of their own lives, for understanding their obligations to others — and to open the door to possibilities that provide them a love of learning and exploration and spirituality and mental health.

Choice Mothers are great role models in these two regards.

STAGE 3

Choosing the Method

If you decide to become a Choice Mom, perhaps after years of debate, you face another uniquely challenging and personal question: How? Will you adopt, use an anonymous donor, or conceive with the help of someone you know?

For some women, reaching this decision can be even more difficult than choosing to become a Choice Mom.

Is adoption the "morally correct" choice — giving a loving home to a child that most likely already faces a life without a father in the home? Or is it cost prohibitive?

Should an older woman with unknown fertility, and few insurance benefits for the procedure, pursue insemination in order to experience pregnancy and birth, and to share genetics with the child? Should she select a completely anonymous donor, or would her child someday prefer an open-identity donor who is reachable when he or she turns 18?

Should a woman who wants the child to know the other biological half use a known donor, or are the risks of legal and emotional complications too great?

Whichever method a single woman uses, there are ethical concerns connected with each one. Some people strongly believe children should not be created with donated "material" when so many already need homes. Others strongly believe that a child has the right to know his or her genetic identity.

Entire books have been written about adoption and insemination, which I encourage readers to refer to. In this section we look as closely as we can (in limited space) at the complexities of the three methods to motherhood.

In "Known Donor: Pros and Cons" we explore in depth what few resources cover: what can happen when you use someone you know to help you conceive a child (as I did). We hear the emotional story of a woman whose agreement with a former boyfriend ended up changing, against her will, as well as the wisdom of lawyers. We discuss the advantages of this method for the child. And we learn about the motivations and emotions of two donors, as well as from a man who has said no to four women.

In "Using Donor Insemination" we examine the merits of the growing open-identity option. We hear from a donor-conceived woman who has mixed emotions about the fact that she is attempting to conceive with an anonymous donor, as well as from a donor who expresses his mixed feelings about not knowing his offspring. We briefly discuss the process of insemination (covered so well in other resources), and how women have chosen their donors.

In "Choosing Adoption" we explore the factors a prospective adoptive parent needs to consider, including costs of domestic and international options, sources of emotional and financial support, and the home study process, and receive special advice on transracial adoptions.

In the next section we will look at how to address the related "daddy" and "identity" questions children naturally will have.

7

Known Donor: Pros and Cons

While in my early thirties, I wrote a short story about a woman who fantasizes about asking for sperm from three male acquaintances she approved of genetically. She would store each man's donation anonymously, so no one would know which man's sperm helped her conceive, thus alleviating everyone of pressure to play the dad role. The flash-forward twist to the story, however, was that the child as a young boy had so many familiar traits that the father's identity was no mystery. When the long-lost donor paid a visit ten years later and excitedly saw himself in the boy, the mother sadly knew she was about to lose her place as the sole nurturer in her son's world. Her carefully constructed attempt to create an intensely reliable one-on-one family structure had failed.

Does this speak to some sort of controlling interest I sought in parenthood? Perhaps. Although I used the story as an opening to tell some people (like my mother) that I might become a single parent someday, my desire to become a mother seriously kicked in when I started dating a divorced father. Sharing visits with him and his son led me to tell him that I might like to have a child with him someday. This pronouncement apparently scared him away; he broke up with me two days after my 35th birthday. I was devastated.

After a solitary retreat on the primitive African island of Madagascar, I returned to the States, plunged energies into my executive position at a publishing company, and spent ten-hour weekend days at a coffeehouse writing my dark novel, *Ocean of the Dead*. Several months later, I shared a drink with a male friend and announced my interest in becoming a single mom someday. My genuine intention was to startle him, by letting him know how fiercely independent I was, but he surprised me instead by offering to be the donor when the time came.

It would be nearly a year before I took him up on his offer. In the meantime, I got to know him well enough to understand his story. Overall, I determined that he had fatal flaws as relationship material, but he was a good man at heart. Importantly, I had time to figure out why he would want to have a child for whom he would not have custody. His motivations were wrapped up with being the divorced father of two kids he missed, longing for family due to an extremely isolated childhood, having a "live for the moment" personal life rooted in his inability to commit to any one person, and a basic lack of time because of his entrepreneurial career. In short, he loved the idea of kids, but couldn't be responsible for them on a regular basis: the perfect known donor.

The decision to become a Choice Mother also was made easier as my salary approached six digits. I owned an apartment large enough for two, had substantial savings, and was nearing the age of 37. It was time to act.

Getting pregnant turned out to be easy. Sophie's biological father and my parents were present for the delivery, which passed smoothly in a drug-free four and a half hours.

I wish I could say that everything was effortless after that, but, of course — as the woman in the short story of my youth discovered — nothing is that simple. My friend was close enough to me to attend Lamaze classes and various prebirth checkups, but he disappeared minutes after the birth. Initially, we both felt awkward about his pseudo role in this beautiful child's life. He suggested that the child be named Sophia, in memory of his grandmother, yet I had to battle to put his name on her birth certificate. He was afraid his name on the official document would make him financially responsible in the eyes of the government, yet I didn't want Sophie to someday think he disavowed his parentage. (In hindsight I've learned that leaving the known donor's name off the birth certificate is advisable, especially if you do any international travel, since it's easier to get through border control without requiring a letter from the "other parent" each time.) He was disappointed that I spent the next three months living with my parents, 1,000 miles away, and that I didn't name him as Sophie's guardian in my will.

Clearly there were emotional and legal wrinkles for both of us to work through. Fortunately we were able to talk through the rough spots. But then the big whammy came. As I was preparing to return to work, my boss informed me that my position had been "eliminated" and, unless I was prepared to take a demotion and major pay cut — which I was not — there was no job to return to. Now insecure financially, and emotionally drained by the responsibilities of single parenthood in that first year of "take care of me!" infancy, I berated my donor at length for not doing enough to help me out.

Eventually I evened out again — using my severance package to facilitate a flexible freelance lifestyle — and moved comfortably into the Choice-Mom role for which I had prepared. But as my donor and I both learned, this route is not an easy one to take.

The ups and downs of having a "father"
The attachment Sophie and her donor developed (for a time) was wonderful to watch. This bonding didn't kick in until she was nearly 3 — when she was more of a person for him to relate to, and when he was less of a stranger for her to get used to. He even scheduled regular visits after Sophie and I moved to Minnesota, to help us settle into our new home. Seeing her rush into his arms at the airport made me extremely proud of the known-donor choice I had made.

But this unusually rich "father" experience came with obvious confusions. Three times in one week Sophie told people that she wanted to go to Disneyland with "her parents" — PANIC! It was the result, I know, of seeing the commercial of a happy family bouncing with joy about their upcoming trip. Did I worry that having a friendship with her donor made it more difficult for her to see him simply as "the nice guy who let mom have a baby?" Yes.

On another occasion, after it had been two months since his last visit, Sophie told a friend of mine that she wished he lived with us — PANIC!

At a boat outing, fascinated with watching members of our group water ski, Sophie told a little girl that "my dad is going to teach me how to ski when I'm 10" — a partial fantasy based, I suppose, on knowing that her donor is an avid skier. Her friend innocently replied, "I didn't think you had a dad." PANIC! I quickly stepped in with the line, "He lives in New York, not with us, so he's not a dad like yours is."

> One obvious reason I prefer the method I chose is that it allows me to give Sophie the security of knowing that two people who cared about each other as friends helped to create her, albeit in an untraditional way.

Of course, using a friend as I did clouds the issue much more than other options would have. Some women pick known donors from advertisements and lists of acquaintances and ex-boyfriends. But our friendship assured me that he would adhere to my parameters because of our ability to communicate and his respect for my role as THE parent.

Sadly, when Sophie was 4, his personal distractions and dramas made him much less reliable. I decided to close the gate — without locking it shut — since he no longer had the time and energy to maintain the attachment she had been forming. Sophie was confused by his absence for a while, but was young enough to adapt to the new arrangement of occasional phone calls. Although their contact is much more limited than it was during her first years, she will continue to benefit from knowing who her donor is. If she wants to develop a stronger relationship with him when she is older, my hope is that she will have that option.

As the Wellesley College researcher Rosanna Hertz described in a study about Choice Moms who use donors, this kind of arrangement places more of a "gatekeeper" burden on the mother.[1] In my case, I must figure out what I think is best for Sophie, given her needs and his lifestyle. With the passage of time, and lack of regular contact, I must also be aware that he might decide not to make himself available even if she is interested, and I need to be able to explain that to her.

I used the same friend to help me create Dylan. Although my son will not have the same early-year experiences with his donor that Sophie had, I am thankful the two are full siblings. They have obvious similarities in appearance. As a family historian who has traced 16 branches, it also is important to me that Sophie and Dylan will be able to fill in some of his sketchy heritage on their family trees. I consider it a blessing that we know his family's medical history, which tends to be extremely healthy and robust. And, as my top concern, I am glad I'm able to give them the option of knowing exactly who helped to give them life.

What Can Go Wrong

Although I have no regrets about the method I chose to motherhood, my experience indicates that the known-donor route requires both parties in the conception process to maintain emotional stability, trust, open lines of communication, and sensitivity to the child's changing needs, whether the sperm is provided for home insemination, clinic insemination, or in the "old-fashioned" way. It's a tall order, which is why a majority of Choice Mothers choose an unknown donor for a "cleaner" route to parenthood.

In my conversations with people for this book, I've learned of a few men who did the "donation favor" for friends, only to be sued later for child support when the women ran into financial and emotional difficulties. I've read stories of the very troubled Australian woman who lost a partial-custody battle with her known donor — and killed herself and her child rather than give him visitation rights. I know of women who allowed themselves to get pregnant by unknowing donors, which raises serious ethical dilemmas.

And I've learned the story of Sarah — and those of at least two other women like her — whose known donor ended up making her life miserable (read on).

Many states have enacted legislation that prevents donors from having any responsibility or rights to the child as long as a licensed physician is used, but these rights only extend to a donor who donates through a licensed physician, clinic, or sperm bank. And the issue isn't as clear-cut for the courts if the recipient is a single woman. Use of a donor by an infertile couple, where a father exists for the child, is sometimes perceived very differently than it is for a single mother.

Even with a paper agreement between a Choice Mother and known donor, it is not guaranteed to work. If either party challenges the agreement (or later, if the maturing child does), many courts will uphold what is in the best interests of the child, which might very well include financial support and time with two parents.

In states with a sperm-donor statute, parties who want legal protection by supplying "directed-donor" sperm for insemination with a doctor must follow the exact language of the law. In California, for example, if the donor gives the sperm to the recipient to use, rather than to the doctor or sperm bank, a court may find he is the father, despite his intention to donate. (See chapter 14 for cases in which donors and mothers didn't get what they bargained for.)

One particularly cautious lawyer told me: "Even if there is a written agreement, if there is sexual intercourse, the sperm contributor is a parent, and the courts will not 'unparent' him. You might not put his name on the birth certificate, and never ask for support, but that doesn't change the fact that he's the father. Everything is up for grabs. Every scenario in which a parent has rights can apply."

On the other hand, the Santa Fe–based BioLaw Group attorney Ami Jaeger told me that a well-drafted agreement can go a long way toward convincing a court of law — if it ever comes to that — what the original intent and expectations were.

> *"In the absence of a contract,"* Jaeger said, *"it becomes a 'he said, she said' debate that you don't want to be in."*

Andrew Vorzimer, a California-based lawyer who specializes in clients who use third-party reproduction, told me, "Although I am loath to generalize, since every state is different, the common theme is that courts will do what they think is in the best interest of the child. Some states uphold the rights of the intended parent. Some states favor the genetic parents. Some pay attention to marital status."

In other words, if a known donor marries and wants visitation rights as part of a couple, some courts might favor that arrangement over that of the single parent. Others might protect the limitations set in the contract, or believe that the child is more secure with the mother, who has been available since birth. And once the child is old enough to assert rights, Vorzimer warned, there is potential for even more complications because "that child is not governed by the contract."

Worst-case scenarios are not limited to custody issues. They could include a donor who refuses to allow a second-parent adoption in the event of the mother's marriage, or alternative guardianship in the event of the mother's death. Conversely, a donor might be sued by the mother not only for child support, but for medical costs if the child has a genetic disease not disclosed in the donor's family history.

Even if the mother and donor are in full agreement, if public assistance is needed — say, the mother uses state-sponsored health coverage — the local government will likely step in and require the father to replenish its coffers. (Sometimes this applies when the

Laws Really Do Vary

✦ One source of information about the wide variations in state donor laws is Human Rights Campaign (www.hrc.org). As its website reported in 2005, "In some states, if a man is known to the woman or couple to whom he provides sperm, he may be required to assume the legal responsibilities of a parent. In California, Ohio and Wisconsin, a known donor releases himself from legal responsibility if the procedure is performed with a physician's involvement. In Colorado and New York, a known donor may be able to assert parental rights; however, it is unclear whether a court would impose any responsibilities on a known donor in these two states. In Pennsylvania and Utah, the law is unclear and a known donor may be assigned some parental responsibility. In the remaining states, there are no laws or cases that assign or allow a donor to assert parental responsibilities."

mother is seeking assistance for herself, and does not apply if the benefits are for the child.)

Although every situation is different, Jody DeSmidt, a Minneapolis-based adoption and assisted-reproduction lawyer, offered these general thoughts:

- **Signing away rights** — A court is unlikely to approve an agreement to terminate parental rights unless there is a second parent waiting to adopt the child.
- **International borders** — Establish with the donor a written agreement that enables you to take the child across international borders, and carry it whenever a passport is required. Because of the quirkiness of the situation, "arguing with a bureaucrat somewhere is not where you want to be."

Pennsylvania Case

✦ In January 2008, the Pennsylvania Supreme Court reversed on appeal a decision involving a known donor and a woman who conceived twins with his sperm through in vitro fertilization when she was married to someone else. Although the woman named her husband as father on the birth certificate, after her divorce — and subsequent financial difficulties — she filed a case against the donor for child support.

Lower courts ruled that it was in the child's best interests to pay more than $1,500 a month in child support plus $66,000 in back support. The courts made their decision based on the tendency for the law to not allow biological parents to waive the interests of a child.[2] The Supreme Court ruled 3-2 that the mother should not be entitled to change her mind about her agreement not to ask for child support.

- **Donor rights** — If the donor has rights specified in an agreement, for contact with the child perhaps, he can take the mother to court for failure to live up to that arrangement.
- **Time** — The longer a child is raised by a particular parent, the less likely that a judge will say it is in the best interests of that child to switch to a co-parenting or shared custody arrangement.
- **Marriage and adoption** — If the mother marries and the donor has never parented, been declared on the birth certificate, or been adjudicated to be the child's parent, notification of the donor is suggested, although not always required.

Because the rules can differ even from county to county, it is highly recommended that anyone using a known donor should first consult with and then have a contract drawn up by an experienced *reproductive lawyer* who is familiar with local statutes. Jaeger recommends taking advantage of the attorney's expertise to talk about what to expect, as well as what could go wrong and how to best protect yourself.

> **Caution:** A family law attorney tends to know more about divorce than assisted reproduction, and may or may not catch all of the issues. A contract lawyer tends to be versed in business transactions, which can be dangerous in a situation like this. "The majority of states want to see the most altruistic contract, which eliminates any commercial aspect," says Vorzimer. Even stipulating payment of $1 for sperm donation, which some might see as a distancing business mechanism, is generally regarded in the field as a no-no because "it raises the specter of baby-selling."

When the Agreement Fails

Sarah asked a friend to be her donor. After agreeing initially, he turned her down because he didn't think he could accept knowing he had a child, yet not be part of the child's life. So she asked an old boyfriend, who was reluctant at first. "He finally agreed, with the stipulation that he would have no responsibilities whatsoever — financial or emotional — and that he would remain anonymous. My child was never to know, and he wanted me to tell everyone that I went to a sperm bank."

After some additional negotiations, they agreed to terms. "I swore that the only time I would contact him would be a life or death situation. He asked if the child would be able to make any claims on him or his family. I assured him that I wanted nothing from him. I went to a lawyer to draw up an agreement, but the lawyer advised me to save my money because if the father decided to become part of the child's life, the agreement would be useless, as the child's rights superseded the parents'. I was so confident that the donor was not going to do this that I didn't pursue it any further.

"At that point, we were still friends, and he was so adamant — to the point of rehearsing what I should say to people if they asked questions — that I convinced myself that it would turn out okay. It was the easy way. We weren't using doctors, there would be no expenses (ah, hindsight). If he had given me any inkling that he wanted to be involved I never would have chosen him."

The donor was 35, and Sarah, 40, assumed he knew what he wanted. But shortly before her child, who we'll call Pat, turned 2, the donor, having appeared casually maybe five times since the birth, showed up to say he had made a mistake and would like to get married and be a father. "I knew I couldn't deny him the right to see Pat, but he became verbally aggressive when he wanted to visit but it wasn't a convenient time for me," she told me. "I felt intimidated, and, since we didn't have an agreement set up, I tended to give in to avoid making a scene around my child."

Between his aggressive nitpicking and her use of avoidance to wish the situation away, it took seven years to work out a co-parenting agreement.

She fought back harder after he enrolled Pat in religious education classes in a faith he knew Sarah disagreed with — one whose church he did not attend in the years she knew him. "In the spirit of compromise, I offered to help look for a less dogmatic religion for my child to be part of, but that wasn't good enough for him. He insisted on the religious classes he wanted. This finally got me out of my 'avoidance' mode and I got the advice from my lawyer to serve him with papers asking for full custody. In the end, I got sole legal custody. I think at that point it was more of an issue of his unwillingness to compromise that made the judge rule in my favor."

When we talked, they were still working out a financial agreement. He started to pay support after deciding he wanted to be part of the child's life, but they had yet to agree on the final details. Sarah has spent more than $10,000 in legal fees; he has had access to legal advice from people he knows.

Were there clues in his personality?

Sarah had dated this man — we'll call him Hank — back in 1986, after five years of friendship. "He seemed like a 'normal,' even-keeled type, which is what I thought I needed. There was no passion there, but he was a nice man. I never noticed much of a backbone until he wanted to become part of my child's life." Sarah has never understood why he ended up battling with her like he did, other than the fact that he says he hadn't thought everything through before he agreed.

How is the child faring?

Sarah said her child has a good relationship with Hank. "I know it is better for Pat to know the father's identity, but emotionally it will always be difficult for me to be forced into raising a child with a man I don't love."

When Pat asked why the biological father suddenly appeared in their lives, "I told Pat he was a friend who helped me to have a child, but not everyone is ready to be a parent at the same time. When he was ready, he became a part of our life together. Pat seemed to accept that.

"My child is wonderful, and seems as well-adjusted as any 9-year-old. Pat has a relationship with the donor's family now, as well as mine, and seems happy about that. Hank's family has a different perspective on issues than I do, but I want Pat to be exposed to different ideas and make decisions based on reasoned and well-rounded thought," she said. "In the meantime, I try to teach Pat good values and to have a good moral compass. Right now I focus on exposing Pat to charitable giving, and we have been doing volunteer work for several years. We all do the best we can."

Regrets

"The emotional toll it took on me, particularly in the first couple of years that Hank became involved, was great. I thought about it day and night. It was an awful time for me. I understand and accept that he made a mistake and that the situation became different for him, but it is difficult for me to see him as a father since I have no emotional attachment to him.

"I love my child more than my life. Pat is the child I was meant to love, and was created because I, and I alone, wanted and desired to give the love I have to a child. If I had gone to a sperm bank instead, the time spent battling for custody, and the financial and emotional turmoil, could have been avoided.

> *"Obviously, in retrospect, I regret using a known donor because of the problems it created in my life. Although I have custody, I have to confer on decisions with someone I have no feelings for, and have to experience not having my child with me all the times that I had expected to."*

"I cannot picture a life without this special child in my life, but if I wanted a second child I would use a sperm bank with open-identity donors."

Sarah's final thoughts

"I feel as if so much of what I have said is negative. My child is the best thing that has ever happened to me. Although I spent four years planning this, it certainly didn't turn out as I expected. As time goes on I am learning to deal with it, but sometimes it is very difficult. Pat loves Hank, and he loves Pat, and it's great to have more people to love you in your lifetime. He and I have a civil relationship, and I never say anything negative about him to Pat and would never deny them their time together. But it's just not what I expected. Other women thinking about this should be aware of what can happen."

On the Other Hand

Some women know that they don't have the stomach for something as potentially complicated as what Sarah has experienced. Others feel strongly that it is important to give a child every opportunity to know their full genetic background. For anyone undecided who lies in between, here are the main reasons some experts think — despite the legal and emotional complexities — that a known donor is the best option to give a child, and why I have no regrets about my choice.

Pro #1: Sense of identity

As we will read in future chapters, children who have been conceived with an anonymous donor or placed for adoption sometimes feel a sense of loss. A child's disconnection from his past can lead to periods of confusion and alienation. "I feel like a cereal box with no ingredients," said one of the adoptees quoted in *Being Adopted: The Lifelong Search for Self*.[3]

This same identity crisis has been applied by some experts to the feeling of loss experienced by children of anonymous donor insemination. Although this "half-adopted" circumstance might alleviate some of the loss, an unknown donor still leaves a child with the potential for feeling like he or she is only half identifiable. Said one such donor offspring, "I'd like to know about my donor's health — half of my health history is missing, and missed. I'd like to 'see' the personality traits I've inherited. I'd like to know what the donor does for a living, what conflicts he's had, how he's resolved them, what issues he struggles with."[4]

The noted Yale child psychiatrist Dr. Kyle Pruett believes that this identity issue alone is why the trend toward known donors will grow. Despite the uncertain strings attached, Pruett thinks the desire to have a "father story," and to have the ability to share the other half of one's genetic history, is beginning to outweigh, for many women choosing a donor conception, the advantages of anonymity.

> *"Having useful information about the donor has a way of keeping the child's identity secure," Pruett told me. "They aren't aliens, created from Kryptonite. They have a stronger sense that they belong to a world in which kids are born of a mother and a father."*

Primarily in response to this identity issue — which affects many, although certainly not all, children — numerous sperm banks are now recruiting donors who agree to be reachable when any resulting child turns 18. This promise can be too tentative, however, for a mother who wants her child to know all genetic quirks and attributes.

For my own children, I desire that they not have gaps in their knowledge about who they are and where they came from — a desire accentuated by my understanding of the difficulties faced by several adopted people I know. That is why I want them to know their donor — not only as I have known him, but as they might come to know him in time.

Unless, of course, they decide they have no interest. That's what happened to Susan, a child therapist who "accidentally on purpose" conceived more than 20 years ago while in a relationship with a charismatic but inappropriate man. Although Susan thought it important for her daughter to develop a relationship with him, the girl declared at age 7 that she wasn't interested. When we talked, she hadn't seen her biological other half for 12 years.

But her daughter does have pictures of the man, and can see how her African-American heritage came from him. "I do think it mattered to her to at least know who he was," Susan told me. And, even more importantly, it now seems, her daughter is getting acquainted with half-siblings from the man's other relationships.

Pro #2: A "creation" story

Having a "father story" to help inform her child's sense of identity and creation is the main reason Beth decided to use the sperm of an old boyfriend, even though his personal issues made it clear that he wasn't the right lifetime partner for her.

"Although I'd ordered long profiles and audio interviews for the sperm donor I'd chosen, I remembered that one of the reasons I wanted to conceive with my old boyfriend is that my child would have an origin narrative," she told me. "I think in some ways, lacking a narrative is even more problematic for DI children than lacking half a genetic history. For me, the story of how my parents met is one I tell over and over again. This way I will be able to tell my child that I met his father because we were both news correspondents who fell in love overseas. That's a good story."

For some, conceiving a child with a vial of sperm is too impersonal. Even if the woman chooses to be inseminated with the sperm of a friend, rather than procreating the old-fashioned way, creating life with someone familiar can seem less faceless, for the mother and eventually for the child. As one donor offspring who obviously was struggling with her creation story said starkly: "Some stranger masturbated into a glass vial and I'm the result."[5]

It can be easy to explain to a young child that "mommy wanted you so badly that she went to a place that gave her what she needed to create you in her tummy." The story might be less satisfying to a teenager or young adult, who wants to feel that he or she was created out of an emotional form of bonding between two people. I can understand Beth's need for a creation story for her child. And I agree with the views of Dr. Pruett, who told me:

"The mother tends to think of the conception story as hers, when in reality it is the child's."

In other words, you might write the words to the story, but ultimately it's the child's book. I know the circumstances surrounding my own birth have been more important to me than to my parents. I was born less than a year after my parents lost their first child at birth, and tended to think of myself as the "miracle" baby they created contrary to doctor's orders.

The point is, while your energies right now might be to choose what feels most comfortable to you — which is important — it is the child that will be impacted most by how he or she came to be. Make every effort to insure that the origin story you write for your child is one you are happy with.

Pro #3: Medical history

With the amazing advances in genetic testing, we are becoming increasingly able to use science and family history to warn us about our predilection for many diseases. These advances will make it more frustrating for children to grow up with large gaps of knowledge about their medical heritage.

Diane Bartel, associate director at the Center for Bioethics at the University of Minnesota, says that there will be growing pressure on adoption agencies and sperm banks to provide full medical histories over time. "There will be even more need to know family histories in the next 10 to 15 years. The lack of health information in the future will have more impact on people than in the past."

Because of my father's and grandfather's histories of heart disease, I know to regularly monitor my cholesterol. In fact, when I was having chest pain at the age of 40 (which, thankfully, turned out to be unrelated to my heart), doctors took it seriously enough — knowing that my father had his first heart attack at age 42 — to keep me in the hospital overnight for monitoring and tests.

Unfortunately, an adopted acquaintance in her midfifties had no such information to go on. Two doctors dismissed her complaints of chest pains as "stress related." Because she was a woman — women are often underdiagnosed with heart disease to begin with — and she had no known family history, they didn't take her concerns seriously. That is, until she collapsed in an emergency room with a massive heart attack a week later, suffering brain damage in the process.

Scary, but true. Especially these days, when, due to overburdened medical clinics, we are responsible for understanding and aggressively protecting our own health. Any child missing such valuable information about medical history is at a disadvantage.

That's the main reason, in fact, that my adoptive brother has periodically considered learning more about his biological parents. He doesn't want to meet them, he has generally dealt with his resulting identity issues; but now, in his forties, with two children, the lack of genetic background is, for him, a significant gap.

Consideration: Cost

We don't like to be crass when it comes to discussing our child's birth, but if you are willing to have intercourse with the donor or use his sperm in home insemination, this method to motherhood is significantly cheaper than adoption and anonymous insemination. Indeed, it is essentially free, except for the ovulation test kits and basal thermometer to pinpoint the timing.

However, health and safety should never be overlooked as a concern, especially for a single parent. Banking the sperm as a "directed donor" runs about $600 — for simple tests and storage — if you can claim a dedicated relationship with the donor, and about $2,000 if you can't, since most clinics are required to quarantine the sperm for six months to test for AIDS and other diseases. (A few will allow you to sign a release absolving them of responsibility if you refuse the testing.)

And as Sarah's story reminds us, using a known donor can become an expensive option if the donor someday asserts his parental rights in court.

If You Say Yes to a Known Donor

If you want to use a known donor, the next big question is: Where do you find one and what do you do if you ask someone and he says yes?

> *As one woman said, "It's got to be someone who is going
> to add more to the equation than just free sperm."*

Some donors are gay acquaintances or friends who want to be partially involved with the life of a child they help to create. Others want to see their DNA continue without getting involved. Many are ex-lovers, or even current lovers who don't have long-term potential as a mate but are willing to be involved in creating new life.

One woman I talked to was in her early thirties when an older man she knew expressed strong interest in being her donor. He had lost his family in concentration camps during World War II, had four grown children from his marriage, and felt he had a debt to pay to "repopulate" his family genes. She wrestled with moral concerns, discussed the option at length with a therapist, and worried if she might be setting a future child up "for something bad" if she chose this route. She had high regard and appreciation for the man, who wanted to be a stable and consistent presence in any life that was created. Ultimately, she went ahead with it, and has two children with the donor, who is very involved in their lives.

Another woman I know took the known-donor option to the next level. She and a childless 50-year-old male friend agreed, after medical and background checks, to co-parent. "We look at it that we will be friends who will have joint custody of a child," she told me. "This is emotionally and financially helpful for me, and I think it is better for the child to have a dad around. We have discussed issues like housing, schedule, child support, will, life insurance. We plan to do activities together, maybe even take vacations together. It's like a divorced couple who get along well and do things with their child. He will help me financially so I can be home for six months, and work part-time another six months." (Postscript: Within a few months of the child's birth, the co-parenting wasn't going as smoothly as she had hoped.)

Any known-donor relationship involves collaborative parenting to some degree. This option requires the Choice Mom to have several talents.

Manage the gate

The Choice Mom largely controls how the child's relationship with the donor develops in the preadolescent years. Young children tend to absorb the cues of their primary caregiver. As Hertz, the Wellesley researcher, has written, one aspect of managing the gate is deciding what to call the man.[6]

I remember how tentatively I introduced Sophie's donor to her with the term of "dad" when she started talking. I didn't have the foresight to understand how confusing the use of that term would make things for all of us, and how hard it would be to reverse the connotation. Now she usually refers to him by his first name, but I'll never forget the inquisitive look she gave me when she called him dad for the first time. Whether she wondered if she was correct in using the word, or whether she wanted to see whether I objected, I'll never know. But it was easy in that moment to see that she was gauging my reaction. Eventually I could see that she was happy to know she had a "dad" (I now prefer the word *donor*), but would adapt to the cues I gave her.

> *Seriously explore your ability to set limits and expectations before you make the choice to use a known donor.*

Understand what kind of relationship with the donor you prefer the child to have. It will be less confusing for everyone if you can monitor this consistently over time. As one lawyer recommends, "Decide in advance whether the contributor of the sperm is a donor or a parent."

This was my weak spot. Although Sophie's donor will always be more than a donor in her creation story, the consistency of their relationship changed significantly during her early years. Those long visits after we moved to Minnesota were fun for Sophie, but, in hindsight, temporarily created expectations that he was unable to fulfill in the long term. She adapted well to the changes, but if she had been older — or we were living closer to him with more frequent contact — it likely would have been much harder.

Know the donor better than he does
In order to manage that gate, you need to be reasonably sure that you can trust the man to respect your boundaries. You need to understand his ability to relinquish control of the child's upbringing,

even if he is unable to articulate it or understand what that lack of control might mean for him emotionally.

A friend of mine — professionally successful, attractive, intelligent — has been asked by several women to "provide seed." He has turned down every request because he knows he would not be willing to relinquish control of the child's upbringing to someone else.

If you know what you want and don't want, and understand the donor intimately enough to feel that he will abide by your wishes — and ultimately the child's — you can likely ride out the inevitable bumps and offer your child the benefits of having a known father.

You might be interested in working out a kind of co-parenting role with the donor, as I did in a limited way with Sophie's donor, accepting gifts, phone conversations, visits — or not. Regardless, be sure the two of you are secure enough as human beings to be able to communicate and negotiate.

As Beth told me: "I do think my boyfriend would abide by my wishes. I would probably want him to be a not-so-involved face and name, and my guess is that he wouldn't challenge that. He has agreed to sign an agreement in which I would ask him to sign away rights. I know those agreements have no legal value, but at least the exercise would help lay out the parameters."

If you can't find a man you trust to respect your wishes about what is best for your child — one who is emotionally mature enough to negotiate fairly — then don't try to force it. This might not be the choice you can safely make.

Be accepting of change
Like any married relationship, the known-donor route requires the ability to accept the ambiguities. With at least three different individuals involved (not including a donor whose future wife might not be as accepting of your arrangement, or a donor whose parents want to be grandparents), things will change over time. Realize that no matter how reasonable you are on paper, there are highly

---

Why I'd Like to Be a Known Donor

✦ Every donor has his own thoughts and motivations. Personally, I haven't found anyone to create a family with. As the years pass by, I've started thinking, what if I die and never leave anything behind? I just want to pass my genes on to someone. I am not in a situation where I want to have any contact — I would only want to do that if I was in a relationship with someone. I know there are a lot of single women out there who want to have a child but have no one to do it with. I personally think helping someone out like this is one of the greatest gifts you can give. And if it is not too much of a hassle for me personally, why not? Part of me lives on somewhere. I take comfort in this. The way I am doing it — not anonymously through a clinic — gives me a little control over it as well. I wouldn't want to help create a baby for a woman that could be abusive. There are a lot of loonies out there and I wouldn't want to donate blindly. Also, going to a clinic can cost a fortune. I met a girl who had spent over $8,000 trying to become pregnant with frozen sperm through a sperm bank, without success. Having a baby shouldn't only be for rich women.

---

unpredictable emotions that come into play. If you are the type of person who can roll with changes and accept what comes — if you know that life never turns out exactly the way you planned it — this would be a reasonable option for you to take.

On the other hand, if you shudder at the possibility of having to negotiate rights and terms with a donor or your adolescent child, then the adoption and insemination routes might be safer. At the very least, plan to be inseminated at a clinic using your "directed donor" sperm, which might give you more protection under the law. It costs more in the beginning, but could save you much in the end.

Be unrelenting on one point

There are many men who would be happy to have uncommitted sex with a woman who wants no responsibility from him if a child is conceived. Several websites, in fact, now offer known donors — who tend to prefer having sex rather than donating in a clinic setting. Be wary of any such offer, no matter how simple and inexpensive it would be. Trust no one who refuses to get an HIV test or sperm motility count for your peace of mind. He's obviously not someone you would want connected to you and your child.

Questions to Ask Yourself

For her 1987 master's thesis, a Choice Mom interviewed 14 women about how they chose the method to motherhood.[7] She explored, among other experiences, the ethical decisions of women who considered "accidentally on purpose" getting pregnant with men they might not forewarn of their intentions. Many of these women agonized over "whether it was morally right" to take advantage of the men. Sometimes women chose men who were likely to "bolt when the pregnancy was announced." As she noted, "A common feeling was that men who take no responsibility for contraception had no right to oppose conscious conception."

Remember your child's right to his or her creation story. What story can you in good conscience tell your child someday? Let that guide your method to motherhood.

As you consider taking steps with someone, ask yourself these questions:

1. What are his motivations in wanting this child with you? Is it to maintain a relationship with you over time . . . to be a

father without the commitment or responsibility . . . out of a desire to give you something you want?

2. Do you want him to be a semi-involved father in the child's life, or a not-so-involved face and name? When you know what you prefer, it might be easier to decide whether he's capable of sticking to the rules that you set.

3. Do you intuitively trust the man? Don't leap in the hopes that it will all work out, or let your own desire for a known donor cloud your vision.

4. How does he handle situations in which he can't get what he wants? Is he capable of compromise? Is he sensitive to the needs of others?

5. Has he thought about the legal issues involved? I wouldn't fully trust a man who hasn't thought things through. (I wouldn't trust yourself either.) That's why I agree with Jaeger that the smartest thing the two of you could do is to sit down and talk over the details, so you both know what to expect, and what you intend. "It's so important to sit down and talk through the paternity issues and birth certificate issues," she told me. "Dealing with 'the law' makes the parties come to terms with what outside, institutional issues they will have to deal with. Too many people think a contract is not enforceable, so it's not worth it. I disagree."

6. How will you both feel if the child wants him to play a larger role than you envision? How will you feel if the donor wants a larger role, or says he'll be available for contact but changes his mind? What if the donor marries and his wife has a role in setting rules? What if you marry — will the donor's role change? Can both of you accept not being able to control this rather emotional area?

7. How will his family react if they are told? Will they be supportive and hands-off, or want to play a role in the child's life?

Why I'm a Known Donor

✦ I love kids, and think everyone should have the opportunity to have them. I've helped several women have their children, and I have no regrets that I'm not playing a bigger role in those children's lives. Yes, it makes me sad sometimes — frequently — especially when I see pictures of how they're growing. But I have no regrets about doing it.

And it's not about me wanting to spread my seed everywhere. At the core, it gives me joy to know that I've given this profound blessing to a mother and her child.

There are emotions involved, but the right type of person can overcome that — to say 'that's life, there's nothing I can do about it.' It takes a realist, someone capable of being firmly grounded in logic and rational thinking, to do this, I think. Men are generally able to detach from their emotions, but not all.

My advice to anyone picking a donor is to look for someone who is pretty damn logical. Maybe someone in sales or business, who is accustomed to brokering business deals without letting emotions get involved. Not someone who is a superpowerful, dominant kind of guy who has to have his way all the time. Not a control freak.

I think it also would help if he has had kids already and has no interest in more. Or if he has enough to keep him occupied so he's less likely to feel lonely. Mainly he has to be capable of being detached. And ask him if he's ever initiated a lawsuit.

You should know him for at least a year, so you can have the confidence that he's capable of accepting whatever comes his way. He shouldn't have a fixed mindset about anything, but be open to change. Above all, he needs to be realistic, and able to tell himself that he can't have everything — that no matter how great the kid is, he's not going to interfere with the agreement. He understands that nothing more will happen, and is okay with it.

Why I'm Not a Known Donor

✦ Four women have honored me by asking me to father a child. These requests mean something different now than when it first happened at age 25. Twenty years ago, I did not grasp the intense feelings of being a parent. As a young person, the responsibility and emotions played a less important role, and I would have been driven mostly by the desire to replicate the pattern of my parents, siblings, peers, and the community in which I was raised, plus satisfy my ego — she likes me, she really likes me!

To contemplate becoming a father at age 45, however, one draws from richer life experience and different personal, economic, and emotional circumstances. As a single gay man, in many respects I have lived autonomously my whole life. The notion of bringing another human being into the world brings a sense of duty and responsibility that I have not experienced before.

Many people have taught me raising any child (not to mention your own child) is an experience unlike any other experience in life. I imagine it's a form of intense self-actualization I would find especially rewarding. So I took the last invitation very seriously.

The reason I said no to being a donor the first three times was because I was too immature and not prepared for the demands of being a parent, even as a sperm donor. Another time it was because the woman and I were unsuccessful navigating the circles of responsibility. I wanted agreement on the principles of how we continuously balance the well-being of child, mother, siblings, grandparents, partners, friends, classmates, teachers, and so forth.

In order to make this decision, I wanted to look beyond the obligations of child rearing to the emotional or spiritual connection I feel exists between parents and children. Which meant a three-part agreement (two parents and child) that gradually shifted choice from the parents to the child.

8. Even if you don't co-parent, how do his values about parenting differ from yours? Will he protest if you raise the child in a way he doesn't agree with?

Another good source of information for you (and the donor) — even if you are not a lesbian couple — is Stephanie Brill's book *The New Essential Guide to Lesbian Conception, Pregnancy & Birth*.[8] The chapter about known donors goes into detail about everything from the success rates of frozen versus fresh sperm, the logistics of providing sperm, how to find a donor, the strong benefit of sperm analysis early in the process and what it will tell you, how to ask, establishing boundaries, asking questions about sexual history.

You'll find more questions and suggestions for negotiating with a known donor, using the advice of Brill, Jaeger, and myself, at www.choicemoms.org.

Final Thoughts

Jenifer Firestone, director of Alternative Families Matter, addressed a conference for the lesbian and gay community in 2001. She talked about how sharing some level of parenting with a non-spouse is a life-long commitment, regardless of the lack of romantic relationship. She talked about the fact that some known-donor arrangements have been disastrous, and that she was "horrified at the cavalier approach taken by some men and women considering these arrangements."

She talked about how the network of family and friends for both parties in the conception process need to acknowledge the complexity of the situation, and make a pact to resolve any conflicts outside of a court of law. She noted that any successful family arrangement involves honoring responsibilities to the child, while recognizing that either party might have a change of heart, mind, or circumstance.

Reflections on Being a Known Donor
by Andrew Berg[9]

✦ *As a 25-year-old gay man, the author was asked to be the donor for a lesbian couple.*

Many of my gay friends didn't quite understand what I was doing or why. My family, although supportive, was worried that I wouldn't be able to handle the emotions that might arise out of having a child who really isn't mine . . . Even the potential mothers wondered if I had ulterior motives. Why would I want to do this knowing full and well that the child would be theirs and not mine?

The potential moms presented me with a contract that spelled out that I would have "no expectation of a relationship with the child." I would have no say in his or her name. No say in how the child would be raised. No say in his or her education or religious upbringing. For my protection, I had no financial obligations to them, ever. And finally, the child would one day come to know that I was his or her father.

Two years have now passed, and the road has been fairly smooth. I visit them almost every five weeks. We talk on the phone. We exchange photos and e-mails. I've developed a very loving and warm relationship with all three of them. We have built a relationship based on trust, caring and, most importantly, honesty. But there will most certainly be awkward moments on the road ahead, and times when I wish things were a little bit different.

Awkward little moments continue to arise even today. We're now at a time where we're discussing whether or not I'll be referred to as "Dad," and how to explain this relationship to a two-year-old who is quickly figuring out that not all kids have two moms.

Whether or not she calls me Dad isn't really all that important. I've slowly come to terms with and understand that there won't necessarily be a call or a card on Father's ▶

Day. I have come to terms with the fact that my parents can't treat her like their other grandchildren and that I won't always be able to see her when I want. But everything I don't get to share with her makes the time I do have that much more special.

I do my best to look at the big picture. And when I do, I see that the only thing that is important is that I continue to have a loving relationship with this special child — that I have the chance to watch her change and grow, discover and learn. That is my reward.

Postscript: Since this article was written, Andrew agreed to help the same couple, and a brother was born. "They are 5 and 7 years old and I still continue to see them on a regular basis. They just found out that I am their biological father (it took the 7-year-old this long to ask) and they're processing the information. They still call me Andy." Andrew and his long-time partner are parents to twins. "The joke (since the twins are biologically my partner's) is that I'm the biological father of two children who aren't legally mine and the legal father of two children who aren't biologically mine."

As Firestone said:[10]

We need to establish our own customs that make sense for our unique families. We can arrange ceremonies to welcome the new baby/child . . . We can publicly assure our children that while life is full of all kinds of changes, this carefully chosen family of parents, donor/dads, etc., will always be their family, and that each family member will forever honor and appreciate that child's relationship with each of them. We could make use of "godparents" or other individuals who are mutually trusted by all of the parents to witness the recognition of these family members, to hear why they chose each other, what they felt the other(s) would bring to the child's life, and to step in and assist if problems threaten the relationships to which the child is accustomed . . .

[Non-couples] who conceive children together do so for the sake of fulfilling the child's need to know, and possibly have relationships with both biological parents, and for the richness these bonds can bring to the act of parenting.

But this fulfillment can only be achieved, she said, if both parties involved accept and understand that "parenting is a life-long commitment you make to the children, regardless of the parents' relationship with each other."

In my conversations with many single women who choose to have a child on their own, I recognize that whether the donor is known or anonymous, or whether open or closed adoption is used, we tend to have very strong feelings about how important the birth parent is or should be to our child.

But my important message is this: Ultimately, it is the child who gets to decide. No matter which method you choose, don't lose sight of the child's intrinsic right to determine who he or she considers important.

8

Using Donor Insemination

Although donor sperm has been used medically since the late 1700s, the first known United States case occurred in 1884, when a couple arrived at a medical school in Philadelphia with an infertility problem. The group of doctors discussing the case chose a good-looking donor and secretly inseminated the woman with sperm. Not until after the birth was the husband told. The wife was never let in on the secret.[1]

It took another 100 years before donor eggs became an option for infertile women, and even longer for the shame and secrecy of insemination to begin to dissipate (thanks partly to the growing availability of the process to Choice Moms who had less to hide). Now insemination is a booming business. One estimate is that 30,000 children are born each year from reproductive technologies.[2] Single women now account for about half of the business at California Cryobank, one of the world's largest sperm banks, and roughly one-third of the insemination business overall.

The process is a complex one: Do I need fertility testing? Which donor should I pick? Which clinics are open-minded regarding single mothers? What do all the acronyms mean — ICI, IUI — and what do I need to be prepared to deal with? How much will everything cost?

Entire books have been written about donor insemination, including my own *Choice Mom Guide to Fertility* (Be-Mondo Publishing, 2007). Check the Resources section for sources that go into greater detail about insemination, egg donors, sperm banks, and storybooks for kids about how they were conceived. Rather than cover ground available elsewhere, this chapter will focus on:

1. why I believe women should seriously consider using an open-identity donor;
2. the views of sperm donors about why they donated and how they feel about it today;
3. the questions to consider when choosing a sperm donor and bank.

In other chapters we discuss insemination costs (chapter 2), how to answer a child's daddy questions (chapter 11), and how some donor offspring feel about their conception story (chapter 12).

Conception Methods: A Comparison

A single woman who wants to conceive has four options in choosing a donor:

1. A known donor (the topic of chapter 7) — This option does not come with legal and emotional protections between donor and mother, as tends to be the case with an anonymous donor. As we learned in the previous chapter, it can be extremely painful and costly to deal with a known donor who changes his mind and wants to be a co-parent after all. However, some women have a strong desire to give a child the opportunity to know as much as possible about his or her full genetic identity and medical history. One woman I talked to stopped pursuing the ADI route and asked an old boyfriend to become her donor. She knew

that using a known donor was more complicated, "but I feel better about knowing who the father is."

2. A "directed" donor — Using a known donor's sperm in a clinic insemination (also called "directed" donor) tends to give greater legal protection. A drawback is timing: In most cases (but not all, if legal release forms for liability are accepted), the sperm needs to be quarantined for six months. This was the case with my donor, even after we had already conceived one child together. There is cost for storage, testing for HIV, and the insemination process, but the donor and mother are *generally* protected from custody and support issues. However, there have been legal cases in which directed donors were granted parental rights, and at least one directed donor for in vitro fertilization has been sued for child support, so legal protection is not ironclad. (See chapter 14 for details about legal cases.)

3. An anonymous donor — This provides the greatest legal protection for donor and mother, although it tends to leave the child with few options for dealing with potential identity issues. Even with anonymous donors, exceptions have been made. In 2000, for example, one 11-year-old girl with a kidney disorder won the rights to information about her donor by a San Francisco court.

   Compared to using a known donor, an anonymous one makes it cleaner for the woman (and the child) to know that there is no partner and no father in the family. Given the emotions involved in creating life, it can be hard to keep clearheaded when using the sperm of a known person. One author of a comprehensive book about insemination used a donor that was known to her and her husband — and eventually divorced and married the donor. Another woman I know fell in love with a potential known donor. He got scared of what he might be getting himself into, and backed out.

4. An open-identity donor — I'll spend a lot of time discuss-

ing this option, because I strongly believe it gives all three parties in the conception a reasonable agreement. Children, who I think are equally entitled to choices, will know that their mother tried to give them the opportunity to contact the donor after the age of 18. Sometimes the child has no interest, sometimes the donor is too nervous in 18 years to be of much help, but at least the mother has selected someone who understands and accepts responsibility for an offspring's curiosity about his or her other genetic half.

Home insemination

It can be very stressful for women to attempt to get pregnant in a clinic setting, often having to secretly fit in one or two last-minute appointments when ovulation is detected. A great deal of emotional energy can be expended waiting and wondering if any of the costly attempts will work — a fertility concern that increases with the woman's age and in fact might contribute to stress-related infertility issues. To avoid the clinical setting, some banks will allow frozen sperm to be shipped to the woman's home so she can use a needleless syringe or cervical cap to inseminate at home. (For tips, see www.fertilityplus.org/faq/homeinsem.html.)

Home shipment generally requires a doctor's sign-off. The success rate of this low-tech option is not high — although it is common, and one bank reports that 54 percent of its clients eventually succeed at home.

One expert on home insemination (and on helping women over the age of 40 conceive) is Stephanie Brill, of Maia Midwifery and Preconception Services.[3] Brill generally recommends that, if the insemination uses frozen sperm (and remember that fresh sperm can be a health hazard), any woman expect a year of attempts, especially if she is over the age of 40. Sperm can be inserted either using a premade kit, available for mail order, or by using a disposable syringe without the needle. In some areas, trained midwives can help perform the procedure, including placing the sperm into the uterus

Alphabet Soup

ART — assisted reproductive technology, in which egg and sperm are handled to help a woman get pregnant.

ICSI — intracytoplasmic sperm injection, when sperm is injected directly into an egg in a laboratory.

IUI — intrauterine insemination, a clinical method that increases the number of sperm that reach the fallopian tube and thus improves the odds of an egg being fertilized. It requires "washing" the sperm to separate it from semen and is timed to occur with ovulation. It is sometimes combined with supervolution induction, which makes multiple eggs available for fertilization.

IVF — in vitro fertilization, the usual treatment for a woman with blocked or damaged fallopian tubes, or to circumvent infertility caused by endometriosis. This process was first used in England in 1978, with the "test-tube baby" Louise Brown, and ushered in the new age of ART. Hundreds of thousands of children have now been born this way. It involves combining egg and sperm in a culture dish and transferring the embryo into the uterus. It requires about two weeks of preparation in order to create a strong environment in the woman, including fertility drugs, ultrasounds, and blood tests.

IVI — intravaginal insemination, which is a method of home insemination that uses a needleless syringe or cervical cap.

(IUI), rather than near the cervix (ICI), for better odds. Careful fertility timing is crucial, and is often related to cervical mucus rather than temperature charting.

Women should turn to a clinic after several months of unsuccessful attempts at home, to check fertility issues and to better the odds of success.

> ### *Important*
>
> ✦ In hindsight, many Choice Moms I've talked with wish they had started before the age of 35, to allow more time with better quality eggs, as well as to give them more time to have a second child without the extra expense and stress of fertility treatments.

The Ethics of Donor Insemination

One area in which Choice Mothers have an advantage over married couples is that they don't have to agonize over whether to tell the child the truth about their origins. Most of today's roughly 1 million donor-conceived children do not know the truth about their conception (one estimate is 80 percent!).[4]

Some children of married couples feel something is "off" — that perhaps their mother had an affair or was raped, for example. Some find out after the father dies, after a divorce, or during a family argument. One teenage girl was told by an angry mother: "You should be grateful. You have no idea how much we paid to have you!"

The secrecy aspect of donor insemination has given the process a bad name. Many research studies reveal that when a couple uses an egg or sperm donor and don't tell the child the truth, the damage of secrecy (or shame and distance of the infertile parent) can have a seriously negative impact on the family dynamic. Someone who learns late in life that he or she is not related biologically to a parent often experiences intense feelings of betrayal, anger, mistrust, resentment, and confusion about who they are. Many of these donor offspring turn to online support groups to vent their emotions.

It is hard to separate whether the emotions of these men and

*One Policy of Openness**

We recognize the concerns regarding the rights to privacy and confidentiality on the part of the sperm donor, the mother, the parenting father and the child. In an attempt to balance these concerns with the real and legitimate needs on the part of the child to know about his or her biological heritage, we have developed a "Policy Of Openness," which includes the following:

1. We have never destroyed patient or donor files and plan to keep the information indefinitely.
2. If, at the age of 18 or older, the child of a recipient requests information about the genetic father we will make all reasonable efforts to supply that information either from our records or by attempting to contact the donor.
3. While we are NOT opposed in principal to breaking anonymity between the donor and the adult (or near adult) child, we do feel strongly it must be by mutual consent of both parties.
4. We do not believe that the semen donor or the mother should be asked today how they might feel about such a sensitive and complex issue 15–30 years from now.
5. We do believe the issues are real. Our task is to maintain our records and prepare ourselves so that we can appropriately respond to individual needs.
6. However, we are obligated by mutual agreements to maintain the anonymity and privacy of both the donor and recipient. The only exception to this would be by mutual consent of the involved individuals.

* *This is the openness policy of one sperm bank found online.*

women are rooted primarily in being misled by their parents, and how much is related to being unable to get a full picture of their genetic identity. Many children who consider their donor conception to be "no big deal" typically were told at a young age and grow up more curious about their origins than angry about it.

Anonymity vs. open identity

Secrecy is not an issue for Choice Mothers, since their children tend to know that a donor was used. But whether to use a donor who can never be identified, or one the child can make contact with after the age of 18, is an important option to consider.

In the United States and elsewhere, anonymity is slowly giving way to the viewpoint that a child's right to know their genetic history should take precedence. Arthur Caplan, the director of the Center for Bioethics at the University of Pennsylvania, says lessons from adoption are opening the door. Nowadays in adoption, he told me, "It doesn't matter if the records are open or not, many judges are starting to allow adopted children to appeal a sealed record. It's still case by case, but if someone says they want to screen for Huntington's disease or breast cancer, a judge is not going to deny the medical need to know more about the person's own genetic background."

Caplan predicts that someday offspring of anonymous donors are likely to be able to do the same.

The Open-Identity Option

To honor the needs of parents who want their children to know more about their genetic identity, a growing number of U.S. sperm banks offer open-identity donors, who agree to be reachable after the child turns 18. In 1983, The Sperm Bank of California (TSBC) in Berkeley was the first to offer Identity-Release (IR) donors. In 2003 alone, 75 percent of the 130 children born from its program had IR donors. Other banks are adapting their policies to suit growing consumer demand. At last count on spermcenter.com, 10 of its 24 listed sperm banks offered some form of open-identity donor. A few banks, on a case-by-case basis, contact anonymous donors retrospectively to see if they are willing to have their identities released to offspring.

Although sperm banks might use similar terms, there is no standard program. Every bank has a different approach and should be studied closely. Sperm from open-identity donors tends to be more expensive per vial than that of anonymous donors; one website I checked reported a difference of $100. One bank doesn't charge more for the vials, but charges a fee when a child is born.

One survey of 115 single women, including lesbian couples and heterosexual couples from a New Mexico clinic,[5] reported that lesbian couples and single women were more likely than married couples to want a donor's identity disclosed (75 percent to 32 percent).

A TSBC survey, however, found both single and married people equally interested in its open-identity donors — nearly 80 percent reported it as an important criterion in choosing a donor.[6]

On the other hand, another TSBC survey reported that children of Choice Moms were slightly more likely to request information about the donor than children of married couples.[7]

Why choose open donors?

Even if a child is told openly about conception by donor sperm or egg, the child sometimes can grow up with a deep curiosity, wanting to understand the missing donors' identity as part of his or her own definition of self. This curiosity is often misinterpreted by worried parents as seeking a 'replacement' parent or an additional parent. The fear tends to be that the donor will become important to the child in a way that cannot be controlled by the parent, rather than being recognized as a natural interest in one's genetic background.

Based on my conversations with Choice Moms and mental health counselors, I believe that the more confidence a parent has about making this choice, the less threatened he or she will be about the donor's existence. I also know that some of us might have strong tendencies toward controlling external factors in our lives, and this too can make it difficult — as it does for some married parents — to see the donor as anything other than an intrusion on our lives, rather than a choice for the child to someday assess and place value on.

As we deepen our understanding of how influential genetics is — compared to what we once thought in the nature versus nurture balance — it can be troubling for offspring to have an incomplete medical history. In most cases, a sperm donor's family health history is available based only on what the donor was able to divulge at the generally young age at which he donated. This is not reliable, especially since so much will occur in his family after that date. I see this as a major weakness of the donor insemination system today, and have been talking with sperm industry leaders about correcting it through a medical updates database.

Sometimes offspring might not feel a compulsion to know more until they are about to become parents themselves. Caplan told me it is common to be ambivalent until issues of heredity make the issue seem more urgent.

One adopted Choice Mother told me it was important to her that she choose open-identity. She had found her own birth family ten years earlier. She defines family as people who raise you, not whoever provide sperm and egg, yet "I wanted to give my son the chance to connect with his biological roots."

Another Choice Mom told me it was her child's right to know his full heritage someday if he desired — that it was not her right to decide what he could and could not discover. Although she ended up using a known donor, she had originally selected an anonymous donor who would allow contact in 18 years. "I don't agree that we can think of our children as only ours. My parents don't own me, and I don't own my son, even if I do call him mine," she said. "Our children will be confused teens and then mature adults one day, with questions and a need to find out who they really are. There will be some kids who are content not finding the donor, but I am sure many will."

Strengthening her opinion was the knowledge of a friend who was conceived to a mother and father via anonymous insemination. "She cannot find her biological father, and she is full of anger and resentment about it."

The trend toward openness — in adoption and donor insemination — makes it more likely that a child conceived today will expect to understand their full genetic legacy tomorrow. Using an open-identity donor will make that expectation easier to satisfy.

Why *not* choose open donors?

Although children benefit from having the opportunity to learn more about their other half if they choose to, it is not always an easy choice for the parent to make.

A primary reason Choice Moms use anonymous donors is that they are more plentiful. At last count, of the 1,500 donors listed on spermcenter.com, only 226 were open-identity. With other important variables — such as resemblance to her family and religious background — it can be tough to pick a donor from such a limited pool.

Some are reluctant to use such popular donors, whose sperm is likely to be used by many families before being retired, depending on bank policy. Others worry that a child who grows up with expectations of having contact with the donor will end up disappointed, either with what they discover, or what they don't.

Many don't feel comfortable accepting the agreement of a man whose life likely will change in unforeseen and substantial ways over 18 years. Rather than infringe on the privacy of the man and his family, an anonymous donation makes it a clean break.

A few women admit that, deep down, they are threatened by the idea that a relationship might someday develop between donor and child, and prefer to keep the family structure more clear. This is a major reason most married couples do not tell their child that a donor is used; fear that the unknown person will have a special place in the child's heart and replace the nonbiological parent.

A TSBC survey reported that nearly 44 percent of its respondents who did not choose an open-identity donor did so because they preferred no contact. Comments included "not wanting to consider the donor as a person" and "not wanting the donor to assume a parental role."[8]

Author comment

There are valid reasons anyone might be reluctant to use an open-identity donor. But in my view, I feel strongly that the donor and parent are affected much less by this decision than the child, who typically is interested in asking questions related to his or her own sense of self, rather than finding another parent. If the child is someday interested in learning more, I believe it's better for the Choice Mother to be an ally in the search for information than to be perceived as someone who didn't think it should matter, or who was trying to protect the donor or child.

I also agree with the motto of a friend of mine who used open adoption. You can live in fear or in love. Many of the reasons for rejecting an open donor are based out of the parent's fear.

On the availability front, the stronger the demand for open donors, the more effort banks will put into recruitment. The sales director of one sperm bank told me that an informal in-house survey revealed that the 20 most popular donors at their bank were open-identity, or had an adult photo, or both.

The TSBC survey found that open-identity status was second in importance only to physical appearance of the donor (generally matching to family) during the selection process.[9]

As more people request donors who are open to revealing information to offspring, banks will work even harder to make them available. Within a year of launching its open-identity program in 2004, one-third of California Cryobank donors were open to contact.[10]

A Worldwide Issue

✦ The United Nations Convention on the Rights of the Child declared formally in 1989 that a child has the right to his or her genetic origins. This "open-identity" right was declared law — and not optional — first in Sweden (1985), and then in Austria, Switzerland, New Zealand, the Australian states, The Netherlands (2004), and the United Kingdom (2005). These countries have made it mandatory for sperm banks to use open-identity donors. All new donors must agree to be contacted at the wishes of any offspring after a certain age. Japan and Norway have considered similar legislation.

Several countries have voluntary national registries to enable adult offspring and donors to find each other.

On the other hand, France allows only anonymous donors, on the theory that the child's best interests are served by having one father. Italy does not allow donor insemination at all.

Finding siblings

Another option available to donor-conceived children is to find half-siblings through websites such as the Donor Sibling Registry (www.donorsiblingregistry.com). Since 2000, the registry has grown to more than 9,000 members, with more than 4,000 matches of half-siblings.

When her son was only a few months old, Teresa was in contact with three families who had daughters using the same donor's sperm (identifiable by his number). "I wasn't sure how I would feel about this, or how much contact I would want with these families, but after hearing from two families and seeing photos of two of the girls, I was surprised at how much happiness I felt," she said. "It was both strange and wonderful to see little faces that bear a resemblance to my son's. I have no idea where this path will take us, but I'm glad I did it, and I look forward to contact with other families as well."

When Open-Identity Children "Come of Age"

Another TSBC research study (available in detail on the bank's website),[11] led by Joanna E. Scheib, revealed that the teenagers born of its Identity-Release program, who were nearly old enough to seek information about the donor, tended to be curious — not resentful — about their donor. All 29 teens in the study said they felt loved and wanted by their family.

Nearly all of them wanted to see a photo of the donor, and most were interested in what his current life was like, what his health was, and more about family history. Most did not intend to make immediate contact, but thought they might write a letter or go through the sperm bank to get more information when the time came. (In fact, only 15 of its eligible 120 children, in 2005, had thus far requested information.[12]) Most reported that contact would be helpful to learn more about what the donor was like, with two-thirds saying that it might help them learn more about themselves.

Scheib and her colleagues also interviewed 27 of its donors who had the potential to be contacted by offspring soon. Most were between 35 and 45 years old, in committed relationships, and about half had their own children. Most were curious about the pending identity process, and only two regretted being an Identity-Release donor. More than half had concerns about the unknown, such as what the offspring would want from them. About a third were concerned that the offspring would be resentful about their origins, although in reality this was not the case.[13]

The first donor meeting of a Choice Mom

Christina was 18 when she met her open-identity donor, Phillip, in 2003. Her mother, Mary, was a librarian and Choice Mom who used The Sperm Bank of California. As Mary told CBS's *The Early Show* at the time, pictures of the donor seen earlier didn't show much of a resemblance. But when she and her daughter met Phillip in person, "The eyes, goodness, it's like looking at her eyes in someone else's face. And they have smiles that are alike. I was amazed."

According to a *Los Angeles Times* story about the meeting, the donor and offspring both have gregarious personalities that aided them both. "I'm completely outgoing and spontaneous," Christina said. "Definitely a wild child. He's a really positive person. Our chemistry just clicked. I think we can be really good friends."[14]

Phillip, who has bungee-jumped and fire-walked in a motivational seminar, said he had long hoped to be able to find out how any of his offspring turned out, and thought it only fair that they know him. During the meeting, he and Christina talked about their mutual love of reggae music.

Mary hoped her daughter and donor would be able to forge a type of long-term relationship. "Any kid who can get more love from wherever, I'm all for it. As long as love is healthy, it's wonderful."

My book series about families and issues impacted by donor insemination (see voicesofdonorconception.com) has enabled me to talk with people on all sides of the donor equation. I know offspring who have met their donors, others who wish they could, and still others who might be curious, but not to the point of wanting contact. One young man who has spent time with his donor on several occasions has found it a very interesting way to understand his own idiosyncrasies. A woman who thinks she knows who her donor is but has been rebuffed in efforts to make contact feels almost ashamed of her birth, and resentful that she is not entitled to know her own history.

Choice Chat with Susan:
A Donor-Conceived Woman Pursues Insemination

✦ *When Susan was 27, her mother told her she had been con-ceived by an anonymous sperm donor. Prior to that, Susan, a single lesbian, had spent months talking to her mother about insemination options before her mother's "cognitive dissonance apparently reached a breaking point." As some-one on both sides of the donor equation, with strong opin-ions about it, Susan offered her story for this book.*

On what she'd like to know about her donor
I know nothing about the donor my parents used. There were no donor catalogs or medical histories or long profiles in 1967. The infertility doctor told my mother he would use a "dark, Eastern European" medical student to match my father. I have no idea if he did this. Although I recognize the value of an accurate medical history, what I most want to know is what he's like. If you gave me a choice of medical history going back four generations and a half-hour con-versation with him, I would take the conversation without hesitation. Is he like me? Am I like him? What are his other children like? What kind of a person is he?

On using a donor herself
I spent a long time trying to find the right known donor among my friends because I really did not want to use a sperm bank. I thought it would be great to have one of my wonderful male friends as the donor and the child would have another person who loved them in his or her life. It was complicated and expensive — legal contracts, having people show up on very short notice for months. But in the end, there were infertility issues. I'm 36 and I really, re-ally want to have a baby. So, now I am working with a ▶

sperm bank that has a large selection of open-identity donors as well as Jewish donors. It's not my first preference,
but I think it strikes a decent balance. I can only hope
that my child will have compassion about my choices, just
as I had compassion for my mother's. And if not, that's
parenting, right? May I be blessed with such problems as
soon as possible.

On the ethics of donor anonymity
We know that many adoptees search for their birth parents.
Not all, but many. And not only the unhappy ones — some
people just feel the need to know these things. Because so
many adopted people grew up and wanted to search, we
have changed public policy on this issue. We have open
adoptions, we have systems in place to help people with
search and reunion. Some states, like Oregon, have opened
sealed adoption records, recognizing that the child has a
RIGHT to know their parentage. Why do we have to start
at square one with gamete donation when we already know
all of this? Giving away your sperm or eggs is not like donating blood. Blood does not become a person with feelings
and identity.

> *It's very frustrating to me when people say that biolog-
> ical connections should not matter. If biological con-
> nections do not matter, why are you going through this
> much trouble just to conceive your own child?*

There are lots of children that need homes. You are trying to have your own child because biological connections
matter. Why should biological connections matter less to
me than they do to you?
I don't understand what people are afraid of. The worst
that could happen is that I don't like him or he doesn't like
me. Okay. Why can't we make that decision as adults? ▶

On the limited pool of open-identity donors
The entire focus of most infertility clinics is "curing" the infertility, getting you pregnant. I understand the desire for a good selection. I just think it pales in comparison to the possible needs of the child. There are many high-quality sperm banks with a good selection of open-identity donors that ship all over the country. I really think it's worth the extra money in order to be able to say to your child, "I thought you might want to know."

All that said, look, sometimes people can't know things they want to know. We're rarely born into the circumstances we would have chosen as adults. I try not to judge individuals for their choices.

I am far more angry at the system than I am at individual people making individual choices in their lives.

On the emotions of donor-conceived kids
In general, it's fair to say that people with strong, loving, positive relationships with their parents seem to enact love and compassion around this issue, and those with weak, traumatized, and problematic relationships tend to enact trauma and pain. So, I'm sure that the general health of the family has some effect.

I do wonder if it's largely a question of personality. Some kids spend lots of time wondering things like "Who am I?" "What is my task in the world?" I was always that kind of kid. Other kids would rather run outside and play and not worry about that stuff. Thank God there are people like that in the world because if everyone were like me, the world would have a serious fun deficiency.

On advice to Choice Moms
You can feel bad that you don't have all the information your child might seek, you can feel bad that you could ▶

not conceive in the way you originally wanted, but do not make apologies about using DI or the conception will be seen as something shameful. Work through whatever emotions you have so that you can convey that you wouldn't trade your child for anyone in the world.

Who Are the Donors?

Views about donors vary among Choice Moms, from those who feel he is simply a provider of material to those who are appreciative of his gift and wish they had the opportunity to thank him personally. Some parents — single and married — have no interest in the donor in the beginning, but curiosity develops as their child grows, exhibits a few unrecognizable traits, and starts asking questions.

The Wellesley researcher Rosanna Hertz reported that one single mom said of her donor, "Initially I didn't talk about him much . . . and I didn't really want to treat him as a person but just a sperm donor. But as time went on . . . I changed my attitude about the whole thing and began to see it more as [my daughter being] half-adopted."[15]

So who are the donors? And what can a Choice Mother tell her child about the unknown person who helped create his or her life?

Sperm donation is much more complicated than sitting in a room with a magazine and a cup, then walking out with cash. Donors are highly probed and tested before they are allowed into a program. As Alice Ruby, executive director of The Sperm Bank of California, explained, their donors go through an extensive screening procedure. "Men hoping to donate sperm must provide blood, urine and semen samples to be tested for transmissible diseases such as HIV, hepatitis and syphilis, and for genetic conditions such as Cystic Fibrosis and Tay-Sachs," she told me.

"They complete a long questionnaire about their personal

health history and health habits, and a four-generation health history detailing the health status of their relatives, including their parents, grandparents, siblings, children, aunts, uncles and cousins. Potential donors also must go through a physical exam and a very detailed HIV risk assessment interview. Becoming a donor takes eight to ten weeks on average. Contrary to popular assumptions, men do not donate semen casually."

Will donors stop giving?

Some countries have made it mandatory to use open-identity donors. The United States is not likely to enter this debate anytime soon. One common concern of those opposed to the option is that donors are involved primarily for money, and will stop donating if they are required to take some responsibility for answering their offsprings' questions in later years.

The Sperm Bank of California conducted an in-house survey of donors in its Identity-Release program:[16]

- 48 percent felt the offspring had the right to know the donor's identity
- 32 percent said they would be curious about the offspring
- 20 percent said that if they were donor offspring they would want to have the option to know

In 2005, a United Kingdom clinic asked 32 donors (who are not paid) if they would continue to donate under the new open-identity requirement. Half said yes, one-quarter said no, and the rest were undecided.[17] A Manchester clinic, in fact, has reported that being more creative about where and how it recruits donors — placing ads in progressive-minded news magazines, for example — has enabled it to find the altruistic, intelligent, responsible donors it needs.

I've interviewed several men who were sperm donors during college — largely for the money — but in later life regretted knowing nothing about the real people who would have been created as a result, or being able to offer updated medical information to the families. Although contact with offspring can complicate things for a donor who has a wife and family of his own, many mature men recognize the gap in knowledge faced by unknown offspring and welcome the chance to correct it, in a controlled and even-handed way.

Choosing a Donor

In the "dark ages" of insemination, even less than two decades ago, doctors decided where to get sperm for insemination, and the parent(s) had no choice in the matter. In many countries today, in fact, the woman still has no choice of donor — a laboratory specialist does the selecting.

Nowadays, long profiles are available at most sperm banks, revealing extensive details about the occupation, education, and personality of the donor, as well as those of several layers of relatives, to give a greater picture of a family's gene pool. Most banks provide profiles with three-generation medical histories. Many include essays from the donor about why they donated, as well as messages to offspring.

Other services offered by some include:

- photo-matching services, in which the bank selects a donor resembling the submitted photo of a family member
- online photos of the donor as an adult or baby
- live audio interviews with donors who answer presubmitted questions
- results of personality assessment tests
- staff impressions of donors
- videotaped interviews with the donor

Doing the research

Policies vary considerably among sperm banks and clinics. As Arthur Caplan advised, "You have to shop carefully. Don't just take the one down the street."

Good resources for comparing and choosing doctors, sperm banks, treatment options, and much more are available online. Check resources on my choicemoms.org website, such as sperm center.com, which gives you a one-stop glance at all donors available in a given month.

Sample questions for banks include: How many offspring are allowed before a donor's sperm is retired? How does the bank plan to keep records of donors and recipients in the long-term? What counseling is provided, for client and donor? If a child with a genetic condition is linked to a donor, are other families who used that donor alerted? One counselor I talked to recommended working with banks that can help you make a plan: if home insemination doesn't work after a few cycles, for example, Plan B will take effect. Otherwise many cycles can go by status quo, without success and without changing the variables.

Note that all clinics should allow you to choose your own donor from the bank of your choice, rather than limiting you to the bank of their choice.

Narrowing the field

Deciding on the "right" donor is a personal decision that varies considerably among single women. One woman I know purposely chose an older man with an existing family, to help insure his comprehension of what his donation meant. Another Choice Mom invited her closest girlfriends over to vote on her potential candidates, using her existing network to be part of the process from the start. Some women report picking donors they might have wanted as a mate.

One organized woman used a bank with donors who supplied photos, audio interviews, temperament sorters, and a long profile, and narrowed her selection to only those men who supplied all four. She read their free short profiles until she had only two remaining choices. After purchasing full packages of information for those two men, she made her choice based on how their essays "felt" to her.

What Donating Has Meant to Me*

✦ *The author of this story learned about donor insemination as a college student, when he saw an advertisement offering money to help infertile couples become parents. He did his own research, and learned that 1 in 10 couples had trouble conceiving, and decided to be of assistance.*

I'll never forget how apprehensive and embarrassed I was walking into the clinic on my first appointment . . . I couldn't have become a donor if I thought that I was being paid for my "services," and I find it difficult to understand how anyone can commit themselves to a fairly de-humanizing and stressful process for a measly [amount of money]. I feel sure that even if most donors expect payment, the majority are primarily motivated for altruistic reasons . . .

I know that many find it difficult to understand how anyone can become a donor knowing that their contributions will be used to create individuals genetically related to them of whom they will have no knowledge. During my counseling I had to confront this reality, but I never let it faze me because I was clear that the reason why I wanted to become a donor was to give others the opportunity to have children . . . In any case . . . donating in the impersonal and sterile setting of a clinic . . . doesn't allow you to form any personal attachment [to any new life] that can be created as a result of your donations.

Pleased as I am to think that my contributions may make a positive difference to some families, I still have my regrets. I regret that I will never know anything about any person born from my donations . . . I often have found myself wondering whether their parents will tell them of the circumstances of their conception. I also wonder what any person conceived as a result of my donations would think of me, if anything, and how their lives might develop.

* From: Donor Conception Network

Recommendations to consider:

- If open-identity is important to you, start with that limited pool.
- If you believe genetics play an important role in a person's personality, make sure you are working with a bank that offers many profiling options — and has a proven plan for updating medical histories. Are you particularly interested in physical characteristics, personality traits, creative talents, athletic skill?
- Do you prefer a donor who believes in a certain set of values? If so, use a bank that provides essays for you to assess.
- Do you hope the child looks like you and your family? Many women attempt to increase the odds by finding similar appearance factors in a donor, or shared ethnicity. Height seems to be an important criteria for many women.
- Check medical history for special concerns you might have.
- Many banks eventually retire a donor's sperm to reduce the potential for too many children coming from the same donor. Some women purchase multiple vials to assure availability for many attempts. Others pay to store these for future use in creating siblings.

Some women consider choosing the donor to be the uncomfortable equivalent of genetic preselection, or are suspicious of the honesty of the profiles, and don't put much thought into the selection process. Others believe the way the child is raised is more significant than genetics. Still others look but do not find a "perfect" donor, and end up choosing from a list of options. As one woman said, for her the donor choice ultimately was a minor part of the process.

Of course, any child's inheritance is imprecise. Picking donor traits may seem logical or fun to some, but should never be considered true science. Your child will be the one you were meant to have.

Survey Says: Being Able to Contact the Donor

✦ *Another study led by Joanna Scheib of the University of California–Davis and research-intensive TSBC explored the perspective of parents whose teenagers had Identity-Release donors.[18] Almost 80 percent of its clients request an IR donor, they wrote, reflecting the desire of parents and children to "avoid a possible sense of futility in having incomplete knowledge about the child's origins and the child becoming preoccupied with this lack of information."*

Emotions about meeting donors — Most of the Choice Mothers represented in the survey felt that open-identity was the right option for their child to have. About half reported some concern and anxiety as their child neared the age of 18, although none indicated they regretted giving the child the option to receive information about the donor. Concerns included:

• whether the donor would live up to the child's expectations;
• the child's reaction if the donor had died;
• whether the donor would respond if many other offspring had already tried to contact him.

The older child's views — With the child now a teenager (only those with DI children aged 12 to 17 were included in the survey), most parents reported that their child still had no negative feelings about their origins. A common reason for this was thought to be because the parent was honest with the child, and that DI was not a major focus — "they had a life outside DI," and "homework [was] more of an issue at this point." Others reported that the child understood that DI was simply part of his or her life, and "did not know any differently." ▶

Other facts that came out of the study:

- Most birth mothers (which included married, lesbian, and single women) had told their child of the circumstances of their birth by the age of 6, with the average age being 4.8 years old.
- Almost all parents (nearly 91 percent) said they expected or knew their child was curious about the donor, with almost two-thirds reporting that the child looked forward to meeting the donor.
- About half (nearly 49 percent) thought their child would want genealogical information, with 42 percent expected to want health information. Parents from six households thought their child would do nothing with the information other than read it and keep it as family history.
- Parents from nearly 83 percent of families thought their child would contact the donor to "learn more about himself or herself/increase sense of identity," and 20.5 percent thought it would help create an ethnic connection.
- Parents from about 47 percent of the households thought their child might want a relationship, generally depending on what the initial contact was like.
- The three top questions listed by the children were: "What is the donor like?" "Is he like me?" "Can I meet him?" All but one wanted a picture of him.

The Process

Many women are optimistic that the first insemination attempt will work, and then supremely disappointed when they find that they are not pregnant. Many women report this crushing news doesn't get easier, no matter how many times it happens.

The process can be intensely emotional, requiring you to wait patiently for the right day, fit in a doctor appointment with little notice, look for signs — "I'm feeling bloated, is that good or bad?" Some women need a demanding series of drugs, which makes the process even more difficult. Several women have told me that in retrospect they wouldn't have told as many people as they did about their attempts to conceive, to avoid the repetitive "Are you pregnant yet?" questions. But do find a select few who can offer you moral support, especially those who have been through the insemination process. There are several online chat options, if that is a method of interaction that appeals to you, including my own Choice Moms group.

One sperm bank reports that 1 in 12 of its clients who used IVI succeeded in conceiving, compared to 1 in 6 for IUI. Depending on the mother's age, cycle regularity, and fertility issues, the American Society for Reproductive Medicine indicates that getting pregnant using frozen sperm has a success rate of 8 to 15 percent. In general, industry trends indicate it takes four to eight attempts to conceive.

A 2002 research report revealed that, per cycle, IUI had a success rate of 18.5 percent for women under 35, 11.9 percent for women 35 to 40, and 5.4 percent for women over the age of 40. In comparison, timed intercourse succeeds at a rate of roughly 20 percent.[19]

Many women on my Choice Moms discussion group report that a combination of ovulation predictor kits and basal body temperatures can help them learn more than a doctor could about their fertility. As Kris told me, "For my first insemination, the doctor argued with me about when I was ovulating, but I knew better than he did when it was happening, after months of charting my temps. So, I timed my next insemination according to my ovulation predictions and got pregnant that way. Bottom line: You know your body better than anyone else does!"

Others prefer to leave the science in someone else's hands. But whether you want to learn everything you can about your own fertility or not, I always advise women to be educated consumers. One Choice Mom I know spent thousands of dollars on the wrong doctors, with the wrong treatment plan, before a new doctor discovered the issues that needed to be fixed before she could conceive.

Final Thoughts

Being conceived from donor sperm is not inherently problematic to a child. One study examined the behavior of donor-conceived children, who averaged 7 years old. The children who were having behavioral or socialization issues were not significantly affected by biological connection, sexual orientation, or relationship status of their parents. Rather, the predominant factor was related to the stress their parent reported simply from being a parent.[20]

Donor children, however, can be affected by the realization that they were not created from a physical union between a man and a woman. Research indicates that it is important to convey that the donor is a real person who cares about the child and the mother, even if they've never met.

Consider the conversation you will someday have with your child about how and why you chose the donor that you did. If you end up with a donor whose information is sketchy, consider creating a general profile about the average donor. For example: someone comfortable doing things in a different way, proactive, interested in helping others, confident, open-minded.

I'd also recommend that you actively participate in any available counseling. Emily, a Choice Mom, wrote a letter to members of the Donor Conception Network that she allowed me to excerpt

Choice Chat with Jeanne: The Value of Hindsight

✦ As someone who did 13 inseminations, one tubal transfer, and seven in vitros, I have a lot of knowledge I wish someone had imparted before I started the process. For the insemination process, if you haven't gotten pregnant within four cycles (twice for each tube) you need to get more proactive. Your doctor should be monitoring your follicle growth, and if you aren't producing eggs you'll need fertility drugs. If after two or three more cycles you haven't gotten pregnant, inseminations probably aren't going to do it. There may be tubal factors, and in vitro may be the best option. It is expensive. This is the point where you want to consider adoption.

If you go the IVF route, check doctors' and clinics' success rates for live birth. My first four attempts were at two hospitals that I later found out had only 20 percent success rates for "chemical pregnancy." I got pregnant with twins at one of them but the fetuses never developed heartbeats and I miscarried. This was recorded as a "successful pregnancy" with this group. Another doctor transferred all 11 embryos at once while I was under general anesthesia, "for a better shot of success." Needless to say, I switched doctors, and clinics. The doctor I eventually used for my first child, and then my twins, had a success rate of 38 percent.

The first two clinics I used were "in-network providers." While for me that didn't cover much, every dollar helps, and I didn't know better. But after that, I figured there was only so much my body could handle, and I decided I'd rather pay myself and get results.

My first try I had an ectopic pregnancy that ruptured my tube. The silver lining here is that we then knew I had "tubal factor infertility" so I could finally get covered with insurance. The second attempt gave me the first of my three wonderful miracles.

here. She said in hindsight she might have approached counseling differently.

> "My own fears of being judged led me to see it as a hurdle rather than an opportunity," she said. "Now I think it would have been good to talk through some things to which I wasn't giving much thought . . . I was oblivious to some significant issues. Don't fear raising vague thoughts, fears, and questions with the clinic counselor. If they're worth their salt, they shouldn't be telling you anything, only helping you find your own answers . . . It's important not to ignore the things that are most difficult: at some later stage, you may well have to answer to your child about the same issues."[21]

· 9 ·

Choosing Adoption

Adoption is about finding families for children, not finding
children for families.

— Lee Varon, author of *Adopting on Your Own*

My parents never sat my brother and I down when we were kids
to talk about the facts of his adoption. It was simply part of who
he was, something we knew at the earliest age. Just as we knew the
three boys down the street were adopted, and two of our cousins
were adopted. It was not a big deal — no deal at all, really. He
never expressed much sentiment about being adopted when we
were growing up.

Eventually, though, as adults, my brother and I started to have
conversations that helped me to recognize that adoption was an
issue for him at times. His red hair and hunting interests were
not the only traits that made him feel like he stood out in our family. He's an outdoorsy, traditional family man who, although quite
intelligent, never enjoyed school. Our parents and I are city folk
who earned college degrees. We are vocal Democrats; he is an
Independent who likes to tease us about his propensity for voting
Republican.

From my perspective, over the years he tended to seem disengaged and disinterested in the family. In hindsight, from his perspective, he likely felt that the connection between my parents and
I excluded him. He occasionally expressed frustration at being
"the last to know" family business.

Some of this has likely been the consequence of the tendency for boys and girls to differ in family attachment. But as I researched this chapter — thinking I knew a lot about adoption and discovering I knew nothing — I recognized how much of my brothers' feelings might be attributable to the "genealogical bewilderment" phenomena social scientists had named.

In short, my brother periodically struggled with "how do I fit into this family?" questions that were never spoken out loud, and not debilitating, but there nonetheless. Likely there were things we could have done as a family to soothe any identity struggles he was having. But none of us, my brother included, recognized that there was anything to talk about. It took decades — and his fatherhood and other events — to realize there was an adoption nerve that sometimes hurt.

The complexities of adoption have been discussed in great detail by excellent resources listed in the back of this book and on my website, choicemoms.org. Four I will name here, for their excellent insight that helped educate me as I wrote this chapter:

1. Lee Varon's book *Adopting on Your Own: The Complete Guide to Adopting as a Single Parent*[1]
2. Lois Gilman, author of *The Adoption Resource Book*[2]
3. Child Welfare Information Gateway website (www.childwelfare.gov)
4. Archives of *Adoptive Families* magazine

In the limited number of pages we have here, I will offer an overview of the adoption process, the general costs, and touch on the potential identity issues of adoptive children, including those of transracial adoptions.

The Adoption Debate

After Tara decided to pursue Choice Motherhood, she debated whether to adopt or conceive. As she told me, she wondered whether she should have a child of her own when the world was overpopulated and there were so many children living in orphanages. Yet she also worried what effect it would have on the child to be removed from country, culture, and family environment.

Bridget, however, went straight to adoption. She wasn't quite 35 when she made her decision, and others counseled her to wait for the right man and conceive, but fertility statistics about women over the age of 35 scared her.

> *She didn't want to spend her savings on insemination, not conceive, and then have no money left for adoption.*

Many women are clear that bearing a child with the sperm of someone they do not know is of no interest to them, nor do they want the complications of a known donor. Adoption is the clear preference for many. But for others, the choice is not as clear. Some are intimidated by the long waiting lists, scrutiny of home studies, and single-parent quotas. Some don't like the lack of knowledge about a birth mother's habits during pregnancy. Others are concerned that an international adoption might involve exploitation of poor families who feel compelled to give up a child. Still others fear that in an open adoption a birth mother might change her mind.

In my case, I briefly considered adoption for my second child, but ultimately decided that the unknown factor of genetics bothered me. For one, I'm a strong believer in the influence of nature, partly because of adoptive children I know who veered considerably from the nurturing they were given. I was uncomfortable not knowing the full history of my children. And I sentimentally wanted my kids to see shared characteristics in each other — so I used the same known donor for both.

Yet another woman I know loved the fact that there were unknown genetics at work with her daughter. She was curious to see how the nature/nurture blend would work out, and joked that she was happy to see some inherited traits stop with her.

A note about grieving

Many women turn to adoption after trying to conceive. A good article on the American Fertility Association website[3] (www.theafa .org) suggests that trying to adopt while continuing infertility treatment can be emotionally draining, and recommends that most women need a point of closure on one before fully engaging with the other.

I have, however, interviewed a few women who happily engaged in both. One married woman, in fact, conceived with a third IUI attempt the day before they boarded a plane to meet their adopted daughter for the first time. Their son was born a few months after she came home with her permanently.

But in the drive to build a family, don't discount your emotions. The adoption book author Dr. Lee Varon is the Choice Mother of two. She was excited about the idea of adoption when she was 14, and as a professional woman years later eagerly adopted a Latino son. It wasn't until she adopted her fair-haired daughter and started hearing comments such as "she looks just like you" that she felt an unexpected pang. "I realized that I would never experience the feeling of being biologically related to my children. My sadness took me by surprise."

As cofounder of the Adoption Network, she counsels women to explore any deep-seated feelings about not conceiving. As she wrote:

> *"Resolving feelings about not having a child by birth is a process, just as coming to terms with parenting without a partner is a process."*

On the other hand

Although many single women who choose to conceive report being criticized for creating new life rather than adopting an existing child who needs a parent, there are — as with any choice in life — those who oppose adoption. Sometimes family and friends fear that an adoptive child might have life-long issues of abandonment, or suffer from the poor health of the birth mother.

At least one website is devoted to minimizing the incidence of adoption. Believing that the multimillion dollar industry of adoption is leading to black-market trafficking of children, and leads to identity issues that result in a higher rate of imprisonment, this group works to keep kids with their birth families and to encourage others to use infertility options.

As with known donors and anonymous donors, there will be fears. The important factor for a Choice Mom is to consciously decide that adoption is the right step for her to take — whether it was the first move or not — and consciously prepare to open herself up with love for whatever child she is chosen to parent.

Phase 1: Deep Thinking

About the age of the child

The typical couple or individual is looking to adopt a newborn, so competition is strongest for that age group. Of the nearly 23,000 international adoptions in 2004, less than half involved children under the age of 1, according to immigration statistics. Of the 118,000 children in U.S. foster care who were waiting to be adopted in 2004, 24 percent were newborns, and the median age was 5. Private, independent U.S. adoptions more commonly involve newborns, but it is sometimes more challenging, although not impossible, for a single parent to get a placement.

About race

If you are white, will you feel comfortable raising a nonwhite child? Are you willing to handle persistent questions, from your child and others, if you become the mother to a son or daughter who clearly does not look like you? Would you consider moving to a more diverse neighborhood? Is a Russian child a stronger match for you than a Chinese child?

Jolene, whose daughter is from Guatemala, told me, "I'm clearly of the mindset that there's no shame in being honest about one's abilities. I personally had no problems adopting a child of another race and ethnic background, with one big exception: I felt in no way equipped to handle the societal issues of a child with African or African-American heritage.

> *"The child could be green and I'd have no problems, nor would most of my family. However, I recognize that in this country there are huge issues around discrimination that as a very WASPy-looking woman I don't have the understanding or energy to tackle."*

She also recognized that her first assumption — that she would adopt a girl from China — was not the right fit for her. "As shallow as this might sound, I don't like Asian art and culture enough to be excited about it, and I felt this alone would be a huge liability for my child."

About special needs of the child

Are you open to exploring the idea of adopting from the foster care system? Would you be willing to adopt siblings? Is a child with special developmental, behavioral, or physical needs someone you would be comfortable with? (Read the essay about the adoptive mother of two special needs children in Chapter 1 if you haven't already.)

There are so many children waiting for adoption from U.S. public agencies and the foster care system that single parents tend to be welcome. In fact, singles are sometimes considered an advantage for a child who needs the attentive nurturing, strength of character, and less crowded environment of a Choice Mother home.

Numbers: According to a Children's Bureau report, the average age of the more than 500,000 children in foster care is 10. In 2004, 118,000 (20 percent) were hoping to be adopted, and had been in the system for three years. Roughly 38 percent were black and 38 percent were white; 53 percent were boys. Of the 52,000 children

Definition of Terms

Closed or confidential adoption — The agency makes a match between birth mother, who presumes the agency will find a good home, and adoptive parent; there is little or no contact. This is becoming rare among private agencies.

Semi-open adoption — Similar to open adoption (described below), although less identifying information is exchanged between birth parent and adoptive parent, and less contact is made between birth parents and child.

Open or cooperative adoption — The birth mother chooses the adoptive parent, with mediation from an agency. Generally there is a pool of prospective applicants to choose from. An agreement can be made for any degree of ongoing contact between child and birth parent — regular contact, sporadic holidays and birthdays, none. According to one study, however, the type and frequency of contact, and individuals involved, typically varies considerably over time.[5]

The open method of adoption is increasingly popular with birth parents. Some estimates are that half of today's roughly 15,000 domestic agency adoptions are open. One study reported that between 1989 and 1999, agencies that offered fully disclosed adoptions had grown from 36 percent to 80 percent.[6]

Note that birth parents in the United States are entitled to change their mind about placing the child for adoption. Some speculate that 1 in 10 do, generally before the birth. An experienced adoption attorney is essential.

The noted adoption therapist Dr. Joyce Maguire Pavao has written, "The success of open adoption depends on clear boundaries, the participants' respect of each other's roles and responsibilities, and the ability of the adults involved to put their egos aside in order to do what is best for the child."

who were adopted from the system in 2004, more than 14,000 (27 percent) were placed with single women.[4]

About contact with the birth family

Like any method to motherhood, the adoptive parent is single only in lifestyle. No child is the sole "property" of any one parent. Even with married couples, the child has a triangular relationship with the birth family, even if they never meet. Today there is a wide range of relationships adoptive families can share with birth parents. Some are interviewed and selected by birth mothers in person, some work through attorneys and agencies with no face-to-face contact, some arrange for sporadic contact with the child over the years, others have no contact whatsoever.

The relationship you feel most comfortable with has a big impact on the type of adoption you should pursue. Will you want to share information and photos about the birth family with your child? Will you want to meet the birth mother so you can talk about her later? Are you afraid that a birth mother might change her mind about placement and derail your plans? Are you comfortable "competing" for a child with other candidates?

About adoption itself

As you explore these fundamental questions, talk to other adoptive parents, parents of multicultural families, and adoption counselors. Read chapter 12 to understand identity questions your child might have someday, and some of the books listed in the Resources section to help you examine these important issues.

An Open Adoption Story

You'd think that of all the single women who would feel skittish about open adoption, it would be Shelly. She had one adoptive son in her life for three months before the birth mother managed to turn her life around and asked that the child be returned to her. Subsequently, five pregnant women picked Shelly to be the mother of their unborn children, sharing months of bonding and ultra-sounds and name-selection processes with her before changing their mind after delivery.

Yet Shelly — an energetic, passionate Choice Mom in every sense — is adamant that, despite the intense pain of loss she experienced in all six cases, the best interest of the child is to be with the birth mother if possible. And it is that spirit of openness and love that led her and her adopted African-American son, Max, to find each other, in Fall 2003.

In fact, mystic though it might be, Shelly feels that the spirit of her unborn child passed into the adoptive son she was destined to have. After the six disrupted adoptions, Shelly had used insemination to conceive a second child (her first son was born years earlier from a known donor). While attending the funeral for her beloved adoption attorney a few weeks later, Shelly experienced painful and unusual symptoms of a miscarriage. The funeral and the heavy bleeding occurred the same day Max was born. A few days after that, she and Max found each other.

Shelly has no doubt that they were meant to be mother and son, as was validated in an entitlement ceremony when Max's foster mother placed him in Shelly's arms as she pledged her life to his.

That feeling of entitlement was a priority for Shelly when she chose her path to motherhood. As an avid traveler who has visited 35 countries and climbed mountains on five continents (including Kilimanjaro), she knew there were many children awaiting strong, stable families in the world. Yet she also knew that she didn't trust some aspects of international adoption. Desperation and poverty sometimes leads birth parents in a direction they might not actually want to go. For Shelly, she needed the sense of entitlement that comes when a birth family says, "I want YOU to raise this child."

How to succeed at domestic adoption

Adoption is a very personal choice. If you are considering open domestic adoption, Shelly has these tips to share from her experience about adopting as a single woman.

Being flexible

Most people reject open adoption as potentially too painful if something "goes wrong." Shelly's philosophy that the right thing for a child is to be with the birth mother if possible helped her to endure that pain. And her passion about the importance of open adoption is what led so many families to consider her for their child in the first place.

In her son's case, his birth parents were both 13 when he was born. The birth mother, an "A" student, hated placing him for adoption, but family shame left her no choice. The birth father, largely raised by a grandmother in a loving but already overburdened extended family, strongly wanted to maintain contact. The trust his family had in Shelly's ability to stay connected, as was the case with the six previous mothers, is a primary reason her single status didn't matter to them. (The birth father coming from a strong matriarchal family didn't hurt either.)

The personal touch

As part of the adoption process, Shelly compiled an extensive, handsome booklet with her letter of introduction and color photographs of family and friends. She wrote about her active community life, parenting classes and books in her arsenal, her diverse network, the local child-friendly activities, her goals as a parent, and her broad appreciation of other human experiences and cultures. The scrapbook she created was filled with color, energy, family, and friends. It was no wonder that she was such an appealing candidate to so many. Her passion, creativity, nurturing, and extended community networks were obvious.

Multiracial blending

Shelly knew that the concept of open domestic adoption in the United States made it likely that she would become the parent of a multiracial family. For many, this is a breaking point. Some people simply feel unable to help a child with the issues of ethnicity and racism that will be an inevitable part of their life together.

Shelly was able to embrace this reality, even as she moved forward without knowing quite how to resolve the issues that would come up. For starters, she became a member of the Minnesota-based Harambee Village before she even knew that she would be the parent of an African-American son. ("Harambee" is a Swahili term for coming together as a group for the betterment of all.) Even her elementary school–aged Caucasian son has participated in African drumming, and workshops about gang violence and father envy.

The strengths of being open

Especially powerful is Shelly's view that birth families are part of a child's right, and that there is nothing to feel threatened about in blending the two. When asked how to respond to people who would naturally be fearful that an involved birth family might someday assert themselves too strongly into the adoptive family's life together, Shelly responds with a quote by a good friend: "All there is in the world is love and fear; make sure you're on the right side of it."

She strongly believes that the more family, the more friends, the more community attachments a child has, the better. She talks five or six times a year with the birth father and his family. They've even flown across the country to meet.

As an example, she brings out the scrapbook of family photos that Max's birth father's family compiled for him. It includes photos and names of all the cousins, aunts, uncles, grandparents. Photos of his young father in football uniform ("That my daddy?" he used to respond as a toddler when he saw it). It includes the wonderfully touching letter of the birth father, who describes himself in the details of a young boy: His sports abilities. The fact that he likes to smile. His height. And, toward the end, these lines: "We thank God for your mother Shelly, just knowing that you are with a loving family. And that they are willing to let us be in your life. So I'm just writing to tell you that I do love you. Love, your birth father."

As Shelly says, "How can it be bad for Max to know that his birth father loves him and wants to remain in contact with him?"

Genealogical Bewilderment

As the British researcher H. J. Sant explained in 1964, adopted children can sometimes feel a sense of loss and crisis of identity, generally starting in their teenage years and reappearing at critical junctures during adulthood. This phenomenon, labeled by a predecessor in 1952, is referred to as "genealogical bewilderment."[7]

The adoption therapist Dr. Joyce Maguire Pavao has said, "Every young person is trying to figure out who they are not, and who they are. For most children, the people around them are mirrors on which they measure themselves, until the adolescent years. At that point they look in the mirror and see themselves. They become more aware of how different they are. I think it is a complicated process for adoptees during the teen years . . . They begin to realize that they do not know another person in the world genetically related to them."[8]

Some adoptive children feel a sense of incompletion and disconnection, resulting in sadness, confusion, and anger. They might feel a lack of control, that they were never consulted about important matters in their life.

A paper presented at an adoption conference in 2001 reported that one adoptee summed up the feeling like this: "Where did I get my red hair? What nationality am I? What kind of body am I growing into? What talents or special skills are in my family line? What hidden illness might show up in my life? All these questions follow me as I move into adulthood and no one has an answer. I feel like I am walking around with gaps and holes in my life that I cannot fill."[9]

Lois Melina wrote in *Raising Adopted Children* that 90 percent of adopted children are well adjusted, according to studies. But every child will need to make sense of what it means to be adopted and will need to understand the influences on his or her identity twice — in relation to an adoptive family as well as to a biological family.[10]

About curiosity

I know many people who were placed for adoption, including a former roommate who debated for years about whether to contact her possible birth mother, and a cousin who met hers. Some have been frustrated at not knowing enough about their birth stories. Others aren't interested, or have dismissed it as an impossible mystery to solve. Many are ambivalent about finding their biological heritage.

When my brother was the 30-year-old father of two young kids, he talked to me for the first time about trying to locate his birth history. Eventually he registered on an adoption site, but never fully followed through on a search. Shortly before his fortieth birthday, he received a phone call from a 38-year-old woman who believed she might be his half-sister. She told him that her father, since deceased, had as a teenager impregnated his 15-year-old girlfriend. A boy was born in a particular city on a particular day and placed for adoption through the Catholic agency that my parents used to adopt a boy born on that same day in that same city.

Although my brother is interested in his medical history for the sake of his kids, even now, years after receiving that phone call, he remains skeptical and ambivalent enough that he has done no DNA testing to see if the woman is related to him biologically. Some adoptees want to know more, others do not. Curiosity is healthy, but is not always acted upon.

According to the American Academy of Pediatrics, a child's interest in biological roots is a sign of healthy emotional growth in the search for identity. One report published in 2002 indicated that feelings of loss might be "more rooted in societal expectations of genetically based attachments rather than in any inherent biological loss." Another study, reported in 2004, found "no evidence that desire to search is the result of poor adoptive family relationships or adolescent maladjustment."[11]

The child's point of view

In the book *Being Adopted: The Lifelong Search for Self,* the authors quote children who experience the emotions of adoption in many different ways.[12]

Some express anger at their birth parents, feeling that "they didn't care enough to keep me." Others believe their birth parents lost them and might be looking for them. Still others worry that they ate or cried too much, which is why they were placed into an adoptive home.

A 9-year-old girl said, "It isn't fair that they could buy me just because they have more money. Kids should be with their real parents. I'm not a toy or something you just decide to buy."

And still others express no such emotions.

In chapter 12, we look at specific and practical ways you can help meet an adoptive child's emotional needs in regards to feelings of belonging and identity. At the end of this chapter we have a special section about transracial adoption issues.

Phase 2: Explore the Expense

There are wide variations in the cost of adoption, depending on the agency and type of adoption you pursue. Consider whether you are receptive to a less expensive adoption from a public agency. If you are open to a "special needs" child — which is defined as someone from a minority group or an older child; someone with physical, developmental, or behavioral issues; or paired siblings — you will likely qualify for reimbursements, subsidies, counseling, medical coverage, child-care aid, and more.

Costs below generally include the cost of a home study (about $1,000 to $3,000), document preparation ($500 to $2,000), and attorney fees ($2,500 to $12,000). Variables are listed. The detailed, up-to-date estimates about costs are available from the Child Welfare Information Gateway (www.childwelfare.gov/adoption/search/) and Adoptive Families (www.adoptivefamilies.com), which indicate these *average* typical expenses:

U.S. foster care

Domestic public agency fees are minimal (generally under $2,500), or waived. In recent years there has been a greater effort to help the more than 100,000 children who are looking for an adoptive family each year, with roughly half finding placement. Many of these are considered "special needs" children. Hundreds of dollars in subsidy payments are often provided each month, as well as Medicaid coverage. A written agreement will specify financial and medical aid, social services, and reimbursements. Asking for a deferred adoption assistance agreement gives the option of seeking funding assistance if the child develops needs that were not noticeable at the time of adoption.

Private domestic

The National Council for Adoption estimates that more than 20,000 U.S.-born infants are placed for adoption each year. The typical domestic adoption requires postplacement supervision, parent physical, attorney fees, and extensive expenses for the birth parent. Some agencies require psychiatric evaluation of the adoptive parent. Requirements vary according to state law.

Domestic private agencies run from $5,000 to $40,000-plus (with an average of $12,000). This typically pays for birth-parent counseling, birth expenses, and other agency costs for overhead and temporary postplacement supervision. Some agencies use sliding fee scales based on the adoptive parents' income. If a birth parent is located by the adoptive parent, an agency will often provide these services at a lower cost. Fees can generally be predicted in advance, but vary considerably from agency to agency.

Domestic independent agencies range from $8,000 to $40,000-plus (with an average of $15,000). Some states allow advertising to locate birth parents; others don't allow independent adoptions at all. Check state laws early in the process. The often unpredictable costs are for legal representation of birth and adoptive parents, as well as birth expenses (roughly $7,500, which tend not to be reimbursed for birth parents who change their mind). An experienced lawyer is needed who can help screen and minimize the risks.

International

Intercountry private agencies and independent agencies are a more costly option: $10,000 to $30,000-plus. The typical international adoption varies considerably according to local law and whether the placement is from a government agency, orphanage, charitable organization, or independent attorney. It costs less to adopt from some countries than others. Expenses include fees for immigration processing. Foreign attorneys, medical professionals, and court fees are usually required. Other variable expenses can include fees for psychological evaluations, translation services, and escorts to accompany the child, as well as a "donation" to the orphanage or foreign agency.

Usually expenses involve travel (and meals, lodging, long-distance phone calls) to process the adoption abroad. Requirements for length of stay and number of trips vary by country. A child's medical care and foster care can be an additional expense. U.S. doctors with familiarity in international adoption can be found at the website for the American Academy of Pediatrics, at aap.org/sections/adoption.

Phase 3: Find Assistance

My *Choice Moms Guide to Adoption* (Be-Mondo Publishing, 2008), as well as the choicemoms.org website, lists a variety of resources.

Financial aid

Before despairing about the expense, check the options available in your state and at your company. There are many incentives designed to help people afford adoption. Current tax law allows a healthy federal adoption tax credit, which can give you a nice "cash back" option at tax time. For 2005 returns, eligible adoptive parents qualified for up to $10,630. The Internal Revenue Service

---

The Numbers

✦ Since 1992, there have been roughly 125,000 adoptions to U.S. families each year. In 2001, about 40 percent of these were adopted from public agencies (up from 18 percent in 1992). More than 15 percent were international adoptions (up from 5 percent in 1992). The remainder were private or tribal adoptions, or children adopted by relatives. The state with the highest number of adoptive parents each year tends to be New York.[13]

Intercountry adoptions have increased significantly over the years. According to the U.S. Department of State, there were 6,536 adopted children brought to the United States in 1992. By 2004, there were 22,884. China, for the fifth year in a row, was the leading country of origin, with 7,044; Russia continued to be second, with 5,865; and Guatemala continued to be third, with 3,264.

---

website (www.irs.ustreas.gov/) has up-to-date details. Some states allow tax credits for children adopted from the public child welfare system. And as we've mentioned, many expenses for special needs children can be reimbursed.

Many large companies offer extra benefits for adoptive families. Human resource departments have details about leave policies, referral services, and reimbursements. The National Adoption Center estimates the average expense reimbursement is $3,750, and can be as much as $10,000 at some places.

Loans, home equity programs, and grants are available from many places, including the National Adoption Foundation.

Seek out adoptive parent groups
Networking with other adoptive parents, online and in local communities, is invaluable. From beginning to end, these experienced

peer advisers will offer information about local agencies, social workers, attorneys, pediatricians, therapists, financial aid, post-placement issues, and much more.

"When I was looking for an agency and attorney for international adoption, the best advice I got was to get on e-mail discussion lists," Jolene told me. "There's at least one for every major country and these are, hands down, the best way to locate an agency that is experienced, reputable, and embraces singles."

Phase 4: Start to Focus

Narrow the type of adoption you prefer

After you have explored the level of openness you prefer, your capacity for building a multiracial family or raising a special needs child, and the expense you are prepared to absorb, you will be ready to pursue the type of adoption that seems right for you.

A domestic agency can be welcoming to single applicants, especially depending on the type of placement preferred. Some are less accepting, but might not say that. It is easier than it used to be for singles (and lesbians) to adopt, partly because studies are finding that children raised by singles are as well adjusted as those in two-parent homes, and because special needs children are experiencing fewer problems in single-parent homes.[14] You will need to do your homework and ask an agency how many placements it has made with single parents.

If public agency adoption is an option for you, books with biographies of waiting children will jump-start the process. Check your library, or look online at the National Resource Center for Special Needs Adoption (www.nrcadoption.org) and AdoptUS Kids (www.adoptuskids.org).

An independent adoption tends to be less restrictive and bogged down with bureaucracy. I know several parents who received a child placement by letting everyone they knew — including gynecologists, social workers, and church personnel — become aware of their interest in adopting. If the birth parent and adoptive parent find each other through word of mouth or advertising, an agency might be involved little or not at all. It is imperative to find an experienced attorney to minimize your risks. It is rare, but possible, for birth parents to change their mind, within a limited time frame after the birth (many change their mind before the birth). Contact with the birth parents can be extensive; sometimes the adoptive parent is even present for delivery. Check online (www.adoptivefamilies.com/adoptionlaws) for up-to-date state rules.

In general, an intercountry adoption will require international travel and extensive paperwork, and will likely involve minimal contact with the birth family.

A few countries do not permit adoption by single parents. It was especially unfortunate in 2007 that China — which traditionally had been a good resource for Choice Moms — stopped allowing singles to adopt. Government policy changes frequently. As of this writing, China and Guatemala require statements that the adoptive parent is heterosexual. One good place to start research about current policies is www.internationaladoptions.org.

Important note: As of 2008, the United States has met the requirements of the Hague Convention on Intercountry Adoption treaty, which requires approval of adoption agencies that engage in international adoptions. New regulations also require pre-approval from the U.S. Department of Homeland Security before parents can finalize an international adoption. Both of these new steps will likely affect the time involved in completing an intercountry adoption.

Research agencies

The agency you end up selecting will have a huge impact on how much you spend, how smoothly you will get through the home-study phase as a single parent, and what kind of information you will have about your child. You should check out the agency as carefully as they will research you. This is where the experience and referrals of adoptive parent groups play a vital role. As you narrow your list, attend informational meetings by the agency to get a feel for their personnel and services.

Get an itemized estimate of costs, including hidden charges and wait time. An excellent source of questions to ask any prospective agency is available on theadoptionguide.com, as well as at adoption.com and adoption.org. Sample questions to ask include:

- What kind of family history will they try to secure? (Some adoptions don't include much.)
- Will they help to get medical and developmental information about the child? (This should be done whether the agency handles it or not.)
- How many children have they placed with single parents?
- Where do the children waiting for adoption come from, and how do they assess the placement services of other countries?
- Which services are included in the overall fee, and which are not?
- How long will you have to decide whether to accept a child?
- What happens if you change your mind after acceptance?
- What counseling services are available for you and the child?

Understand an agency's criteria

Most agencies, domestic and international, have a set of criteria they are looking for in applicants. Many have a small quota of single parents they will place children with each year. Although it is legal in all U.S. states for single people to adopt, and generally for gays and lesbians to adopt (see chapter 14 for exceptions), that does not mean that an agency will consider the loving and stable home of a Choice Mom to be suitable, even if they cannot say so. Some will go through many intensive steps with you — including home study — only to drop the ball when it comes time to find a referral. Ask how many children the agency has placed in single-parent homes.

In general, most domestic agencies are looking for candidates

TIP: Don't Pay Up Front

✦ The bulk of payment is usually required after an actual assignment to a child has been made and accepted. Be suspicious of anyone who might be preying on the vulnerabilities of a single woman eager to be a mother.

who are at least 25 years old and show stability, maturity, and flexibility. With single parents they'll want to see a solid plan for childcare, a support network, and role models. A large income and home ownership are not required.

Find an attorney
It is advisable to consult with your own attorney. A good source is the American Academy of Adoption Attorneys (adoptionattorneys .org).

Phase 5: Prepare Yourself

The home study
Beyond the underlying requirements of an agency, there are certain things every adoption process will examine closely in a home study, which takes from three to six months to complete. Independent private adoptions are usually less extensive, and every state varies in its requirements. Some private adoptions require only a postplacement home study. The process involves extensive written comments and face-to-face interviews with one person or a group.

Many people worry that this part of the process is a close scrutiny of flaws, but it is also an opportunity for any reputable agency or social worker to help prepare prospective parents for the adoption experience. The home study will look into your full family, religious, educational, and professional background. It will examine your neighborhood, home, and community ties, as well as your health, support network, and financial situation.

Note that if you are a lesbian, Varon has good advice in her book about whether to disclose sexual orientation to the agency.[15] As she wrote, "Although it is legal to omit information (don't ask/ don't tell), it is illegal to lie if you are asked a direct question. To do so can be grounds for denying the adoption."

Be open to advice from your social worker, who might help you uncover emotions you have not yet allowed yourself to explore, such as whether you are "grieving the childhood dream" of a two-parent family, or are unhappy about being unable to conceive, or are concerned about adopting a child from a culture that is not your own. In many cases, it might simply take time to work through these issues and does not mean the door is permanently closed.

In the end, the home study agents want to see that you are resolving issues, confronting fears, committed to adoption, and realistic about parenthood.

Paperwork

The paperwork is intense, particularly for intercountry adoptions, since there are two countries to satisfy. You will likely need: the record of your home study, your birth certificate, medical clearance, divorce decree if applicable, letters of reference, employer financial information, tax returns, bank statements, photos of your home, criminal record clearance, and copies of passports.

The waiting game

Many Choice Mothers recommend waiting before you tell many people your plans, or you will have months of tedious "Have you heard yet?" questions. The process of getting from home study to placement generally takes from six months to two years, whether adopting domestically or independently. It can take that long to

---

TIP: Get Duplicate Records

✦ Ask for multiple copies of certified birth records and adoption decrees, especially with an international adoption. It can be difficult to get them later, and they will be important throughout your child's life.

---

find a birth mother in independent adoptions as well. In some cases, the referral might come faster, but the paperwork doesn't.

After referral

With an international referral, Varon recommends that you try to get a videotape with sound that shows how the child interacts with other people in her environment. In her book, she details psychosocial history questions you should get answered, including: How many moves has the child experienced, why did the moves happen, and how did the child react? Does the child have siblings, and if so, where are they?

Get a full history, including any issues related to abuse, neglect, or drug and alcohol use. Find a pediatrician familiar with adoption to check the child's developmental and medical issues (check the website www.fwcc.org/doclist.htm for referrals).

As Varon says: "Adoption is a miracle just as birth is. I believe there is a reason we are led to adopt a particular child. Once you have made the decision to adopt, hold fast to the belief that somewhere in the world there is a child waiting for you and that eventually you will meet. I have heard countless stories of people who lost assignments and were devastated. Eventually they did adopt, and all of them have come to feel there was a reason for their previous disappointments, and that they ended up adopting the child they were meant to parent."

Choice Chat: The Day I Met My Child

✦ When I was 37, the relationship I was in ended and I cried all day about how I would never have a baby. But I read a story about women who were having children on their own, and realized, "Why not me too?"

I tried donor insemination first, but after a series of infertility issues I realized that adoption was my obvious next step. I became obsessed with having a baby. One day, a friend called me about a malnourished child at the hospital (no longer an infant) whose birth mother was unable to take care of her. After a frenzied process of paperwork, I was cleared to pursue adoption.

The first time I met this child, she was screaming at the top of her lungs, trying to break ropes the hospital personnel had used to restrain her. I could see in her eyes that she was trying to figure out a way to get out. I picked her up and she stroked my cheek. I was hooked.

It was a struggle for many years. She had trouble sleeping, tended to be hyperactive, and even crawled, fully clothed, into the bathtub with me because of her need for connection. For me it was a long path of coping, without collapsing, so that I could allow this child to get on with her life. Sometimes I wondered how suburban me got to this point: What am I doing here? But with age, therapy, love, and nurturing, she outgrew it all.

I never doubted my decision to become her mother. At times I wondered how we would get through everything together. But I have had enormous respect for her, from that moment I saw her trying to break through the ropes. She wanted life, and I became totally absorbed in enabling her to experience it in her unique way.

✦ BONUS SECTION ✦

Transracial Adoption

The transracial family has two separate issues to address: loss of birth culture and absence of genetic identity. As with everything in this book, challenges are not meant to be ignored or denied, but to be acknowledged and tackled with honesty.

Adoption experts agree that ignoring the differences between a parent's race and a child's race is not helpful. A multicultural family needs to have a multicultural approach to life. There will be issues and there will be conflicts. The Choice Mom who builds a transracial family needs to be prepared to embrace this inevitability in order to deal with it in a healthy way.

There is bias and prejudice in every community, and the adoptive parent of a non-Caucasian child will need to help her child confront it. It is a very hurtful and often demeaning place to be, and it can be difficult to find the words to explain it or resolve it with a child. The balancing act of helping a child prepare, while not overburdening them with self-consciousness about skin color, is difficult.

Cheri Register, author of *Beyond Good Intentions: A Mother Reflects on Raising Internationally Adopted Children,* said in an online conversation with members of the "As Simple As That" community,[16] "What I have come to feel most sorely is what one daughter calls her 'perpetual foreigner' status. It comes clear in the stupid questions people ask, like 'Where are you from?' or 'How did you learn to speak English so well?' The notion that they don't really belong here turns Asian Americans invisible — in public life and in popular culture. It still hurts to think how excited my daughter was about buying her first *Teen* magazine, and how she thumbed through it looking in vain for the Asian faces. I encouraged her to write to the editor, which she did. I truly believed she'd get a response, which she didn't."

Choice Chat with Leslie:
How We Are Creating Our Multicultural Family

✦ I adopted my two girls from China. I have had people say that I 'rescued' my daughters. This doesn't take into account what they left behind: family, language, culture. There are many ways that we have incorporated Chinese heritage into our lives, even in our modest midwestern community, such as:

1. We have artwork and other mementos from China on display in our home. I have been careful to intermix these with other pieces from my travels, as well as multigenerational family photos, and similar mementos. I don't want my house to look like a Chinese museum, but I do want it to be a natural part of who we are as a family.
2. Both girls attend Chinese language and dance classes.
3. We celebrate Chinese New Year by decorating our home as traditionally as possible and going out for a special dinner. We participate in the Chinese New Year event sponsored by Families with Children from China.
4. I have at least a dozen books about China, its folklore, and adoption from China that are readily available for the girls to look at and ask me about.
5. Each year on the anniversary of their adoption, we go out for a Chinese dinner at which the girls receive one of 18 small gifts I purchased for each of them when I was in China adopting them.

I plan to return to China with the girls in a few years. I want them to have a foundational knowledge of where they came from before they hit adolescence.

"Most people believe they are aware of racial issues, but a large majority don't have as clear an understanding as they are going to need," Amanda Baden, a New York City psychologist, told me. For some people, their "differentness" from others — sexual orientation, for example — can be hidden. But a child growing up in a community and extended family in which no one else looks like them can find it extremely difficult.

Baden was adopted from Hong Kong and has extensive experience with members of transracial families as a therapist and adoption researcher. She suggests that the goal is not for the parent to simply decide she will cope with issues as they arise. "I don't encourage prospective parents to get past this," she told me. "Some people turn to international adoption because they think it gives them more options to become a parent, but convenience, or altruistic goals, are not enough to sustain that relationship over time. If someone is questioning her ability to confront issues of race before an adoption takes place, that's a good thing to know. It might be a good idea to parent a child who is not so different from you. Often, my advice is to look somewhere else."

One of Cheri Register's points is this: If you would never consider living for a time in a certain country and can't imagine marrying a person of that ethnicity, then don't adopt a child from that country either.

STAGE 4

❧

Day-to-Day Parenting

We've discussed the various psychological issues related to the "should I or shouldn't I?" debate single women face. Now let's get down to the bald truth that everyone wants to understand better: How *do* Choice Moms cope with the stress and the questions that inevitably come when their potential child turns into actual baby, toddler, child, and teen? If you want to understand what you might need to deal with someday — or are a Choice Mom looking for advice — this is the section for you.

First fact is this: After a single woman becomes a mother, the issues she thought were important as she made her decision ultimately become faded memories of doubts and fears. For example, the typical Choice Mother cares much more about earaches and how to pick a preschool than on how to deal with disapproval in the community.

Second fact: There are far too many questions that a typical mom has on any given day for us to deal with in this book. We won't, for example, discuss real concerns such as: "What happens if I get seriously sick?" "Do you leave your baby inside the house alone while you're shoveling snow?" "How do you deal with the boredom of taking care of an infant all day?" "Should I take steps to help my child find donor siblings?"

What we will discuss in this section is the foundation of what Choice Moms can do right, for themselves and for their child, as they are:

- "Dealing with the Stress," including a special section on having two kids;
- "Answering the Daddy Question" at each age and stage;
- "Confronting Identity Issues" for adopted and donor-conceived children;
- Learning "How to Raise a Well-Balanced Child," including a specific plan of execution for raising happy and healthy children without the help of a father.

· 10 ·

Dealing with the Stress

I discovered that being a parent was the most difficult, frustrating job in the world. I wanted to be an accepting, nurturing parent — the great earth mother — but I was totally unprepared for the reality of coping with two active, imperfect children. I found that I had a terrible temper and amazingly little self-control. I wanted to be empathic, but I was critical. I wanted the boys to get along well, but they were always quarreling. I wanted them to treat me with respect, but they talked back to me. I wanted them to listen, but they tuned me out.

— Nancy Samalin, author of *Loving Your Child Is Not Enough: Positive Discipline That Works*[1]

You have to have multiple game plans for dealing with the stress of Choice Motherhood. Yes, there will be many beautiful moments when your child says the funniest thing, or you are watching your angel sleep peacefully, or you are giddy singing loudly together to a favorite song.

But that doesn't help when you are dropping your infant off at daycare while rushing to meet with a client, and she spits up on your red silk shirt. It doesn't help when your tired child is in a heap on the floor of a dirty airport bathroom, screaming as if you are trying to abduct him, when all you want to do is get to the gate with carry-on luggage before your flight takes off. It doesn't help when your seventh grader is embarrassed that she has no "father" side to the family tree for her social science project, and instead of telling you about it she's become unusually hostile and resentful about ever being born.

My daughter has always been a rather easy-going, self-sufficient child. But when she was 4, she entered a phase in which whining and crying over little things increased. Undoubtedly this had something to do with me suddenly having a boyfriend, adding her new brother to the house, and having a future stepsister who liked to pull her hair.

I could rationalize the reasons for it, but to be honest, that didn't help me when she was sitting on icy steps in below-zero temperature, wearing a thin skirt and insisting that her pregnant mom carry her to the car. Or when she and my beau locked horns for ten minutes about her saying "please" before he would pass the ketchup. Or when I was trying to rest after a long night with my infant son and she demanded that I pick out her clothes for the day — knowing that she would reject whatever I picked.

After any contentious behavior had worn me down I would yell, or want to yell: "Can't you see that I have my hands full? You should be old enough to help, instead of simply adding to the problem!"

The parenting expert Mary Sheedy Kurcinka has a beautiful way of expressing this inevitable rollercoaster aspect of parenthood in her recommended book *Raising Your Spirited Child*.[2] "The good [days] couldn't be better . . . Profound statements roll from his mouth, much too mature and intellectual for a child of his age. He remembers experiences you've long since forgotten and drags you to the window to watch the raindrops, falling like diamonds from the sky. On the good days, being the parent of a spirited child is astounding, dumbfounding, wonderful, funny, interesting, and interspersed with moments of brilliance," she wrote.

"The dreadful days are another story," Kurcinka went on. "On those days you're not sure you can face another twenty-four hours with him. It's hard to feel good as a parent when you can't even get his socks on, when every word you've said to him has been a reprimand, when the innocent act of serving tuna casserole instead of the expected tacos incites a riot, when you realize you've left more public places in a huff with your child in five years than most parents do in a lifetime. You feel weary, drained, and much too old for this . . . It's hard to love a kid who keeps you up at night and embarrasses you in shopping centers . . . You may wonder if you are the only parent with a kid like this, scared of what is to come in the teen years if you don't figure out what to do now, in the early years."

Most of the stages of parenting are predictable and universal. Another author I recommend, Karen Maezen Miller (*Momma Zen*),[3] has written of the natural feeling mothers have that the other mothers have it all figured out: how to keep their hair perfectly coifed and raise their children effortlessly. But the perfect mother is a myth.

Even when you know it's not your fault, and you've read the theoretical tips about how to correct imperfect behavior over time, it's still difficult to cope with the dark side of motherhood in the moment that it's happening.

There are a few things you can do, however, to help yourself deal with the inevitable stress, especially when you don't have a partner to unload on. We won't reinvent the wheel here. Good advice is available every day in magazines and bookstores and websites. But here is what most of the advice says in a nutshell.

How to Reduce the Impact of Stress

Take care of yourself
We know we're supposed to eat, sleep, exercise, and be merry.

And, by the way, don't forget to shower, get dressed, brush teeth and hair, cook, clean, work, pay bills, nurture and humor the little one, turn the TV off, help with homework, keep up with friends and family, chauffeur, shop, do laundry, take time to pamper, open the mail, read the paper, organize family entertainment, read to your child every day, mend, repair, garden, do home improvement, attend functions and school meetings, record your child's history in albums and journals, read about how to be a good parent, play, plan, save for college and retirement, get involved in the community, show your child the value of volunteering, keep up with e-mails, drink water.

I didn't even take care of myself well when I was without children.

The best any of us can do is to make a priority list for each day and week, and then see how much we can cross off before we make the next list. Just don't forget that if you eat well, exercise, and get enough sleep, it will be easier to deal with. Nearly any time that I've snapped excessively at Sophie, it's because at least one of us hasn't had enough good food or sleep that day. And it's usually me.

Embrace community
This is nonnegotiable. When I lived in New York, I had a wonderful babysitter who handled much of the cooking and cleaning, as well as taking excellent care of Sophie. I had an easier life as a Choice Mom with her, ironically, than when I was simply a single woman. Yet it wasn't enough. And it wasn't until I moved to Minnesota that I discovered why.

Without realizing it, my New York life had become too isolated. I was upset that my single friends didn't seem to have time anymore. The few that I did see regularly didn't seem to offer enough. I felt like a machine, eventually getting more uninspired, hating work, stressing about my small apartment, wishing I had more money for travel.

I considered this a byproduct of new motherhood, until I moved and discovered a better life. One in which I made the effort to talk to people at the playground instead of sitting on the bench reading. One in which I discovered the joy of being able to drop off my child with another mom simply so I could go to the dentist without using up valuable child-care time. Of course, I could have discovered this in New York. But until I moved, I didn't make an effort to widen the circle I had before I became a mom.

> *I assumed the friends I had would carry me through — but you need more when you become someone else's caretaker. You need to be part of a larger network.*

After I moved, I was closer to my brother's family and my parents — which was huge — but I also started to, slowly, become more connected to people I didn't already have a relationship with. Other Choice Moms, other stay-at-home moms, other work-from-home parents, fellow PTA board members, Unitarian Universalist church teaching colleagues and committee members.

It does take a village to raise a child well. It's not simply a matter of having your work hours covered, or being able to go out one night a week, or being able to run errands unencumbered. It's also being able to have someone take over for a few hours when you have the stomach flu. It's having someone teach your child how to make a beaded bracelet that you don't have the ability to make yourself. It's having someone stronger than you help your child swing from bar to bar at the playground. It's giving your child the experience of boating and fishing and camping if you're a city girl. It's having someone in addition to you teach concepts about religion, world culture, sportsmanship, family, patriotism. Your child needs many teachers.

To be a good Choice Mom, you need to cultivate your network. Find the secure base of family and friends your child will grow up with while getting acquainted with neighbors, community groups, and recreation instructors.

Find the people you can turn to for emergency childcare at the same time that you're finding people who will introduce your child to new things, like how to tell the difference between a sparrow and a robin.

If you're like me — and maybe half of you are — widening the circle is not something that comes naturally. As I got older, I found my network getting smaller. I knew who I liked and why, and didn't "waste" my time and energy adding anyone to the mix. But you can't be a good mother that way, whether you like it or not. And you won't be able to maintain your own mental health either. Talk to people, open up your world — one person at a time. Most of them won't become close, long-term friends. But being engaged with others is a very necessary step to keeping your own balance, as well as your child's.

How to Reduce Stress

Learn to be adaptable

My daughter was never a napper, which meant that when she was younger I had little time to myself without paying a babysitter. That could have been tough, but thankfully, by 3 months, she easily slept ten hours every night, so I learned to work with her schedule.

My son, on the other hand, is a light sleeper who woke up several times a night until his first birthday, and was usually persistent enough to cry himself awake rather than back to sleep. By the time he was 7 months I had already tested three strategies — until I threw in the towel and gave him a watered down bottle of formula to get him to relax enough to stop crying and fall easily back to sleep. It was against the rules, but it worked.

Being a mother does mean that you compromise much more than you'd like in order to get what you need done. You discipline and instruct and give timeouts when they misbehave, but if your children are exhausted, there is no amount of rational conversation that will get them from Point A to Point B. It is always you who needs to think on your feet, find a creative solution, revise plans if needed.

This also includes picking your battles. I can be embarrassed when Sophie wants to go out with five pigtails in her hair, or sparkle "makeup" on her lips and eyes, but ultimately her appearance isn't worth fighting about unless we're getting a portrait done. I let her choose her methods of self-expression and save my "absolutely not's" for matters of safety, health, and behavior.

The happiest Choice Moms I know are the ones who can "go with the flow," rather than feel the need to stick to an agenda their children aren't capable of meeting. Flexibility, ability to compromise, and a calm demeanor are definite strengths.

One woman who was contemplating this decision talked to single mothers.[4] She found that the ones who said the lifestyle was tough tended to be "women who might find very easy things to be difficult, or were women who refused to modify activities that would lessen their load."

Ultimately the woman ended up having two children. "This isn't brave or courageous," she said. "It is simply that I gave in to a great need and desire to nurture a family. It would take courage to try to live a life without this experience."

Understand your child

Children don't usually misbehave because they want to make our lives miserable. Yes, they test us, and the limits we set for them, to see what happens, but most of that is the result of going through predictable phases of development when they are learning to assert their own independence — a necessary ingredient to maturing into a nondependent adult. The child expert Michael Gurian calls these "little bursts of behavior" a natural part of the child's process of discovering how to be his or her own boss. This usually starts with about a year of willful behavior in the toddler stage — which Gurian says can be a foreshadowing of the teenage years — then again around age 5, in prepuberty, in puberty, and in adolescence.

It is normal for a toddler to become aggressive when frustrated, and emotionally manipulative, easily distracted, and wound up. Starting at about 18 months, your child is ready to be trained with discipline, which enables you to regulate natural urges in a way that builds character, tests self-esteem, and teaches social skills. Being able to remain calm in the face of adversity is another personality strength — although it will frequently fail even with the most serene parent. (Now that I am a parent, I have a much shorter fuse than I thought possible.) Advice from Choice Moms is to remind yourself that "this too shall pass."

Help them express themselves

The stubborn and irrational resistance of a child is one of the most common triggers of stress in a parent's life. To be able to break through the wall requires communication skills more than discipline — because often the behavior isn't prompted by willful disobedience as much as the inability to navigate frustration. Understanding that simple bit of psychology can help a parent a lot.

I was referred to Ross Greene's book *The Explosive Child*[5] by a specialist in child aggression. Because my new husband had an adolescent daughter whose special needs issues include difficulty controlling aggressive impulses, I read this book to understand her meltdowns. Greene's wisdom about dealing with verbally and physically aggressive children had some useful advice for any parent dealing with the inevitable tantrums of a child.

In Greene's view, a toddler starts to freak out over little things — putting on pull-ups, getting shoes on, exiting the playground — because he or she doesn't yet have the ability to understand why something is bothersome and then articulate it in a mature manner. As he wrote: "Instead of asking yourself, 'What's it going to take to motivate this kid to behave differently?' you need to ask yourself 'Why is this so hard for my child? What's getting in his way? How can I help?'"

One example Greene used was of a girl who carefully saved the last popsicle so she could eat it the next day, and then became incomprehensively unglued when her brother took it. If she'd had the capacity to say "I wanted to eat that tomorrow, so perhaps we can ask mom to buy more before then," the crisis could have been averted. (When an adult's reactions get triggered in a seemingly irrational way, we call it "pushing our buttons.")

Usually, as a child matures, they develop — with the help of their parent — the ability to express themselves and find a workable solution. Thankfully this capacity generally begins to kick in around the age of 5 for normally developing children whose parents don't end up needing the advice of experts like Greene. But it's not a seamless process, and takes effort on the part of the parents to see signs of wearing down that are particular to the child.

When that child is recognizably moving toward the edge — perhaps exhibiting restlessness, irritability, intense reaction to routine tasks — Greene recommends using empathy to help the child put the frustration into words and come up with logical solutions. You might offer choices or compromise, or use humor as a distraction. Once the meltdown occurs, it's too late, so the key is to recognize the warning signs. Communication skills are a personality strength.

Take your own timeout

Yes, this is a good technique to give you and your kids the space to cool down. But here I'm talking about something even broader. Actually take the time to come up with a creative strategy for coping with patterned behavior — yours and theirs — rather than simply repeating the same tired "kid acts out, mom gets mad" syndrome. Melissa is one Choice Mom I admire for her ability to find imaginative solutions.

"The six months between 4½ and 5 were the closest I came to committing homicide in my entire life," she admitted about living with her daughter. "The constant talking, the constant need for attention, the oppositional attitude and behavior." She came up with several effective coping mechanisms to address any new hot button. Such as:

• When they spend entire days together, for at least one hour they have to be in separate spaces with closed doors between them.
• They agreed on a code word that Mom uses to indicate it's time to stop talking. "For some reason, it works!"
• "There's nothing to get her out of a black mood, and us out of

a power struggle, faster than something silly. It is hard to do, since I'm usually madder than a wet hen myself, but it really makes a difference. When I get the 'I'm too tired to get into my pajamas' whine, I turn into the mommy monster who chases a shrieking, laughing child around the apartment. Within a minute she is dressed."

Other helpful strategies moms (and child experts) devise involve giving the child a sense of control at early points of combat: Do you want to wear the green pants or the purple pants? Do you want to eat carrots or tomatoes? Which shoe goes on first?

One of the most common struggles for Choice Moms is getting kids out the door in the morning and into bed at night. This is where rituals play a great role in keeping things on track. Some families put together schedules, using kids' drawings of a toothbrush, hair comb, and other bedtime needs. Others combat distractions by turning it into a "beat the clock" game, using timers to keep focused on each task. A good imagination — of both mother and child — will help.

How Do We Handle It Alone?

Trick question. As I'll repeat a few more times, no one can handle parenting alone. Many Thinkers feel that if they embark on motherhood without a partner, they'll be worn out from providing for, supervising, and carrying the emotional and physical load single-handedly. And they're right.

What can be easy to forget is that even married mothers need outside help. You need many people around you — not simply one amazingly helpful, attentive, sensitive partner — to raise your child. You're still the one who needs to have the stamina to get through 365 days a year of diapering, feeding, cleaning, consoling, transporting. It can be a pain in the neck, monotonous, and irritating to be on call so much. So how do we do it?

Don't feel sorry for yourself

It's easy to think that all of the troubles of our world have something to do with being single. It's also too simple to point out that married women usually have partner stress in addition to basic mom stress. Life is about dealing with stress, every day. The sooner you get over thinking your situation would be better "if only," the sooner you will do something about it.

Even if you had the most loving spouse imaginable, your adoring infant who simply needed to be fed, clothed, comforted, and loved will still turn into the preschooler who drives you crazy, bouncing from fiercely independent ("I can button this myself," — even though the buttons are in the back), to whiner ("I can't walk anyyyy morrrre . . . carrrrry meeee"), to "smarty pants devil" who tirelessly rebuts everything you say.

When I lived in New York, feeling sorry for myself that I didn't have anyone to lift the folded stroller onto the bus while I carried my daughter and a shopping bag, I would get angry that no one offered to help — instead of swallowing my pride, and my pity, and simply asking a stranger to give me a hand. When you stop focusing on the negativity, it's easier to find a solution.

Embrace the challenge

Most of us have experienced the scary thrill of going traveling or off to college, away from our parents for the first time. Before my kids were born, I found travel to far-flung places like Russia and Hungary and Madagascar exciting. I glowed during a three-week solo trip through Ireland, proud of being able to handle every detail myself. In my first years after divorce, I proved to myself that I could handle any mishap, hardship, and change that the adventures of travel threw at me.

In my late thirties and early forties, I became a Choice Mom twice. It has been like living the challenge of travel or college all over again. It's difficult . . . lonely . . . exciting . . . empowering . . . satisfying.

When we were younger, maybe we gained the freshman weight,

Choice Chat with Marlene: My Favorite "Stress" Story

✦ My daughter was not quite two and I had been working nonstop, 50 hours a week, for months without time off. It was Memorial Day weekend and I was desperate for that extra day off. Well, wouldn't you know, she got up at 5:00 A.M. Single mom, no one around to help, I put on cartoons, gave her a juice box and some toast, and went back to bed for an hour thinking that I would hear her if anything went wrong. I dozed for a while, no sounds from the other room, then finally figured I wasn't going back to sleep anyway, so got up.

In less than one hour, my daughter had:

• gotten up onto the kitchen counter and into the candy jar, there were about 20 candy wrappers on the floor;
• gotten into the magic markers and colored on my beige carpet;
• gotten into a box of Band-Aids and put them all over the long haired cat (I had to cut them out of his fur);
• gotten a pair of scissors and cut two fist-sized holes in her brand-new pajamas.

She was calmly watching cartoons when I got up. Did I cry? Did I punish her? No. I realized that this is my lot in life and I knew when I took on single parenthood that the responsibility was ALL MINE. I took a deep breath, cleaned it all up, and never again left her unsupervised for more than five minutes, no matter how sick or tired I was.

or missed our train connection, or got a D in that early-morning history class, or suffered from Montezuma's revenge. But we learned and adjusted and did what it took to get by — with as much fun along the way as we could. That's the same determined, self-fulfilling mindset the Choice Mom needs. Maybe we'd rather stay in beach resorts than cheap youth hostels now, but we still have the same capability to find our rhythm and survive everything.

The most obvious advice

Besides reminding yourself that your child is going through a rite of passage that will change over time — one that you didn't cause and that you can't prevent — commiserate with other moms, single and married. And if you are feeling overwhelmed, hopeless, or depressed, see a therapist. An unhappy parent can be as detrimental as smoking or drinking while pregnant.

The Difference a Partner Makes

When a partner essentially fell into my lap — after nearly five years of Choice parenting and another five months of pregnancy — the primary advantage was to give me more "me" time: date nights without kids, back rubs, snuggling. Sure, on paper I could have accomplished the same things by going out once a week with friends, paying a massage therapist, being satisfied with my daughter's embraces. But truthfully — even for someone like myself who didn't feel the need for a man in my life — it's not the same. Plus, his experience at parenting, including his four years as a single dad, has made him a solid role model for my kids to look up to.

Yet in the pre-Dave days, I functioned quite well with the logistics of running a Choice household. With Sophie, I got used to the mindless diapering and feeding duties. I had my priceless parents to help with the first months and vacations. My babysitter was a godsend. My unexpected return to the self-employed lifestyle was a blessing because of the flexibility. In short, I found solutions to get through the day-to-day without much fuss. Otherwise I wouldn't have decided to have two.

There were obviously times when it would have been easier to handle situations with a second pair of hands around — such as carrying my sleeping daughter out of the car when I was suffering from intense lower back pain during my second pregnancy. But when I met Dave, I was not longing for a partner to "save me" from the demands of Choice Mothering. Even now, as the primary caregiver for Sophie and Dylan — with a partner who works, volunteers, and has two children and a house of his own — I handle the job largely alone, with my community of helpers.

Three years in, Dave is one of my stressbusters — thanks to scheduled date nights — more so than a parenting partner, just as my parents, friends, sister-in-law, and babysitters are. When I originally wrote this chapter, Dave was in the second week of a hiking trip in New Mexico with his son. There were no phone calls, no e-mails, no contact at all since he entered the wilderness. Sophie was on summer vacation, my son was not sleeping through the night, I had only two days of childcare per week, I was planning a wedding, and finishing this book. Yet I felt on top of the world parenting-wise.

I was delighting in my son's smiles, his enthusiasm for new taste sensations, his fascination with every sound and movement. I was doing morning yoga with my daughter and teaching her about other countries as we watched the Summer Olympics together. She was helping me prepare wedding invitations, pick out bridal accessories, choose music for the reception. The three of us were enjoying bike rides around the lake, with stops at the beach and the playground. We spent a wonderful day at an Irish Festival, watching sheep-herding, learning step-dancing, bouncing to live bands. We were looking forward to the Renaissance Festival and State Fair.

This, for me, is what being a mother is all about. Not the baths and the laundry and the relentless need to get food ready. And none of these activities are less in the absence of my partner. In fact, I appreciate this threesome time even more.

Not unlike most two-parent households, Dave and I have different approaches to parenting — as man and woman — enhanced by the fact that we're both independent and strong-minded

From: Anne, a Married Mom

✦ Honestly, we went through about a year (maybe it was only months — felt like a year) where Clare had a fit about the car seat if it made her shirt, skirt, or whatever stick up or out in any way that she deemed "puffy." Much screaming ensued along the lines of "No, no, no, it's too puffy — it's tooooo puuuuuffffyyyy!!!" All delivered as if being brutally murdered with an ice pick. And forget about coats. Coats can only be worn in the car seat EXTREMELY RARELY. Coats, you see, are definitely "too puffy," not just in the car seat, but sometimes in general.

I have resorted to an "it's okay to take your coat off to ride in the car and then put it back on again" policy on coats in the car seat. This sometimes leads my husband — who is not 100 percent behind my "no coats in the car seat" policy since he doesn't ride in the car with her so often — to screaming fits of his own. In general, I've adopted an "it's okay not to wear your coat, but we'll bring it along just in case" policy. Believe it or not, Clare originally had a problem even with the idea of bringing it along (this is me carrying it, not her), but has now come to love saying, as if it's her own idea. "I don't think I want to wear my coat, but how about if you bring one along, Mom, just in case?"

Humor sometimes works and usually at least helps (if Mom can manage to keep it together to find some humor, which I must say, I can't always).

Personally, I've come to believe all children are relatively nuts — or at least the really brilliant, creative, and interesting (and they are!) kids we seem to know. I mainly keep plugging away on helping Clare learn to identify and find positive ways to express, or release, her emotions.

Sometimes I feel as if I'm making no progress at all, and then one day she'll suddenly say to me (as she did, one day), "Mama, did you notice when you said no to me, I didn't cry or scream or get angry; I just said, 'Okay, Mom.' Wasn't that good?"

people who have developed our own child-rearing systems. I'm not surprised that a typical point of stress between couples is how to raise the children. Truthfully, I don't mind the fact that we are not co-parenting (an advantage to living apart). As a married friend told me, when her husband is traveling on business, being a mom tends to be less stressful. "Sometimes I don't like what he says to the kids, or how he says it. Or I don't like what he does. When there's no other adult around to chime in, it can be easier in many ways."

Accept that Stress Doesn't End

When I interviewed Wendy Kramer for this book, I presumed that for her the stress of single parenting was over. Her son Ryan is a remarkably well-balanced and happy young man — able to make numerous TV appearances to talk about the Donor Sibling Registry website the two of them launched, as well as to enter college at age 14 because of his status as a gifted student. But I presumed wrong.

"This past fall was one of the most difficult times I'd ever been through, and pushed me beyond where I thought I could go stresswise," she told me.

Ryan had started his first semester at college, and she had closed a restaurant of eight years and was laid off from a job of ten years. "We both had complete meltdowns. Ryan was struggling at school, emotionally, mentally, and academically. I thought I was a bad parent. 'How could I have put him in such a situation?' It was brutal. I thought I'd set him up for failure. 'What have I done?' For about two months it was almost unbearable. We were walking around here like zombies."

Because of the strong relationship Wendy had developed with her son, however, even at that rebellious age of 14 he wasn't acting out against her. The way she had handled stress and anger with him in past years paid off (read more in chapter 15). "We kept in touch with each other about what we were going through," she

Choice Chat with Teresa:
Surviving with an Infant

1. **Be shameless about asking for help.** At the baby showers I passed around two sign-up sheets. One was for meals. A friend coordinated this by contacting people on the list after the baby came. This was great! I think I had meals delivered to my house three to four times per week for about six weeks. The second sign-up sheet was for other help. People indicated how they wished to help (run errands, babysit, other chores). I personally contacted people on this list throughout my maternity leave. It allowed me to go out without the baby for about an hour or two twice a week. It also gave me a reason to call people, and that contact was very important during the first few months. I still call people on this list.

2. **Take walks (inside malls or out).** I should have done this regularly, but it seemed I usually didn't do this until I was losing my patience. It always calmed him down, and it was good for me to get some exercise and fresh air.

3. **Pay for services.** I hired out lawn work and had my groceries delivered. These were unplanned expenses, but there's no way I could have kept up without them. I could have used cleaning services as well, but let it go. Laundry and dishes were all I did.

4. **Daycare.** I was pretty close to losing my mind from sleep deprivation. Once I did go back to work and he started daycare, life got easier. It was such a relief to have a few hours a day where I wasn't consumed with his needs. There are drop-off centers that will take infants (6 weeks or older) on an hourly basis.

said. "We were on each other's teams, even if it felt like our teams were losing. He saw me panic, but we did the best we could do and we both came through it. We relied on each other."

Everyone — single or married, parent or not — needs to accept that life always will be visited by stress, sometimes big (boiler broke down and will cost thousands to fix), sometimes small (I've got to be somewhere in 15 minutes and he just pooped all the way up the back of himself).

Being a mom adds to the stress list on a daily basis. Be prepared to accept this, develop your skills of creativity and empathy to minimize it, and don't let yourself be a martyr about it.

Tips for the Caregiver's Soul

A lovely book by James E. Miller, titled *The Caregiver's Book: Caring for Another, Caring for Yourself*,[6] has several good recommendations for anyone who is taking care of another human being, including:

1. List things you can do to restore yourself. Examples might be "order Chinese food" or "read a mystery." Put this long list in a place you'll see every day and make a check mark next to each entry when you do it. Be sure that you are making several check marks each day.
2. Schedule time off. You should always have short breaks and long breaks planned in advance so you have downtime to look forward to.
3. Talk to someone honestly. Every caregiver needs someone to open up to without judgment in order to unplug, get perspective, and listen to their own emotions while explaining them to someone else.
4. Create a "timeout" sign. As Melissa has done, when your

child is old enough, each of you should have a sign — wearing a certain hat or pin, for example — to signal that you simply want time to yourself without talking, interruptions, or demands.

5. Keep a notebook of the gifts you receive from caregiving. Write about how your child inspires, educates, touches you.

6. Accept caregiving from others. As a single woman who consciously chose motherhood, it might be tempting to pretend to be superwoman, especially around people who warned how hard it would be. Don't let that happen. Graciously allow them to help you. People gain a lot from helping others.

7. Make emergency plans. Don't wait for illness to strike to devise options and strategies. Make sure anyone involved is willing to help when asked.

8. Start a co-op. Share shopping, driving, cooking with other caregivers. Exchange a skill you have for one they have.

9. Create a sacred space. Especially for homes that are overrun with plastic toys and baby equipment, set up a quiet place filled with items of special significance to you. Perhaps photos, art, candles, incense, travel mementos.

As Miller wrote, "It's not easy being a caregiver. There are days when your vitality runs low, when your spirit sags, when your anxiety peaks. There are times when the hours are too long, when the demands seem too many, when the rewards feel too few . . . Yet through the discipline of your caregiving, you will experience marvelous new awareness.

> *"In being a blessing for another, you are blessed. In being a vehicle for growth, you grow. You will realize that you are cared for on the grandest scale possible. And the most fitting response you can make is a prayer that contains only four words: Thank you. Thank you."*

Final Thoughts

Have you heard the parable of the glass of water? Lift a glass of water and it doesn't take much effort. One minute, okay. One hour, your arm starts to ache. One day, you need a doctor. The weight never changes, but the longer you lift it without a break, the heavier it becomes. You need to put it down and rest before holding it again. After we're refreshed, it doesn't seem like such an effort again.

No one can truly "conquer" the stress of parenting. It will always be there, especially without a partner to hold the glass of water for a while.

But the most relaxed moments of single parenting can come after you master three requirements. These three strategies are boiled down from this chapter and explored in more detail in chapter 13.

1. Establish daily rituals that calm and connect, such as eating breakfast, cooking, and washing dishes together.
2. Schedule predictable breaks from your child.
3. Find support. Many parents, married and single, largely handle the job alone. The important step is to have many friends, fellow parents, and others who will give you time and space for the needed breaks.

✦ BONUS SECTION ✦

Having Two

Once upon a time pioneering single women decided to have one child on their own. Some of them have told me they regretted not having two kids. Today, a growing number of Choice Mothers are having two (or three) kids.

For some women (including me) the decision to have a second

child is harder to make than the first decision to become a Choice Mom. Others, especially with enhanced fertility, accidentally conceive multiples and have to get used to the idea. Still others — more than a few I've talked to — are elated to have two at once.

Morgan was "totally delighted" when she learned that two of three embryos had survived in vitro fertilization. "At that stage, I was only ever really, really happy and grateful and desperate for both babies to be okay."

On the other hand, Patty initially had no intention of becoming a Choice Mother even to one child, knowing how hard it had been for her mother after her father left. But when she was 33, with no partner on the horizon, she decided it was time to act.

> *Enhanced by fertility drugs for her fourth cycle, she conceived. "When I saw two embryos on the ultrasound screen I was SHOCKED! How was I going to raise two babies on a single income? How was I going to raise two babies with one set of hands! I started to cry."*

Others have every intention of having more than one from the start. Dina, for example, has two boys three years apart and would have a third if she were younger. She doesn't feel she is under any more stress than a married mother. "Of course, I am only one mom, and I can't be in two places at the same time, but that is true of any mom. We are all experiencing similar difficulties and stresses. Mine are not different or worse because of my marital status."

Choice Moms who want two generally hesitate not because of stress and logistical issues, but because of financial issues. It's simply harder to save up for another round of insemination or adoption costs when you're paying for childcare. As Leslie said, "The financial piece was very scary. I had to consider the cost of the actual adoption as well as other child-related expenses. I have stretched the equity in my house pretty far, both through refinancing and a home equity loan. However, I believe if people waited until all their finances were completely the way they wanted them to be, no one would ever have kids."

For those who are debating the choice of having two — or struggling simply with the decision to have one — here is what some Choice Mothers of two have told me.

Support is always important, but especially when there are two kids. Before she proceeded with her second adoption, Leslie talked with her mother and other close friends and family members to make sure she had their support.

House-wise, cooking and shopping needs are about the same, laundry is slightly more frequent, tidying up takes longer. As Marlene put it, "The majority of the extra effort is for refereeing fights and trying to give equal time to each child."

Health is doubly affected with two kids. The school-aged one brings new viruses home, and it's impossible to keep siblings from sharing germs, even if they won't share toys.

"Being the single parent to twins who pass bugs back and forth — and to me too — is impossible to deal with, but you just do," said Morgan. "I vividly remember crawling around my home at 3:00 A.M. with one baby tucked under my arm and the other crying upstairs, and me having a temperature of 104 degrees with mastitis and thrush, and still recovering from my C-section . . . barely making it to the bathroom to throw up and knowing there was no end to this in the near future."

Personality dynamics can become more complicated when the simpler one-on-one relationship changes between parent and child. That was the one thing I worried about most with Sophie — she and I had such a wonderful bond and I hesitated to affect it. But the unanticipated plus is that she and I sometimes feel like partners in affection as we watch Dylan grow up.

Dina found that "not only did my heart expand to encompass my love for my second son, it expanded in a third direction to encompass my love for them as brothers. I love my older son, I love my younger son, and I love their relationship with each other — that relationship is like a third dynamic in our family."

Patty got over her initial shock about having twins and ended up embracing the idea. "I've been raised to believe that you are given what you can handle, and I ran with it. I loved being pregnant, and kept a diary of the experience to remind myself — and later, them — how wonderful it is to be pregnant with twins."

Her daughter was born easily a few hours after the water broke, but her son was breech and Patty had to be put under for an emergency C-section. She cried because "I wasn't going to see my little man until the next day."

Age difference

The dynamic is not always perfect, of course. Timing seems to be a crucial variable: How many years apart is best? Can Mom handle diapering and feeding two young ones at the same time? Or can Mom handle the diverse emotions and activities of two kids who are several years apart? For this, there is no easy answer, since every situation depends on unique temperaments.

For me, having nearly five years between the two has thus far been great. Sophie enjoys Dylan's cuteness, sometimes getting tearful at how "adorable he is." It really does feel like a shared adventure we are having together. Plus, she is old enough to take care of many of her own basic needs while I tend to "the little guy." She generally enjoys entertaining him, and gets him to giggle like no one else. Another benefit of the five-year split was that Sophie was in free public school before I needed childcare for Dylan, so I never had to pay for two at once.

Marlene, on the other hand, has a similar age difference between her two girls, but her circumstances haven't been ideal. Her youngest was adopted at 20 months, when her oldest was 6. "In my experience, this is a bad split. Perhaps if I had brought an infant home to my 5-year-old, things would have been okay. I have dealt with horrible jealousy and tormenting from the older one, who had much more trouble adjusting than the little one. She has reverted to 3-year-old tantrums, and picks fights constantly. There is a huge territory war about what is 'my stuff' and what has to be shared. If I had it to do over again, I would try to adopt a 4-year-old or would have done this a few years earlier. I think bringing a toddler home who touches everything and breaks small toys was probably a form of torture for my oldest."

Age difference also can have a big impact in the early years, with varying nap and bed routines. As the kids get older, the more years between the two, the tougher it will be to find mutually satisfying activities. A benefit of having them close in age is that they can eventually take recreational classes together.

With twins you don't have the age difference issues — and sometimes wish you did. "It's definitely been harder than I expected," Morgan said. "But maybe not any different to the huge shock that hits all new parents at how hard it all is. The worst part was sleep deprivation. Total deprivation. My babies were almost six weeks premature and put onto a three-hour feeding schedule. As I was determined to breastfeed (with bottle feeding augmentation) this meant every three hours I spent all but maybe 15 minutes feeding, sterilizing equipment, pumping milk, changing babies — then the cycle would start all over again.

> *"I was hallucinating with lack of sleep, often going days and nights without any sleep at all, and this went on for six to eight months at least. But I managed to breastfeed until they were 28 months old."*

Morgan has no family nearby, or experienced friends who can help, so she fully takes care of her twin boys with paid help. "Initially I hired an expensive mother's help for a few hours a day. I wish now I'd paid out even more just to get some sleep in that first year. After that, once I returned to work when the babies were 6 months old, I had nannies and home daycare providers, then part-time school."

Patty's mother helped her for the first two months. "I'm really not sure how I would have handled being alone after the birth. I hemorrhaged 10 days later and was bedridden for 24 hours." Her breastfeeding and pumping demands also were exhausting. She had her "one and only breakdown" at the end of the first month.

About stress

The old adage is that having two more than doubles the energy required. But other than the difficulty of keeping track of two, this did not seem to be the complaint of most women I talked to.

Dina says, "I have absolutely not found two twice as difficult as one. In many ways, having two is easier than having one. They entertain each other and are more self-sufficient than my older son was until his brother came along. In other words, mommy is not the sole source of entertainment. In fact, as they grow older, in some ways life is becoming a little easier — if one of them wants me to get something, it is possible that the other one will actually do it, so I get to keep sitting on the couch (ha!). Don't get me wrong, life with a 3-year-old and newborn was hard, and I still don't get enough sleep, but again, my married friends don't have it much better."

What can be lost when a young one enters the picture, however, are private moments that were savored when the older child was beginning to be away from home for longer periods of time with babysitters, teachers, and drop-off play dates. One woman told me that with two kids she had less money to spend, and found herself limited to chauffeuring the oldest to activities while still maintaining a nap schedule for the other.

> *"Going shopping with two kids is like trying to herd cats," Marlene said. "One you can hang onto, but two are impossible unless both fit in the shopping cart. I do almost all my shopping on my lunch hour now."*

Morgan said she has her nearly 4-year-old twins strapped into strollers or toddler reins instead of letting them run free as she'd prefer. "Having twins on my own has meant their lives have been more restricted. We can't easily do family activities, like swimming and going to cafés, as there's only me to supervise. They still tend to run off in opposite directions, to different dangers, and I'm forever having to assess the potential dangers in a split second and leap towards the greater need. It keeps me very fit, physically."

Patty says she's happy she doesn't have the added stress of validating her parenting decisions with someone else. "I truly believe that life would be much more difficult with a spouse," she said. "In my world, I make the decisions and I live with the results. There is no one else to blame or hand off to or hug. Just mommy."

Regrets are few, no matter what the path has been. In the big picture, the stress of motherhood tends to be minimized.

"Do I sound sorry for going for two?" Marlene said. "I'm not. Just stressed and frazzled, like having an infant with colic all the time. I figure that if they survive childhood without killing each other, they will be great friends and finally appreciate each other. Of course, when the youngest turns 18, I'm packing up and moving to the tropics with no forwarding address."

Morgan's only regret is that she rarely gets time alone with each twin. "They're so completely different from each other, with different needs, that I wish I could give each more unique Mommy time."

Leslie says, "Bottom line, having a second child has added a wonderful new dimension to our family. I love watching the girls be sisters and hope they will always share a special bond. I want them to have someone to share hopes, fears, and memories with, now and in the future. Even on the toughest days, I cannot imagine a world without either one of them. I never thought I could love someone as much as I love my first daughter. Then along came my second daughter. She adds such a wonderful new dimension to our family. I have no regrets about my decision to adopt again."

Coping mechanisms

Patty says she "didn't know a THING about raising a baby, let alone two at the same time. It has all been flying by the seat of my pants. I didn't have patience to start with, but have gained an

The Author's Journey to Two

✦ After 9/11, and after a beautiful trip to Hawaii for my fortieth birthday that reminded me of quality of life elsewhere, the piece of the puzzle I had never considered before dropped into my lap: I would move out of my beloved city of 18 years. After leaving New York City, I realized that what I wanted to accomplish more than anything was to add a sibling to Sophie's life.

Oddly, the love for my daughter really did impel me to think of a second child as a gift for her, rather than for me. Even throughout the pregnancy, I wasn't as excited about the new arrival as I thought I would be. I worried, as many mothers do, whether I would be able to love the new one as much as my first.

Being nearly five years older than I was the first time, I was unexpectedly more concerned about the pain of childbirth. I felt more back pain, more hemorrhoids, more exhaustion. I still loved the sensations of having a child in the womb, but I was much more nervous about whether I was up to the challenge. I had gotten used to having a well-behaved daughter and knew this time I was having a son — whose kicks were more intense!

When Dylan made his arrival, my daughter was there to witness the miracle. She squealed with delight when she saw his head emerge, and was mesmerized for the rest of the day, barely letting anyone else (including me!) hold him.

That night, however, when the hospital room was quiet and it was just Dylan and I, the bonding began. It amazes me, the capacity for the human heart to open wider, when you thought it was already as wide as it could get.

I have enjoyed motherhood even more the second time around — although he didn't let me sleep through the night the first year. Since I know what I'm doing this time, I'm finding it much easier to relax and enjoy our simple moments.

ounce a day since my cubs came to me. Laughter is a must. And the reminder to myself that I chose them, they didn't choose me."

Morgan says her planning and thinking about Choice Motherhood in advance of pregnancy — "being very sure I wanted children so much" — has helped her cope with twins in a way she might not have if she'd had children in a traditional relationship, without as much thought about becoming a mother.

"My children have a mommy who can at least laugh at herself for her crazy moments, apologize to them for her mistakes, and beyond everything, feel deeply grateful to have such beautiful little beings in my life," she said.

> *"It's really the first time in my life that I've experienced something so incredibly and impossibly hard that, at the same time, is so incredibly and unbelievably wonderful. A unique paradox!"*

11

Answering the Daddy Question

Sooner or later every Choice Mom will be answering the "where is my daddy?" question. It likely will come up many times over the years. And it often will appear out of the blue — while you're watching a TV show about dogs, or standing in line at the grocery store, or driving to church.

So it pays to be prepared ahead of time. But many women I've talked to who are worried about how they will answer this question generally are focused on the complex background they themselves might feel guilty or emotional about: Why did you bring me into this home without also giving me a father? Why don't you know anything about my donor, or my birth mother? Why did my father reject us when you were pregnant? If that man helped you create me, why don't you let him live with us?

Look at any single-parent website and you'll find some of the agony women can put themselves through about answering the daddy question. Wrote one woman on Single Parent Central: "My boyfriend left me when I was six months pregnant, moved to another state, and was never heard from again. My daughter is almost three and has been asking who her daddy is. She is very intelligent and I don't want to lie to her. She asks me everyday, and even the daycare teachers have said that she tells them almost daily that she doesn't have a father. I feel worthless and don't want to say the wrong thing, something that will mentally harm her!"

A Choice Mom I know who used a known donor didn't struggle with the daddy question when her son's donor was living in another country, but after the man unexpectedly returned to live in their state she was not sure how to answer her inquisitive boy's questions. Should she tell him his father lived nearby, or stick to the "other country" story, even though it was no longer true? How would her boy react if he knew that the man had no real interest in meeting him? Wouldn't it be simpler to lie about his whereabouts?

A woman who used an anonymous donor confided in another who had done the same about the pain she was going through watching her daughter struggle with identity issues as she entered her teens. The first mother had long worried about this day, when her daughter might resent not knowing her other half. The second mother wondered if, deep down, that's why the struggle was happening — years of unspoken apology for the way the daughter was conceived were being passed down.

Some women worry that this is the conversation that will determine whether their child will be happy and how they will be perceived by their child going forward. That the words have to be "just right."

Interestingly, for several lesbian women I know, the daddy question doesn't have as much weight as it does for many heterosexual women. Since many families in their inner circle don't have a traditional dad, and never would, the daddy question seems less oppressive to think about and respond to.

This makes me wonder, of course, how much of the concern about answering the inevitable daddy question has to do with a woman's own feeling of "lack" in not having a partner. My personal theory is that the less self-conscious a woman feels about that, the easier it will be to answer a child's questions naturally.

On the other hand, I also know women who feel genetic connections are not important, and that the biological father (or mother, in the case of donor egg or adoption) should not be con-

Choice Chat with Dina:
"The Question"

✦ "Where is my daddy?" was my elder son's first question about his father, spoken when he was about 3½. I thought I was prepared for it. My son knew the story of his creation from infancy. From birth I had told him a bedtime story about a lady named mommy who wanted a baby, couldn't have one by herself, and met a very, very, very nice man who helped her make a baby. I tried to make the point of how much he was the focus of the story, not the failed relationship between the man and the woman. As he got older, I would ask if he knew who the lady named mommy was, and he'd point at me and yell "MOMMY!" The answer to who the baby was came even more quickly: "ME!" he'd yell with delight.

My son asked The Question after seeing his friends with daddies. Although I thought I was prepared, The Question drove a stake through my heart.

I immediately felt guilty — guilty that I had not managed to make a successful relationship with an alcoholic, guilty that I did not mind that the man did not want to be part of his son's life, guilty that I had accidentally gotten pregnant in the first place, guilty that I hadn't waited until Mr. Right or Mr. Almost Right came along. There was a little silence after my son asked The Question. I took a deep breath and was about to launch into some kind of explanation about grownups, responsibility, alcoholism, and assorted other adult issues. But my son looked so innocent, so unaware of how loaded his question was, that I paused.

"What do you mean?" I asked.

"Where does he live?" he clarified. "Florida," I answered truthfully. "We don't have a daddy in our family, but we have a mommy and a grandma and . . ." ▶

My son seemed satisfied, and that was the end of the conversation. A few months later, we were at a play date. The other little boy (then about 4) asked my son where his dad was. My son said, matter-of-factly, "Florida, but," — and then he pointed at me — "my mommy is right over there and she loves me a lot!"

For myself, I learned an important lesson. The Question, when spoken by a small child, is not laden with all the questions and nuances imbued and implied when spoken by an adult. For virtually all questions now, I pause and think about what could be their simplest, most concrete meaning. I ask for clarification about exactly what he is asking, and I try to answer only that question.

Sometimes, I ask an additional question or two to make sure I've completely answered the question to my son's satisfaction.

My elder son is now 6, happy and well-adjusted. He seems content with the fact that our family has no daddy and that his father lives in another state. He knows now that his father can't be a daddy because he's sick from drinking wine.

I was a little chagrined recently to discover that he told a friend that he has met his father (he hasn't), but realized that he was confused after meeting his paternal uncle when his paternal grandmother (Nana) was in town. Once I cleared up the confusion, my son was fine.

Daddy questions haven't come up much recently, especially after I showed him a picture of his father and offered to call his Nana if he had any questions. He didn't, and hasn't brought up his father in about six months, but when he does I'll answer honestly, in an age-appropriate manner.

My younger son (now 3) was conceived via ADI. His bedtime story is a continuation of my older son's. The lady named mommy wants another baby but can't have one by herself, so the doctor gives her the seeds to make a baby. (In addition, through an Internet donor registry, I discovered a ▶

woman on the East Coast who used the same donor to conceive her daughter. So, the bedtime story ends with the discovery of another lady named mommy who used the same
seeds to make her baby.) My younger son has not yet
brought up The Question, but when he does, my answer
will be honest: "We don't have a daddy in our family."

I believe each person has his or her own "baggage." For
my sons, not having a father may be theirs, but who
knows? The most important thing, I think, is that I am at
peace with my decision to have my children.

*I tell them that I'm the luckiest mommy in the world,
and I mean it. They may wonder about their fathers,
but they will never wonder about whether they were
wanted and loved.*

sidered important. Sometimes they think it's simply too confusing
for a child to have a "father" who has never been part of their life,
and they prefer to dismiss it after one or two talks of "we don't
have a dad in our family."

Yet a mother's feelings about why there is no father, and
whether it is important, has little to do with the child's budding
curiosity about family. And when those first natural questions
come, no matter what the situation, it is the parent's openness to
discussion that experts concur is of consequence, more so than the
words. Shame or a sense of lack or guilt or a dismissive attitude
will have more impact than the actual story.

As children grow up, they decide for themselves what importance family plays in their life. After all, don't we as adults vary
about who we want to spend Thanksgiving dinner with (Family?
Friends? Soup kitchen volunteer work?). In a similar way, children
will differ as they grow about whether they consider a biological
father to be important to their life, and when they might express
curiosity about who he is. I don't know a teenager or adult who

doesn't think they have the right to decide who is important to their life and identity and who is not.

What we want as parents is to support their interest and emotions about this and other issues in their life. To empower them to ask questions and find answers.

What Kids Really Want to Know

Jamie told me of an experience she had with her 5-year-old adopted son. He asked why he doesn't have a father. "I started to give him the 'all different kinds of families' response, and he stopped me. He said he knows that, but why doesn't he have a father? So I decided to give it to him straight. I said because I hadn't found a man I wanted to spend the rest of my life with, but I was ready to become a mom. His response: 'Well, I'll marry you.' When I said that moms and sons can't marry, he said he'd marry me when he was an adult. I said no, moms and sons can't marry then either. But when he found someone he wanted to spend the rest of his life with, he could get married. He said, 'I want to spend the rest of my life with you.'"

As we'll discuss further in this chapter, a child's daddy questions spring out of their own predictable concerns. For young children, that includes feeling secure that a parent will never abandon them — that family is permanent. At first, they want to understand not how babies are made, but how exciting their arrival was. As they get a little older, they want to be reassured that they are the same as other kids, created in the same way.

> *Understanding the basic developmental phases of each age — and really listening to what your child is asking — can take pressure off the mother who worries that she won't give the "right" answer.*

In the early years, the idea is simply to lay groundwork for more complex discussions that can come later.

Keeping It Simple

It took me a while to understand what my daughter really was asking in some of our "deep" conversations. It wasn't as instinctive for me as deciphering when she was hungry or tired. Our early talks ended up not feeling satisfying because I was thinking about what I wanted my smart little girl to grow up understanding, rather than understanding what she was needing to hear.

When Sophie was 3 I explained — since she had a known donor — that he is her biological father, but not the kind of daddy who lives with us. But she didn't understand yet that some dads are integral to family life, so for her the distinction wasn't important. The only thing she wanted to know, I realized later, was that she had a dad, like other kids.

When she was 4, I explained that many people are married when they have kids, but I was one of those women, like others we'd met, who had a baby but hadn't yet found someone I wanted to marry — that her "donor dad" (we now simply call him by his first name) helped me to create her, but wasn't the right person for me to marry. The explanation was too complicated. The only thing she needed to know was that there was a mom and a "gene man" (another term some use) who created her.

When she was almost 5 and Dave had entered our lives, I explained, when she asked what she should call him, that she could call him Dave, and that someday maybe he would be like a daddy to her. "Then I have two dads!" she said gleefully. Initially she decided to call him her "pretend daddy," and her donor became known as her "real daddy." Eventually, because she liked my ex-husband and thought the fact that I was once married to him should make a difference to her (even though we divorced six years before she was born), she added him to the list and called him her "other daddy." (That phase lasted until she was 7.)

When Dave and I married, I explained the "stepfather" term to her — but since he doesn't live with us, or co-parent, she continues to call him by his first name. What she most cares about are not the terms, but that her family is bigger, and that's good enough for her.

The code phrase here, as I've been told several times but have a hard time managing, is: "Keep it simple." As I'm learning, when a child first starts asking about dad, often what the child wants to know is simply whether he has what his friend on the playground has. Any answer that doesn't respond to that simple question won't really be what the child is looking for.

> *Our kids have their own agenda when they ask questions, and generally it's MUCH less complicated than what we feel we need to impart to them. When the questions get more complicated, the answers can.*

One approach to telling a child's story, proposed in an article about donor insemination, but applicable to any origins story, suggested that a child's beginnings initially do not need to be told in biological terms (seed and egg coming together) or as the parent's story (child created to make Mom happy). Rather, it can be told as an important step toward building family.

"In this approach, the emphasis is on 'us' as a family rather than 'you' as a child," the authors wrote. "It means parents are sharing information concerning how they, as a family, were formed/built/created . . . It is 'our family' story that is being told to the child rather than the child's story."[1]

Basic Dos and Don'ts

My conversations with child experts and Choice Moms, especially those familiar with children conceived from donors, reveal simple rules:

1. Work through your own issues about why there is no daddy for your child. Children who are conflicted about their origins often have parents who are conflicted about it. As the psychotherapist Patricia Mendell said in a good arti-

cle published on the American Fertility Association website (www.theafa.org), there is a growing consensus that "a child's understanding and adjustment is profoundly influenced by how the parent(s) feel about forming that family in the first place."[2]

2. Start early. One strategy used by many Choice Moms is to tell the story out loud from babyhood, so that the words get comfortable before the child is old enough to comprehend them. Lay the groundwork early, so the term "dad" or "donor" is never considered a taboo word or dismissed as unimportant. The goal is to make the child feel secure and loved, to tell the story simply and honestly.

3. Shrugging off the "dad" concept is never a good strategy. Even if you are happy not having a dad in the home, don't expect your child to feel the same. And if you used a known donor, never disparage him in front of the child, even if he hasn't played by the rules you expected of him.

4. Emphasize the normality of being different. Every young child wants to be perceived as normal. They will notice earlier than you think that having a father is normal. Be sure they know by then that there are many ways to create a family. There are recommended storybooks on my website that tell the stories of different normal families.

5. Always remember that the birth story is theirs. As Dr. Kyle Pruett indicated, it is easy to forget that ultimately the way a child came to be is more important to him or her than to the parent. If your child is sensitive about the way he or she was created, don't push it in the hopes of making him or her embrace it.

6. Keep in mind that privacy can be very important to children. Many Choice Moms report that their school-aged children aren't comfortable sharing their story with friends. Sometimes they don't want to appear to be different. Sometimes they understandably don't want to explain the concepts they've learned about conception,

donors who help people have babies, and how biology doesn't always relate to who your family is.

7. Realize that every child processes differently. My daughter, for example, is the type to ponder before finally asking a question, and even then it isn't always directed at me. She asked my housemate, for example, why her real daddy doesn't live with us. She mentioned to my mother that "all the other kids had daddies there," but never gave me a clue that this was a distinction she had noticed. She does talk to me about important issues, but sometimes only after she's had a chance to digest them. I need to be ready when she is — and make sure she knows the door is open when she's ready to ask.

Expert Opinion

Anne C. Bernstein, author of *Flight of the Stork: How Children Think (and When) About Sex and Family Building,*[3] has given parents good information about what adopted or donor children need to know and when. My thanks to her for allowing me to excerpt her findings in this book.

In her 30 years as a family psychologist who studied how children understand sex and birth, she found that children question their own birth story in parallel to their growing comprehension of how other things in their world come to be. It starts with the young child's interest in where babies come from. As their understanding evolves, so too will the curiosity about their birth.

Another great source of information about this topic comes from the Donor Conception Network, which in 2006 published a series of Telling and Talking booklets for parents of donor-conceived children about what to tell children, and how, about the way they were added to the family. Written by Olivia Montuschi, they also include tips for those who use a known donor, for talking with relatives and friends, and for communicating with a child's school. (Free downloadable versions, for different age groups, can be found at www.dcnetwork.org.)[4]

In this chapter I've gleaned tips and insight from both sources, as well as from other child development experts such as Dr. Kyle Pruett, that are applicable to any Choice Mom, no matter which method to motherhood was used.

Toddlers: "Do I have a daddy?"

The first thing kids of 2 and 3 begin to notice is that most kids seem to have a father, even if he doesn't live with them. As Pruett pointed out to me, the big question at this age is, "WHERE is he?" Bernstein in particular advises:

- Understand what they are asking before you jump in with an answer.
- Reaffirm that you will be in their life forever. Especially in the case of adoptive children, your unwavering commitment to them as a parent is what they need to hear. This is when you can start delivering the message that genetic connection is not the same as devoted parenting.
- Create an atmosphere of trust and openness. Early discussions should be considered a first installment on what will be a continuing discussion. It is not the details or terminology that will have a lasting impact, but the emotions.

Preschoolers: "Why don't we have a daddy?"

Innocent curiosity leads to interesting questions, and exposure to other kids who have their own understanding of biology and relationships will lead to interesting situations.

- Relate to their need to understand relationships. Kids this age tend to see people as connected to each other because they want to be. This is when the basic idea of wanting to be a mother, but not knowing an adult to love and live with, is appropriate.

Dads, Trucks, and Babies
From: Wendy Kramer

✦ I wasn't prepared when my 2½-year-old son asked, "So did my dad die or what?" I thought the question would come up later than that. I walked him down the driveway, explained about women having eggs and men having sperm, and that I used some donated by a nice man. A passing truck caught his attention, and that was the end of that conversation.

After that, I would always take his cues when he brought it up. Every time he asked a question we'd go a little deeper into it. It usually happened every six months or so. Eventually he was mostly curious about how people have babies. He wasn't so much missing the dad thing as showing overall curiosity about the process. By the time he was 6, he'd introduce himself by shaking hands and saying, "Hi, I'm Ryan and I'm a donor baby." It wasn't intended to shock people. For him it was simply part of who he was. It was how he identified himself.

- Talk about what makes a parent real, as well as the many ways to be a parent. Bernstein suggests asking the child to list what other children's daddies do, so that he or she can begin to understand the distinctive role of parenting.
- Give the foundation for their birth story. As the Telling and Talking booklet points out, kids become curious about how a baby gets inside a mother much as an adult might wonder how a ship gets into a bottle. This doesn't mean they want to know about sex and biological detail. The appropriate basics are that it takes an egg from a woman and sperm or "seed" from a man to make a baby.

Note that children start comparing notes on this topic sooner than you might expect them to. It's best to arm your child early on with the knowledge that it takes both a male and a female to create a baby.

As Ellen told me, after kids in her son's preschool asked about his dad, he replied that he didn't have one. They told him that was impossible. He asked Mom, and she told him about the role of his birth father and the doctor in helping her to conceive. The next day, his preschool teacher reported that he excitedly told everyone, "I do have a dad! My mom just doesn't know who he is or where he lives!"

When the conversations get more complex

- Confront your own conflicts, on an ongoing basis. Many therapists tell me that it is very often the adult's conflicts about how the child was brought into the world that a child picks up on. Don't let any guilt or resentment or grief about how you became a Choice Mom linger. And don't avoid answering your child's questions because you're afraid of saying the wrong thing. Start talking to someone to resolve your own emotions long before your child starts looking to you for conversation.

- Acknowledge, if it's the case, that the subject is difficult for you to talk about. Be sure to mention that you are glad the child asked and that you will try your best to answer.

- Don't assume your child comprehends certain concepts. One common source of confusion is that food and babies both seem to be in the same "tummy" space, and some young children worry that eating might be harmful. Another common misunderstanding is that the "nice man who helped" couldn't have children of his own and thus gave up part of himself to help Mom. While there is ample opportunity over time for mix-ups to get straightened out, check your child's understanding of concepts before a new layer of conversation begins.

Levels of child development

David Brodzinsky, an adoption expert, subscribed to the behavioral therapist Erik Erickson's seven stages of life conflict. Bernstein's study used Piaget's theories about the ages and stages of a child's thinking process, described at length in her book. She told me that while subsequent research has refuted some key aspects of Piaget's theory, the descriptions of children's thinking at different ages — as long as it is not taken as an unvarying and universal progression — still tells us a lot about how children are processing information about sex and birth.

Whatever the theory, it's important to understand that children have natural levels of development, so answering their questions appropriately will vary according to the stage or age they are in.

A preschooler, for example, uses words without having much of an idea about what they mean. Such as my daughter using "pretend daddy" and "real daddy" and "other daddy" to describe the three important men of Mom's past and present life.

As Patricia Mendell has said, young children don't usually push for more information, and are likely to create their own imaginative twist to anything you say, so choose your language carefully, but don't be surprised at how it is digested. For example, "If you talk about eggs, kids often picture a carton in the supermarket," she noted.

Another understandable one I've heard is referring to a sperm bank, which then becomes associated with going to the ATM and getting a handful of sperm.

Children between ages 4 and 8 will often concoct magical, imaginative fantasies about how things work. (My 7-year-old daughter is certainly creative, but is starting to transition toward wanting to understand things accurately.)

Starting around the age of 6, they will start to understand basic concepts of reproduction — such as the role of sperm and egg — and that a man and woman need to love each other to be in a relationship. Pruett told me this is when children start to move from questions of "Where is my daddy?" to "WHO is my daddy?"

Some children might be less inclined to ask questions. If that describes your child, consider using triggers to bring the topic up. The Telling and Talking guide suggests using the birth of a friend's sibling, or a story about diverse families, as hooks. Such as: "It's funny how we are all different but every human baby starts in the same way, with a tiny egg that comes from a woman, and an even tinier seed that comes from a man. Do you remember . . ."

After the age of 8, they become more concerned with accuracy, and begin to understand the context of their birth story in more nuanced ways. Most experts point out that this is when sadness might set in about, for example, being placed for adoption by a birth mother.

By the age of 12, a child is able to combine all the information they have been given into a complete story. They might be angry that they were not conceived to a man and woman like their friends were. They might have a growing urge to know more about a donor or birth mother. They might be self-conscious about appearing "normal" with friends. Their questions might be more uncomfortable to answer. But the groundwork you've laid together over the years will help.

Montuschi writes: "It is easy to feel bad about not being able to provide everything your child wants. But don't beat yourself up. By being honest, listening, acknowledging feelings, and generally being there for them you are doing everything you can to provide them with the tools (resilience, high self-esteem, self-awareness) to cope with what life throws at them."

Advice in a nutshell

- Don't worry about giving the perfect story. As several experts pointed out to me, you will get many opportunities to get this answer right.
- Every child will react differently. Some will be open with friends about their story, others won't. Some will be frustrated or sad about the lack of full information about a donor

or birth parent, others will not. This reflects much more the natural temperament of your child than anything you have "done wrong" in the telling.

✦ BONUS SECTION ✦

Blurring Lines:
Meeting Donor Dads and Birth Fathers

One of the most common areas of concern, particularly with parents who use open-identity donors or have used open adoption, is how to navigate the relationship between their children and "birth others," as author Diane Ehrensaft calls them.[5] This is, in fact, why many single women choose to use an anonymous donor, for fear of what might happen if an unknown donor (or half-siblings from the same man) become part of her child's life. And it's a primary reason why closed adoptions are chosen instead of open.

When we invest as much time and thought as we do into raising our children, it can be understandably threatening to think that someone we don't really know could somehow usurp our authority or leadership or importance as the parent, or could claim some ownership to our child based on biological connection, or could impose values on our child that we don't want them to have.

I know adults who have met their birth parents after adoption. I know anonymous donors who have met offspring. I have also spoken with many offspring about what that type of contact means to them, whether it has happened already, or whether it is still an unfulfilled desire.

My Voices of Donor Conception book series is designed to collect and disseminate some of these stories about meetings with half-siblings, and between offspring and donor. (See www .voicesofdonorconception.com for details.)

For some, understandably, making contact is a nerve-wracking process, akin to meeting in-laws for the first time — you can't simply put them back if you don't like them. I know several adoptive offspring, my brother included, who have turned down an opportunity to meet potential birth family. Many offspring who have contact information for their open-identity donor don't reach out right away.

Fear of disappointment and discomfort, as well as a general lack of guidance on how to talk with someone who might define or expect more of the "family" label, are predictable reasons for avoiding the opportunity.

Some gregarious individuals have jumped in easily and felt energized by the contact. Others tentatively make contact with half-sibling families, generally found via the Donor Sibling Registry, to seek information while their kids are young, and perhaps to swap photos. Still others use cybersleuthing to try to learn the identity of their donors from the information they have.

In 2007, I led a two-hour workshop in Canada that invited participants to discuss how and why we define family as we do. The attendees included a woman who learned at 15 that she'd been placed for adoption, and reported feeling a great connection with the birth parents she was invited to meet. Another young woman in attendance felt her adoptive family was all she needed, and had no desire to consider birth parents part of her community. An older man who had been a long-time donor said he felt no sense of love or paternity toward any unknown offspring, yet did feel he and they had a right to meet if they chose to, and should not be prevented from doing so simply because paperwork and outside-party policy restricted it.

Most people prefer to meet and develop potential relationships privately, but there have been a few publicly reported stories of meetings between offspring and birth others. There is the story of Bobby, a donor who was plagued with questions after coming into contact with his 21-year-old offspring Katie, as reported by Judith Graham of the *Chicago Tribune*.[6]

Katie, who was raised by married parents, learned as a teenager, during an argument with her mother, that she was conceived by donor insemination. She told Graham that she wasn't hurt or angry, but confused. She contacted the sperm bank, and someone there made a phone call to the donor. He accepted a letter from Katie, who wrote, "No matter what contact we have, half of my chromosomes are yours."

Bobby agreed to meet with her not so much because of what she said, but because of his own experience as an adopted child who searched for his birth parents, and because he recognized so much of himself in the photo of the girl.

The two had regular contact, and visits, before the girl's divorced mother moved with her daughter to the donor's city so a stronger relationship could build with him and his family. Graham reported that the girl's mother and the donor's wife had become friends. The girl occasionally babysat her half-brothers. All of them spent Father's Day and Mother's Day together.

But the donor said he was "reeling" from the intense emotional impact of the encounters with the girl. "There's no book you can go to and learn what is the etiquette," he told Graham. He wondered what he was supposed to do when the girl wasn't doing well in school, or wore low-cut shirts. Act like a dad and say something? Or not?

As his wife told Graham, "To think about all the interactions and make sure they're appropriate and healthy and don't hurt people, it's taken a tremendous amount of energy. People don't want to comprehend the power of a biological connection. These kids, they're going to find their donors, they're going to look for their half-siblings — it's going to happen because there's a fundamental drive to do it, and these sperm banks need to start counseling families that this is what could come."

Two Young Kids Meet "Daddy"

In a similar story, this one involving a Choice Mom, reported in a *Washington Post* magazine article by Michael Leahy,[7] 44-year-old

Raechel flew with her two young children to stay in the home of their formerly anonymous donor, Mike.

In their case, both parties found each other because of the Donor Sibling Registry, where Mike had made himself available for contact by anyone who was conceived from his sperm. He is a 45-year-old divorced, childless artist. The Choice Mom is a psychotherapist. When they met, Aaron was nearly 7, eager to meet someone he could call "Dad," and Leah, at 3, was more shy.

Raechel made a point of conveying tidbits about the donor to her kids from an early age, wanting them always to think of him as the real person he is. For example, she would hold up a drawing and point out that red was one of the donor's favorite colors, or encourage them to send hugs and kisses to the donor on Father's Day.

After Raechel became acquainted with Mike in e-mail and phone conversations, Leahy reported, the kids started mailing him cards and drawings, and he sent gifts. Eventually the visit was planned.

Raechel herself was excited, Leahy wrote, "especially about the possibilities for her son, who had not had a chance to bond closely with a man. Her own father had died many years earlier, and she had no brother or brother-in-law. A T-ball coach had been kind to Aaron, as well as a hockey coach and a playmate's father, but none of the men could possibly be more than a pale substitute for a committed and unencumbered man."

For his part, the donor placed pictures of the kids in his home, referring to them as his "children" with friends. He told Raechel that if the kids felt comfortable, he hoped during the visit that they would call him Dad. He was clear in his own mind that he did not see himself as a family man in the conventional, day-to-day sense.

After the trip, Raechel began making plans to move her therapy practice and children closer to the donor so the relationship between the kids and donor could grow. With Mike's approval, she redid her will to give custody of the children to him, and she changed their names to include his last name as well as hers.

Potential Pitfalls

There are many complications to work out when meeting a birth other, as these stories reveal. Interestingly, one of the most loaded issues is what terms to use: "daddy," "donor," "brother," "sister," "birth mom"?

Offspring will often use terms that the parents would not. Although, as the example of my daughter showed me, those terms will — and should — change naturally over time as they redefine the words and relationships.

A speculation of bystanders was that Raechel was trying to form a partnership with Mike that enhanced her life, as well as the lives of her kids. (Interestingly, the same criticism wasn't applied to Mike.) By turning an anonymous man into a known donor, the assumption of many who reacted to the story was that she was trying to make him into a mate, rather than simply encouraging her kids to know more about who they are, with a man who had an invested interest, eventually, in their well-being.

In an online chat with the reporter, one reader bluntly wrote, "How in God's name does Raechel think she's not going to be confusing her kids by introducing them to a man she doesn't know and calling him Daddy? You have better things to do than dip into such fanciful nonsense as a woman chasing a man to the other side of the country and making her children hostage to her fantasy. What the heck are the kids going to do when Daddy says he can't see them for a month because he's painting and needs his solitude? Or has a beautiful model posing?"

A less strident reader commented, "I am 100 percent in favor of unconventional families, and totally support whatever path an individual or couple decides to take in order to fulfill their dreams bringing children into their lives and hearts. But every time she referred to [the donor] as 'your daddy' to the children, I grit my teeth. No, this is NOT their daddy, this is the DONOR. A daddy has a loving, permanent, committed relationship with a child — whether he is the biological father or not. As a psychotherapist, she should know that *daddy* is a loaded word, and should not be thrown about lightly, especially when there are vulnerable children involved."

Regardless of the terms, another complication after meeting is how to steer through inevitable conflicts about expectations. Is a birth father allowed to offer parental advice? What do you say when children want to live with or near each other?

One wife of a donor admitted to me a fear that her younger children will suffer, as her husband becomes enamored with his older, donor offspring, perhaps even paying for their college tuition or including them in his will.

Therapists respond

I contacted two women who have special insight into nontraditional families, and asked them to comment on the story about Raechel and her kids. One of them was Anne Bernstein, whose advice about answering the daddy question we've discussed in this chapter. The other was Ellen Sarasohn Glazer, a clinical social worker with 20 years of experience focusing on infertility, adoption, and related issues.

Bernstein told me she is a strong supporter of the view that all donors should be knowable, even if they are not "known donors," and that she would support a move toward allowing only open-identity donors. She indicated that the story seemed to capture a "so far so good" moment in Raechel's children's history with the donor. She does not know the people or dynamic, but it seemed to her that the decision to relocate was made quickly, "given that the father's commitment to parenting might be more sustainable when contact is for a week or two at a time, at most a few times a year, than when proximity offers the promise (and the challenge) of more day-to-day involvement."

Glazer, too, said that it is difficult to comment from a distance, but that she would caution anyone from assuming that a donor will become a father. "A relation-

ship can still be there, even if it's not a parenting one,"
she told me.

"On the positive side," Glazer said, "I feel strongly that children need to know where they came from and that these children are better off knowing who their donor is."

It also can be helpful for children to have influences from two prominent individuals in their life, to help balance out the influence of one. But Glazer, too, was concerned by the possible impulsiveness of the decision to more fully incorporate Mike into the existing family structure. She felt that contact could have been made with the donor without involving an at-home visit, using the "daddy" term, and making plans to move.

As Bernstein pointed out, it also could potentially be a difficult position for Mike, given that he might have dozens of offspring. "Developing ongoing, consistent relationships with more than a few would be an unsustainable responsibility, leading to inevitable disappointment should other mothers seek similar relationships."

In short, both women agree — as do I — that it can be emotionally difficult for young children to navigate relationships with donors. But I also feel that letting fear of potential pitfalls constrict us is not nearly as powerful as confidently (and wisely) embracing the potential rewards.

After all, it also can be difficult for children to navigate emotions about not having a father to form a relationship with, even those conceived to a married couple with a distant parent. The challenge is to make whatever bonds form be as enriching as possible.

We all define family in our own ways, and making biology part of the formula is, if you think about it differently — as our adopted and donor-conceived children must — a matter of choice.

Key to all of it (one theme of this book) is that the Choice Mom must truly have the best interest of her child at heart, and the judgment to make sound, loving decisions. No one knows yet how offspring like Aaron and Leah and Katie will be influenced by knowing their donor. In large part it depends on how receptive and open the donors remain, as well as the kids' interest levels.

As we discussed in the chapter about known donors, expectations of all parties need to be clearly communicated and negotiated on a continuing basis, which can be difficult, but highly rewarding, when done well.

And it is this openness with our kids, this bond of respect and trust we place with them as we share our family building stories — their very personal life origin stories — that enhances our relationship with them.

12

Confronting Identity Issues

Every young person [is] . . . trying to play different roles, experiment with different looks and figure out who they are along
the way. I think for [some] . . . there is an awareness that they
don't really have the genetic information to do that kind of
sorting out of their identity. They are basing it on their family
of intimacy, their adoptive family, but that's not necessarily
where their abilities, interests and traits have come from.

— Dr. Joyce Maguire Pavao, adoption therapist[1]

General industry estimates are that each year there are roughly
125,000 adoptions involving U.S. families, and 30,000 conceptions using a donor. If that's true, and a reliable average, in a typical year more than 150,000 children become part of a family that
doesn't include both biological parents.

Of the donor-conceived children who are told the truth of their
origins (many are not; some learn or make the discovery later in
life), and the adopted children who have no contact with their
birth families, many will be curious about the missing pieces of
their history. Some will feel loss, anger, or resentment. Others will
be ambivalent, or show no particular interest.

No one knows why some kids feel compelled to learn about
their donor or birth family while others don't. In the case of donor
offspring, a child whose conception has been an open book since
birth is less likely to consider it a big deal compared to someone
who learned later in life. Many kids who report insemination as a

nonissue in their lives attribute it to the parents' up-front and casual attitude. But regarding insemination as a nonissue is not necessarily the same as not having curiosity.

Even those who are told early can grow up with identity-related questions that can manifest in three ways: (1) desire to understand more about genetic and medical history, (2) desire to know more about the unknown donor as a reflection of self, and (3) less commonly, but most powerfully when it occurs, the sense that knowing one's origins is a personal right, not the right of a parent who might have contracted it away or dismissed it as unimportant.

In the cases of those who care very deeply, some speculate that a parent who feels guilty might unwittingly prompt the child to feel deprived of something. A glance at the varied stories of children, however, reveals that there is no fixed pattern. At best, it's the unpredictable and uncontrollable temperament of a child that determines how deeply they look at questions of identity. As one donor-conceived adult told me, "How much of who I am can be traced to the DNA of a man I've never met?"

As we look in this chapter at the typical issues children face at stages of their life, and what Choice Mothers can do to help, I am grateful to the wisdom of many people, including the authors Diane Ehrensaft (author of *Mommies, Daddies, Donors, Surrogates: Answering Tough Questions and Building Strong Families*)[2] and David Brodzinsky (co-author of *Being Adopted: The Lifelong Search for Self*[3] and referred to throughout as Brodzinsky and colleagues). I've also learned many things from people involved in raising awareness about donor insemination issues — an effort that lags behind the adoption industry but is gaining ground — including Diane Allen of Infertility Network, Wendy Kramer of Donor Sibling Registry, and Olivia Montuschi of Donor Conception Network.

Why Do Kids Care?

Most parents understand why a child might want to know more about their genetic history. A growing number of parents have learned from the example of adoption, or from listening to donor-conceived adults, that the "right to know" issue can be powerful. But the common curiosity of kids to understand their origins as an extension of self is less understood.

We'll focus most of the energy of this chapter on the latter, as well as offering solutions for the parent and child to work on together.

The biggest misperception of a child's desire to know is that the child wants to establish a parental relationship with the donor or birth parent, or that seeking contact will weaken ties to the existing parent (especially if it's a nonbiological connection). I've interviewed many donor-conceived children and adults, as well as several adoptive children, and the pervasive urge they report is not to replace someone, but to add in a way meaningful to the child, by having the opportunity to ask questions that might seem unimportant to outsiders: Does my aptitude for math come from him? Do we like the same music? Is that where my big feet come from? For most, interest in the donor or birth parent doesn't usually start until the child is about 7, but maybe not until 12, as adolescent questioning begins, or 15, as teenage identity issues take shape, or much later as that child becomes a parent.

In addition to "who is he, or she (in the case of donor egg), and how much of me comes from that person?" children and adults face other nagging questions over time.

In the case of adoption, children naturally will wonder if they were to blame for the adoption, if their adoptive parents might also give them up, why their birth parents couldn't raise them, and if their adoptive parents will be hurt by questions about birth parents. Some kids will openly ask these questions, and some will not.

In the highly recommended book *Being Adopted*, Brodzinsky and colleagues point out that sometimes the internal search can manifest itself in unusual ways, such as a 7-year-old boy who seemed to stop blinking. Eventually it was discovered that he was afraid to blink in case he lost sight of his birth mother passing by on the street or on the TV screen.

In her excellent book for donor-conceived families, Ehrensaft writes that the unknown donor can sometimes be seen as a mythic hero or villain in a child's (and parent's) fantasies. Such as the daydream that a child's interest in piano might stem from an anonymous donor who is a musical genius. Or that the donor might try to steal the child away before the age of 18 if there was any contact before then. As I've heard from many sources, not talking about the donor as a regular human being (rather than a flawless individual, or a set of tissues, or a nobody that is never discussed) can lead to unhealthy delusions.

Many kids won't pursue a full-blown investigation of their origins, such as hiring a private investigator, or doing DNA testing for clues, or tracking down information from the donor profile. But they will wonder, and ask, what can be known about the stranger who helped them to exist. And often times this is when the Choice Mother realizes she wished she knew more.

The birth "other"

There are important differences between adopted children and donor-conceived offspring. In adoption, there is no biological connection between parent and child, there is no pregnancy process for the adoptive parent, and it is a live baby — rather than donor "material" — that is offered. Yet there are important similarities as well, which is why donor offspring are sometimes referred to as "half-adopted."

One important commonality for all Choice Moms is that there is a "birth other" in her child's life — a wonderful term coined by Ehrensaft in *Mommies, Daddies, Donors, Surrogates*. A birth other is the parent who places a child for adoption, whether in an open or closed situation. A birth other is the anonymous or known donor who provides the seed. Or the egg donor or surrogate who enables conception to happen. And, in the case of donor-conceived children, I would add to that list the half-siblings, created from a shared donor, that other families are raising.

Whether we acknowledge and talk about the birth other or not, whether we think that person is important to our family life or not, the basic fact is that people exist outside of our family who have a genetic connection to our child.

And while I would not go so far as to say that the birth other has a legal or emotional right to be part of our family life, I would say that the child will someday have the right to make up their own mind about whether they want to extend their definition of family to include birth others.

I've become friends with Shelly, a Choice Mom of two who adopted her African-American son, Max, in an open adoption. She maintains contact with her toddler's teenage birth father, swapping photos and phone calls on a regular basis. She has a letter from the young man, acknowledging how happy he is that they found a good mother and open home for Max, how sad he was that he couldn't provide the kind of home life that would be best, describing some of his interests, and ending with the heartfelt sentiment that he will always love and care about the boy. As Shelly has told me, "Now how can it be bad for Max to know that?"

I also know some Choice Moms who don't want to hear the donor number of other moms, for fear of discovering a half-sibling connection they don't want to pursue. I know one-half of a lesbian couple, who is opposed to letting their kids know that family friends used the same donor, because she doesn't want to complicate their definition of family. I know a woman who took away her teenage daughter's cell phone and Internet access after she made contact with a half-sibling.

For better or worse, depending on your perspective, we have no choice, as married couples do, but to be open with our kids about how they were brought into our life. And with that honesty comes the responsibility to grow up with them in their acknowledgement, acceptance, and curiosity about the birth other. As they get older, we might not agree with who they want to bring into their circle, but it is my strong view that trying to control it does a disservice to the parent-child bond.

Ehrensaft, in fact, points out that so much attention is paid to the potential damage of telling or not telling the child details about his or her origins, we lose sight of it as a growth-enhancing and positive experience that builds trust, respect, and a shared curiosity between parent and child.

The Donor Insemination Industry Debate

> We have an infertility industry that is built on the desire for biological connections, and then these same people turn around and tell the kids that biological connections do not matter.
>
> — Susan, a donor-conceived adult
> who is using a donor to conceive

A child's right to know his or her genetic legacy can arouse intense emotions, on both sides of the debate. Many of the most vocal are those who learned late in life that their genetic inheritance is not from the parents who raised them, and parents who are afraid of losing the opportunity to build a family. This is a lesson that people in the adoption community started to understand a few decades ago. But the donor insemination industry is still catching up. Many married couples, for example, are not advised that telling the child the truth is considered by most mental health experts to be the best policy.

Confusing the debate is the notion of whether a child's right to know necessarily leads to invasion of the donor's privacy.

After an *Oprah* segment aired in 2003 about donor offspring, viewers commented at great length on a website message board. Wrote one woman, "The sperm donor is just like the parent who adopts out a child. He deserves his privacy."

Another concurred, saying, "I think it's dangerous to say the donor's privacy is less important than the right of the child to know his or her parentage. Saying that sperm and egg donors must be willing to meet the children later is forcing an issue that would cause many people to refuse to become part of the donor programs. As someone who doesn't have the ability to have a child with my husband, I prefer having as many options as possible."

Although many agree that giving a donor the right to choose whether or not to remain anonymous is fair, some feel that a child's right to know should outweigh that choice. Others fear that children who cannot get access to their donor will resent the fact that others can.

As one woman wrote, "The only person who didn't agree to anything at the time of anonymous DI is the child, and that child should be the one who decides whether or not to contact the biological father. I have a child from anonymous DI and he has a very loving dad, but that doesn't negate the fact that he still wants to know who his biological father is and what he's like."

Wrote another: "Medical info taken at the time of [donation] is sometimes useless. As an adoptee who adores my family, I must say that it is time that society quit denying us birth rights of our identity, in all of its complexity."

And another: "I am adopted. I love my family. The only thing I can advise someone who is considering sperm donation is: Please think about what the needs of your child might later become. I am 35 and still stuck with answers I will never have."

What Is the Identity Issue?

An adoptee who successfully searched for her heritage said that looking for her biological connections was not to replace her parents, but to complete the picture of identity, and to "get the answers every other kid has."

Comments and comparisons about how children look like their parents will follow the offspring throughout life. The process by which an adoptee or DI child comes into his or her family will leave gaps of knowledge that most people take for granted, and may leave the individual feeling cheated. As the adoptee said, "When I found my birth family, I got many of the missing pieces. My birth family had many parts to my identity that I needed in order to move on and feel confident about who I was, where I came from."

When Christine, the 18-year-old daughter of a Choice Mom, was allowed by the sperm bank contract to get in touch with her donor, one of the first things she asked him was whether he had big feet. "I knew it," she exclaimed excitedly into the phone when he said yes. Her next question was whether his sense of humor sometimes got him into trouble, as hers did.[4]

Not pressing questions, perhaps, but for this enthusiastic young woman, the need to attribute certain unexplained traits to her mysterious donor had been strong since the age of 10.

Others have written that children who do not know both biological parents sometimes grow up struggling with "a sense of unreality, of not being born properly, not being real."[5]

To better understand this tendency — sometimes known as "genealogical bewilderment," two British researchers, A. J. Turner and A. Coyle, solicited the perspectives of adult donor offspring who were members of support networks, and reported their findings in *Human Reproduction*.[6] Said one adult they talked to, "I needed to know whose face I was looking at in the mirror. I needed to know who I was and how I came to be. It was a very primal and unrelenting force which propelled the search, and it was inescapable and undeniable."

Others expressed feelings of being part of a science experiment. One woman bluntly stated that "some stranger masturbated into a glass vial and I'm the result."

Susan, the donor-conceived adult we met in chapter 8 who learned of her origins at the age of 27, told me that none of the roughly 50 donor-conceived people she knows of in an online community are happy about donor anonymity. "It is pretty powerful to me that absolutely no one in the group feels that it's 'okay' that they cannot find out who their biological fathers are. No one feels that this is right or fair. All of us feel that something has been taken from us."

Of course, people who seek out support networks tend to have something they are trying to confront and heal. Many kids don't grow up feeling the issues as intensely. According to the U.S. Census Bureau, 5 million people listed in the 2000 census were adopted (1.5 million of them under the age of 18). Despite such high numbers, relatively few seem to be reporting major identity issues.

But whether or not they seek answers and resolutions actively, all children start to ponder who they are by comparing themselves to the people who helped create them. A report available from the Committee on Early Childhood, Adoption and Dependent Care of the American Academy of Pediatrics indicates that interest in biological heritage is healthy.[7]

An Anonymous Donor and Offspring Meet

As part of my Voices of Donor Conception book series, as well as ongoing talks with Choice Moms, I've become acquainted with many stories of meetings among half-siblings and between offspring and donors. One of these stories involves a young man who has made contact with his anonymous donor. The two have met on several occasions, even including an extended visit with the donor's parents.

As the young man, who I will call Ted, has told me, meeting the donor has not only satisfied his curiosity about who the mysterious biological father was, but has enabled him to look in the face of the person responsible for half his genetic history, hear him talk, make comparisons with himself, and know that yes, he had similarities with another human being that hadn't been taught.

For example, it was a strange sort of satisfaction Ted got simply noticing that he and the donor had the same way of stretching after meals or when bored. An odd pose that Ted did several times in the day, arms in the air, elbows in each hand, curling first to this side and then the other. Not necessarily something a geneticist would look for, or an earth-shattering insight that would affect Ted's life, but interesting just the same.

Their voices sound alike, they answer questions in similar ways, they have the same laugh. Ted had always known the things he had in common with his mother, but now he was able to find parts of himself in another person who was an important part of who he is. For him, it didn't fill a profound gap so much as give a greater sense of connection with the parallel universe of people that were part of his lineage. It gave him a sense of relaxation, to now have a face and name for an essential aspect of his being. No longer was he lost, or invisible, to a side of his own genetic family.

Importantly, Ted did not at all feel like he had found a missing parent. This is one of the most common misperceptions about seeking out birth others. In fact, he reported feeling even closer to his mother, who supported his decision to meet his donor.

There is also an almost laughable misunderstanding by the general public of why offspring seek out donors. After it was reported in *New Science* that a teenager used the Internet and DNA to trace his donor, online comments ranged from:

> Why would you want to know where the sperm came from? I'm pretty sure it has everything to do with the kid needing money. Still, who the hell cares? You're alive, be grateful!

> Isn't that the reason why all these people try to find out who their real parents are? Hoping to score some gold . . . that's why.

> The next call the father will receive is from a lawyer demanding past child support.

That kid is screwed up. Why would he want to know who his dad was? The "dad" doesn't want to find some "son" that he never knew. What is the "dad" going to say to his son? This isn't like a lost baby caused by adoption. It's just a sperm donation. Or is that what this "son" hopes to do. Find this sperm donor "dad" and have him give him a hug and have him say, "Oh, I'm so glad you found me. Now we can be father and son forever."

Ted, like most donor-conceived offspring I've talked to, has no interest in acquiring a father, or an inheritance. Although a few of his talks with the donor did involve general advice, it felt much more to him like that of a male role model attempting to share wisdom than as any kind of surreal father-son conversation. A parenting role, Ted understood even at a younger age, is something that is earned, not simply granted by virtue of birth connection.

In fact, the more stories like these that I collect, the more I can report that it is the sharing of fundamental childhood experiences, pivotal life moments, and meaningful rituals that unite people, even more than genetic characteristics. "Family" is people who choose to embrace each other for what they share. Whether it is soldiers who battle together, partners on the police force, high school classmates who reunite every five years, cousins who gather together for Thanksgiving every year.

There is a profound difference between wanting to understand and absorb your roots, and wanting to remake your community. Some half-siblings who have met find an energy in their kinship and commit to building a relationship; others simply satisfy curiosity, swap notes about similarities, and move on.

But whether new bonds are created or not isn't the point. Sometimes children seeking answers to questions of identity are simply looking for reassurance, the calm that comes from knowing what was once unknowable, and feeling more in control of their own origin story. Sometimes it is very much about being able to "own" the information about whose lives created theirs, which most kids believe should belong to them — not simply relegated to a closed file folder among thousands in some storage center.

Typical Ages and Stages

No matter how a child is conceived or whether he or she is adopted, every child ponders similar questions at certain ages, as we saw in the previous chapter about answering the daddy question. Understanding normal developmental stages will help the Choice Mother understand what questions her child is trying to resolve — especially helpful when the answers are harder to come by.

Most Choice Mothers start telling the birth story to their child at a very young age, before the words are even comprehensible, which builds a sense of attachment and trust, and avoids the "shock factor" that can come if the story is delayed until later.

No matter how many times the story is told, the meaning of it doesn't usually start to sink in until the age of 4 or 5. Some children, for example, will assume everyone comes from a donor or is adopted.

Preschoolers do start to recognize racial differences, even if they don't understand how it came to be. Children in multiethnic families, for example, start to react early to differences in skin color and hair type, sometimes attempting to paint their skin or change their hair color in an attempt to look more similar to their parents.

Many young donor-conceived children, interviewed in a study we'll learn more about later in this chapter, believe their donors were unable to marry and have children of their own, so gave up part of themselves.

Children don't have the context to understand what their origin story means to their life until about the age of 6 or 7. In early childhood, they define family as whoever lives in the house. They don't see biological connection as a factor, and don't realize that blood relationships are a common part of the family definition. Children initially might feel special about being "chosen" by their parents, but often will feel less positive over time when the process is more fully understood, sometimes via peers.[8]

After they are old enough to understand basic biology (seed and egg), it will be easier to help them understand the distinction between "bio dad" or "donor dad" and the term "father." This is when it becomes more useful to have conversations that let them know the donor is a real person who helped to bring them into the world.[9]

When context starts to set in

After the age of 6, children start to feel odd or confused about being different from peers or family. They begin to understand that blood connections exist with people not living in their family. Some become more reticent about discussing their origins.

This is when a lack of similarity with parents — especially in multiethnic families — can be disconcerting to a child (and sometimes even to a parent). Or when family tree assignments at school can confuse a child.

Brodzinsky and colleagues tell the story of a 6-year-old black child who was adopted by a white couple. He noticed that other black children in his kindergarten class had black parents, and the white children had white parents. "Am I black or white?" he asked. After he was reminded of his adoption story, he replied, "I know that, but I still don't know if I'm supposed to be black or white."

Some children embrace the emerging awareness of their origins as part of their self-identity. At the age of 6, one donor-conceived son started introducing himself to others enthusiastically as a "donor baby." As his mother explained to me, it was simply part of how he identified himself. As a teenager, he continued to see his origins positively and as a unique part of who he was.

At this stage of life, children begin to understand not only the "family building" concepts their parents have explained to them, but they also independently recognize the correlating factor of "family loss." That to be proudly placed or created within their family, someone else had to give them away.

Donor-conceived children go through the same processing steps as adopted children, although the comprehension of their story will vary at this age. A preteen is not likely to put the picture together of how their conception differs from that of others — that a relationship between a man and woman tends to be the preferred way to bring a child into the world.

Grieving is a natural part of the process. Some grieve quietly and for a brief time. Some deny and avoid their feelings. Some welcome opportunities to talk about them. Some become infused with a mask of bravado and oppositional behavior. Some will concoct fantasies, such as the girl who thought a Hollywood star she resembled was her birth mother.

The young child who shows little interest is not guaranteed to feel the same ambivalence at 14. The job of the parent is to keep in step with the child — not push for interest that is not there, and not ignore questions that are. Setting the stage for openness is the goal.

Many children naturally begin to feel envious and jealous of others, and this is especially true of those who feel their origin story makes them "different." They might struggle with feeling unconnected from their "normal" friends, or that something important has been denied them. Their self-esteem can suffer if they feel ashamed or are teased, unwittingly or purposefully, by peers.

One piece of advice for developing healthy self-esteem comes from the pages of the behavioral theorist Erik Erikson. He said the middle childhood years (between 6 and 12) need to offer a sense of mastery.[10] How children cope with the natural sense of grief and loss about their origins can be influenced at this age by how well they feel they are able to have an impact on their surroundings.

Brodzinsky and colleagues wrote that, as difficult as it is for parents to watch their children try to deal with emotions related to their origin story, "They can do nothing to spare them. They can,

---

Empowering Your Child
From: Wendy, cofounder of Donor Sibling Registry

✦ When my son was 7 and curious about his donor, I encouraged him to write the sperm bank so he wouldn't feel powerless. He wrote a cute letter to "Dear Hospital," saying he would appreciate hearing from them if they had any information, even if he had to wait until he was 18 to get it. We slowly started putting a profile together, like pieces of a puzzle. (I didn't even know the ethnic background of the donor.) Together we've found ways to help him feel proactive.

---

however, help ease the process by providing a supportive, nurturing environment in which the emotional storms of grieving can be weathered."

That means being available to listen, to put emotions into words, to accept sadness and anger as part of the process. The idea is to be there nonjudgmentally in the ups and downs so that the child develops trust, as well as the understanding that emotions are normal, short-term, and allowed.

Inevitable questions of independence
In late adolescence, no longer is right and wrong a matter of what gets punished, as it is with young children. And no longer is it defined by behavior that wins approval from others, as it is in preteen years. Starting around the age of 12 or 13, young people feel they can set standards in their own unique way. Young adolescents begin to pull away from authority, especially parents, in order to make discoveries about who they are in relation to other people. Friendships become intense, and conformity to peers is more important than ever.

Note that Erikson coined the term "identity crisis" to describe the intense analysis and experimentation with different ideas of self that is acutely felt in the teenage years. He believed that each stage of life involves a conflict between two directions. When the struggle is resolved, its inherent issues recede in importance — although never completely disappear — and the individual moves on to the next stage. One of the most important of the seven phases, he felt, is the Identity stage.

Teenagers tend to test what they are "given" with what they are able to create. (One's inherited hair color, for example, might be considered in a shade of purple.) Appearance, temperament, strengths, weaknesses, and values tend to be inherited in many ways, and teens are uniquely intent on trying variations on the themes until they are able, ideally, to commit to a particular identity that suits them.

It is a very confusing, open-ended time of inner conflict, and many experts feel it goes easier if the teen has a strong sense of what has actually been inherited — where the roots are. Like the toddler who starts to walk away from Mom, yet keeps looking over the shoulder for reassurance that she's still there, the identity crisis of teenagers often requires a solid attachment as a starting point. (Erikson himself was very Scandinavian in appearance, yet raised Jewish, and didn't feel he fit in with either group, which apparently fueled his strong interest in identity issues.)

The impact of being adopted or donor-conceived can take an added significance during these inner-focused years, when the child is searching for clues about who they are, who they will be, who they relate to, who is important to them. Some teens will consider their missing pieces to be intriguing, while others will find it unsettling. Some will consider themselves special in a positive or pioneering way, while the self-esteem of others will be affected negatively. Some will build fantasies, while others will distance themselves from the idea.

Sometimes our children will become angry teenagers who resent being created from a stranger's seed. But more commonly, as that child moves into adulthood and pursues career interests that seem unrelated to Mom, or becomes a parent, or wonders whether to monitor for heart disease or cancer, the concerns about identity will be more gentle and nuanced.

What can you do to help?

Sometimes a confused teenager might act out in disruptive ways as a way to test out what the unknown inheritance might be. Discovering more information about the missing players of his or her life can help simplify the usual age-appropriate task of separating from family, simply by giving a more well-rounded image of what to separate from. In the case of adoption, a trip can be taken to the birthplace, or to the agency that helped to facilitate placement. In the case of donor insemination, contact with the sperm bank can sometimes be helpful in learning more information.

Brodzinsky and colleagues recommend two-way correspondence between child and missing donor, written by the child. It gives the child an opportunity to express emotions, fantasies, frustrations about the unknowns — as well as to imagine the perspective of the other party. Sometimes this helps foster acceptance and understanding.

Adult comprehension

The sense of loss can be even more intense when the child is a young adult, especially when considering having his or her own children, or getting involved in intimate relationships. Young adults may feel that part of themselves is missing, that there is an unfilled void. Some recognize this as being part of the nature of having unanswered questions about their history — others don't know what to attribute it to.

Brodzinsky and colleagues reported the stories of new parents who suffered unexpected emotional pain with the birth of a child, many of them confronting for the first time the absence of their own genetic links. Some pregnant women worry about hereditary surprises that might occur. Some parents find themselves jealous that their child knows more about his or her physical and behavioral history than they themselves did. Some grieve not having the same bond with both birth parents that their child has.

Despite the committed support of family throughout childhood, sometimes children can still grow up with an irrational and unarticulated view of being abandoned or rejected. They might decide, for example, that they aren't worth being committed to.

Some donor-conceived children have reported feeling a loss about being created in a sterile environment from a commodity that was bought and sold. This stark view was offered by an unhappy woman conceived by donor sperm, as excerpted from literature available from the Infertility Network: "My biological father was paid for his 'services.' I feel like a product. I was sold, bought, frozen, and defrosted. I feel illegitimate and manufactured. My mother paid for the little vial containing 50 percent of my genetic material. Most people enter this world freely; my conception was contractual, a mere transaction between two strangers. I regard it as putting a price on the value of my creation, my existence. It's dehumanizing and degrading."

What does it all mean?
The conflicts brought up here are not intended to dissuade anyone from adopting or using a donor. And certainly, if you already are a Choice Mother, the idea is not to beat yourself up about particular choices made. Rather, it is hoped that the parent who consciously wants to understand and assist her child through the inevitable stages of development can learn from the experience of those who have had identity issues, particularly those who were placed for adoption or conceived from a donor.

In the next pages, we will focus separately on the donor-conceived child and the adopted child for perspectives and advice particular to their origins. Also included is a section on building a multiethnic family, as well as the story of someone who sought out and found his anonymous donor.

Harvard-Educated Adult
Conceived with an Unknown Donor
From: Rebecca

✦ As a young adult, it is sometimes very difficult to cope with the feeling of sheer helplessness about not being able to obtain information about my donor. Lines of inquiry through doctors and the hospital have all been fruitless.

People say I should simply be happy that an anonymous man's donation enabled me to exist, because if it wasn't for him I wouldn't be here. I worked with displaced populations in Sudan. I interviewed women in camps who were traumatized beyond recognition and yet who still chose life over nonexistence. The desire to exist does not mean you need to be content about the conditions of that life.

People tell me that I am special because my parents wanted me so much. But lots of children are wanted by their parents. Being wanted is not a substitute for having access to one's full identity.

People tell me that perhaps if I met my biological father I wouldn't like him anyway, and that many people who know their fathers wish they didn't. Give me that option.

The Donor-Conceived Child

For her doctorate in psychology from Yeshiva University, Elizabeth Groisser did in-depth interviews with 22 children, ages 5 to 10, who were conceived by Choice Mothers using donor insemination. All of the children had mothers who were open with them about their conception at an early age. My thanks to her for allowing me to excerpt her findings from the dissertation she completed in 2003.[11]

Imagined characteristics — Many children considered donors to be adult versions of themselves. One 7-year-old boy believed his donor worked at a company that made Nintendo and Gameboy "'cause I like electronics and if you have people in your family, or that helped, you kind of like the same things." Others attribute traits they cannot find in the mother to the donor. One 10-year-old said she must have inherited her swimming ability from the donor because her mother "hates cold water" and doesn't like to swim.

Imagined relationships — An 8-year-old boy said his donor would allow him to have a pet snake or lizard, that he would have a beard and be very cool, and he would do anything with him except girly stuff. A 6-year-old girl imagined her donor to have red hair and red overalls. She wished she knew his name since then "it would feel like he was here." Another 6-year-old girl called her donor her "fake dad," and described him in great (and largely made-up) detail. She then said he was like a man she saw on the news with dark glasses, hat, and a microphone, "and I would say, oh brother, that guy looks like my dad, and one day I would find out he was my dad."

Ambivalence — Others are much less attached emotionally to the idea of their donor, and prefer to avoid the topic. One 7-year-old corrected the interviewer who referred to his donor as "dad." Some said they were too busy to think about the donor. One 6-year-old girl had a detailed image of her donor as a photographer (which was a known detail from the sperm bank). But she was clear that she didn't want to meet him because he was "not part of my family and not part of my life," and said that the letter *f* reminded her of him — because it was part of the word *father* but not the whole thing.

Another 6-year-old girl alternated using distancing mechanisms in the conversation — saying she believed he ran in marathons like she would like to; that he had curly hair like hers, although she had just straightened her hair; and that he was "a million years old," but she would like to meet him. One boy said his donor was like the middle of a ball you couldn't get to, but said he didn't want to know more about him because he wasn't going to meet him or "be what he is."

Understanding insemination — Most of the children described their donors as nice men who gave their mother sperm or seed so they could be born. Some attributed this to the desire of the man to help other people, others thought it was because he couldn't find anyone to marry and so had to give up his sperm. One 7-year-old boy believed his donor to be brave because he had to have surgery to give up pieces of his body. Several children were unclear about the process, and believed it to be an invasive procedure. Some believed that after the donor gave his sperm he could never get married and have his own children. One imaginative boy believed he once lived in a different mom, died, his spirit rose up and collided with an alien ship, then came back to earth as a spirit in sperm that went into his mother.

Factors influencing a child's reaction

Most of the single mothers interviewed as part of Groisser's research project had a permissive attitude about allowing their child to meet the donor (even though most of the sperm banks did not offer that option), which likely contributed to their child feeling free to understand the donor as a real person. Many of the Choice Moms provided the child with known details about the donor's appearance, occupation, education, hobbies, and ethnicity. One mother of 10-year-old twin boys worked with her sons on projects tracing the ethnic background of the donor.

In a literature review, Groisser included the story of a 7-year-old boy conceived to a couple with donor sperm. His parents did not talk about what they knew about the donor. Perhaps as a result, the boy believed that the unknown donor could steal him away, which is why he needed to remain hidden until he was 18. Eventually this family was convinced that it was healthy to encourage their son's imagination about the donor, in order to build a "family romance" together.[12]

Another factor thought to be important in the children's feelings about their donor was having male role models to help them understand men on a real level, rather than as fantasy or negative influence.

One researcher speculated that some mothers deny the existence of the donor, thinking of him as nothing more than a vial of sperm, perhaps to avoid acknowledging feelings of "shame, loss, and disappointment." Other women might construct the donor as a glorified member of the family who completes a picture, often resulting in an unhealthy fantasy for the child that this wonderful man might someday show up. In either case, the children might end up with negative feelings about insemination, as did one 10-year-old boy who said, "Nice man, yeah, right. I bet you he just did it for the money."[13]

Groisser also quotes the Wellesley College researcher Rosanna Hertz, who we met earlier in this book. Hertz discovered that Choice Moms who used donors — both anonymous and known — tend to create a picture of the father as the child grows to give him or her a broader sense of genetic kinship. She wrote that this "ghost father" image is important to validate the child's sense of self.[14]

Hertz concluded that the mother needs to acknowledge and embrace elements of her child that derive from the donor. In so doing, the child can avoid feeling rejected by a genetic father, and can feel he or she was produced from a human being rather than from a "deconstructed part of a man."

Be a role model in telling the story
Someday the donor-conceived child will be telling other people about her origins, and answering questions from others. The way

the parent tells the story — to loved ones as well as strangers — will be the model for how the child responds someday. Elizabeth Carr, who was the first U.S. baby conceived through in vitro fertilization, was 7 when she finally understood how much effort her parents went through in order to conceive her, according to an excellent American Fertility Association online fact sheet.[15] She says that every parent who uses unusual means to have a child must be prepared to handle the child's eventual reaction to it. For her, it hasn't been a negative experience, she says, because her parents never communicated her origins as something different or abnormal. "If the parents are comfortable and can talk to the child openly, then I don't think the child will have any problems," she said.

Most Choice Moms find themselves telling the conception story to their child by the age of 3. Some start the story earlier, so that the words become comfortable by the time the child is more aware of them. Many kids want to hear the story again and again. A few children ask practical questions about the donor, such as "Does he have a family?" "Why can't I know his name?" Other parents report their children give no real response or reaction to the story. Both reactions are common.

Seven-year-old Helen would like to meet her donor someday, and doesn't mind not having a father since she likes getting all of Mom's attention. But as her Choice Mom told me, the difficulty for Helen is "when other children ask questions that she finds hard to answer. She tried to explain donor insemination to them, but said they didn't understand because they didn't know what sperm was."

When kids get teased, some parents report that it doesn't seem to bother their children as much as being kidded about their hairstyles or sports prowess.[16]

A 14-year-old girl reported that a friend once threatened during an argument to tell everyone in school about her donor-conceived status and that it meant that she didn't have a father. Although her friend's threat (not carried out) was upsetting, the girl said she was able to withstand it without feeling self-conscious "because of the way I have been raised to believe in myself."

What can you do to help?

1. Whether you choose an open-identity donor or not (this question is explored in chapter 8), my advice is that you have a method for determining which donor you choose, to someday help your child respect the fact that there was, indeed, a process you went through to create his or her unique self.

2. If you've used an open-identity donor, be sure the child recognizes that there is no guarantee that he will be reachable, and that they probably won't have a relationship, but that he or she is entitled to know as much about this person as the two of you can find together.

3. Especially if you don't have much information about the donor himself, consider gathering articles and videotapes of shows about donor insemination, for your own special library collection you can offer to your child. Acknowledge that it might be difficult to have unanswered questions — just as it's sometimes difficult to not have a father — and that together you are creating a family with a loving network of friends and relatives.

4. Create a life/family book, described in the next section.

The Adopted Child

As we've already discussed, adopted children might be ashamed of their origins, or angry about not having a simpler, more "normal" story to share with others. These emotions will often appear periodically over the child's lifetime, and can hit hardest anytime after about the age of 10.

Particularly in the middle childhood years, these growing problem solvers might begin to ponder other choices that might have been made. Brodzinsky and colleagues quote children of this age who suggest:

> *"If she didn't know how to be a mommy, then someone should have taught her. She should have gone to school to learn, then it wouldn't have happened."*

> *"If she didn't have enough money to keep me, why didn't she get a job?"*

> *"I often wonder why she and my first dad didn't get married. Together they probably would have been able to keep me. That gets me angry, that my first dad probably just left and didn't care enough to try."*

One Choice Mom told me her 7-year-old daughter tends to ask questions such as: Do you think my birth mother is all right? Does she miss me? She rarely asked about simple biographical details, such as favorite color or food. "The sophistication of her questions is amazing to me when you realize she is 7 and thinking about these things already. I wonder about the questions she isn't asking me."

Although every adopted child wonders about the birth parents, few take the step — even as adults — to mount an actual search for information or contact. On the other hand, one man gave this reason for his search: "I want to stop running from life, to feel complete, to stop looking at every stranger wondering if I'm related, to settle my self-image anxiety."

Often the search is triggered by a life event, such as a marriage, birth of a child, or death of an adoptive parent. It usually has nothing to do with dissatisfaction with family members, and tends to be a much more personal quest about self.

What can you do to help?
Even if the questions and confusions cannot be avoided, there are proactive steps that parents can take to help an adopted child em-

brace the knowns and unknowns of his or her past. Suggestions from a variety of adoption experts, particularly Lee Varon (author of *Adopting on Your Own*, which we discussed in chapter 9) include:

1. Provide the child with as much information as possible about the birth family and culture, the circumstances of the adoption, and other available details (without making them up).

2. Through your example, help your child learn how to answer prying questions such as: What happened to her parents? Why did they "give up" the child? One Choice Mom was rudely asked, in front of her daughter, how much she had to pay for her. The trick is to be matter-of-fact, nondefensive, and, if possible, humorous when dealing with questions that are no one else's business. The excellent Maryland-based Center for Adoption Support and Education offers several proactive guidebooks about educating teachers and others about the adoptive experience (See www.adoptionsupport.org).

3. Make a life/family book. A life book tells the story of where the child was before placement, as well as the story of the adoption. It can include photos, souvenirs or information about the birth country, family history, religious history, birth information, letters from birth parents, special events, stories, and the parent's early memories of the child and important people in the birth country. It can include thoughts and emotions about events (especially meeting the child for the first time), description of the parent's own childhood and process of becoming a parent, information about the birth parents, and first-day stories.[17]

4. Update your vocabulary. Varon includes a list of positive and negative terms in her book. In reading over the list, I realized that my "old" vocabulary was tied to the language

used in the 1960s, when my brother was adopted, and is quite out of date. For example, it is a *birth* parent, not a "real" parent, who decides to *terminate parental rights* or *make an adoption plan,* rather than "give up" a child. The birth parent does not decide whether to "keep" the child, but whether to *parent.* If the *child in need of a family* (not an "available" child) decides *to locate* or *to contact* the birth parents someday, this is not referred to as "tracking down" the *biological relatives* (not "natural" or "blood" relatives).[18]

The Transracial Family

According to 2000 U.S. census information, 17 percent of the 1.5 million adopted children under the age of 18 were a different race than that of the head of their household.[19] That makes for a lot of multicultural families.

It should never be the goal in a multiethnic family to leave the child's cultural references in the past, and effectively force the child to think of himself or herself as "white." That is a supreme disservice to the child, akin to asking him or her to pretend to be of the opposite sex.

Experts say that adopting across racial or cultural lines requires parents to no longer think of themselves as a "black" or "white" family, but as a multiethnic family. This requires meaningful inclusion of cultural traditions and events into the family, such as interaction with others from the same background, celebration of holidays, and perhaps trips to the originating country.

This is not to say, however, that all children will welcome and react to the multiethnic component in the same way. Some kids will be reassured by the interactions. Others will be less confident, or confused or conflicted about identity issues.

Transracial families can encounter unusual challenges. Tips for dealing with them, from a variety of experts, include:

1. Do not ignore the fact of racism and discrimination, but attempt to define and explain it in ways your child might understand.
2. Work out possible responses to prejudice with your child, emphasizing the protection of his or her rights. Methods should include both confrontation and avoidance, as well as occasional intervention and advocacy by Mom as a model.
3. Actively seek out role models from the child's community, and proactively embrace diversity yourself. Consider relocating to a more diverse neighborhood or school. (And note that living in a multiethnic neighborhood is not the same as having members of the child's particular culture available — such as a sports coach, or manager of a favorite store or restaurant.)
4. Together seek out greater understanding of your child's cultural history. See chapter 9 for the ways a Choice Mother of two has incorporated her daughters' Chinese heritage into their daily life.
5. Make sure your child grows up feeling proud of his or her culture, but also independent of it. The goal is to identify with members of the community, and not be ashamed about being part or apart from the culture.
6. Be sensitive to the religious background of your child, and be willing to observe services or find a mentor who will accompany your child.

One excellent article about raising a child of another race was written by Jana Wolff for *Adoptive Families*.[20] As she wrote, she finally realized that she could never completely master transracial parenting, simply because she and her husband would never be their child's color or part of his cultural heritage.

She wrote about sitting through a Sunday morning service in an all-black Baptist church. "Sure, Ari got to see lots of lovely and friendly black families, but since we are Jewish we could never truly belong to a different religious community. We have since learned to customize our family traditions so they fit our particular combination of cultures. One December, when Kwanzaa and Hanukkah overlapped, we hosted a Kwanzukah party, which has since become a tradition bringing together our African-American and Jewish friends."

She reported that transracial parenting requires becoming more boldly public, such as asking men of color for clues on how to raise their son. And that above all, it requires understanding that ultimately the job of identity formation becomes the child's. "Parents can nourish young kids with healthy foods, but young adults pick their own menus. We hope that when that time of searching for himself comes, Ari's early experiences will resonate with a deep meaning. We also want Ari to know how much we care about who he is, as a unique individual."

Many Choice Mothers of multicultural families have been careful to move to a more diverse community. This is a good step — although it doesn't resolve every issue. One such mother I talked to discovered years after moving that her tough-minded daughter had not been telling her that other girls were taunting her because she was middle class and they were not.

More than anything, this mother told me, it was the race difference between parent and child that became a focus of attention for her daughter over time. Of little or no consequence was being raised by a single parent, the basic fact of being adopted, or missing the presence of a father in the home. "She was fascinated by our different skin colors, our different hair textures, our different religious backgrounds."

Through it all, Mom followed her daughter's lead, allowing her to become attuned to issues of ethnicity in her own way. "I didn't make a big deal of it, I just exposed her to it in whatever ways I could." Today, cultural differences are a big part of her daughter's life. She has lived in and traveled to a variety of countries and is in-

terested in cultural anthropology and identity. Although she struggled greatly with some issues growing up, she is now a highly dynamic and active young woman.

Final Thoughts

As we know from our own childhoods, every child will grow
up with issues. The Choice Mom should be prepared to be yelled
at by her child someday for the way he or she was added to the
family. If you are confident in your decision, however, it will be
easier to accept the tirade and not feel threatened by it. Providing
the child with as much truthful information as you can about inherited traits and characteristics can alleviate a child's sense of dis-
connectedness. And respecting the need to know can go a long way
toward helping a child cope with any identity crises.

As Anne Bernstein (whom we met in the previous chapter) has
written: "The most important factor in children's psychological
adjustment to the circumstances of his origins is how parents feel
about how they formed a family. A parent who can discuss these
issues matter-of-factly and without defensiveness, who is open to a
child's questions about key figures in her conception and birth, will
foster the child's positive self-regard."[21]

Santa Monica–based clinical psychologist Elaine Gordon[22] also
told me about the importance of welcoming open discussion of a
child's biological origins. Speaking about donor insemination, she
said, "Hopefully the acknowledgement of there being a father is
answered and discussed both from the genetic and social perspective. One of the most destructive things I see in my practice is that
single women, both lesbian and straight, will sometimes try to
deny the existence of a father, which is not in the best interest of
the child. Children want to be like everyone else, and were born
like everyone else, albeit into different circumstances."

Whether you are the parent to an adopted or donor-conceived
child, there are several steps you can take to help your child.

1. Build strong family connections and rituals, especially if the child indicates a sense of feeling abandoned or rejected.

2. Use family consultations as part of the decision-making process, especially if the child expresses a need for a better sense of control.

3. Ensure the child feels able to talk easily and openly in the home about identity issues or his or her origins.

4. Form friendships with other families with similar histories so that the kids grow up knowing others with diverse backgrounds.

5. Embrace the origin story in a matter-of-fact way, rather than treating it as unimportant. Discuss it casually — but openly — with friends and teachers as needed until the child is ready to handle it in his or her own way.

6. Be an advocate. Varon wrote about a woman whose adopted son came home in tears after his class starting doing a family-tree assignment. The woman realized that she needed to be proactive on behalf of her child. "Part of this involved sharing information about adoption and single-parent families rather than blaming other people for not having taken the time to do this work," the woman told Varon.[23]

7. Respect the child's privacy. Tread softly on advocacy, however, based on your child's comfort zone. By the age of 6, some children are reluctant to disclose their story to others. Ask before sharing a life book or initiating public discussions. By the age of 10, many children are deciding whether or how to disclose the story.

8. Other kids might not retell your child's origin story the way you or your child prefer. Be prepared to help your child with self-consciousness about loss of privacy if curiosity compels peers to ask personal questions. Often the most awkward stage (about anything) is between the ages of 10 and 14. It's best to arm them — with your example of poise, confidence, and words — before the age of 10. After that, they will likely want you to butt out.

13

How to Raise a Well-Balanced Child

The ambitious cultural shift I am hoping for is this: that adults come to view appreciating and being generous to others, acting with fairness and integrity, and formulating mature and resilient ideals as evolving and subtle capacities. This shift is especially important for adults who are becoming parents. For parenting itself is clearly a prime instance when adults are faced with hugely complex challenges to their core moral qualities: their capacity for empathy and fairness, their ability to disentangle their own interests from those of others, their generosity.

— Richard Weissbourd, essay in *The American Prospect*[1]

It is a daunting task for any couple to raise a healthy, well-balanced child. It can be even more challenging for a single parent, since there is no solid partner available to help alleviate stress, play "good cop, bad cop" in matters of discipline and enforcement, and provide a child with two different sets of skills, perspectives, and networks of family and friends.

As we read in previous chapters, growing up in a single-parent home, without a biological father, can affect a child. But as we also read, good parenting requires skills and supplements that are not exclusive to married couples.

The challenge of any parent is to find the time to create and implement a vision — a strategy for molding a confident, hopeful, and happy moral character out of the little personality you have been given. After that baby enters the house, parenting can easily dissolve into a daily struggle to earn, nurture, enjoy, discipline, and stress.

On the front end, we are consumed asking ourselves if we're prepared to be Choice Mothers. The middle years of parenthood involve an even longer list of questions. Is this the right child-care provider? Why won't he sleep? Shouldn't she be talking more by now? Why won't he eat? Am I letting her watch too much TV? Is he becoming resentful about not having a dad? Is she doing well enough at school? How do I get him to talk about what is bothering him? Should I trust her to go out with her friends un-chaperoned?

A mother loves her child like no one else, yet in the end, after the child is grown, after we breathe a heavy sigh as the door closes and she eagerly departs for college and family and friends of her own making, what will our years of questions and hard work have added up to? How will our child turn out? Will we have raised a well-balanced person?

One of the basic needs of any individual is to feel connected to a larger universe. Our well-being depends on it. And our children will increasingly look to this wider universe for their lifetime of meaningful experiences and relationships. How will they do when they are navigating on their own? How will we have prepared them? Will they embrace their future with hope and optimism? Will they be able to commit to intimate relationships? Will they achieve goals, respect others, act responsibly?

This, after all, ends up being what the stuff of successful parenting is. More than whether they were breastfed or bottle-fed, cared for in a daycare center or a home, out the door on time with hair combed and teeth brushed, it is the quality of the connections they will make — how they fit into the larger community — that will determine if they are the happy and healthy individuals we want them to be.

Developing a child's inner core is the most important thing a parent can do, yet it is often lost when the juggling act begins. Michael Gurian, one of the experts we talk with in this chapter, has said, "Most of us are too busy to think of our children as being anything other than 'boys' or 'girls.' This, like thinking of them as 'kids,' is worthy and important, but how little we think of them as souls."

In this chapter, we will hear from nationally respected child development experts I consulted for this book. Each of them offers a particular specialization and insight helpful to Choice Moms. We will boil down their theories, and other things we have learned throughout this book, into a definition of what children need in order to become well-balanced individuals. Then we will turn these concepts into a game plan that any Choice Mother can use as a guide until her guiding days are done.

In a nutshell, I propose that the plan we develop in this ambitious chapter is the minimum requirement for any parent. Any Choice Mom must be prepared not only to consider the expense and logistics of raising a child alone, but to contemplate how she will single-handedly cultivate that child's connection to the world.

The Experts

There are countless experts across the country who offer good insight about what makes "good kids" and what makes "bad kids." The Parenting shelves at bookstores and libraries are filled with their wisdom. Sometimes the advice focuses on dealing with an overwhelming list of things that can go wrong with the kids we love so much: violence, drug use, depression, eating disorders, learning disabilities, promiscuity, delinquency.

Although there is wisdom from many quarters for this chapter, I have singled out four experts for advice specific to Choice Moms. These four have written excellent books about their philosophies. They are:

Mary Sheedy Kurcinka
Parent educator; speaker; author of books and workbooks, including Raising Your Spirited Child *and* Kids, Parents and Power Struggles[2]

Kurcinka's advice about how to understand a child's temperament and emotions — as well as the parents' own — is helpful for the busy Choice Mother who needs to communicate effectively with her child in order to establish mutual respect and the essential authoritative style of parenting. The stress of being the sole disciplinarian and conflict mender is great, making it vital for the Choice Mom to have keys to unlock power struggles.

Her highly regarded books have enabled parents to see the temperament behind their children, how the child's personality matches and clashes with their own, and how to create a better "fit" together. The idea is not to rewire parent or child, but to better understand and enjoy each other so parenting doesn't dissolve into a depressing and never-ending tug-of-war.

For example, in *Raising Your Spirited Child,* Kurcinka speculates the inventor Thomas Edison was likely a frustrating child. She wonders how many times he forgot to come home for dinner, how many times he got yelled at for taking things apart in the house. Edison's persistence and focus, when he was an adult, were great assets, but when he was a child, they likely were sometimes difficult to deal with.

"You don't get to choose your child's temperament nor does your child, but you do make a big difference," Kurcinka writes. "It is you who helps your child understand his temperament, emphasizes his strengths, and provides him with the guidance he needs to express himself appropriately."

Kyle Pruett
Child psychiatrist, Yale Child Study Center and Medical School; president of Zero to Three: National Center for Infants, Toddlers and Their Families; author of Fatherneed: Why Father Care Is as Essential as Mother Care for Your Child[3]

As Pruett and others discussed in chapter 6, children need men in their life. Men and women naturally offer different skills and temperaments that help a child grow up in a balanced way. It is difficult, and not advisable, for any one person to attempt to handle the yin and yang of every situation. As he points out, "Men are the single greatest untapped resource in the lives of American children. Natural, renewable, and by and large nontoxic, they couldn't be healthier for the country's children. We can't afford to let another one get away."

Among other things, his book offers suggestions to help ease a child's need for a father at different stages of development.

Michael Gurian
Therapist, educator, and long-time specialist in male development; author of many books, including The Good Son *and* The Wonder of Children[4]

Anyone who has ever been in a relationship or watched toddlers of different sexes knows that "Men Are from Mars, Women Are from Venus," as John Gray put it. But neuroscience, enhanced by new imaging technologies, gives us evidence about why, as Gurian details in his books. For example, the differences between the brains help explain why males tend to try to problem-solve quickly, compared to females who tend to delve into emotional issues.

Gurian also writes at length about the importance of community and ritual in a child's life. What kids need besides a primary caregiver, he says, are elders to help them understand how everything they experience is helping to form them into adults. Not unlike the useful aspects of a kibbutz, he wrote: "With many voices teaching the child, the child hears echoes of values, wisdom, self-worth . . . Parents have back-up systems, babysitters, respected partners in child-raising . . . When children make their inevitable moves toward independence, there are other community members with whom they've bonded and to whom they can turn for advice, help, or embrace."

Richard Weissbourd

Harvard-based lecturer, child psychologist, and author of The Vulnerable Child: What Really Hurts America's Children and What We Can Do About It[5]

Weissbourd, whom we heard from in chapter 5, says important things about the big-picture aspect of quality parenting. Namely, that national debates about family structure and income level tend to overlook a vital aspect of quality parenting: the emotional stability of the caregiver. It is common, he has written, for social workers to find children whose needs are not being met because a primary caregiver feels helpless and hopeless.

Concept #1: The Basics

Children do not need perfect lives in order to grow up whole. They learn from mistakes (yes, even mom's) and can develop strength from bad times. What they do need are a few essentials designed to make them feel secure, connected, accepted, and hopeful.

Weissbourd suggests in *The Vulnerable Child* that a well-balanced child needs:

- order and consistency;
- a continuous relationship with a caring adult who sees the child as special;
- interaction with an adult who stimulates, engages, challenges, and provides a compass for meeting social and moral expectations;
- strong friendships and community ties;
- protection from exploitation and discrimination, as well as a sense of justice and opportunity for achievement;
- attention to any special health, social, and educational needs.

In his review of research, he has found that when children grow up with these ingredients, they are more likely to have trust in themselves and in the world. They have the strength and inner resources to find enjoyment in relationships and work, and survive tough times. He points out that these ingredients are missing in many homes, not simply those of particular ethnicities or income levels or family structures. His ongoing research about vulnerable children and moral parenting finds that many families are not serving their children well, in communities across the country.

Concept #2: Understanding the Child

Gurian, Kurcinka, and others talk a great deal about "nature-based parenting." Rather than attempt to mold children to a parent's vision of who they should be, the attentive parent reaches in to understand a child's strengths and weaknesses, and teaches that child how to recognize and handle his or her own feelings.

The more "emotional intelligence" a child develops in this way, the more able he or she is to make connections, tackle challenges with confidence, negotiate differences, maintain self-esteem, cope with ups and downs — and cooperate with Mom.

As Kurcinka explains, if a parent realizes her child is introverted, for example, she will understand that he needs time alone in order to feel energized after a long day at school. When he starts to get surly, she will help him recognize that he needs alone-time, and enable him to get it until he's recharged — rather than push him to talk about his day and get upset when he grunts.

Extroverted children provide a special challenge to the single parent. They are at their best when they can be engaged in activities and need regular feedback. "There is no way one parent, especially an introverted parent, can keep up with the interaction needs of an extroverted spirited child," Kurcinka says. This kind of child needs to be taught to ask for attention and encouragement from grandparents, mentors, friends, and neighbors, rather than simply annoying mom until she yells, "Give me a break!"

It is easy for a Choice Mom to agree with this philosophy. It is more difficult to implement. But understanding how the brains of boys and girls are wired differently helps (see Gurian's books). Understanding the innate temperamental styles of children — which you can't yell out of them — helps (see Kurcinka's books). And letting the child know that mom is attempting to understand helps tremendously.

Concept #3: Community, Community

There are so many reasons community is vital to a child that it has appeared in many chapters of this book already — and every child development expert I talked to specifically for Choice Mothers brought it up as an essential component of successful parenting.

As we discussed in chapters 5 and 6, research indicates that children grow up best when they have a balance of influences that single parents will struggle with alone. One of the (stereotypical) benefits of having a father in the home, for example, is generally to serve as the rule-driven parent of authority, compared to mom's flexible stature as nurturer.

This is one reason why Pruett and others recommend that a team of secondary caregivers — at least one of them male — be in place at the earliest age to help mom:

- encourage both connection to others and independence;
- instill a sense of personal safety as well as assertiveness;
- offer predictability and flexibility;
- have respect for relationships and rules;
- be duty-bound as well as empathetic;
- provide an environment that is demanding and responsive.

Gurian talks about the importance of community to help form character in an even larger sense. "Mentors and intimate role models rarely exist to show in any long-term and consistent way how both to serve a group and flourish as an independent self," he wrote in *The Wonder of Boys*. With busy parents and little emphasis today on cultivating the soul, celebrities too often become the heroes, peers the role models.

The typical Choice Mom–in-the-making is considering what family and friends can help her get through the first few years as a mother — but community is so much more than that. And the sooner she develops a creative list of outlets, the better able she will head off the often predictable stages of loneliness and isolation that can occur in single parenthood.

Community organizations and individuals should be found early to give parents predictable breaks from their child. This benefits more than Mom's sanity. As Weissbourd points out, "Children of all ages should have a variety of opportunities for exploring their environment and talking with adults."

That means communities, not just parents, need to offer meaningful activities for children that build trust, self-confidence, and a sense of hopefulness and excitement about the future. "Decent environments not only provide clear discipline and encourage children to absorb basic social expectations and norms," he writes, "they also give children the knowledge and skills, the practical strokes — such as how to ask for directions or for change — that will enable them to swim in the mainstream."

This emphasis on community means you need to identify adults in your neighborhood whom children respect, who look out for their safety as if they were their own. You need to generate or find informal networks and events that support kids. You need to help build communities that believe that all adults are responsible for all children — not just their own. And it means, even as a busy single parent, you eventually need to get out of the house and the workplace and participate in that community. A dedicated Choice Mother will volunteer to coach or teach a skill at the community center or church where her child is learning.

In my case, I am an active volunteer at Sophie's school and our Unitarian Universalist church, have served in civic education projects, and am involved in building links between diverse cultures.

Concept #4: Establish Mutual Respect

Some believe a child without two loving parents in the home misses out on the lessons of seeing adults work out conflicts in a healthy way and relate to each other with love, trust, and respect. However, many of the young adult children I spoke with for chapter 15 didn't agree with this concern, indicating that the strong relationship they have with mom (for those who did) was example enough.

What I did see, with those kids who had loving connections with their Choice Moms, was a great deal of mutual respect. And this, I believe, is the key ingredient to building healthy relationships with anyone. It also correlates directly to the other concepts we've discussed.

When a child has a mother who attempts to understand the innate personality within, and helps him or her find words to express frustration as well as appropriate outlets for energy and emotion, that child grows up not only with self-respect, but with respect for the authority and the nurturer that is Mom. And when that child and mother have several others to turn to for support and encouragement, the parent-child relationship doesn't get overburdened and overwhelmed.

The parenting expert and author Nancy Samalin[6] suggested, in her book *Loving Your Child Is Not Enough,* the importance of not only inviting the child to be the problem solver, but acknowledging the child's right to feel the way he or she does. Often we try to fix emotional hurts fast, she wrote. "We may unwittingly deny or minimize their feelings with such comments as 'there's nothing to be afraid of' or . . . 'it can't be that bad.' Or we point out the sunny side, or try to talk them out of emotions with logic. That response convinces them that they aren't being heard.

Also, as your child matures and seems to stop listening, she says, talk less. The long, automatic response, she writes, is: "How many times have I told you to take your boots off on the porch? Look at this mess you've made. You think I have all the time in the world to spend mopping up floors? You're inconsiderate. Why can't you remember something as simple as taking off your boots outside?" The short version that might succeed in getting their attention is: "Boots."

I know several Choice Moms who use humor to diffuse arguments. Samalin also suggests playing with fantasy: "If I had a million dollars a year I'd . . . [do what the child wants]." Or you can use drama to defuse demands: "I guess you've mixed me up with the Wicked Witch of the West," or, "Let's hit rewind and start over."

The key thing, as Samalin and others point out, is to let our children see us as their allies when they are being gripped by strong emotions. By rephrasing their sentences when they are upset, instead of counteracting, we let them know we are not sitting in judgment, but rather respect and understand their position.

Wendy and her son are one of several teams I interviewed who I greatly admire for their strength in this area. Wendy is not a Choice Mom — she was married when she conceived using a donor, but divorced soon after. She was relieved that her son wouldn't grow up in an atmosphere of hostility, but was intimidated by the awesome responsibility of nurturing "this little human being alone. Any mistakes that are made, it's all me. I would get the glory, but also all the blame."

Like most women who actively choose to raise a child without a partner, Wendy embraced her role as Choice Mom as "the most important job I would ever have in my life. I worked on my own issues so they wouldn't be passed along. I knew I couldn't be a perfect mother, but I would ask for forgiveness when I made mistakes. I would keep the playing ground equal so we would both be very accepting of each other — and then hopefully he would be with himself too."

More than a decade later, Wendy's strategy has paid off. Even in private, her teenage son had terrific things to say about the way she raised him. "I have a great, involved mom," he told me. "From handling almost every aspect of my education to instilling in me a sense of right and wrong, she's done it all. And to be perfectly honest, I feel that she has done most everything right. She gives me all the freedom a teen needs, without having to worry about me trying pot or a cigarette or anything like that."

Concept #5: Authoritative Parenting

Wendy brought up another important aspect of quality parenting: maintaining the division between parent and child by establishing the mother's authority. In fact, mutual respect enhanced her ability to be The Enforcer. She has never needed to yell or threaten her son, she told me. All she needed to do was give him "the look."

"Even now, he towers over me, is 50 pounds heavier, and I can almost bring him to tears with 'the look,'" she said. "It comes from having respect for each other, I think. At this age, he sees friends yelling at their moms, and families where the teenager becomes the boss. But he would never say anything disrespectful to me.

"It's challenging — you need to have a friendship, when it's mom and one kid together so much of the time you need to like each other. But having clearly defined boundaries between parent and child is very important."

Diana, whose college-age daughter also expresses great respect for Mom, said establishing authority was difficult at first. "I didn't know how to say no," she told me. She adopted her daughter at 13 months from a family that had provided little nurturing. "I just wanted to hold her. For a long time when she was a child, all she wanted to do was sit on my lap. It was hard for me to learn how to discipline her."

But slowly she managed to put rules in place that helped establish her authority. *When I'm eating, you can't interrupt me. There is no time it is appropriate for you to hit someone.*

It helped Diana to realize that setting limits didn't have to involve anger, but involved developing her daughter's sense of empathy. *It hurts my feelings when you do that. When you wake me up at night it makes me tired and more likely to get colds.* Diana's daughter is now a highly disciplined, moral young adult. As Diana told me, "I recently asked her whether I was a successful authority figure. She said, 'Absolutely not. You were never any kind of authority figure. What you always had was an ethic that what you communicated was inviolable.'"

Establishing rules is naturally harder for a single parent — even a strong one. Speaking from experience, with the wisdom of many other Choice Moms I have talked with, it is difficult to always be the "heavy" with your child. And it is tough to avoid caving into demands without the support of another adult. Especially since, as Pruett says, any parent working alone gets "old," with a natural lessening of authority over time.

Research by gender-identity specialist Barbara Risman[7] revealed that even in single-father households there tend to be weaker controls and fewer demands, suggesting that it is the logistical factor of solo parenthood, rather than the sex of the parent, that makes the difference in establishing an authoritative approach to parenting. Kids in single-parent households tend to seem more mature, which leads the parent to be more permissive and take less of a supervisory role.

But not only is it easier to avert trouble with kids if the parent consistently establishes her authority, but, as Wendy and her son are a good example of, it helps to create respect.

As the child expert and Temple University psychology professor Laurence Steinberg wrote with coauthor Ann Levine in the highly regarded *You and Your Adolescent: A Parent's Guide for Ages 10–20*,[8] the authoritative parent:

- solicits the child's opinion;
- allows the child to voice disagreements;
- can be persuaded to reconsider a decision;
- values curiosity and self-direction;

- wants their child to understand the reasons for their demands and restrictions, so explains why behavior is inappropriate;
- does not hesitate to assert their authority if reasoning fails;
- does not demand unquestioning obedience;
- sets limits based on love.

"This is in contrast to 'permissive' or 'indulgent' parents, who love their children dearly but have difficulty setting limits or imposing rules, and 'authoritarian' or 'autocratic' parents, who are controlling and in charge, but who discipline their children harshly and without sufficient affection or discussion," they wrote.

They echo the concerns raised in chapter 5 and in Risman's research, pointing out that the biggest issue for single parents with adolescents is maintaining control, because they grant more independence, don't have the time or energy for authoritative parenting, and have only one set of eyes and ears for monitoring a teen's activities. They also point out, "If a single parent maintains an authoritative relationship, however, any problems that might develop can be averted."

The Four-Point Game Plan

So we've learned a lot of mumbo-jumbo psychology and philosophy. How is a typical, busy Choice Mom to make sense of it and turn it into action?

Here are the basics of a suggested game plan. Make these steps part of your planning process before you jump into Choice Motherhood — just as you would assess and improve on your financial health.

Step #1: Develop a strong child-care plan
Research suggests that the importance of the quality of early child-care is not a myth. The first few months in particular, and the first two years in general, are crucial for helping a child develop the attachment and security that will serve him or her in later years. This

is why programs like Head Start have been, in strong economic times, a priority for funding initiatives. Most researchers agree that getting adequate childcare is more important than family structure. And this requires not only money, but identifying the most loving caregivers for your child before you need them.

As we discussed in chapter 2, there are many caregiver options to consider. No matter what you end up choosing, make the effort to develop a rapport with the caregiver, since this person is your backup parent. And check out the staff-child ratio; suggested standards are no less than one adult for every four infants, every five toddlers, or every ten preschoolers. Are employees well paid and educated? Is the turnover low? How well is the place managed?

Ideally, your child will be taken care of by a secondary caregiver who is consistently present when mom is not — available to snuggle, talk, and play like a second mom (or a dad). Without this level of attachment, research tells us, he or she will grow up spending more time trying to be safe and loved than growing emotionally healthy and strong. And, as Gurian points out, a mother who feels guilty about the care situation her child is in will ultimately damage her authority — by overcompensating, avoiding discipline — and the child, picking up on signals that "mom wants me to punish her," will do just that by pushing her away.

Most Choice Moms do feel guilty for not being available full-time to their child. Make sure you are capable of devising a loving community of caregivers.

Step #2: Pick your mentors and male role models
Based on Weissbourd's checklist of requirements for a successful childhood earlier in this chapter, and the balance/counterbalance needs we've discussed elsewhere in the book, identify your weak spots and take steps to correct them. That includes actively bringing people into your life — family, friends, community members — who not only support your needs, but can provide the yin to your yang. If you happen to be strong at setting rules and limits, identify someone who provides a model of flexibility. If you are an

accountant and strong in mathematical abilities and problem solving, find someone to nurture the creative side of your child.

Don't hesitate to start adding to your tribe. You will need them as soon as you become a Choice Mom, and will need different ones as your child matures. Look to godparents, the parents of your child's friends, Boy Scouts and Girl Scouts, Big Brothers, religious organizations, extracurricular school activities, youth groups, coaches, and teachers. These are not simply sources to keep your child busy. They should be actively explored as places to find good people. (Interestingly, I met my husband because I was looking for male role models for my kids.)

There is no shame in not being able to offer everything to your child. As Pruett says, "Children need you to be who you're best at being, not who you think you should be." Pruett's recommended secondary caregiving, as detailed in his book, includes:

Infancy — Invite close male friends and relatives to hold, walk, rock, play, and babysit (before stranger awareness takes hold around 7 to 9 months) so your child gets a sense of the body, face, smell, voice, and comforting styles of others.

Toddlerhood — Have close male friends and relatives engage in rough-and-tumble exploration with your boy or girl; they should also read and comfort, as the different behavioral styles of "not-the-mother" time are stimulating and fascinating.

Preschool years — Find someone in your closest circle to offer toilet-training boys a demonstration of standup peeing; encourage reading by men, since this is an important activity that men and children can do together; as gender identification begins, boys will want to practice "being a guy" with male role models and girls will want to explore the "power of their femininity."

Early and middle school years — Look for men engaged in religious education, recreational sports, Scouts, Big Brothers, and other community activities that typically begin at this age. My daughter's capoeira instructor, who taught her the Brazilian martial art for two years, was an excellent role model of strength, discipline, and respect.

Adolescence — At this age, kids make their own choices about adults they want to be with, are more private, and pay attention to your dating behavior, which serves as a model. Make sure they have an open line of communication with other adults, including a masculine one. Look for a close male family member who loves your children to help affirm and clarify expectations and limits.

Step #3: Establish rituals

An essential tool for busy parents is to create rituals that provide connection between parent and child, and with community.

Kurcinka advises Choice Moms to create daily rituals designed to help calm and soothe: eating breakfast together, cooking together, washing dishes together instead of tossing them into the dishwasher, sitting next to the bathtub while the child relaxes and plays, dimming lights and putting on soft music in the evening, making time for walks and exercise.

Gurian stresses the importance of developing rituals at an early age — for bedtime, reading, family meals, drives, family get-togethers, family storytelling. The connection that comes from rituals is even more important as the child gets older — and nearly impossible to implement if they haven't already been put in place.

In Gurian's family, for example, Thursdays have been Extended Clan Gathering time. Several families with kids, elders, and godparents enjoy talk, Ping-Pong, and food. "This kind of ritual is a complete celebration of child, family, and community . . . As the children leave infancy and grow older, they have people to turn to, they have a night to look forward to, and they have a big family close to home," he says.

The less involved that children are with their parents and extended clan, the more susceptible they are to bad influences among peers and in the media. The strongest relationships, Gurian indicates, are forged by mothers who "keep communicating, keep talking, keep family rituals strong, keep having dinner together, family time together, reading time together."

Respected family therapist William Doherty has written a book about the importance of ritual, *The Intentional Family: Simple Rituals to Strengthen Family Ties*.[9] As he wrote, "Entropy — the loss of energy, connection, and focus — is the wolf at the door of all families, but especially threatens overburdened, full-time single-parent families and part-time nonresidential families. Single parenting is one of the most difficult tasks in contemporary society. But it also offers the opportunity to start family life anew, to be creative about family rituals, and to involve the children in shaping the family's values and its future.

"Some of the most highly intentional families I know are single-parent families, as are some of the most overwhelmed. The key differences appear to be the ability to focus on what is most important about family rituals of connection and celebration, and on the degree of support from the extended family and community."

It's easy to lapse in connection time when you're too stressed and overworked to take a breath. Don't let yourself get isolated, overwhelmed, or depressed enough to lose conscious daily moments with your child. Find your rituals, tribe, and relaxation techniques before you need them.

Step #4: Be happy as a nonmother

As Steinberg and Levine wrote: "The best of us have bad days. When parents are under stress, tired, or preoccupied, they often slip into domination ('Just do it because I say so') or permissiveness ('Do whatever you want') . . . A bad day or a pressured decision will not have a profound effect on a child. What matters is the general pattern, over time."

To be a loving, authoritative, and successful Choice Mom, you need to pay attention to your own mental and physical balance. As they advise on airplanes, put the oxygen mask over your own mouth before assisting your child — you cannot help anyone if you're passed out.

Weissbourd reports that even the child in a low-income household who has one loving and attentive parent is generally much better off than the child in a middle-class household with a parent who is withdrawn or self-involved.

Narcissistic and cold the Choice Mother generally is not. But the single parent who finds herself disconnected from others can become depressed, overwhelmed, unfocused, and burdensome to her child. Who will you turn to, what nonmother activities will you be involved with, as you help your child mature?

Gurian writes that the greatest gift a single mother can give her child is her stability. In the beginning, she is the only anchor. As the child begins to reach out to others, she must roll up the anchor, notch by notch. It is a disservice to children to make them feel that they are your life, he points out. When they start feeling secure enough to pull away, it is the emotionally healthy moms who are able to let them go — who can see them as emotionally powerful and as competent as she is.

He writes in *The Wonder of Boys* about a man he counseled who said, "My mother and I were always so close. I remember one time when I was about fourteen she started to cry and said, 'How am I ever going to live without you?' I felt so sorry for her, so sad." The man grew up to have several loving relationships with women, but eventually he would resent the woman, get distant, and the relationship would end. "To this day," the man said, "I still don't have the heart to tell [mother] I had become her little man but never became my own."

As Gurian puts it, the message mothers need to give their children — male and female — as they go through adolescence is this: "Every day you need me less and less, both physically and emotionally, and I need you less and less. And that's okay."

A mother needs her own emotional health in order to maintain her separateness — and allow her child to do the same. Again, in order to maintain authority and success as a parent, the Choice Mom needs a community of people and rituals to support her.

Final Thoughts

The strategy behind most of this game plan, and indeed much of the advice in this book, boils down to two words: "Community" and "Authority." The reality is — as it has been throughout centuries of child rearing — that it takes a village to raise a child well. If community ties are weak or resources are insufficient, it is the kids who suffer, and ultimately society.

At the same time, since there is one face of parenting for a child, that face had better be the reasonable, affectionate, responsive, respectful, and authoritative parent that every child needs.

If your day-to-day life consists primarily of working and caretaking, it might seem like you are being responsible to your child, but you are not doing enough. We are self-sufficient women, capable of doing incredible things, but none of us can raise a child alone — or even with one partner. Offering children the authoritative voice that raises them up in a well-balanced way over time demands poise, which requires keeping the stress level down.

Your responsibility, as someone who wants to raise a child in the best way that you can, is to be involved in your community . . . help build your community into a stronger one . . . find members of your community who have something to give — for your child and for yourself.

In the end, the secret to raising a well-balanced child is to navigate both of you through a variety of activities and experiences that foster interaction with a variety of important people — encouraging your child's development of self-control and self-esteem — until the one you have been chosen to guide is old enough to hold the compass alone.

✦ BONUS SECTION ✦

If You Are Raising a Boy

As the male development expert Michael Gurian told me: "Males raised in homes of single mothers are definitely at more risk for social and personal problems than males raised in two-parent homes. I don't believe there is any credible research that denies this. However, I don't condemn a single parent, nor do I argue she/ he can't raise great kids."

There are many reasons why it is more challenging for single mothers to raise boys — and knowing those reasons can help a Choice Mother do it better.

Brain Science
Because male brains are wired differently than female brains — in addition to boys' and girls' differing hormone levels and social expectations — boys are in some ways more challenging to teach, Gurian says. They are naturally more impulsive, for example, because their prefrontal cortex is less active than girls' and develops at a later age, and because they have less serotonin in their bloodstream and brain.

Girls and women have 15 percent more blood flow in the brain, are able to process more things simultaneously, and have stronger neural connectors, enabling them to retain more from the senses and to detect tones of voice more easily. Girls use more parts of their brain for verbal and emotional functioning, whereas boys use more areas for spatial and mechanical functioning.

Since a girl's brain "lights up" in more areas than a boy's, Gurian says, "She is often more flexible and adaptable and full-brained in her responses to the world around her. He is often more narrowly focused, and may end up with a narrower emotional, behavioral and therefore moral range of response."

So what does this mean? Do we throw up our hands and let innate behavior take its course?

Gurian says the science tells us that boys generally need more love, discipline, and modeling behavior than they are getting today in order to learn how to respond to situations in a less simplistic way. As he told me, "no one is saying girls are more moral than boys. What we are saying is that boys need a greater concerted effort on the part of the mom, the family, the elders, the community, and the social institutions in order to inculcate all the moral coding of a social group."

Girls need the same training, of course. But not only do girls absorb these relational skills more easily, a girl's mother is more likely to understand the way she behaves and processes experience.

Boys and emotions

In the early years, it's easy for a mom to recognize when something is bothering her son: he cries, he hits, he yells. But as the brain grows from that of a toddler to that of a child, around the age of 5 or 6, boys start processing their emotions differently. Some of this is because boys are taught to hide pain more than girls. But a lot of it is natural to a male brain.

"Unlike many of my colleagues, I don't worry about boys masking their feelings," Gurian told me. "Most boys are going to naturally grow into males who cry less than girls and talk about feelings less than women. It begins in childhood and continues when puberty hits and testosterone becomes a very big influence. I disagree with some colleagues who feel that the salvation for males is to learn how to feel through the use of talking and crying.

"I prefer that each child be provided profound attachment by primary and secondary caregivers — attachment so useful to the child that he will develop his own personal system for handling emotion. That system will include masculinity, masking, femininity, physical exercise, problem-solving, repression, free-expression through art or sport. The list is endless."

Gurian told me that the best thing a Choice Mother can do to help her son be emotionally healthy is not necessarily to get him to talk more, but to make sure he is attached to at least four other caregivers: grandparent, godparent, male mentor, teacher. An unconnected boy is more worrisome than a quiet one.

Communication strategy

Male development experts tend to agree that one way single mothers raising sons are at a disadvantage is that they have very different styles of communication. As Gurian explains, girls have a much greater need to connect and attach than boys do. He refers to this as the "intimacy imperative." Females will bond by chatting before playing together, for example, whereas males will bond simply by the process of playing.

A Choice Mother needs to learn new strategies of conversation. As Gurian told me:

> *A mom with a father involved in the boy's life typically does not have to do too much to extend out beyond who she already is. If she is alone in raising her son, however, then she has to hold onto her own identity as a woman and try to extend toward the masculine.*
>
> *She finds herself trying to learn how to play basketball with her son. She finds herself trying to learn other ways of processing emotion than feeling-talk or eye-to-eye conversation.*

There are things a mother can do to encourage his connection with her, as Gurian and others have detailed. Boys do much better bonding while doing, rather than simply sitting and talking. William Pollack calls this "action talk." For example, start a conversation after engaging him in physical play, or while driving or biking together.

A discussion starter: "You look like you feel angry," or "What do you think about that thing that happened?" Less effective: "How do you feel?"

STAGE 5

The Legacy of Choice

Think for yourselves and let others enjoy the privilege
to do so too.

— Voltaire, *Essays on Tolerance*

I have never considered myself to be a strongly political
person. But I am a huge believer in protecting the principle
of Choice in its myriad forms. I believe that any healthy, responsible person who desires to be a parent, or marry, or not,
should be allowed to make that decision if he or she can
pledge to meet the needs of the other people affected by that
choice over time.

In most U.S. states, single women are not prohibited from
becoming mothers. But that does not mean that they are
given the same access as married women. Clinics, insurance
companies, and adoption agencies are free to develop their
own policies — and they do, resulting in variance from place
to place, state to state.

In the chapter that follows, "Of Politics and Policy," we
will look at ways family life is decided in legislative and judicial halls, as well as in clinic and agency board rooms.
Although the news is largely good for single heterosexual
women, the chapter will look at obstacles designed to dis-

courage "nontraditional" families. I think it is important for us, as a community, to be always mindful of the ways in which decisions are being made about how families can be created, so that we can lend our voice to the discussion.

In "How Are the Kids Turning Out?" we will hear directly from the older children of pioneering Choice Moms about how they have been influenced by the way they were raised, and what they think about the lifestyle as a family model. I continue to collect these stories — positive and negative — so that we can continue to honestly understand the legacy of Choice parenthood.

· 14 ·

Of Politics and Policy

After often painful self-scrutiny and debate, intense scrimping and saving, and time-consuming research, a single woman who is resolved and ready to take the next step toward becoming a Choice Mom sometimes meets with powerful opposition: laws, regulations, politics, and policy.

The new reproductive technologies and loosened adoption criteria have made it much more possible than it used to be for single women to become mothers, gay couples to become parents, and infertile couples to raise children using sperm or egg donors. But the yellow caution flag is being raised by some who believe the parenting field is being confused by too many biological and nonbiological players. Or that marriage is being devalued. Or that men are being considered irrelevant to a woman's life.

Some who set policy throw up their own red flag, believing that a single mother (or a homosexual parent) is not "fit" to have a child, and thus should not be aided in the effort to do so. Some policy makers believe strongly that every child should have a mother and a father, and enact rules to discourage single parents or lesbian couples from adopting or conceiving — even though research indicates children do quite well in "nontraditional" environments where devoted, quality parenting is present. In Florida, for exam-

ple, a policy was reinforced in a 2005 decision that forbids gays
and lesbians to adopt (a bill that would repeal this has since been
suggested).

Many countries today are establishing laws that affect adoption, open-identity donors, and access to reproductive services.
Several are supportive of single parenthood. A few are not. For
now, the United States is less involved in regulating the adoption
and insemination industries than Australia, Canada, the United
Kingdom, and other European nations.[1]

By and large, single women are finding little resistance from
doctors and clinics. But tell that to Carol, who was turned away by
two clinics because she wanted to use the sperm of a gay friend.
Tell that to a Minnesota woman I know whose long-time female
gynecologist wouldn't help her get pregnant because she was not
married — and to Gretchen, who was dismissed by five doctors
for the same reason. Tell that to all the lesbian women in Florida
who have to withhold truth, or move to another state, in order to
have children.

In this chapter we will look at how some women face obstacles
to motherhood because of their marital status or sexual orientation. We also will look at the general state of insurance coverage,
open-identity donors, and adoption law, as well as court cases that
have attempted to address the complicated ethical issues that arise
with the new reproductive technologies.

Who Gets to Try?

Some believe that any healthy person has the right to use medical
technology in order to conceive a child, and that the role of the
provider is to offer it, without judgment. Others believe that those
who need medical assistance to conceive should not be offered services unless the provider has verified that the resulting child will be
brought up in a proper home. In between these two views, of
course, is a lot of gray area. When is someone "too old" to be a
parent? Will a single woman, or a lesbian couple, provide a "fit"

environment for a child — and should the same scrutiny be applied to married couples? Is it ethical for a child to have many unknown half-siblings? If contact is made with half-siblings and donors, who decides whether to call each other family, and whether the terms "brother," "sister," "father" apply? And, importantly, who is entitled to make this judgment — and on what basis?

There are many players involved in insemination: donors, sperm banks, doctors. All of them are subject to scrutiny by outside forces, such as reproductive medicine society guidelines, FDA regulations, judicial review, state and federal legislation, and insurance company policies that decide what is covered and what is not. Yet the industry is relatively unregulated in terms of broader, ethical issues, which is why individuals find very different policies from place to place.

For example, in the case of assisted reproduction technology (ART), which involves advanced fertility treatment (such as in vitro fertilization), a study sponsored by the Center for Bioethics at the University of Pennsylvania School of Medicine indicated, "There is no guarantee of access to ART in the law."[2]

Study results were based on responses to questionnaires by 210 program directors (out of 369 contacted). Many respondents indicated a belief that it is wrong to help bring a child into the world to be cared for by a parent who would be unfit, and that the program has a responsibility to consider a parent's fitness.

Ironically, however, a substantial number of programs reported being likely to turn away candidates on the basis of characteristics that they did not actually collect information about, such as sexual orientation. And on average, programs offering these expensive services report turning away only 4 percent of their candidates each year (3 percent for medical reasons, 1 percent for emotional or psychological reasons). Responses revealed that:

• At only 18 percent of the programs do candidates meet with a social worker or psychologist; 80 percent meet with a financial coordinator.

- Overall, 59 percent of directors agreed that everyone has a right to have a child, and 43 percent feel they do not have the right to stop anyone from attempting to conceive.
- On the other hand, 64 percent believe it is their responsibility to consider a parent's fitness before helping them conceive. But judgment about who is fit and who is not varies considerably. Given a series of hypothetical situations, respondents indicated they would be most likely to turn away a couple in which the man has been physically abusive to his existing child (81 percent very or extremely likely to turn away, compared to 5 percent not likely or slightly unlikely to turn away).
- A couple on welfare is not likely to be turned away by 46 percent of programs, yet is very likely to be turned away by 38 percent.
- A single man looking for surrogacy services is likely to be helped by 37 percent, but likely to be turned away by 53 percent.
- A single woman is likely to be helped by 77 percent, but turned away by 20 percent.
- A lesbian couple is likely to be helped by 82 percent, but turned away by 17 percent.
- A couple in which both partners are at least 43 years old is likely to be helped by 77 percent, but likely to be turned away by 18 percent.

Researchers involved in the study recommend that the United States begin to formalize guidelines to ensure equality among the programs. However, one of the authors of the study, Arthur Caplan, told me that regulations aren't likely to happen anytime soon. Unlike countries such as Canada and the United Kingdom, the United States has no federal regulatory agency in place to oversee assisted reproduction issues. It is a largely self-regulated industry that, as of this writing, is in the process of re-examining itself, but is still a long way off from reaching consensus on what it needs to do differently.

Choice Chat with Gretchen: I Was Turned Away Five Times

✦ As a straight women with decent finances and a terrific doctor, I naively thought the two years I spent thinking and soul-searching about this choice would be the hard part. After getting a thumb's up from my doctor about my ability to conceive, he told me his practice did not help single women get pregnant. I was surprised — could people who didn't know me decide I can't do this? My doctor apologized and referred me to someone who worked with a different practice. Seven weeks into a ten-week waiting period for first-time appointments, after I had returned some standard paperwork, that clinic called to verify that I was single. When I said yes, I was told that the referral doctor wouldn't work with a single woman either.

I was referred to another doctor, who had no trouble with me being single, but didn't work with insurance company paperwork. Okay, this was important to me — I would pay out of pocket and file claims myself. We started a cycle on my first appointment, after he laid out the facts based on my age, weight, medical history, and other necessary information. After it was determined that I was not developing enough follicles on a low dose of Clomid, on our second appointment he said I wasn't going to be able to get pregnant. It felt like I didn't fit his success parameters so he cut me loose.

Back to my original doctor, whose office referred me to the first doctor again. I pointed out their mistake, and was given a new referral, to a woman. Turns out she, too, wouldn't see me because I was single — although if I'd been part of a lesbian couple it would have been okay.

I called for yet another referral, and was told that my original doctor would help me after all. I was confused, but didn't protest. We started a cycle of Clomid. The day of the ▶

ultrasound, a different doctor was there who told me, as I was sitting there with follicles ready to go, that they did not do this at their clinic and this cycle would be wasted.

I was crushed and had no idea what to do. Didn't they understand how important this was to me? That I am a sane, intelligent woman who would also like to be a mother? My own doctor called to apologize for the confusion. He referred me to doctor #4. It took six weeks to get in, and when I met with him he said I would need genetic counseling, a psychological evaluation, and fertility testing. After that, he would meet with his partners and they'd decide whether to move forward. He said not to take it personally. How was that possible? If I had shown up with an abusive husband, none of these steps would be required because I'd be married. But, as irritated as I was, I realized if I didn't take the steps, the process would end.

Which brings me to today. I passed all my "tests" and am waiting to see if I am pregnant from a third attempt at donor insemination.

The process has been much more emotionally draining than I expected. But without a doubt, I would truly regret not trying.

Caplan believes that single women and the gay and lesbian community would benefit from regulations, since they'd likely be approved as "fit" parent material, and thus clinics would not be allowed to turn them down.

A question of age

Some people are critical of older women who are allowed to use donated eggs and bear children who will have an aged parent earlier than peers. When a 66-year-old Romanian woman gave birth to a 3.2 lb. baby in 2004, it raised questions about whether there should be stronger guidelines to determine who should be eligible to have a child. Later that year, a 56-year-old New York woman gave birth to twins.

According to the *Boston Globe*,[3] in 2002 alone there were 286 births to U.S. women in their early fifties, and more than 5,000 in their late forties. The age at which a clinic will not work with a woman varies considerably. At 18 percent of clinics in the Center for Bioethics study, there was a formal or informal cutoff of age 43.

Most American adoption agencies will not work with women over the age of 45, although that, too, varies considerably.

Who Can Be a Donor?

In New York State, where gay rights tend to be strong, two clinics rejected a woman's gay donor because of their (erroneous) interpretation of state regulations. Although donor sperm in New York, like everywhere, is tested and quarantined for six months before being retested and used by a recipient, Carol was surprised to find that her donor's frozen sperm could not be used. Her donor agreed to offer fresh samples for clinic inseminations, but was told state regulations wouldn't allow that either, since she did not have an intimate relationship with him.

"I feel trapped by regulations that exist purely to absolve institutions and practitioners of liability," she told me at the time. "Neither my known donor nor I have a problem with a single lie ("no, he is not gay") but a lot of insemination clinics want a session with a psychologist, a long verbal interview, access to the donor's medical records, and more — all of which would reveal that he is gay, or would require extensive lying and concealment, which we're not okay with."

She considered pursuing insemination in nearby New Jersey, where regulations are more lenient. The early morning commutes would be exhausting and challenging, but doable. "However, it's depressing to have to select an RE based on whether they practice over the state line rather than who is the best doctor for me to work with."

Her story had a simpler solution, however. The truth is that it is not generally prohibited to use a known (or "directed") donor who is gay. The first two places she went to simply followed unusual policies. On her third attempt, she consulted with an RE in private practice who "did not care at all about my donor being gay, and in fact said it was irrelevant to what he was doing for me medically. I loved that he was so sane about it."

The doctor agreed that a donor who does not have HIV posed no risk to her health. "I was incredibly relieved to hear his position at my initial consult. I just wanted the best medical care I could get from someone I trusted and respected, and that is what I feel I am getting." She and her donor did need to sign paperwork that acknowledged the man as the biological father. "This type of document would not be acceptable to everyone, but it was for us."

FDA controversy

In 2005, Food and Drug Administration (FDA) guidelines (12 years in the making) were released that recommended that any man who had had sex with another man during the previous five years be disallowed as an anonymous sperm donor. The reason given was that gay men as a group were at a higher risk of carrying the AIDS virus.

Sperm from a healthy gay man is no different than sperm from a healthy heterosexual man. Since all sperm is tested, quarantined and retested after six months before being used, there is no scientific reason to believe that anyone will contract HIV from unaffected sperm. There have been no known cases of AIDS passed on through donation since testing procedures were enacted in the 1980s.

One person who was incensed by the proposed guidelines was Leland Traiman, director of the California-based Rainbow Flag sperm bank, which offers gay sperm donors. The only people categorized as "criminals" by the FDA in this way, he pointed out, were IV drug users, prostitutes, and male homosexuals. "A heterosexual man who has had sex with an HIV prostitute could donate after one year," he told me, "but a gay man in a long-term relationship could not. It's clearly not based on science, but on bigotry."

And it gave a false sense of security to think that if gay men are removed as donors there is no HIV threat, he indicated. Some opponents of the guidelines suggested that anyone who has had sex with an individual of unknown HIV status should be rejected as a prospective donor. The point should be the sexual behavior of the candidate, not the sexual orientation.

As Aubrey Noelle Stimola, the assistant director of public health at the American Council on Science and Health, wrote at the time: "I would hope that even a genetic masterpiece who attended Harvard and who has never been ill a day in his life would be tested for HIV, regardless of claims that he had never used intravenous drugs, had sex with a man, or received a blood transfusion before HIV testing became routine. What is accomplished by barring homosexuals from donating sperm? Does it save money? I don't see how. Will it save lives? Nope. Is it mere bias? It seems so, given the fact that while homosexual men do have a higher risk of HIV — tests for which are now extremely accurate — heterosexual men are by no means without risk."[4]

The guidelines are simply that — suggested protocol that excludes gay donors. Sperm banks technically are free to use gay donors, although most do not want to run afoul of the FDA's recommendations.

FDA rules currently do not prohibit gay men from being a known or directed donor.

Taking It to Court

While most women who meet with resistance find a more receptive doctor, clinic, or agency, some women attempt to change the system by doing battle in court.

As Women's eNews reported,[5] a Florida woman named Melinda helped deliver thousands of babies in her 20 years as a nurse. When she was 39 and unmarried, she looked to her hospital for help getting inseminated, and was shocked when they refused, indicating donor sperm was used only for married heterosexual couples. She argued with doctors that she had a stable job and a strong support network. She argued that 50 percent of marriages end in divorce. But six clinics turned her down.

After six years of battling her employer in federal court, the woman, then 45, lost both her legal case and her hopes of having a biological child, since her eggs were no longer viable. "If I had just brought a man with me to the clinic six years ago, I would have received treatment," Melinda said. "But I didn't want to have to lie to get health care and I don't think millions of other single women should either."

In Ontario, a 39-year-old lesbian also challenged laws governing sperm donors. After the woman was unsuccessful at self-insemination, she turned to a doctor. Since she was attempting to use a known donor who was over the age of 40 and gay, he was automatically disqualified on two counts as a donor for assisted conception.

For a fee of more than $600, and a great deal of time, the federal government would have granted her special permission to use him as her donor. But she hired an attorney to attempt to change the law instead. Her attorney argued that it was unfair for fertile women to conceive with men who are over the age of 40, or who have a history of genetic defects, but not allow those seeking assistance from a doctor the same right. The case was lost at the Superior Court level and on appeal.[6]

Four cases, four judgments

One needs only to look to California for examples of the many ways insemination in particular can find itself in the courtroom. Here are four examples. (Reminder that state laws, and judges, vary considerably.)

1. Known Donor Is *Not* Dad (March 2005)[7]

Steven and Deborah were sometimes intimate friends. He provided semen to a doctor to inseminate her. After one miscarriage, they had sexual intercourse for a few months, which did not result in a pregnancy. Deborah ended the sexual relationship and went back to the doctor, using the sperm Steven had originally provided. She became pregnant and gave birth to Trevor.

In the initial judgment, Steven — who had petitioned to establish a parental relationship in 2003 with Trevor, then 3 years old — was granted that right in a trial court. However, Deborah won on appeal.

Citing the language of California law, the Superior Court opinion indicated there can be "no paternity claim from a sperm donor who is not married to the woman who becomes pregnant with the donated semen, so long as it was provided to a licensed physician. The statute does not make an exception for known sperm donors, who will be denied a paternity claim so long as the semen was provided to a licensed physician for insemination of an unmarried woman."

2. Known Donor *Is* Dad (March 1986)[8]

Mary and Victoria chose Jhordan as their known donor. He provided semen to Mary several times over a six-month period. She performed home insemination herself until she became pregnant and gave birth to Devin. After the birth, Jhordan pursued rights as a parent — they disagreed in court about whether this had been verbally agreed upon prior to insemination, and there was no written document. In a related issue, Victoria sought joint legal custody of the child as co-parent with Mary and requested parenting rights.

As the court opinion stated, in cases of insemination in which a licensed physician is not used, there is no protection from a paternity claim by (or for) the sperm donor. The trial court determined Jhordan was Devin's legal father, but awarded sole legal and physical custody to Mary and denied Jhordan input into decisions about Devin's schooling, medical care, and day-to-day life. He did, however, receive substantial visitation rights as recommended by a court-appointed psychologist. Victoria was determined not to be a parent, but was also awarded visitation rights. The judgment held up in appeal.

In this case, it was determined that California law gave married and unmarried women equal rights to protect themselves from paternity claims of donors, but using a licensed physician is a requirement for this protection.

In an important detail, however, the opinion stated that the physician is not required to perform the insemination. In cases when a woman prefers the atmosphere of a home insemination, the opinion stated, California's legal protection is allowed if the sperm is simply provided to a licensed physician.

Author's note: One woman told me that a friend who was a licensed physician accepted a donor's sperm at her front door, then handed it off for use in home insemination.

3. When an Anonymous Donor Is *Not* Anonymous
(May 2000)[9]

A married couple filed a lawsuit against a sperm bank, claiming that it failed to disclose that the sperm they used came from a donor with family history of a serious genetic kidney disease. Their daughter was conceived with this sperm. The family requested that the donor's identity be divulged as part of a court disposition.

A trial court denied the motion, ruling that the donor's anonymity and privacy interests should be maintained as part of the confidentiality agreement he signed with the sperm bank. The court found that the family had access to other relevant medical information, and that the donor would not provide new insight into the medical condition.

On appeal, however, the superior court determined that the agreement between the sperm bank and the donor went too far in providing for anonymity "and thus conflicts with public policy."

The opinion stated that the sperm bank agreement includes a provision that "good cause" by court order could preclude privacy. As the opinion stated, "a contract that completely forecloses the opportunity of a child conceived by artificial insemination to discover the relevant and needed medical history of his or her genetic father is inconsistent with the best interests of the child."

It also stated that since the donor deposited more than 320 specimens of his semen, for more than $11,000, the substantial commercial transaction involved makes it "unreasonable for donor No. 276 to expect that his genetic and medical history, and possibly even his identity, would never be disclosed."

The court determined that the state's interest, and the petitioner's, outweighed the donor's interests. It required him to appear at a deposition, answer all questions, and produce documents needed. But it also ruled that full identity might not be required, and that all efforts to retain some anonymity should be attempted.

4. An "Oops" Error (June 2003)[10]

Susan, a single woman, went to a fertility clinic for help conceiving with an embryo created from anonymously donated ova and sperm. She used anonymous donors to avoid any paternity issues. Robert and Denise went to the same clinic to fertilize a donated ovum with Robert's sperm, and signed a contract stating they would be the parents of any children produced from the resulting embryos.

Robert and Denise produced about 13 embryos. Because of a clinic error, three of those embryos were implanted in Susan. Both women got pregnant around the same time and gave birth to full genetic siblings ten days apart.

After the families were made aware of the error, Robert and Denise sought parenting rights of Daniel, the boy Susan had given birth to from the embryo created with Robert's sperm. A trial court determined that Susan is Daniel's mother, Robert is his father and Denise had no standing as a parent.

Susan appealed, stating that California law should protect her from any paternity claim, since she contracted for anonymous sperm that a licensed doctor used to inseminate her. Superior court, however, denied her appeal, stating that Robert did not provide his semen for the purpose of inseminating anyone other than his wife, thus the anonymous donor regulation was not applicable in her case. Robert has visitation rights.

A surrogacy case

A 2005 case in Pennsylvania involving a well-off couple and a surrogate mother indicated an interesting twist on questions of biological parenthood and what is best for children.[11] A woman gave birth to triplets on behalf of an older couple — using donated eggs and the man's sperm — but grew uneasy after leaving the hospital because the adoptive parents had not been an active presence in the hospital during the first week of the children's lives. With the hospital preparing to put the children into foster care, the woman named the triplets and brought them home with her.

The intended father was a 63-year-old math professor who said complicated paperwork had kept him away from the hospital, that he could provide a better life for the children, and that he "wanted to leave something behind when I die." His girlfriend was a 60-year-old woman with two grown kids. The couple did not marry because they relied on the pension she received as a policeman's widow.

He testified that the surrogate and her family lived in a small and dirty home, in a depressed city with a poor school system. In contrast, he said his salary of $136,000 would allow him to raise the children in an affluent community, and that he and his girlfriend had more time to spend with them.

Hospital personnel testified that the older couple's primary concerns in that first week seemed to be about insurance coverage and equipment, but not about the newborns.

Fourteen months after the triplets were born, a court decided the 30-year-old surrogate and her husband, who lived well below the poverty line already with three other children, could have permanent custody of the triplets. The judge declared the mother, who had filed for bankruptcy a few months before the birth, was "the better caretaker by far."

The judge indicated that the math professor alternated between complaining about his legal costs and boasting about his affluent community. He questioned why the man didn't take any days off from work when the triplets were with him for 12 days during the summer. He ordered the man to pay $1,750 a month for child support, and gave him weekend visitation rights. The three children were given his last name.

Rights Around the World

Many countries are ahead of the United States on establishing formal regulations for the insemination industry. Here are some of them: (My thanks to Diane Allen for her invaluable work with Infertility Network.)

New Zealand — In 2005, a report was given to Parliament to examine the legal definition of parenthood and recommend several changes to existing laws to reflect changing family structures and developments in reproductive technologies. The emphasis in the proposals is on protecting the child's best interests, from an early age; access to genetic information; desirability of collaborative parenting; and the equality of children regardless of the circumstances of their creation or family form. One of the suggested reforms is to give donors of egg and sperm legal parenthood status, which could mean that a child would have more than two parents.

Sweden — Approved IVF for lesbian couples, and declared that both women should be regarded as the child's mother. (Although gay marriages remain illegal in Sweden, they do allow civil unions and adoption by gay couples.) Only open-identity or known donors are legal; anonymous donors were disallowed in 1985.

Denmark, the Netherlands, Finland, Great Britain, Russia, and Spain also allow IVF for lesbian couples.

Australia — At the end of 2007, the state government in Victoria decided that same-sex couples and single women should be eligible to receive fertility treatment, as married couples do, even without being declared medically infertile. The intent was partially to reduce the cases of women conceiving without clinic intervention and thereby limit the risks of transmissible diseases, as well as to provide offspring with better records of donor identity for future use.

Ireland — The Irish Commission on Assisted Human Reproduction issued a report in 2005 that, among other things, recommended that fertility treatments be available to unmarried parents, including lesbians. A highly controversial recommendation in the report proposes that children born through a surrogate mother should be presumed to be the offspring of the commissioning parents. Typically, the surrogate is regarded as the legal mother until an event such as formal adoption takes place. (In the United States, Illinois and California are notable exceptions.)

Italy — In 2004, Italy passed legislation forbidding anyone to use donated eggs or sperm. Only heterosexual couples are allowed to use in vitro fertilization. Many infertile Italians reportedly are traveling elsewhere for services.

Croatia — The Catholic Church condemned IVF as a "crime against human life," believing that to bear children from any method other than intercourse between a man and a woman transforms the child "into an object." A bill has been in the wings for many years that would allow infertility treatments for single women, but has not been turned into law, many believe because of strong church opposition.

Wales — Guidelines that were being considered in 2005 include prohibiting IVF treatment for a couple if one of them already has a child, and requiring participation in a smoking cessation program for smokers seeking IVF services.

India — Proposed guidelines by the Indian Council on Medical Research allow single women access to fertility services. It was considering the prohibition of known donor sperm.

> *Anonymous donors are not allowed in Sweden, Switzerland, Austria, the Netherlands, New Zealand, the United Kingdom, and the states of Victoria and Western Australia. Germany and Japan are both considering, in public debate, whether single women should have access to sperm donors.*

Open-identity issues in the United Kingdom

A British regulatory agency decided, after consultation with many experts, that it is in the best interests of children to know about their conception. Although it might lead to fewer men being willing to donate at the beginning, the agency determined that the rights of children are paramount — leading to a sweeping change in the law, effective in 2005, which reversed a 1990 decision to authorize anonymity.

The director of the London Fertility Centre coauthored a column after the law was enacted, emphasizing the need for additional monies to be spent on donor recruitment.[12] According to its survey of egg donors, of the nearly 200 past donors who responded, 52.1 percent said they would donate again even if they were not anonymous, and 36.4 percent said they would not. A survey sent to past recipients indicated that 53.5 percent would not use fertility services again if the donor was not anonymous. One concern raised by the authors was that its clients would go elsewhere for treatment.

Elsewhere, another fertility clinic reported that by changing its recruitment practices — gearing toward progressive, altruistic donors rather than younger college men — it was building up its donor pool to acceptable levels.

The United Kingdom regulatory agency also considered a requirement to change the birth certificates of DI children. Instead of listing the nonbiological parent's name, a proposed change would be to say "Donor," making it impossible for married couples to hide the truth from children.

A U.K. court case in 2002 fought to establish a voluntary register of sperm and egg donors, in order to make it easier for donor offspring to trace their genetic parents.[13] The suit was based on the argument that everyone has the right to form a personal identity, and that without full knowledge of genetic inheritance, people can never truly know who they are. The suit invoked an anti-discrimination provision to argue that donor offspring should have the same rights as adopted children to trace their biological parents. And it sought to force a regulatory agency to collect and store a greater range of information about donors, including a requirement that donors report any medical conditions that develop after donating their sperm or eggs.

A similar voluntary donor registry was established in the Australian state of Victoria in 1978. Although donors are free not to register, Victoria clinics report that nearly all do.

A movement for open identity is building slowly in the United States. But inevitably there will be a strong number of parents and donors who want the option for anonymity. Infertile husbands and wives who don't want to complicate their child's definition of family (as well as many Choice Moms and lesbian couples) are often threatened by the existence of a donor, for example. And many donors might opt not to participate otherwise, leading to a supply and demand problem that ultimately will favor those parents able to pay higher prices for fertility services.

So, even though I highly favor the open-identity option, I personally think it's doubtful that a one-size-fits-all approach will be implemented in the U.S. anytime soon. Not enough doctors and fertility clinics care to bring up the emotional issues with parents yet. And many parents prefer to keep any use of donors private, to avoid the potential for becoming wedded to donor families. I have, however, been part of interesting conversations that will lead to changes in the way the donor industry may do business, particularly in regard to accessing updated medical histories of donors.

Changes in Adoption

As of 2005, adult adoptees in New Hampshire, Alabama, Alaska, Kansas, Tennessee, Delaware, and Oregon have access to their original birth certificates. In Ontario, Canada, a similar law was being considered. Britain allows any birth relative of an adoptee to use public records and legal documents.[14]

Some believe strongly that this is a violation of the rights to privacy of past birth parents. Others believe that every individual has the right to know who they are, where they come from, and what their ethnicity is — and that there should not be "haves" and "have nots" in adoption information access. Some point out that confidentiality was not necessarily a guaranteed part of the adoption process.

Another interesting development in U.S. adoption policy is related to the rights of gays and lesbians. In New Jersey, for example, in 2005, a judge granted full co-parenting rights to the lesbian partner of a woman who bore the child they intended to raise together, without requiring the usual lengthy adoption proceedings.[15] Both the American Medical Association and the American Psychological Association support partner co-adoptions.

About 60 percent of U.S. adoption agencies accept applications from gays and lesbians, according to a 2003 survey from the Evan B. Donaldson Adoption Institute.[16] As the institute's executive director, Adam Pertman, has said, agencies are evidently concurring with research that gays and lesbians make good parents. The survey included 307 adoption agencies and found that 40 percent of the agencies had placed children with gay and lesbian parents.

"The child who is older, who is of color, who has special needs — those are the children who are more likely to be adopted by gays and lesbians," Pertman said. He said agencies that deal with children in foster care, with adoptions from abroad, and Jewish- and Lutheran-affiliated agencies were most likely to work with gays and lesbians.

As the survey said: "Although stereotypes and misconceptions still perpetuate policy and practice . . . the willingness of adoption agencies to accept gay and lesbian adults as parents means more and more waiting children are moving into permanent, loving families."

Note: Pertman told me that the institute has not explored how many agencies accept applications — and make placements with — single parents, but he suggested that it is safe to assume that there are more agencies that accept single applicants (including a growing number of men) than gay and lesbian ones.

Where Gays and Lesbians Need Not Apply

The American Psychological Association released a 1995 review of research, *Lesbian and Gay Parenting: A Resource for Psychologists,* that reported that "not a single study has found children of gay or lesbian parents to be disadvantaged in any significant respect relative to children of heterosexual parents," and concluded that "home environments provided by gay and lesbian parents are as likely as those provided by heterosexual parents to support and enable children's psychosocial growth."[17]

Yet Florida — which had more than 8,000 children awaiting

adoption in 2002 — prohibits gays from adopting children, either as couples or single parents. Four gay men there — foster parents attempting to adopt children in their care — challenged the law at the U.S. Supreme Court level. Although the Child Welfare League of America urged the Court to review the restriction, and defended the parenting abilities of gays, the Court refused to hear the case. A majority of the judges in the 11th U.S. Circuit Court of Appeals was required to grant a rehearing, but the ban was upheld by a 6–6 decision.[18]

According to an Associated Press story, the state's attorney wrote in his filing to the court, "It is rational to believe that children need male and female influences to develop optimally, particularly in the areas of sexual and gender identity, and heterosexual role modeling."[19]

And the president of a conservative Florida law group, Liberty Counsel, said the Court's refusal to hear the case sends a message to other states that "you can follow Florida's lead with policies that encourage kids to be placed with moms and dads." In fact, anti-gay adoption bills were subsequently introduced (but rejected) in Tennessee, Virginia, and Arkansas.

The law prohibiting adoption by gays in Florida was passed in 1977, at the height of Anita Bryant's anti-homosexual campaign. Governor Jeb Bush of Florida maintains that adoptive children, who often come from unstable backgrounds, should have a mother and a father. Florida does, however, allow divorcées, singles, and people with disabilities to adopt — and reportedly does not specifically ban people convicted of abuse or molestation from adopting.

In recent years, there have been efforts in at least 16 states to create laws to prevent gays and lesbians from adopting. At last count, Florida is the only state to prohibit it. But Mississippi, Nebraska, Oklahoma, Utah, and North Dakota are not welcoming to gay and lesbian applicants. Alabama, Arkansas, Georgia, Kentucky, Missouri, and Texas have had bans suggested. Ohio has taken a stronger lead in recent years to bar adoptions and foster care by gays and lesbians, although popular opinion there indicates a majority of its voters would oppose a ban.

According to the latest information, six states specifically allow adoptions by gays: California, Connecticut, Massachusetts, New York, Pennsylvania, and Vermont, as well as the District of Columbia.[20]

Family structure research redux

As the social scientist Louise Silverstein reported,[21] a qualitative study of 200 men of different subcultures — including Haitian, gay, Latino, divorced, Greek, and Orthodox Jew — all of whom were actively involved with their children, revealed that "a wide variety of family structures can support positive child outcomes. We have concluded that children need at least one responsible, caretaking adult who has a positive emotional connection to them, and with whom they have a consistent relationship.

"Because of the emotional and practical stress involved in childrearing," the report went on to say, "a family structure that includes more than one such adult is more likely to contribute to positive child outcomes. Neither the sex of the adult(s), nor the biological relationship to the child has emerged as a significant variable in predicting positive development."

Insurance News

Some advocacy groups, such as RESOLVE: The National Infertility Association, are pushing for stronger, all-inclusive polices governing coverage for infertility treatments, believing the option to pursue treatment should be available to all. (They also lobby on behalf of increasing benefits to adoptive families.) But whether a fertile single woman is entitled to assistance in paying for treatments is a wider philosophical question not likely to be mandated anytime soon, especially with health insurance already as costly as it is.

In most cases, single women who find supportive sperm banks and doctors have to pay for insemination services themselves, since only one-fourth of health plans offered at companies with more than ten employees cover infertility treatment, according to RE-SOLVE. And usually, women are eligible for coverage only if they are unable to conceive after a year or more of unprotected sexual intercourse.

Insemination can be cost-prohibitive for many women. Each insemination attempt also includes fees for donor sperm, consultations, physical exams, and the preparation, storage, and shipping of sperm. Since the chances of conceiving using frozen sperm is about 8 to 15 percent per monthly cycle, insemination without insurance can be quite expensive, especially for those who require fertility treatment.

According to a 2003 Women's eNews article,[22] artificial insemination can cost from $500 to $5,000; in vitro fertilization (when a woman's eggs are harvested from her body, fertilized with sperm, then implanted back in her uterus) from $25,000 to $75,000; and gestational surrogacy (when the embryo from in vitro fertilization is implanted in the womb of a surrogate carrier) from $50,000 to $100,000.

Some states allow women to use anonymous donor sperm for home insemination, which is significantly less expensive. A danger to single women who are not inseminated at a clinic is that they sometimes use the sperm of a donor who hasn't been tested for sexually transmitted diseases.

According to the reporter Felicia R. Lee, the average cost of one in vitro attempt in the United States is $12,400. She wrote an article for the *New York Times* in January 2005 about American fertility clients who go overseas in pursuit of less expensive options. In Israel, for example, in vitro is free for citizens, and about $6,500 per cycle for others.[23] One married woman she talked to priced fertility services in many countries and ended up with two IVF efforts in Naples, Italy, for less than $8,500.

At last count, 15 states had laws requiring insurance policies to cover some fertility issues, but many policies do not consider lack of partner to qualify as infertility.[24]

How Marriage Policy Pertains

The political debate about gay marriage, which became part of the platform during the 2004 presidential election, has ties to Choice Motherhood.

In decrying the idea of gay marriage, for example, the conservative James C. Dobson quoted David Popenoe as saying: "We should disavow the notion that mommies can make good daddies, just as we should disavow the popular notion of radical feminists that daddies can make good mommies. The two sexes are different to the core, and each is necessary — culturally and biologically — for the optimal development of a human being."[25]

In a less headline-grabbing way, some continue to consider marriage to be a solution to poverty. In his infamous speech of 1992, Vice President Dan Quayle said, "For those concerned about children growing up in poverty, we should know this: marriage is probably the best antipoverty program of all."

Social policy advocates who agree with this position tend to resurrect arguments about how single parenthood is detrimental to kids. Many believe that single parents should not receive the same benefits as married parents.

The long-time family values commentator Barbara Dafoe Whitehead testified to the U.S. Senate subcommittee on children and families in 2004 about the importance of marriage to children, adults, and society, 11 years after she authored her *Atlantic Monthly* article titled "Dan Quayle Was Right."[26]

She indicated that "researchers now agree that, except in cases of high and unremitting parental conflict, children who grow up in households with their married mother and father do better on a wide range of economic, social, educational, and emotional measures than do children in other kinds of family arrangements."

This is one reason policymakers in the George W. Bush administration created government-subsidized programs that give aid to married couples, and men who live with their families, in the form of specialized housing, economic assistance, and job training. It has especially invested in marriage promotion programs, to help couples avoid divorce. In 2002 and 2003, the U.S. Department of Health and Human Services committed at least $90 million for marriage-related grants, research, and assistance.[27]

According to the Center for Law and Social Policy,[28] 19 states offer state-funded welfare programs that make it easier for married couples to receive financial assistance. Florida requires four hours of relationship and marriage education for high school graduation. West Virginia gives a $100 monthly "bonus" to married welfare recipients. Tennessee and Vermont forgive child support debts to the state if the parents marry or reunite. In Louisiana, about $1.4 million has been spent since September 2002 to develop, among many other things, products for unmarried parents emphasizing the value of marriage.

While there is nothing wrong with attempts to strengthen marriage, those who promote marriage policies often disparage single parenthood in the process, without noticing the existence of Choice Moms as a community of self-sufficient single women who tend to be highly attentive to their children's needs.

Final Thoughts

Does an agency, clinic, or doctor have an obligation to provide service to single women, or not? In the United States, this has been a generally unregulated area of the law.

As more women turn to the Choice option, questions that affect them are increasingly being raised and addressed in clinic and agency board rooms, and in legislative and judicial chambers — and will continue to be raised.

For that reason, as well as for the sake of women who face opposition from agencies and clinics in their communities, it's important that readers of this book and visitors to choicemoms.org be aware not only of rules that might affect them, but of the policies that could be enacted if the collective successes of Choice Moms are not reported.

Just as the success of Choice pioneers made it easier for single women today to make this decision, I hope the legacy of today's Choice Mothers will be to collectively help others see that our families should not be feared or prohibited. We need help to raise our children, just as every parent does. And ours is not a model that will work for everyone. But as responsible, thinking women we can raise wonderful, loving children — despite the absence of a father.

When policymakers need to hear about our family model, I want the stories of Choice Moms and Choice Kids to be heard. The chapter that follows is a start in that direction.

How Are the Kids Turning Out?

I want to do it myself," used to be the phrase that made me swell up with pride that Sophie was turning out to be like her mom. But then I realized that she was in the first stage of independence, and the phrase was not uncommon for kids her age.

In those first years, however, I was ever vigilant for ways in which she might be similar to me, or how she was dissimilar to me and thus perhaps taking after her biological father, as well as how she might be impacted by the lack of a father in her life. For a while, my little girl wasn't given credit for any natural inclinations she might have. It was as if every personality trait, strength, or weakness had a reason behind it that I had some control over.

When she felt overwhelmed on her first day of kindergarten, sitting in a lunchroom with 60 other first-timers who were experiencing a range of comfort levels, I worried that she'd either inherited my tendency for shyness, without an outgoing parent to counteract. She wasn't like her classmate Dante, who was chatting it up with every adult he saw that first day, finding it hard to stay in his seat. But neither was she like the little boy who quietly cried because his older sister had left him with his class and gone off to her own.

Sophie (and Dylan, I'm now finding) tends to be an observer in unfamiliar situations, hanging back to study others before putting herself out there. Although I have the same tendency, I did worry through her first-grade year whether this presumed lack of confidence was related to growing up without a father. An admittedly strange leap, but not uncommon — even for a mother like me, who is confident in many other ways that I hoped would rub off on her someday.

But as I let her grow naturally, and pay less attention to the quirks and emotions that are simply her, without deep root causes, I can see some amazing things.

When that first day of school started, Sophie was proud of her ability to write her name, do basic addition, and read several words. As the year progressed, she made friends easily — boys and girls — and showed a surprising zeal for competition. Most people who worked with her commented on how quickly she learned, and how attentive she was in class. She especially stood out, as the lone white and female participant, in the Brazilian martial art capoeira, where she was at least two years younger than her cohorts. She always had an energy for learning, but I had never expected her to be so interested in challenging herself physically. In a matter of weeks she was proudly doing unaided handstands, and had noticeably improved in cartwheels and pushups.

By third grade she tested in the ninetieth percentile for both reading and math. She had an interest in science, as well as the creative arts, and continues to surprise me with her determination and abilities in skating, skiing, body slides, tumbling, and hip-hop dance.

Clearly the lack of a father in the home has not crimped her in stereotypical ways.

From the looks of it, her little brother will be a social one. He smiles easily and has noticed that he gets attention with his charming grins and enthusiastic zeal. Like his sister, by 18 months he showed an ability to focus for good lengths of time at independent play, was extremely attentive to sights and sounds, and learned quickly. He isn't much of a talker, but at age 3 has a strong ability to detect patterns, which serves him well in completing 100-piece puzzles. Although not yet in kindergarten, he can already write his name and read a few words.

> *I find that my fears no longer have anything to do with single parenthood. I know I can handle things on a day-to-day basis. But there are those nagging questions that can't be answered until they grow up.*

Will my irritability when I am exhausted from multitasking make them rebellious teens? Will they reject me someday because I didn't play with them enough? Will the minimal contact with their biological father hurt them in some way?

In this chapter we consider some of the stereotypical weaknesses of the Choice lifestyle: lack of time for parenting, lack of a model of trust and intimacy for developing adult relationships, intense attachments that might hinder separation, absence of a father's influence on development. And we consider some of the strengths of Choice Moms: genuine love and desire to nurture a child, independence, self-sufficiency, ability to set and achieve goals for personal fulfillment.

I boiled these stereotypes down into a standard set of questions asked for the first time of Choice Kids — young people raised by a single mother who consciously decided to raise them on her own. For this chapter, my interviews with several Choice Kids are included to help answer the big question: How are they turning out?

The young people featured here, who range in age from 11 to 30, were discovered in a random fashion. The kids chosen for this chapter were not selected because of the answers they gave, but because they represent different age groups and methods to motherhood.

I spoke with everyone confidentially, away from mothers. All of them were advised that they could ask for greater anonymity if they didn't want to be recognized in the book. I asked them how they felt growing up without a father, the strengths and weaknesses of the Choice lifestyle in their view, and how they feel their personality and life goals were impacted by their family structure.

I found that most of them were not shy about their opinions. However, several that I wanted to interview were not interested in participating, and likely would have offered worthwhile perspectives.

With such a small sample included here — the conversations are a separate book unto themselves — there are no grand generalizations that can be made, especially since I am talking only to kids willing to be interviewed. But as I continue these conversations, and as the large generation of today's young children mature, I hope to publish another book specifically about this topic in a few years. (Stay tuned to the website for more about this topic, and for the results of an extensive, long-term survey of Choice Mom families, launched in 2008. The survey is being conducted by a research team that includes a noted expert in nontraditional family building.)

Before getting to the perspectives of the Choice Kids, I will briefly summarize what my conversations with them have helped me discover so far.

Overall Findings (So Far)

Social development

Some sociologists have suggested that boys raised by single mothers sometimes make better partners, who listen and show greater compassion and respect than boys from other backgrounds, and that girls grow up with a can-do attitude of open possibilities that serves them well professionally.

Others, who primarily have talked to children of divorce, report that a sudden drop into an impoverished environment, feelings of rejection, and the inability to trust can have a great impact on a child's self-esteem and life choices.

Considering how randomly the kids I talked to were found, one thing that stood out for me was how accomplished most of them were. Many of them were unusually intelligent and precocious — even gifted. One boy entered college at the age of 14, and most were top students.

Was this genetic? Several had anonymous donors who were bright. Many Choice Moms have master's degrees, and obviously are strong-minded individuals.

In general, the kids I have talked to so far are confident and secure, likely because of the commitment and attention to parenting offered by their mothers.

Socially, a few of them seemed withdrawn, but most had close friendships with friends and family. And yes, most of them — not all — seemed to have very close relationships with their mothers.

The effect of stigma

When she was 3, Sophie seemed obsessed with prince-and-princess stories of romance. This too concerned me — might she feel she's missing something? — until I realized that most young girls had the same fascination, regardless of family structure.

The desire to fit in is typically a natural part of childhood. The model of "mommy, daddy, and me" is valued in general society. As one therapist told me, especially in early adolescence, the emphasis is on being just like one's peers, so if a teen differs from his or her friends, it may be a source of personal friction and stress.

Of course, kids can feel bad or be teased about lots of issues (being too fat, too thin, too tall, too short). As she said, "The best remedy is a supportive home environment in which adolescents can learn to love and care for themselves, and maybe get some coaching about how to cope with teasing and other experiences of being made to feel different."

The gender identity researcher Barbara Risman[1] discovered that children raised in untraditional households tend to grow up with more egalitarian attitudes about male and female roles and responsibilities. But because the child's identity is still developed largely from the influence of peers, they can struggle as they attempt to reconcile contradictions between how society sees things and life at home.

Do the children of Choice pioneers feel stigmatized or odd by not growing up in a "traditional" household?

In general, the ones I have talked to so far do not. A 30-year-old woman clearly had struggled with this issue — she articulated how she felt unusual growing up — but in hindsight, she said it had more to do with her mother's evasion of the topic than from a desire to fit in with other kids.

The young people I have talked to so far tend to be highly independent, with little shame about not coming from a "normal" family. One young man, for example, expressed disdain for the notion of conformity — not an uncommon response for his generation. He said that although he appreciated regular contact with a male role model, and although he was sure it did have an impact on him to grow up without a father, it didn't bother him to come from a Choice household when he was growing up, especially since so many kids came from divorced families.

However, a lack of shame or embarrassment doesn't equate with being an open book. Many kids don't want others to know the full, private details of their lives, which doesn't seem unusual.

The daddy story
Even if it wasn't a matter of stigma in their community, a basic question I ask every Choice Kid I interview is whether they wish they had a father.

One girl was 7 when she told her mother, after a few visits with her biological father, that she didn't want a relationship with him, even though the mother thought it would be a healthy option for her to pursue. Now an adult, the girl still has little interest in her father, but is developing a close relationship with her half-siblings.

One of the younger boys wished that he had a father to play with him when his mom was busy — playtime was clearly a priority in his young life.

In fact, many children believe that having a second parent would free up mom's time to spend with them. As one Choice Mom told me, she was explaining to her daughter why she needed her to go to bed, in order for mom to get chores done and have quiet time. "But mom," the girl told her, "if we had a dad in the house he would clean the cat box, do the dishes, and finish folding the laundry so you could cuddle with me."

Another young woman told me that when she was younger she wished she had a dad to make the card for on Father's Day. In kindergarten, she wished she had a father to bring to school when dads were expected. She also wanted one so she wouldn't have to keep explaining why she *didn't* have one. "Now that I'm older, I have no qualms about it. And I've gotten better at explaining it."

On the other hand, a boy who did not want to talk to me was 13 when he started expressing hostility to his mother for denying him a father. Research indicates this is a natural age for this type of resentment to show. Which is one reason I was surprised to find less reluctance or ambivalence from a few other teenage boys I spoke with. A 14-year-old boy expressed open affection for his mother, in fact, proudly declaring that she had done nearly everything right in raising him.

Several children I know who were conceived by an anonymous donor were in their early teens when the "unknowns" started to bother them — but others had no interest.

Will Choice Kids marry?

In 2004, David Popenoe and Barbara Dafoe Whitehead released a report titled "The Marrying Kind," which examined men ages 25 to 34 to determine who marries and who doesn't.[2] In short, they determined that young men whose parents were married were more likely to "express readiness" to be married than men from other backgrounds. They reported as well that young men from married households had more positive attitudes toward women, children, and family life.

One teenage girl I know of thought her mother's single status was working out so well for them that she didn't see any negatives to the lifestyle. Another teenager didn't feel comfortable in solo dating situations, and preferred group dating. Another extroverted girl dates, but hadn't yet met anyone she thought was worth investing time with, and seemed wise to the "use them and lose them" tendencies of some of the men on her college campus.

One girl I was not able to talk to was timid around men, which her mother attributed to the mother's conflicted feelings after a difficult breakup. But others were strong-minded and open in developing relationships with the opposite sex.

One young man reported having good friendships with women as well as normal "hanging out" time with men. He was not opposed to the idea of marriage, and although he dated infrequently in college, he was embarking on more serious relationships in later years.

The older the child, the more introspection they are able to give to what, really, their upbringing meant to them. That's why I intend to continue conversations with young adults who have had more time to reflect. I do not expect there will be big surprises in store about what they have to tell us, but there are more complex insights to be gained as Choice Kids make their own lifelong commitments as partners and parents.

The Mothers' Perspective

I had several conversations with experienced Choice Moms — many of them in the psychology profession, and all of them with kids who were at least 14 — who had interesting perspectives about how their children were turning out and why.

Relationships
One woman said her daughter didn't seem to miss having a father, but did tend to have boyfriends who served as a buffer between mother and child in the teenage years. The relationships weren't serious, but seemed to satisfy her hunger for cuddling.

The girl had reserves of inner strength, however. The mother reported that "she's more radicalized than I — a professional reformer." She seemed able to handle anything, as a top student, with passionate interests and a thirst for knowledge. How she handled the men in her life "blows me away," the mother reported. For example, one of the "players" at her school pursued the young woman for a long time before she told him that she didn't want to be friends because she didn't respect him.

Respect and integrity were important values to several young women. One young girl told her mother she no longer wanted to visit with her known donor because she didn't respect him. Another teenager tended to be suspicious of the intentions of boys who crossed her path. When she started dating, she did not feel comfortable in one-on-one situations and preferred group dating. "I have worried about her not having a model of a good relationship," said her mother. "But in my work, I see kids who get terrible models of relationships. Ideally kids would see perfectly communicating men and women, but many do not. And when divorce happens, that's torture on children. The experts tend to compare parenting to an image of perfection, but life doesn't work out that way."

Another mother, whose child was still too young for serious dating, also worried about whether the lack of a relationship model would be a problem for her child. "My concerns might be totally unfounded, but that does concern me," she said. "I know that he respects women, and has self-respect. He's got a good core, and maybe that's what it takes. Maybe his relationships will be modeled after him and me — mutual respect and kindness."

And in fact, many kids I talked to did specifically mention their strong connection with mom as the model they would use in future relationships.

One woman said her network didn't include many male role models for her daughter, except for one. "I think my father has been a father substitute for her," she said. "They're very close, more so than he and I ever were."

A question to be answered, as our children mature into relationships of their own, is whether they have the healthy connecting skills we hope for them, even without a positive male influence in the home.

Identity

A mother told me her daughter started to confront identity issues around the age of 14. "No one else in the family has a mole on the side of their face," the girl remarked one day. She became ultra-aware of how her conception story differed from others, and declared that she didn't want to have to explain everything to friends and teachers.

"My advice to other single mothers," the woman shared, "is that you should bring it up. You open the door. They might be nervous talking about it. But they'll be much less likely to be nervous if you help them discuss it openly. Even though my daughter is an extroverted child, she still wouldn't bring it up."

A biracial girl didn't have many questions about her father growing up; issues of race concerned her more. After she entered college, she embraced the African-American community for the first time. She also confronted head-on her loneliness as a teenager growing up without siblings. As a young adult, she started connecting with her many half-siblings, and formed a particularly good relationship with a half-brother close to her in age.

This is an area I consider to be of prime importance for Choice Moms to be sensitive about, as it is largely our children who have to answer these questions for themselves.

Strengths

In terms of what children gain by growing up in a one-parent family, one mother said the relationship with her child was so deeply complex — "a wonderful model for creating intimacy" — that her child, even in the turbulent teenage years, seemed able to talk to her about everything.

Another said that her daughter's former boyfriend had once

said, "'She knows how to do everything. She doesn't need a man around for the things men do' — and that's true," the mother said. "I'm not complaining. I'm glad she is self-sufficient. She definitely learned that from me. I think I'm a little obnoxious about not asking for help. She's much more independent than a lot of kids grow up to be."

One woman talked about how lucky she and her son were to be able to spend so much time together, "so much more than most families I know. We've had it very special." She said she had raised him to understand that his opinions do matter. "When we bought a new car, I asked for his opinion. He knows I want him to speak his mind. Some days that makes me want to pull my hair out, but the good far outweighs any negatives." When he became an Eagle Scout, he asked to pin both the "mom" and "dad" recognitions on her.

One young adult I read about, who was adopted from El Salvador and raised by a Jewish Choice Mom, said in an article that appeared in *Hadassah Magazine*,[3] "I always felt like an outsider in the synagogue and in Hebrew school. I was the only person of color, with a white mom. I'm comfortable culturally. I celebrate Passover and Hanukkah, but I don't have much of a Jewish identity."

It wasn't until college that the young woman found a racially mixed community she felt comfortable with. She majored in African-American studies and spent a semester in Namibia. Despite the racial disparities of her youth, the young woman was highly positive about her upbringing. "There's nothing more empowering than being raised by a single, amazing, independent woman," she said. "My mom led this alternative lifestyle by choice — one most people would not have chosen."

Weaknesses

One woman admitted that her child was spoiled — "materially, no, but attention-wise, yes. I definitely think that's the product of growing up with one parent." Another said her teenager seemed a

---

Choice Chat with Diana (a Therapist):
From My Experience . . .

✦ My daughter has clearly learned much from our relationship over the years about how to maintain a trusting, committed connection. But there are some vulnerabilities of Choice Motherhood that I do think we need to be mindful of:

• The intense attachment between mother and child might hinder separation; the mother must be conscious of supporting age-appropriate separation.
• There is no other influence to buffer or moderate the parent's world views and emotional reactions.
• The demands could be overwhelming without another primary caregiver.
• No matter how many other supportive figures there are in the child's life, there is only one primary caregiver for that child to turn to. As my daughter has said, "If my mom isn't there, it is up to me."

---

little selfish and self-centered — "but aren't they all at this age? I'm sure I'm not as disciplined about asking for help and support around the house as I should be."

Another reported that her child was easy from the beginning — good at following rules — but that it might have had something to do with not having anyone else to compete with. "I remember when she was 5, we went to the zoo with her friends. My daughter wanted to get popsicles, they wanted ice cream cones, and there was a big hassle over which one to get. It was the first time she acted like a brat. She'd never had to compromise with others like that."

One woman said she and her son had some regret about not

having a larger family. She tried to adopt when she was in her forties, but it didn't happen.

In fact, it has been quite common for me to hear kids talk about feeling more loss at not having a sibling than at not having a second parent.

Conversations with the Kids

Kyla, adult

Her mother was one of the earliest Choice Moms — she used an anonymous donor in 1975 — and perhaps as a result she missed the benefit of accumulated wisdom that today's single mothers enjoy, as they attempt to communicate about their Choice Kid's origins.

I felt some resentment about not having a traditional dad, mostly when I was a school-age kid. It wasn't so much missing a dad as feeling weary about being an oddity, weary of explaining something I really didn't understand myself.

I think it is selfish in a sense, although my mom was not aware of it at the time, to have a child in such a way that the father is anonymous and remains anonymous. I think a person has a right to know the identities of both parents. I do not think it is selfish to single-parent. Is it selfish to carelessly happen upon parenthood as a couple that has no inspiration for long-term commitment?

> *Selfishness seems unrelated to the form of conception. We all act upon our desires. Whether or not we are willing to take responsibility for the consequences of our desires is what ultimately measures our "selfishness."*

My mother did so many things right. She was devoted to me. She was on my side — irrationally so at times, which I believe is absolutely necessary for normal development. She was more interested in discovering who I was than in molding me into any preconceived image. Her parenting style was relatively hands-off; she trusted me to make choices that would aid me in my own process of knowing myself. So even when she didn't approve of the choice, she was more likely to let it run its course than to interfere.

The tragedy of my childhood was that my mom failed to stay in communication with me about some essential features of my existence. First, she didn't stay current with me about my understanding of how I was conceived. She told me about it when I was too young to understand, and then dropped it, so that I really didn't know what "artificial insemination" was, but only remembered that clinical term. I made up stories about a dead dad to avoid what seemed a humiliating and incomprehensible truth.

Second, and more important, when I was 7 we moved in with my mom's (female) partner, who ignored me to such an extent that I'd guess we exchanged less than a dozen words in the last eight of the nine years we lived together. My mom acted as though this was not happening.

I think part of her confusion or motivation here was the financial and emotional security the partner provided. It allowed her to give me material things I wanted, and also to work half-time in order to be more available to me. These were certainly not conscious choices, but they were part of the fear that kept her from changing what became an ugly and painful home.

My mom also never communicated with me about being a lesbian, but, instead, called her partner our "housemate." So this was another thing I knew but didn't really know in an articulate way, and so lied about.

What I do see in myself now is a lack of attachment for men. I have chosen female partners (in spite of every wish not to become what I saw modeled by my mom and her partner), and although I have had male lovers, I have not ever felt attached to them. I do not have a clear sense of whether this is directly related to the lack of a man who I was close to when I was a child. It may just be my nature, or it may just be circumstantial. It seems possible that tomorrow I might feel attached to a man, or not. Either way, this is not intrinsic to single-momhood. It's rather specific to my story that, in addition to not having a dad, I did not have a brother, or uncle, or grandpa, or friend, who was close and present.

Q: Some feel that a child who grows up in a Choice home might consider marriage unnecessary to happiness. Your thoughts?

Again, this seems unrelated to a Choice home. Choice conception does not preclude a loving relationship between adult role models. I do consider marriage unnecessary to happiness. I consider just about any external circumstance to be irrelevant to happiness. If my upbringing helped me see this, I credit it for that.

I felt a lot of stigma about our family structure when I was young, but I believe this was due to lack of communication rather than the family structure itself.

If a proud and open approach to our "difference" was modeled for me, I'm sure I'd have spoken with pride and openness. As it was, I lied, felt enormous shame, and evaded all inquiries.

About my donor — I just want to know who he is. I want to sit across from him, see him, hear him speak, experience him. I'm not looking for someone to fill the role of father. I do think the identity of a donor should belong to the child.

And I do feel there is a hole in my knowledge of myself. Before I made a concerted effort to find him, it was a conceptual idea — a curiosity more than an emotionally-driven need. It's hard to feel much of anything about an absence. In the course of my looking, however, I was surprised by how raw, how tender I felt every time I thought I might have found him.

Greg, young adult
His biological father left when his mother was pregnant.

I don't think I had many "daddy" questions, but I did grow up with a strong disregard for fitting in. I wasn't a wild child, but I was extremely independent. I tend to make my own conclusions, set my own values, rather than feel bound by social expectations. I definitely would like to get married and have kids, although I was shy about dating for a long time because of some self-confidence issues. I have resolved most of my issues through lots of introspection, and have dated a few women since graduating from college. I am currently seeing someone.

I wasn't ostracized for our different family structure. It wasn't like I was seen as some kind of freak. Maybe more so by the parents of kids, if anybody.

> I used to be asked if I missed having a dad, and my standard answer was that you can't miss what you don't have. In hindsight, I think by being raised by a single parent, I wasn't exposed to the same levels and varieties of social interaction, so when I was a kid I probably developed socially more slowly than others.

As far as fears some have that a guy like me will grow up overly aggressive, or less analytical, because of the lack of a father in the home — it doesn't make sense. I was excellent as a math and science student in high school. (I was only average in subjects like history and English.) I went to a competitive prep school, and graduated Phi Beta Kappa from college as a computer science major. There are a lot of stereotypes about single parenting, and it seems as if we're all clumped into the same category.

On the role-model front, though, since the mother is the one and only parent, it is clearly important that she be an excellent role model. With no one to dispute her or argue with her, it may be easy for the child to think that mom is infallible, especially when they are too young to know any better.

An advantage to the way I grew up, I think, is that I never witnessed my parents fighting. My mother is a very independent woman, and I think I got that personality trait specifically from her, not from single parenthood itself. I definitely learned from her example that you don't always have to do things the way everyone else does. Especially through my college years, I tended to question everything. I wasn't so eager to fit in. In the years since, though, I've seen the benefits of "fitting in" and, although I am still pretty independent, I don't have as strong a need to be different and I don't always mind if I'm doing things the way everyone else does. I'm still not trendy, but I think that's mostly because I know trends don't last.

Money and material things aren't so important to me. I don't mind living alone. I don't really relate to the stereotypical jocks, or get into macho competition. I consider it a waste of time. People tell me I'm easy to talk to, maybe a little more sensitive than some. In college I had several one-to-one relationships with girls. At this point in my life, though, I definitely prefer having drinks with a group of guys than having intense one-on-one conversations with girls.

The weak points of the family structure are just common sense: you don't have a dad around to teach you to do the guy things. It's more the missing of someone who could be a good role model. The husband of my mom's college friend was my godfather, and a good role model. From about the age of 7 to 13, I saw him maybe once a week, and we are still very close — as I am with my godmother. After that I was in the Big Brother program for a few years. I was against it at first, but it turned out to be fantastic. He was about 30, married, with no kids then. He lives in Texas now, with three kids, so we don't talk as much.

When you try to determine the source of a child's personality, it's difficult to tell what came from the lack of a father and what came from the mother's own personality. These days I tend to think that any personality traits one can attribute to the lack of a father are probably just social handicaps due to less exposure to social interactions at home. I have a hunch that having a sibling probably would have made up for some of that.

As far as inherited personality traits from the mother, I think it's important to expose the kid to many different role models, because with only one parent, the kid may end up inheriting an unusual amount of that parent's personality.

I think every kid of a single mom will have a different experience, but the effects of a missing father might be visible in most of them. I am pretty interested whether or not that's true.

Cambra, young adult
Her pioneering mother was inseminated in 1982, after a difficult search for a doctor who would work with a single woman. She had a rough pregnancy and a difficult delivery, and told Cambra as she grew that she had been a fighter from the start.

Mom has been open with me about her choice and my conception ever since I was old enough to understand it. I was never confused about my origins, and always understood what she had done and why. I never begrudged her her decision, never wished she'd done it differently. On the contrary, I was always grateful that she made the choice, that she wanted me enough to fight for me, that she loved me that much even before "I" existed. I've never felt ostracized because of it, was never teased or stigmatized. The usual response I got from kids was "Cool!"

But it hasn't been easy. Mainly because it has just been the two of us for 25 years! We are very close, but since I was a teenager I have tried to distance myself from her a bit so as not to feel smothered. The school system I was at when I was 13 was a mess. We couldn't afford private school. But a teacher recommended a small boarding school with great academics. I won a full scholarship, left home at age 14, and haven't lived with my mother since. I honestly think that my going to boarding school was the best thing that ever happened to our relationship. She was forced to let go a little, I was forced to grow up a little, and I think we both learned to stand on our own two feet.

I think that the line between "closeness" and smothering was a very fine one for us, both because of our personalities and because of the fact that it was just the two of us, all the time. My mother is a very strong, independent woman, but she is also a highly sensitive, emotional creature. I think when I was born I became the vessel for all of her love and attention, but also the protector of all of her insecurities and weaknesses. While she had to be strong in the rest of the world, she could be weak with me. She was supportive to a fault, but also overprotective and incredibly invested in my actions and emotions. I felt like I had an enormous amount of power over her happiness. She loved me with her whole being, but that can be a heavy weight to bear when you are young and trying to figure out who you are, what kind of person you are becoming. It was hard to separate myself from her. And without another parent, without a sibling, there was nowhere for the energy to go except back and forth between us.

I have often been asked if I wished "I had a father." My ready response has always been, "No, not really," but I suppose it is more complicated than that. I have always had a very strong desire to know who my donor is. I've always wondered what he looks like, how his voice sounds, if he can wiggle his ears like I can, if he is really as tall as the paper says he is (and if so, then why am I so short?!), if he likes to read, what his eyes look like. But I have never wanted him to be a "father" to me. I don't feel like I missed out on something by not having him around when I was growing up. And if I met him now, I know I would want to get to know him, and perhaps be a part of his life, but I also know that I don't need anything from him. My life is complete as it is.

The only time in my life I remember wishing I had a "Daddy" was in my early teenage years, when I was beginning to date and learned how awful teenage boys can be. I have distinct memories of wanting a father to run to, to tell me that I was beautiful and boys were icky and that he would always love me. But I learned to seek out support from teachers, coaches, older male friends of the family, and mentors.

I have often wished, however, that my mother had a partner. It has been hard to be the "other" in her life, to be the primary source of love and comfort, or the primary object of anger and frustration. It was a very small world, just Mom and me — no one to come in between, no one to ask a second opinion, no one for me to run to for comfort, no one for her to look to for support.

While I did not see my mother in very many "intimate" relationships during my childhood, she taught me everything I know about loving. She is an extremely selfless person, always ready to sacrifice for others, always ready to give or do or act for her friends. She had close, loving friendships with both men and women, and many of them became my extended family. But while I saw readily the joy she took from loving, I also saw her hurt deeply by the occasional neglect of those she loved, and I myself hurt her with my own desire for distance and separation. I learned from her that when you love and give so freely, you open yourself up to pain and rejection. I have found that in my adult life, as I have loved and learned and moved through relationships, that I seek to embody many of the qualities my mother possesses — selflessness, generosity, honesty, openness, and above all a willingness to love and share and give. However, I also find myself from time to time falling into the same patterns of dependence and need that I felt from her, and being hurt by them as she was. I've learned as I've grown older to seek out those who share similar desires for loving and nurturing, so that together we can balance each other out.

Growing up the daughter of a single woman has given me a lot of strength. Because my mother always treated me like her equal, I have a very strong sense of my own abilities and self-worth. Because she struggled, I understand struggle and persistence. Because she was a strong woman, I became a strong woman. I have an independent spirit, and am not easily cowed or discouraged. While I have a lot of respect for others, I have never been intimidated by men, or my elders, or those in positions of authority. At the same time, I have learned through my close and loving relationship with my mother how important it is to reach out and love and try to form those sorts of bonds in life.

Laurabeth, young adult

Adopted at 13 months, Laurabeth had some rough periods in her earliest years, but when I met her, in the middle of her college years at an Ivy League school, she was thriving — socially, academically, emotionally.

The way I grew up — with a mother and no father — was never an issue at all. In fact, it took me a long time to realize that there were fathers who played a role in their kids' lives. And I never felt like an oddball growing up. Several of my friends thought it was kind of neat that I didn't have a dad. I certainly never felt resentment about it.

I don't really agree with the idea that men do some things better than women, and vice versa — the idea that you need a man and a woman to balance the parenting. People are complex. One person can do so many things, in many different ways. And as far as needing to see a man and a woman as a couple in order to learn how to relate to others — you don't need two parents for that.

I also don't agree with the theory that the absence of a father might make men seem like inferior beings. I think men are great. I've had a number of serious relationships. One great thing about living with a single parent is that it teaches you a lot about compromise.

My mother and I have always been extremely close. Although we have really intense arguments. When there's no other parent to run to, no third opinion on anything, it can be frustrating.

I think the strengths I got from the way I was raised are that I work well with people, I'm honest — the relationship I had with my mom was a good thing for me to learn from. It also made me stronger, as I needed to fend for myself when mom wasn't around.

What I especially learned from my mom was to do what you feel really strongly about, and have integrity in doing it. Those are major character traits I got from her. She's very intelligent and knows what she's doing.

Ryan, teenager

He is a celebrity in the donor insemination industry because he launched a donor sibling registry with his mother. He is an exceptionally mature young man who entered college at the age of 14.

For the most part, I don't feel resentful about not having a father, because I have had such a great, involved mom. Most of the time not having a traditional dad never crosses my mind. There are occasions though, like wondering if college would be easier, or if I would be in Calculus 5 by now, if I had a mathematics-oriented father who could help me. Other than occasional thoughts like that, I am more than okay that it's just my mother and I.

I don't understand why some people would consider it selfish for a single woman to want a child. Perhaps the thought is that it's not fair to the child to subject him or her to a life without a father figure? But as long as the woman is committed to raising the child herself in a responsible way, then I believe it to be preposterous to think that would be a "selfish act."

What has my mother done that was "right" in raising me? I'm not sure how to answer this question without sounding like I'm bragging. To be perfectly honest, I feel that she has done most everything right. She gives me all the freedom a teen needs, without ever having to worry about me trying pot or a cigarette or anything like that. Going to college early, as I did, is a big challenge for anyone, and she has been there 100 percent of the time. From handling almost every aspect of my education to instilling in me a sense of right and wrong, I would say she's done it. In fact, that's probably the primary reason that I'd be scared to have a child of my own. I'd know that I could never do as good a job raising him or her as she has with me.

Q: Some child experts feel that a boy who grows up without a father will lack a sense of discipline, be overly aggressive, lack analytical skills and/or have trouble understanding what it is to be a man. Do you see any of that in yourself?

I have friends who have grown up in a traditional family. As far as analytical skills, discipline, aggressiveness, and "manliness," I see very little difference. Consciously or not, I have learned to acquire those qualities elsewhere. Sure, my mother probably isn't the best at teaching me to be a man, but I think father or no, much of that comes from within. The day any guy is born, they have some element of this already established, and I think that it's going to show through no matter how you're raised. All my life, I've been dragged through clothing stores and jewelry stores and I still hate it. Just because I was raised with it doesn't mean that I'm gonna like it. Father figure or not, I'm always gonna like hurting myself on my bike, gadgets, welding, building, and all that stuff that comes naturally with being a man. I really feel that a lot more of who a person is comes from instinct, rather than their upbringing.

I have found male role models in many forms over the years. The earliest I can think of was a mentor named Sean. He taught me a lot about math and science and mechanics and engineering. I looked up to him perhaps because he was so smart. Over the years I found role models in teachers and friends and mountain biking coaches, and sometimes even on television. The person I probably most admire is late night talk show host Conan O'Brien. He's basically what I want to be when I grow up. Smart, hilarious, witty, Harvard-educated, tall, and fun loving. I think that's basically the definition of a role model — someone I aspire to be.

Q: *Have you felt stigma from others about your family structure?*

Only once that I can recall. It was from a high school physics teacher whom I loathed, and she loathed me. She would openly attack me in front of classmates about what I've done to establish the donor sibling registry. It was a horrid situation, but I no longer attend that school. Other than that, people seem to really embrace what I've done, and where I came from.

I think that one great thing about being raised by only

my mother is that it has given us an unusually strong bond. My mother means the world to me, and I mean the world to her. I think that had I been raised by two parents, that bond would logically be decreased by half. But it's hard to say how my life would have been different with a father.

I am extremely curious about my donor. I feel it is a curiosity that can only be understood if you grow up with half of your family missing. Imagine looking in the mirror and not knowing a damned thing about half of yourself. Half of your physical characteristics, half of your interests, half of everything.

What would I like to know? EVERYTHING. Why do I like engineering? How did I end up with OCD? Where did you go to college? What are my other grandparents like? What Scottish clan am I? How many uncles and aunts do I have? How many half-siblings do I have? Are you married? Where do you live? What do you do for a living? The list goes on. I could ask him questions for years before I caught up with all of the things that I would have known by now.

Do I think donors should remain anonymous? Absolutely not. They should have a total openness policy. Because sooner or later, if the children aren't lied to about origins (and even in some cases if they are) the children are going to be curious about where they came from. And the donor has to be prepared to satisfy that curiosity.

Grace, teenager
Her mother used a known donor, who unexpectedly died when Grace was 4. Before he died, Grace traveled to his state twice a year to visit. She still stays in touch with his family. As a high school sophomore, she was considering following in her mother's steps as a psychologist.

The main difference between me and other friends is that I'm a lot more honest with my mom about what's going on in my life. Maybe because my mom is more laidback. Of course, I don't al-

ways like her being so involved in my business. It's annoying sometimes. But I'd rather have her more involved than not in knowing
about my life.

The father of two of my friends has been kind of like a dad to
me, and I have a friend who is like a brother to me. I'm not a girly
person. I never wear skirts or makeup. I consider myself sometimes
to be like one of the guys, so I wouldn't say the lack of a male influence in the house has had any impact. Like at the fair, with this
screaming death-trap ride, I was the only girl in the group that
would go on it.

Sometimes when friends are busy with family things, I feel a little isolated because I don't have as much family. I wish I had a sibling sometimes, someone to bond with other than my mother. But
I'm very social, and love spending time with friends, so I don't usually feel very alone.

*Q: What kind of connection did you feel with your biological
father? Even though he's not alive anymore, what kind of role do
you think he has played in your life?*

I like analyzing myself, discovering what makes me, me. I have
a natural ability in math, and he was a mathematician, so I know
that came from him. My mom can't read music, and I'm an insane
music person and play two instruments. I got that from him. I can
sing, and I've learned that he loved to sing.

If I didn't know who he was, and wasn't able to ask these questions, I know I'd be really, really curious. On the one hand, you
might be afraid to know things about the person, but I'd really
want to find out what I could.

If I'd grown up with a father, I'd probably hope he might do
some things my mom won't do. Like go to theme parks. But there
aren't really things I miss that my friends have with their dads.

After he died, I handled it like any 4-year-old might. I watched
Lion King on repeat forever. I do get sad now sometimes that he
died, and wonder what it might be like if he was still alive. My

mom tells me how proud he would have been because I'm so much like him.

Q: *What are the advantages to growing up with a Choice Mom?*

Personally, I think it has taught me independence. There are many girls my age who feel this inexplicable need for a boyfriend. While I always enjoy when I have boyfriends, I've never been one to be called boy crazy. I know I don't need a boyfriend and I'm perfectly fine being single. Though crushes are always fun.

Q: *What are the disadvantages?*

Well, there's the obvious ones, like you can't get rides to places all the time, and there's just less opportunities to do things. One psychological thing, I suppose, is that I don't get to see a relationship between my parents. I don't get to see firsthand how a relationship should or shouldn't work, so I have had to learn myself, through movies, friends, and experience.

Q: *What do you think would be different about your life if you had a dad?*

Well, I'd certainly have to ask friends for rides less often! I doubt I'd be this close to my mother, but I can't really say. I don't want to make a prediction about anything because there are so many different ways it could be. It really depends on what my dad was like, how well my parents got along, and so many other factors.

Zac, preteen
This precocious boy acquired a stepfather when he was 6. Together the threesome went to China to adopt his sister. Zac has the unique benefit of having a donor who wrote a letter to be given to any offspring.

My donor wrote a letter telling me about his family, and about his ups and downs through college. He talked about growing up in a multiethnic neighborhood — basically, he's not racist. He was very good at sports, like tennis and running. He always wanted to go to medical school, since he was in seventh grade.

He wrote this message: "I wish the very best to your parents. I hope they give you the love that I got from mine. And to you, I wish you all the best in life. I hope you can become whomever you want to be, and I will always have a place for you in my heart."

I think I was 7 when I decided I wanted to meet him. I thought about it, but didn't really mention it. That's the youngest I remember being interested. I've asked my mom a lot about meeting him. I'm very curious about him. Even though he sent me an entire four-page letter, there are still some questions unanswered. One of them was: Why did he donate his sperm to create kids?

Mom answers my questions, but I do have one she can't. What does he think, truly, about me, myself? Not just any kid that he donated sperm to create. (Not that he really knows I exist, but if he did.)

When I was younger, I was sad about not having a dad. Whenever my mom was doing things, I had nothing to do and no one to play with. All my friends would have dads and they would be playing with them all the time and saying what a good time they had with them. I wasn't angry, but just plain sad. When my mom would play with me, though, I didn't think much about having a father then. She would show me pictures of my donor and also tell me what he wrote to me, so I felt a bit better about that.

Now, because of having a stepdad, I also have brothers and sisters. I liked it when my mom started dating my dad, because he was really nice. He played with me a lot. But there was a bad side to it. His son was the meanest person ever to me. That has cleared up by now, four years later, but there are still some rough spots with him.

Q: Some people consider it selfish for a woman to decide to have a child on her own. What is your opinion on that?

Why would she only care about herself when she was giving birth to me and helping me to grow up to be a great man?

Q: What has your mom done that is "right" in the way she raised you?

She would play with me a lot. She buys me ice cream and lets me have sleepovers whenever I want. She takes me around the world. She played with me when I was a baby and takes pictures of me. She says I was a cute baby. She is very fond of me.

Q: What would you suggest for future single moms about ways they could avoid making mistakes in raising their child?

First of all, don't keep anything from your kids. My mom told me absolutely every secret. For example, she told me as soon as I was 6 that Santa Claus wasn't real. She tells me everything. My mom also told me everything about my donor. She showed me pictures of him and the note that he wrote.

Q: What strengths and weaknesses do you have that you feel are related to being raised only by your mom when you were little?

I'm not jerky like my brother is. I got lots of privileges that normally a father wouldn't permit. For instance, sleepovers, trips to the ice cream shop, playing with friends a lot.

Final Thoughts

Most of the young people I have talked to so far have healthy and nurturing relationships with their mothers, which is perhaps why they talked to me in the first place. And, reluctant commentators or not, most of the Choice Kids I know seem to be well-balanced, highly individualized young men and women.

There is perhaps a streak of self-absorption, which might have something to do with the age, something to do with the self-sufficiency of their mothers, or something to do with the tendency for the earlier generation of Choice Kids to have no siblings. Another tendency I expect to explore over time is whether a subset of Choice Kids have grown up more socially isolated than others, and what impact this has. Although support networks and role models are highly recommended in this book, not all kids have grown up with them, and I'm curious about the effect of growing up in such a one-on-one household.

Perhaps the most logical issue in Choice Households is separation difficulty. "Letting go feels harder when you're a single parent," said one woman. "We share things and are close in a way unique to a one-on-one parent-child relationship."

We will learn much from Choice Kids. I continue to welcome them to contact me through the choicemoms.org website.

Conclusion

❧

Connecting the Dots

As I was finishing this book, preparing to write my final words, several interesting points from my life came together over a period of two weeks that offered me a "wrinkle in time" glimpse at the journey I have taken thus far.

I attended my 25-year class reunion, where we celebrated balding heads, the first grandparents among us, and a heartening number of classmates in their second decade of marriage. I watched an old friend — always the ambitious, studious one among us — let loose on the dance floor, having remade herself from a Pentagon consultant into a California vineyard owner. I admired the self-possessed Texas sheriff who strode into our small Minnesota conclave with cowboy hat and twang. And I marveled at the ability of so many in our class of 200 to remain connected to the community we grew up in, living the classic American dream of family, work, and simple pleasures.

I was reminded that there are many different lifestyles, and that I am very content with the rather nonconformist path I have taken.

A few days later, I was in northern Minnesota with an old college friend and her large family of siblings, watching their second generations bond during the summer ritual of a week together with little else but boating, swimming, fishing, and food.

I have long enjoyed being an "adopted" member of the family, and admire the matriarch for raising such a close family of seven kids largely on her own. Over the years I have seen all four of my friend's brothers turn into active, hands-on fathers, now spread out around the continent but faithful to the semiannual family get-together. I was eager to retain connection to these excellent role models so that my kids could see good, "traditional" family living up close.

I was reminded that many kids have great fathers who offer them something special, and that even those who had less-than-ideal upbringings can turn into good people — and was confident that my kids always would have solid role models and experiences to draw from over time.

A few days after that, Sophie and I returned to New York City for the first time since selling our home there, to show off Dylan and reconnect with old friends and favorite places. Our first stop was the apartment I had shared with my ex-husband before we separated in 1993. Creative, generous, and genuine as he and his second wife are, they opened up their home to us for three days, and it was wonderful to see my children bond with the man who had once been such a large part of my life.

> *I was reminded that once upon a time I did not foresee having children on my own, and that in my twenties I was focused on goals rather than listening to instinct, emotions, and needs. I was thankful that I have since then learned to be more vulnerable and openhearted, and that conflict is not to be avoided but dealt with.*

As the New York trip unfolded, I proudly talked with a documentary filmmaker about Choice Motherhood, met with a mother and her college-age daughter featured in this book, and relaxed with my former therapist as we watched my children play.

Then, it happened. After we had relocated from the spacious digs of my ex-husband to the darker, smaller, typical New York City apartment of a friend, an old, familiar depression started to creep in. The sense of isolation I had felt in my early days of Mom-hood was coming back to me — the feeling of being someone I didn't quite recognize in a place that no longer seemed to fit. With kids in tow, I noticed the garbage, congestion, noise, unsavory characters, and disparity between economic classes much more than I had when I was single and carefree. I felt out of place and adrift.

At our first playground of the day, I found my daughter in tears, telling two girls they had hurt her feelings by saying they didn't want to play with her. I brought us back to my friend's apartment to recharge and hide from the hot, midday sun. While I was in one room — trying to keep Dylan from rearranging my friend's shoes, jewelry, and clothes — and Sophie was watching TV in the other, she suddenly, uncharacteristically, said, "I'm lonely." I panicked. Had she picked up on my own plummeting mood? Was she, too, feeling exhausted from the disparity of being in a city that no longer felt like home?

Although we were only 20 feet apart, Sophie asked me to come closer. I picked up Dylan and the three of us huddled together on the living room futon, propped up against sequined pillows, watching cartoons. It felt better, but still not great. So I got us outside again, to yet another playground. Almost instantly, a 2-year-old girl attached herself to Sophie. The two of them jumped and splashed and slid, and I knew "big sister" Sophie was no longer feeling lonely. Dylan, too, was gleeful (as usual) in the fresh air.

I knew I should be happier, but still I felt alone. Surrounded by honking, rushing, busy people, I felt like an insignificant bystander sitting uncomfortably on the edge of a sandbox in Central Park. I was lonely too, I could have told Sophie — being Mom in a space where I had once been something else. I wondered if I could shorten our one-week visit to the city that had been mine for 18 years.

But then an interesting thing happened. I struck up a conversa-tion with the mother of the 2-year-old. We sat together, with our feet in the sandbox, and she mentioned that she and her daughter would be moving to Pennsylvania soon. Something about the way she phrased it reminded me of myself. "Are you a single mother?" I asked. "Yes, I adopted from Russia," she said.

And just like that, we made a connection. We talked about how we became Choice Moms, how we unexpectedly transformed our lives because of our children (she had lived in New York 15 years and quit a lucrative but time-intensive profession), the difficulties and the joys. My fog lifted. I had found the sense of community I had been missing. Being with my kids wasn't enough. Seeing old friends wasn't enough. Introducing Sophie and Dylan to the Statue of Liberty and favorite stretches of real estate wasn't enough. Talking proudly about Choice Motherhood wasn't enough.

What I rediscovered, in my moments talking with this Choice Mom, was a kindred spirit. The conversation was relatively brief, and we barely exchanged names, but she had become, in that fleeting period of time, a much-needed member of my support network — and perhaps vice versa.

Our daughters too seemed to feed off of the energy of each other. They held hands and, when it was finally time to go separate ways, sweetly hugged goodbye. Many days later, after returning to Minnesota, when people asked Sophie about favorite moments of the trip, she mentioned meeting that little girl.

> *The moral of this extended story I am telling is this: Connections to people become even more important after we become Choice Mothers, because we need more energy and support than we did before, when we were able to fill our days with work, or solitude, or shopping, or travel, or boyfriends.*

Our connections don't have to be simply with other Choice Moms — although they help, and I hope the women you've met in this book help you over a few humps. But if you decide to transform your life, the Old You will be invigorated by meeting people who understand the transforming nature of shaking out life and becoming something altogether New. Your old friends help, but might not intersect with you in the same way. Your beloved child(ren) will bring you great joy, but cannot fill the spaces when you feel disconnected from the world beyond diapers and playgrounds and moody adolescence.

Parenting is not always light and sunshine. There are dark clouds and claustrophobic spaces as well. Especially absent a partner to share the highs and the lows, the Choice Mother needs to make sure solo parenting will not become an isolating experience.

The Real and Remarkable Journey

Personally, I think Choice Motherhood is one of the most remarkable journeys a single woman can take. There are many unremarkable moments of parenthood (in my case, for example, Dylan peeing through his saturated diaper onto my lap after we barely made our connecting flight back to Minnesota). And many of us consider our lives — married or not, childfree or not — relatively unremarkable. Sometimes that fills us with angst, sometimes not.

But when you stop and listen to the moments of our lives, interesting stories emerge. In the last few weeks I've heard a classmate talk about how his family of six keep communication lines open by sharing family time in the hot tub, and another classmate talk about moving his family farther into the country so they could continue to see the stars. I've seen three generations enthusiastically toss squishy balls around a living room while bopping for more than an hour to the "I Like to Move It" song from the *Madagascar* soundtrack. I've watched a non-kid-oriented friend bond with my 6-year-old fashion queen daughter by trying on "New York chic" shoes together. I've watched my son squeal with delight at every bubble that seemed to magically appear from the wave of a wand — and the 50-year-old bubble-maker giggle along with him because of the contagious joy.

These scenes might not seem remarkable enough to qualify for a reality TV show. But they are part of the wonderfully simple, connect-the-dot moments of our lives that end up meaning so much.

When you are a single woman facing 24-hour-a-day, 7-day-a-week responsibility for the well-being of a malleable child, it is easy to sometimes feel despair. When you are a teenager growing up with one parent or in a transracial family, it is easy to sometimes feel lost confronting questions of identity. When you are a young child with a mother stressed from juggling work, family, and a minimal social life, it is easy to sometimes feel afraid and powerless.

The simple moments when we connect with other human beings in a warm, relaxed, openhearted way are fleeting, but the memories of being part of a larger universe are what sustain us — and help lift us out of low points when we are detached, isolated, lonely. That is why anyone embarking on Choice Motherhood must be capable of building community consciously, serendipitously, and everything in between. She must actively seek out role models and rituals that will help her and her child connect to the larger world.

The Choice Mother must surround herself with positive, nurturing, enlightened people so that she and her child will grow up together in an environment that cultivates strengths and balances out weaknesses.

Hippy-dippy as this might sound, I unabashedly maintain that the most essential tool of any successful parent is a strong, extended support network made up of men and women, young and old, single and married — family, friends, teachers, spiritual guides, people down the street . . . even pets. (An adult man raised by a Choice Mom told me one of the smart things his mother did was bring a dog into their home so that he would have more than one place to share attention and affection.)

In short, developing a village for a child is how you become a responsible parent, and no one should build a family without it.

In the words of my daughter

After we returned from New York, Sophie took a Rhythm and Rhyme class at a local writing center. Over the course of a week, while learning some drumming patterns as accompaniment, she was encouraged to write a poem that answered questions about who she was and where she comes from. Her teacher sent her home with questions to consider. I purposely let others help spell out her answers so that I wouldn't end up influencing her.

I was curious, of course, to learn how she would define herself and the six years she had experienced thus far. I was able to hear it, loud and clear, during the performance she and her classmates gave at the end of the week.

What made it into her poem were not profound things like "Who do you most admire?" (her answer: the women in our family because they're so smart) or "Who would you most like to meet?" (God), or the American Idols concert I had just taken her to as our special (pricey) date, or that she was mad at her biological father for not being around, or that her Mom was too busy writing a book to play dolls.

Rather, her poem defined herself in the context of her own simple connect-the-dot moments: her growing skills and strength in capoeira, family time (months earlier!) spent bowling, the lefse-making tradition with Dave's family at Thanksgiving, the special Fourth of July cake she and I made together.

If she'd been a few years older, and able to read complex sentences, I would have wondered if she'd been reading my book. I had just days before finished writing about how the simple moments of connection with others sustain us.

The Eloquence of Choice Motherhood

Back in 2003, one of the Choice Mothers I've never met, but long admired for her eloquent postings on the Single Mothers by Choice website, wrote an excellent encapsulation of this life we lead. I thank Melissa for sharing her thoughts, online and in this book (and thank Jane Mattes, founder of the SMC network, for agreeing to let me excerpt the post here):

I am totally and completely in love with and aston-ished by my child. And I have been, all through the times I've hated her behavior and been amazed at how angry such a small person can make me feel. I really love being a mother.

Yes, there are bad times, sometimes a lot of them. But there are so many good times that I literally can't count them. Like one day during Winter Break when we just lounged around in our pjs all day, playing games and drawing pictures and cuddling and reading and watching TV and playing dolls and having a "beauty day."

I can't begin to tell you how much more I laugh since I became a mother. I watch my kid flying around the apart-ment dressed as Wonder Woman, complete with fake boobs, and I crack right up. And she makes jokes! Some-times they are moronic kid jokes, but sometimes they are totally unexpected one-liners that lay me on the floor.

I have made new friends since becoming a parent — people I would never have met otherwise, who have be-come important parts of my life. I have a renewed inter-est in my faith and ancestry. I live each day more aware of the world around me because I see it with fresh eyes — my daughter's eyes — because experiences are so new to her.

I have become a better person in myself — stronger, more self-reliant, able to stand up for what's important to me and for my child. I'm more well-rounded than I used to be — my life is no longer mostly about my work. I always had a good relationship with my parents, but becoming a parent myself has improved that. My ex-

tended family in general treats me differently — as a person with a family, not as the spinster adjunct.

It is impossible to adequately convey the joy I feel when I pick up my daughter at the end of the day and she comes flying into my arms. To know that I am loved as fiercely as I love. I'm lucky to have a physically affectionate child; she tells me in a thousand non-verbal ways how deeply we are connected. I try to do the same. We never part without saying "I love you."

I take the responsibility of shaping her morals and ethics very seriously. When I see my daughter applying the principles of equality and justice and compassion that I have tried to teach her, I feel that I am doing my part to improve our collective future.

I look at the joy and involvement my daughter has given to me, to her grandparents (she's their only grandchild), to my brother, who is still tickled at the thought that he's an uncle, and I can't imagine my life without her as being anywhere near as rewarding and invigorating as my life with her.

Do I worry? You bet! How am I going to afford college? What if I get hit by a bus? What if the teacher thinks I did all the work on this school project? Did I do all the work on this school project? Does she say she loves me when I'm angry as a manipulative tactic? How will she react when I tell her I won't be home for Halloween this year? If I take off a day in one week to do something at school, and the kid gets sick the following week, will my boss be really pissed when I take time off again? Is she going to hate me when she's a teenager because she has no father? Is she going to grow up thinking that she's responsible for my happiness?

Nonetheless, this was the right choice for me. The payoff's been hugely positive, and gets more so every year.

Coming Full Circle

As I wrote at the beginning of this chapter of final thoughts, I had dipped into a bout of loneliness, while sitting in yet another sandbox during a return trip to the New York City of my younger, childless days. A serendipitous chat with a Choice Mom I met helped lift me out of the dip I had taken, and reminded me how essential it is to surround yourself with a network of people who can support you and your child — emotionally, logistically — throughout the Choice Motherhood journey.

Later during that sandbox day, I was sharing pizza and wine with a single friend I used to club-hop with in my childfree days. We were sitting in a back room I never knew existed, where kids were free to be, in a restaurant where I had years earlier flirted over drinks with a short-lived beau. Sophie was excitedly making her own pizza, wearing a plastic chef's apron supplied by the staff. Dylan seemed intent on chewing a hole into a large purple balloon.

"You're really digging being a mom," my friend exclaimed. And I acknowledged that yes, with all the different lives I had experienced in the 25 years since high school, in the 21 years since I had moved to New York as a naïve but ambitious young career girl, in the 18 years since I had married (and 12 since I had divorced), I had played with many interesting roles — and this "Mom" title was definitely suiting me better than I ever imagined.

Sometimes it is difficult to be a Choice Mom. Some days I think I'm doing a great job at it, and other days I know I'm not.

It is never my intent to encourage women to take this step lightly. While I believe everyone can, I recognize that many should not. Yes, there are issues of finances, fatherlessness, biological identity, energy, and ability to offer basic, quality parenting skills: open communication, authoritative discipline, respect, and effective stress management. But what it boils down to is whether each one of us has the heart to raise a child.

To be a responsible parent, quite simply, requires the capacity to love. If your heart is open, and you have the good judgment required to be responsive to someone else's needs, as well as the capacity to set limits, then you have the ingredients needed to build a Choice Home filled with the simple, connect-the-dot moments that every child needs.

Notes

Introduction

1. Jane Lawler Dye, "Fertility of American Women: June 2004," in *Current Population Reports P20–555* (U.S. Census Bureau, December 2005): 2, 5. Note that birth certificate information collected by the U.S. National Center for Health Statistics reported that in 2002 there were 83,000 births to unmarried women over 35.
2. W. Sigle-Rushton and S. McLanahan, "The Living Arrangements of New Unmarried Mothers," *Demography* 39, no.3 (2002): 415–33.
3. Barbara Kantrowitz and Pat Wingert, "Unmarried with Children," *Newsweek*, May 28, 2001, 50.
4. Kantrowitz and Wingert, *Newsweek*, 50.
5. Lori Gottlieb, "The XY Files: Forgoing a Trip Down the Aisle, Our Correspondent Heads Straight to the Sperm Bank," *Atlantic Monthly*, September 2005, 144.

1. Am I Single-Mother Material?

1. Malia Rulon, "Juggling Congress, Adoption Not Easy: Single White Mom Raises Black Baby," Associated Press, May 29, 2005.
2. Shari Thurer, *The Myths of Motherhood: How Culture Reinvents the Good Mother* (New York: Penguin Books, 1995), xii.

4. Will My Community Accept Us?

1. Jane Bock, "Doing the Right Thing: Single Mothers by Choice and the Struggle for Legitimacy," *Gender & Society* 14, no.1 (February 2000): 62–86.

2. Rochelle Furstenberg, "Family Matters: Single Orthodox Mothers," *Hadassah Magazine* 86, no.7 (March 2005): 12.
3. Mary Ann Mason, *From Father's Property to Children's Rights: A History of Child Custody* (New York: Columbia University Press, 1994), x–xi.
4. Barbara Dafoe Whitehead, "Dan Quayle Was Right," *Atlantic Monthly* (April 1993): 47–84.
5. Stephanie Coontz, "Nostalgia as Ideology," *The American Prospect* 13, no.8 (April 2002).
6. Quayle addressed the Commonwealth Club of San Francisco on May 19, 1992.
7. Tobin Beck, "Quayle 10 Years After Murphy Brown," *Insight,* May 10, 2002. See also: Bob Costantini, "Murphy Brown Redux: Quayle Looks Back on the Big Speech," evote.com (accessed September 28, 2002).
8. David Popenoe, *Life Without Father: Compelling New Evidence That Fatherhood and Marriage Are Indispensable for the Good of Children and Society* (New York: The Free Press, 1996), 53.
9. Sara McLanahan and Irwin Garfinkel, *Single Mothers and Their Children* (Washington, D.C.: Urban Institute Press, 1988).
10. Dan Quayle, "Why I Think I'm Still Right: Since the Flap over *Murphy Brown,* American Families Have Come Under Even More Pressure," *Newsweek,* May 28, 2001, 52.
11. Steven Mintz, "The History of Private Life: An Overview," Digital History website, Gilder Lehrman Institute of American History, http://www.digitalhistory.uh.edu/historyonline/plife_overview.cfm (accessed March 2002).

5. The Impact of a Single-Parent Home

1. E. Mavis Hetherington and John Kelly, *For Better or For Worse: Divorce Reconsidered* (New York: W. W. Norton, 2002), 67–93, 110–162, 227–274.
2. Marilyn Ford-Gilboe, "Dispelling Myths and Creating Opportunity: A Comparison of the Strengths of Single-Parent and Two-Parent Families," *Advances in Nursing Science* 23, no.1 (September 2000): 41.
3. Michael Slavkin, "Gender Role Differences in College Students from One- and Two-Parent Families," *Sex Roles: A Journal of Research* (January 2000).
4. Clare Murray and Susan Golombok, "Solo Mothers and Their Donor Insemination Infants: Follow-up at Age 2 Years," *Human Reproduction* 20 (June 2005): 1655–60. See also Golombok's concise and thorough research review in her book *Parenting: What Really Counts?* (Routledge, 2000).

5. Fiona MacCallum and Susan Golombok, "Children Raised in Father-less Families from Infancy: a Follow-up of Children of Lesbian and Single Heterosexual Mothers at Early Adolescence," *Journal of Child Psychology and Psychiatry* 45, no.8 (November 2004): 1407–19. The first interviews were conducted in 1997, and then again six years later, when all the mothers tended to be in their forties. At the age of 12, some children from all three comparison groups were experiencing more emotional and behavioral issues, but school adjustment, peer relationships, self-esteem, and gender-role orientation showed no major differences between the groups. Teachers, too, did not report more problems for children from father-absent families.

6. Peggy Drexler, *Raising Boys Without Men: How Maverick Moms Are Creating the Next Generation of Exceptional Men* (New York: Rodale Books, 2005).

7. Such as Sara McLanahan and Larry Bumpass, "Intergenerational Consequences of Family Disruption," *American Journal of Sociology* 94, no.1 (1988): 130–148.

8. Sara McLanahan and Gary Sandefur, *Growing Up with a Single Parent: What Hurts, What Helps* (Cambridge, MA: Harvard University Press, 1994).

9. Richard Weissbourd, "Moral Parent, Moral Child," *The American Prospect* (July 14, 2002): 24–26.

10. Stephanie Coontz, "Nostalgia as Ideology," *The American Prospect* (April 8, 2002).

6. Growing Up Without a Father

1. See "Family Structure," Child Trends Data report, based on calculations from "America's Families and Living Arrangements: 2004," *Current Population Survey: 2004 Annual Social and Economic Supplement*, U.S. Census Bureau.

2. David Blankenhorn, *Fatherless America: Confronting Our Most Urgent Social Problem* (New York: Harper Perennial, 1996), 26.

3. William Pollack, *Real Boys: Rescuing Our Sons from the Myths of Boyhood* (Owl Books, 1999). As quoted in Jennifer Wolcott, "Solo with a Son: Single Moms Face Challenges in Raising Sons, but with a Little Help, Boys Do Just Fine," *Christian Science Monitor,* September 13, 2000.

4. Myriam Miedzian, *Boys Will Be Boys* (New York: Lantern Books, 2002).

5. Some of Michael Gurian's several books include: *The Wonder of Boys: What Parents, Mentors and Educators Can Do to Shape Boys into Exceptional Men* (New York: Jeremy P. Tarcher/Putnam Books, 1996);

and *The Good Son: Shaping the Moral Development of Our Boys and Young Men* (New York: Jeremy P. Tarcher/Putnam Books, 1999).

6. See Judith S. Musick, *Young, Poor and Pregnant: The Psychology of Teenage Motherhood* (New Haven, CT: Yale University Press, 1993), 60. Blankenhorn also cites E. Mavis Hetherington, "Effects of Father Absence on Personality Development in Adolescent Daughters," *Developmental Psychology* 7, no.3 (1972): 313–26.

7. David Popenoe, *Life Without Father* (New York: Free Press, 1996), 12.

8. Kyle D. Pruett, *Fatherneed: Why Father Care Is as Essential as Mother Care for Your Child* (New York: Free Press, 2000). See especially chapters 1 and 2.

9. See also Eleanor E. Maccoby, *The Two Sexes: Growing Up Apart; Coming Together* (Cambridge, MA: Harvard University Press, 1999).

10. Head Start Bureau, Administration on Children, Youth and Families, U.S. Department of Health and Human Services, as prepared by the National Head Start Training and Technical Assistance Resource Center, 1000 Wilson Boulevard, Suite 1000, Arlington, VA 22209.

11. John Snarey, *How Fathers Care for the Next Generation: A Four Decade Study* (Cambridge, MA: Harvard University Press, 1993), 35–36.

12. As reported in: Nancy A. Crowell and Ethel M. Leeper, eds., *America's Fathers and Public Policy: Report of a Workshop,* Commission on Behavioral and Social Sciences and Education, National Research Council (Washington, D.C.: National Academy Press, 1994), 8.

13. Richard Weissbourd is the author of *The Vulnerable Child: What Really Hurts America's Children and What We Can Do About It* (Reading, MA: Addison-Wesley, 1996), 28. See especially pages 3–29, 60–62.

14. See, for example, Bruce D. Perry, "Incubated in Terror: Neurodevelopmental Factors in the 'Cycle of Violence.'" In *Children, Youth and Violence: The Search for Solutions,* ed. Joy Doninger Osofsky (New York: Guilford Press, 1997), 124–48. See also Felton Earls, "Violence and Today's Youth," *The Future of Children: Critical Health Issues for Children and Youth* 4, no.3 (Winter 1994).

15. Elizabeth E. Groisser, "Children's Object Representations of Anonymous Donor 'Fathers' and Impact on Self-Concept" (dissertation for doctorate, Ferkauf Graduate School of Psychology, Yeshiva University, New York, May 2003), 62–63, 69–70.

16. M. K. Rose, "Elective Single Mothers and Their Children: The Missing Fathers," *Child and Adolescent Social Work* 9, no.1 (1992): 21–33.

17. As reported in Pruett, *Fatherneed* (2000). See also: Henry B. Biller, *Fathers and Families: Paternal Factors in Child Development* (Westport, CT: Auburn House, 1993); Ellen Bing, "The Effect of Child-Rearing

Practices on the Development of Differential Cognitive Abilities," *Child Development* 34 (1963); Norma Radin, "Father-Child Interaction and the Intellectual Functioning of Four-Year-Old Boys," *Developmental Psychology* 6 (1972); Biller, "The Father and Personality Development: Paternal Deprivation and Sex-Role Development," in *The Role of the Father in Child Development*, ed. Michael E. Lamb, (Hoboken, NJ: Wiley & Sons, 2004).

18. Richard Koestner, Carol Franz, and Joel Weinberger, "The Family Origins of Empathic Concern: A Twenty-Six Year Longitudinal Study," *Journal of Personality and Social Psychology* 58 (1990): 709–17.

19. Henry B. Biller, "The Father Factor and the Two-Parent Advantage: Reducing the Paternal Deficit" (paper presented to the father-to-father working group meeting with the White House adviser William Galston, December 17, 1993; April 15, 1994).

20. Peter L. Benson, *The Troubled Journey: A Portrait of 6ᵗʰ–12ᵗʰ Grade Youth* (Minneapolis, MN: Search Institute, 1993).

21. Mary Pipher, *Reviving Ophelia: Saving the Selves of Adolescent Girls* (New York: Random House, 2002), 130–32.

7. *Known Donor: Pros and Cons*

1. Rosanna Hertz, "The Father as an Idea: A Challenge to Kinship Boundaries by Single Mothers," *Symbolic Interaction* 25, no.1 (2001): 1–31.

2. Barbara White Stack, "Sperm Donor Fights Order to Support Two Children," *Pittsburgh Post-Gazette*, May 20, 2005. Wendy McElroy, "Case Could Freeze Sperm Donation," foxnews.com, May 31, 2005.

3. David M. Brodzinsky, Marshall D. Schechter, and Robin Marantz Henig, *Being Adopted: The Lifelong Search for Self* (New York: Anchor Books, 1993), 129.

4. Quoted in A. J. Turner and A. Coyle, "What Does It Mean to Be a Donor Offspring? The Identity Experiences of Adults Conceived by Donor Insemination and the Implications for Counseling and Therapy," *Human Reproduction* 15, no. 9 (2000): 2046. See 2041–51.

5. Turner and Coyle, *Human Reproduction* (2000): 2047.

6. See Rosanna Hertz, *Single by Chance, Mothers by Choice* (New York: Oxford University Press, 2006). See especially 61–85.

7. Karen Kessler, "Single Mothers by Choice: Deciding on a Known or Unknown Donor" (master's thesis, University of Wisconsin, 1987), 57.

8. Stephanie Brill, *The New Essential Guide to Lesbian Conception, Pregnancy & Birth* (New York: Alyson Books, 2006), 81–118.

9. Andrew Berg, "A Gay Man Reflects on His Decision to Become a Known Donor," Alternative Family website, 2005.

10. Jenifer Firestone, "Lesbians and Gay Men Having Children Together," (keynote address presented at the Lesbian and Gay Community Services Center conference, December 1, 2001).

8. Using Donor Insemination

1. As reported in Carol Frost Vercollone, Heidi Moss, and Robert Moss, *Helping the Stork: The Choices and Challenges of Donor Insemination* (New York: MacMillan, 1997), 27.
2. The industry is not in the habit of compiling aggregate numbers, but the source of this estimate seems to go back to 1987, based on a survey published by the U.S. Congress, Office of Technology Assessment (1988). At the time, anonymous or directed donor sperm was the way to go for infertile couples. Today, couples have more sophisticated options to choose from, including IVF and ICSI, that can include collecting a partner's gametes and injecting them in a laboratory setting. As the number of married couples using anonymous sperm insemination has declined, lesbian couples and single women have risen to take their place. It's unclear what the accurate numbers really are. On the low side, one industry expert who conducted a preliminary survey of 22 major sperm banks suspects that there were roughly 5,000 births from anonymous sperm in 2005.
3. Stephanie Brill, *The New Essential Guide for Lesbian Conception, Pregnancy and Birth* (New York: Alyson Books, 2006), 282–90. For women considering home insemination, or interested in advice about fertility over 40, check out the website www.maiamidwifery.com.
4. Judith Graham, "Sperm Donors' Offspring Reach Out into Past," *Chicago Tribune* June 19, 2005.
5. Claire I. Wendland, Francis Byrn, and Cynde Hill, "Donor Insemination: A Comparison of Lesbian Couples, Heterosexual Couples and Single Women," *Fertility and Sterility* 65, no.4 (April 1996): 764–70.
6. Joanna E. Scheib, Maura Riordan, and Phillip R. Shaver, "Choosing Between Anonymous and Identity-Release Donors: Recipient and Donor Characteristics," *Reproductive Technologies* 10, no.1 (January 2000): 50–58.
7. J. E. Scheib, M. Riordan, and S. Rubin, "Choosing Identity-Release Sperm Donors: The Parents' Perspective 13–18 Years Later," *Human Reproduction* 18, no.5 (2003): 1115–27.
8. Scheib, *Reproductive Technologies,* 50–58.
9. Ibid..
10. According to California Cryobank's medical director, Dr. Cappy Rothman, as reported in *Chicago Tribune,* June 19, 2005,.
11. J. E. Scheib, M. Riordan, and S. Rubin, "Adolescents with Open-

Identity Sperm Donors: Reports from 12–17-year-olds," *Human Reproduction* 20 (2005): 239–52.

12. Judith Graham, *Chicago Tribune,* June 19, 2005.
13. J. E. Scheib, M. Riordan, S. Rubin, "Identity-Release Sperm Donors 10–16 Years Later," manuscript in preparation (2005).
14. Scott Duke Harris, "Runs in the Family," *Los Angeles Times,* July 4, 2003.
15. Rosanna Hertz, "The Father as an Idea: A Challenge to Kinship Boundaries by Single Mothers," *Symbolic Interaction* 25, no.1 (2002): 9.
16. Scheib, "Identity-Release Sperm Donors 10–16 Years Later."
17. Ken Daniels, "Recruitment of Semen Donors Still Possible Under Open System," *Human Reproduction* 20, no.6 (2005): 1670–75.
18. Scheib, "Choosing Identity-Release Sperm Donors: The Parents' Perspective 13–18 Years Later," *Human Reproduction,* 1116.
19. I. Ferrara, R. Balet, and J. G. Grudzinskas, "Intrauterine Insemination with Frozen Donor Sperm. Pregnancy Outcome in Relation to Age and Ovarian Stimulation Regime," *Human Reproduction* 17, no.9 (2002): 2320–24.
20. Raymond W. Chan, Barbara Raboy, and Charlotte J. Patterson, "Psychosocial Adjustment Among Children Conceived via Donor Insemination by Lesbian and Heterosexual Mothers," *Child Development* 69, vol.2 (1998): 443–57.
21. "Planning a Family on Your Own: A Letter from Emily to Single Women," published by Donor Conception Network, http://dcnetwork.org/.

9. Choosing Adoption

1. Lee Varon, *Adopting on Your Own: The Complete Guide to Adopting as a Single Parent* (New York: Farrar, Straus & Giroux, 2000). See especially pages 77–113, 131–245.
2. Lois Gilman, *The Adoption Resource Book* (New York: Harper Perennial, 1998). See also: Gilman and Susan Freivalds, "Adopting Smart: How Adoption Works and How Much It Costs," available at http://adoptivefamilies.com/adoption.php.
3. See "Shifting Gears: The Adoption Option" at http://www.afafamilymatters.com/familybuild/adoptionoption.html.
4. Per U.S. Department of Health and Human Services, Administration for Children and Families, Administration on Children, Youth and Families, Children's Bureau.
5. Harold D. Grotevant, Yvette V. Perry, and Ruth G. McRoy, "Openness in Adoption: Outcomes for Adolescents with Their Adoptive Kinship Networks," in D. Brodzinsky and J. Palacios, eds., *Psychological Issues*

in Adoption: Theory, Research and Application (Westport, CT: Greenwood Publishing, 2005), 167–186.

6. Susan M. Henney et al., "The Impact of Openness on Adoption Agency Practices: A Longitudinal Perspective," *Adoption Quarterly* 6, no.3 (2003): 31–51. See also: Lois Gilman and Susan Freivalds, "Adoption Options: Thinking About Adoption but Not Sure Which Kind Is Right for You? Here's an Overview of Options — How They Work and What They Cost," *Adoptive Families 2006 Adoption Guide.*

7. E. Wellisch, "Children Without Genealogy: A Problem of Adoption," *Mental Health* 13, no.1 (1952): 41–42. See also: H. J. Sants, "Genealogical Bewilderment in Children with Substitute Parents," *British Journal of Medical Psychology* 37 (1964): 133–41. Michael Humphrey, "A Fresh Look at Genealogical Bewilderment," *British Journal of Medical Psychology* 59 (1986): 133–40.

8. As quoted in Jayne Schooler, "Telling the Whole Truth to Adoption and Foster Care Children" (paper presented to the 12th Annual Statewide Adoption Training Conference, Albany, New York, May 2001). Schooler's paper was adapted from work by Lois Melina and Dr. John Powell Young.

9. Ibid. (http://www.nysccc.org/Conferences/Conf2001/whytell.html). See also: Betsy Keefer and Jayne E. Schooler, *Telling the Truth to Your Adopted or Foster Child: Making Sense of the Past* (Westport, CT: Greenwood Publishing, 2000).

10. Lois Ruskai Melina, *Raising Adopted Children: Practical Reassuring Advice for Every Adoptive Parent* (New York: HarperCollins, 1998). See especially pages 83–252.

11. Deborah Borchers, "Families and Adoption: The Pediatrician's Role in Supporting Communication," written with the Committee on Early Childhood, Adoption, and Dependent Care, *Pediatrics* 112, no.6 (December 2003): 1437–41. See also: I. G. Leon, "Adoption Losses: Naturally Occurring or Socially Constructed?" *Child Development* 73 (2000): 652–63. Gretchen Miller Wrobel, Harold D. Grotevant, and Ruth G. McRoy, "Adolescent Search for Birthparents: Who Moves Forward?" *Journal of Adolescent Research* 19, no.1 (January 2004).

12. David M. Brodzinsky, Marshall D. Schechter, and Robin Marantz Henig, *Being Adopted: The Lifelong Search for Self* (New York: Anchor Books, 1993), 79. See especially pages 61–119.

13. "How Many Children Were Adopted in 2000 and 2001," U.S. Department of Health and Human Services, National Adoption Information Clearinghouse (2004).

14. See: W. Feigelman and A. R. Silverman, "Single Parent Adoption," *The Handbook for Single Adoptive Parents* (National Council for Single Adoptive Parents, 1997). V. K. Groze and J. A. Rosenthal, "Single Par-

ents and Their Adopted Children: A Psychosocial Analysis," *The Journal of Contemporary Human Services* (1991). C. Murray and S. Golombok, "Solo Mothers and Their Donor Insemination Infants: Follow-up at Age 2 Years" *Human Reproduction* 20, no.6 (February 2005): 1655–60. Fiona MacCallum and Susan Golombok, "Children Raised in Fatherless Families from Infancy: A Follow-up of Children of Lesbian and Single Heterosexual Mothers at Early Adolescence," *Journal of Child Psychology and Psychiatry* 45, no.8 (November 2004).

15. Varon, *Adopting on Your Own*, 2000. See especially pages 129–245.
16. "Five Questions with Cheri Register," featured on "As Simple As That" website (www.simpleasthat.com), July 2005.

10. Dealing with the Stress

1. Nancy Samalin with Martha Moraghan Jablow, *Loving Your Child Is Not Enough: Positive Discipline That Works* (New York: Penguin Books, 1998).
2. Mary Sheedy Kurcinka, *Raising Your Spirited Child: A Guide for Parents Whose Child Is More Intense, Sensitive, Perceptive, Persistent, Energetic* (New York: Harper Perennial, 1998), 7–8.
3. Karen Maezen Miller, *Momma Zen: Walking the Crooked Path of Motherhood* (Boston: Shambhala, 2006).
4. As reported in Valerie S. Mannis, "The Adopting Single Mother: Four Portraits of American Women Adopting from China," *Adoption Quarterly* 4, no.2 (2000): 38–39.
5. Ross W. Greene, *The Explosive Child: A New Approach for Understanding and Parenting Easily Frustrated, Chronically Inflexible Children* (New York: Harper, 2001). See especially 9–56, 192–216.
6. James E. Miller, *The Caregiver's Book: Caring for Another, Caring for Yourself* (Fort Wayne, IN: Willowgreen, 1996). Available at www.willowgreen.com.

11. Answering the Daddy Question

1. Ken R. Daniels and P. Thorn, "Sharing Information with Donor Insemination Offspring: A Child-conception Versus a Family-building Approach," *Human Reproduction* 16, no.9 (2001): 1792–96. See also: Ken Daniels, *Building a Family with the Assistance of Donor Insemination* (New Zealand: Dunmore Press, 2004).
2. Patricia Mendell, "Out of the Dish: Talking to Children About Their IVF Origins," online article prepared by American Fertility Association (2004), http://www.afafamilymatters.com/pregnancyparenting/kidsandivf.html.

3. Anne C. Bernstein, *Flight of the Stork: What Children Think (and When) About Sex and Family Building* (Indianapolis, IN: Perspectives Press, 1994), 41–148. See also: Bernstein and P. A. Cowan, "Children's Concepts of How People Get Babies," *Child Development* 46 (1975): 77–91.

4. Olivia Montuschi, Telling and Talking series (Donor Conception Network, 2006). Available for free download at dcnetwork.org.

5. Diane Ehrensaft, *Mommies, Daddies, Donors, Surrogates: Answering Tough Questions and Building Strong Families* (New York: Guilford Press, 2005), 14.

6. Judith Graham, "Sperm Donors' Offspring Reach Out into Past: But Those Searching for Roots Can Run into Rules and Dead Ends," *Chicago Tribune,* June 19, 2005.

7. Michael Leahy, "Family Vacation: Why Would Raechel McGhee Fly Her Two Beloved Children Across the Country to Stay with a Man They Had Never Met? Because He Is Their Father," *Washington Post,* June 19, 2005. Online question-and-answer session took place June 20, 2005.

12. Confronting Identity Issues

1. Dr. Joyce Maguire Pavao is the author of *The Family of Adoption* (Boston: Beacon Press, 2005). For more from Pavao, see kinnect.org, the website of Center for Family Connections.

2. Diane Ehrensaft, *Mommies, Daddies, Donors, Surrogates: Answering Tough Questions and Building Strong Families* (New York: Guilford Press, 2005).

3. David M. Brodzinsky, Marshall D. Schechter, and Robin Marantz Henig, *Being Adopted: The Lifelong Search for Self* (New York: Anchor Books, 1993), 55–86. See also: Schechter and D. Bertocci, "The Meaning of the Search," in D. Brodzinsky and M. Schechter, eds., *The Psychology of Adoption* (New York: Oxford University Press, 1990).

4. Christina Cheakalos and Vicki Sheff-Cahan, "Discovering Dad: At 18, Christina Hall Introduces Herself to Phillip, Her Sperm-donor Parent," *People,* July 14, 2003, 109.

5. As quoted in Jayne Schooler, "Telling the Whole Truth to Adoptive and Foster Care Children" (paper presented to the 12th Annual Statewide Adoption Training Conference, Albany, New York, May 2001). Schooler's paper was adapted from work by Lois Melina and Dr. John Powell Young.

6. A. J. Turner and A. Coyle, "What Does It Mean to Be a Donor Offspring? The Identity Experiences of Adults Conceived by Donor Insem-

ination and the Implications for Counseling and Therapy," *Human Reproduction* 15, no.9 (2000): 2046–47. Their findings were based on questionnaires filled out by 16 participants, ages 26 to 55, who were recruited from donor insemination support networks.

7. Deborah Borchers and the Committee on Early Childhood, Adoption and Dependent Care, "Families and Adoption: The Pediatrician's Role in Supporting Communication," *Pediatrics* 112, no.6 (December 2003): 1437–41.

8. David M. Brodzinsky, Leslie M. Singer, and Anne M. Braff, "Children's Understanding of Adoption," *Child Development* 55 (1984): 869–78. See also D. Brodzinsky, C. Pappas, L. M. Singer, and A. M. Braff, "Children's Conception of Adoption: A Preliminary Investigation," *Journal of Pediatric Psychology* 6, no.2 (1981): 177–89.

9. As suggested in Kyle D. Pruett, "Strange Bedfellows? Reproductive Technology and Child Development," *Infant Mental Health Journal* 13, no.4 (Winter 1992): 312–18.

10. For more on Erikson's stages of life, see the Child Development Institute's website: http://www.childdevelopmentinfo.com/development/erickson.shtml. For more on middle childhood and the stage of mastery, see Robin F. Goodman, "A View from the Middle: Life Through the Eyes of Middle Childhood," based on Sesame Workshop research (2001). See online article at http://www.aboutourkids.org/aboutour/articles/middle.html.

11. Elizabeth E. Groisser, "Children's Object Representations of Anonymous Donor 'Fathers' and Impact on Self-Concept" (dissertation for doctorate, Ferkauf Graduate School of Psychology, Yeshiva University, New York, May 2003), 67–79.

12. Ken Corbett, "Nontraditional Family Romance," *Psychoanalytic Quarterly* 70, no.3 (2001): 599–624.

13. Diane Ehrensaft, "Alternatives to the Stork: Fatherhood Fantasies in Donor Insemination Families," *Studies in Gender and Sexuality* 1, no.4 (2000): 371–97.

14. Rosanna Hertz, "The father as an Idea: A Challenge to Kinship Boundaries by Single Mothers," *Symbolic Interaction* 25, no.1 (2002): 1–32.

15. "Out of the Dish: Talking to Children About Their IVF Origins," online article prepared by American Fertility Association, 2004, http://www.afafamilymatters.com/pregancyparenting/kidsandivf.html.

16. Sharon Pettle and Jen Burns, "Choosing to Be Open about Donor Conception: The Experiences of Parents," brochure available at the Donor Conception Network website, dcnetwork.org.

17. See, for example, Holly van Gulden and Lisa Bartels-Rabb, *Real Parents, Real Children: Parenting the Adopted Child* (Crossroad Classic, 1995). See also Todd Parr, *The Family Book* (Megan Tingley, 2003);

Beth O'Malley, *Waiting Adoptive and Foster Families and Lifebooks*, at adoptionlifebooks.com (2001).

18. See also "Positive Adoption Language," a fact sheet available from adoptivefamilies.com, as reprinted from *Ours* magazine (May/June 1992).

19. "Adopted Children and Stepchildren," U.S. Census Bureau, Census 2000 special report (October 2003).

20. Jana Wolff, "Raising a Child of Another Race: Deliberate Parenting Can Make a Difference," available at adoptivefamilies.com. See also its excellent resource list.

21. Anne Bernstein, "Making Sense of New Conceptions . . . in a Family Way," *Family Therapy News* 26, no.1 (February 1995).

22. Dr. Elaine R. Gordon is author of *Mommy, Did I Grow in Your Tummy: Where Some Babies Come From* (E. M. Greenberg Press, 1992), available at elainegordon.com. See the website also for her article "Talking to Children About Their Adoption."

23. See also articles available at adoptivefamilies.com, such as "Dear Teacher," "What Your Child's Teacher Needs to Know," "Tips for Helping Your Child Cope with Intrusive Questions," "Becoming an Advocate at School," "The Family Tree," and much more.

13. How to Raise a Well-Balanced Child

1. Richard Weissbourd, "Moral Parent, Moral Child," *The American Prospect* (July 14, 2002): A24–26.

2. Kurcinka's books include: *Raising Your Spirited Child: A Guide for Parents Whose Child Is More Intense, Sensitive, Perceptive, Persistent, Energetic* (New York: HarperCollins, 1998); *Kids, Parents and Power Struggles: Winning for a Lifetime* (New York: HarperCollins, 2001).

3. Pruett's publications include: *Fatherneed: Why Father Care Is as Essential as Mother Care for Your Child* (New York: Broadway Books, 2001); *Me, Myself and I: How Children Build Their Sense of Self 18 to 36 Months* (New York: Goddard Press, 1999).

4. Gurian's many books include: *The Nurture of Nature: Understanding and Supporting Your Child's Unique Core Personality* (New York: Jossey-Bass, 2007); *The Wonder of Boys: What Parents, Mentors and Educators Can Do to Shape Boys into Exceptional Men* (Tarcher/Putnam, 1997); and *The Good Son: Shaping the Moral Development of Our Boys and Young Men* (New York: Tarcher/Putnam, 2000).

5. Weissbourd's publications include: *The Vulnerable Child: What Really Hurts America's Children and What We Can Do About It* (New York: Addison-Wesley, 1996), and *The Unintended Ways Parents Are Eroding Children's Moral Development* (Boston: Houghton Mifflin, 2007).

6. Nancy Samalin with Martha Moraghan Jablow, *Loving Your Child Is Not Enough: Positive Discipline That Works* (New York: Penguin, 1987). See especially pages 5–54.
7. See Barbara Risman with Kyung Park, "Just the Two of Us: Parent-Child Relationships in Single Parent Homes," *Journal of Marriage and the Family* (November 1988): 1049–62.
8. Laurence Steinberg and Ann Levine, *You and Your Adolescent: A Parent's Guide for Ages 10–20* (New York: HarperPerennial, 1997), 11–12, 58–59.
9. William Doherty, *The Intentional Family: Simple Rituals to Strengthen Family Ties* (New York: Avon, 1997), 175.

14. Of Politics and Policy

1. For more on international regulations in the insemination industry, see infertilitynetwork.org. For adoption regulations, see adoptivefamilies.com.
2. Andrea D. Gurmankin, Arthur L. Caplan, and Andrea M. Braverman, "Screening Practices and Beliefs of Assisted Reproductive Technology Programs," *Fertility and Sterility* 83, no.1 (January 2005): 61–67.
3. Carey Goldberg, "Parenthood: How Old Is Too Old?" *Boston Globe*, April 5, 2005.
4. Aubrey Noelle Stimola, "Wanted: Scientific Reason for FDA's Gay Sperm Ban," posted on May 23, 2005, to the Health Facts and Fears section of the American Council on Science and Health website.
5. Molly M. Ginty, "Single Mothers-to-Be Face Bias, Race Ticking Clock," Women's eNews, June 18, 2004.
6. Tracey Tyler, "Lesbians Protest Rules on Donors: Regulations Seen Causing Unsafe Self-procedures; Approvals Needed for Gay, Older Men Called Unfair," *Toronto Star*, February 15, 2005. See also: "Jane and Sue Make Two in Battle for Sperm Access," April 27, 2005.
7. *Steven S. v. Deborah D.*, Cal. App. 4th [No. B175996. Second Dist., Div. Four] (March 3, 2005).
8. *Jhordan C. v. Mary K.*, 179 Cal.App.3d 386, 224 Cal.Rptr.530 [No. A027810. Court of Appeals of California, First Appellate District, Division Five] (March 28, 1986).
9. *Diane L. Johnston et al. v. The Superior Court of Los Angeles, California Cryobank, Inc., et al.*, 80 Cal.App.4th 1050, 95 Cal.Rptr.2d 864 [No. B137002. Second Dist., Div. Two] (May 18, 2000).
10. *Robert B., Denise B. v. Susan B.*, 109 Cal.App.4th 1109, Cal.Rptr.2d [No. H024926. Sixth Dist.] (June 13, 2003).
11. "Surrogate Mother Wins Custody of Triplets: Pennsylvania Judge Awards Custody to Surrogate Mother Who Gave Birth to Triplets," As-

sociated Press, January 7, 2005. Also: "Surrogate Mom, Biological Dad Battle over Triplets," Associated Press, May 1, 2005, and "Surrogate Mom Perseveres in Battle Against Biological Father," as appeared on www.observer-reporter.com (May 13, 2005).

12. Alan Thornhill and Ian Craft, of London Fertility Centre, "Recruiting Egg Donors After the Removal of Anonymity," as appeared on www.bionews.org.uk (March 14, 2005).

13. See: "Plea from Sperm Donor Children," as reported on www.news .bbc.co.uk, May 22, 2002. Also: "Liberty Wins Contact Register for Children of Sperm Donors," press release, October 9, 2003.

14. For up-to-date state adoption laws, see naic.acf.hhs.gov/laws/info accessap.cfm.

15. Wayne Parry, "Lesbian Wins Full Co-parenting Rights to Partner's Newborn Daughter," Associated Press, May 16, 2005.

16. "Adoption Becoming Easier for Gays," CBS Radio News, October 29, 2003. See also: "Adoption by Gays and Lesbians: A National Survey of Adoption Agency Policies, Practices, and Attitudes," released by the Evan D. Donaldson Adoption Institute, October 29, 2003.

17. "Lesbian and Gay Parenting: A Resource for Psychologists," review released 1995 by American Psychological Association, co-published by APA's Committee on Women in Psychology, Committee on Lesbian and Gay Concerns, and Committee on Children, Youth, and Families. See also, Charlotte J. Patterson, "Children of Lesbian and Gay Parents," *Child Development* 63 (1992): 1025–42; "Families of the Lesbian Baby Boom: Parent's Division of Labor and Children's Adjustments," *Developmental Psychology* 31 (1995): 115–23; "Lesbian Mothers, Gay Fathers, and Their Children," in A. R. D'Augelli and C. J. Patterson, eds., *Lesbian, Gay, and Bisexual Identities over the Lifespan: Psychological Perspectives* (New York: Oxford University Press, 1995).

18. The court's opinion appears at www.ca11.uscourts.gov/opinions/ops/ 200116723.pdf.

19. Gina Holland, "U.S. Supreme Court Sidesteps Gay Adoption Case; Conservatives Cheer Decision," Associated Press, January 10, 2005.

20. Another source for up-to-date state laws is the Human Rights Campaign website at www.hrc.org.

21. Louise B. Silverstein and Carl F. Auerbach, "Deconstructing the Essential Father," *American Psychologist* 54, no.6 (June 1999): 397–407.

22. Shauna Curphey, "Lesbian, Single-mother Families Still Face Hurdles," *Women's eNews*, January 14, 2003.

23. Felicia R. Lee, "Driven by Costs, Fertility Clients Head Overseas," *New York Times*, January 25, 2005. On the other hand, see also: Su-

zanne Leigh, "Reproductive Tourism: Foreign Moms Flock to USA for In Vitro Procedures," *USA Today,* May 2, 2005.
24. For up-to-date state laws, see the RESOLVE website at www.resolve.org.
25. As reported by the Focus on the Family founder James C. Dobson, Freedom Club Report (May 2004).
26. Whitehead's testimony before the Committee on Health, Education, Labor and Pensions Subcommittee on Children and Families, U.S. Senate, took place April 28, 2004.
27. See the Healthy Marriage Initiative, Administration for Children and Families, U.S. Department of Health and Human Services, www.acf.hhs.gov/healthymarriage/index.html.
28. Theodora Ooms, Stacey Bouchet, and Mary Parke, "Beyond Marriage Licenses: Efforts in States to Strengthen Marriage and Two-parent Families," Center for Law and Social Policy, April 2004. See also: Testimony of Theodora Ooms before the Committee on Finance Subcommittee on Social Security and Family Policy, U.S. Senate, hearing on "The Benefits of a Healthy Marriage" (May 5, 2004).

15. How Are the Kids Turning Out?

1. Barbara Risman, *Gender Vertigo: American Families in Transition* (New Haven, CT: Yale University Press, 1998). See especially pages 128–62.
2. David Popenoe and Barbara Dafoe Whitehead, "The Marrying Kind: Why Men Marry and Why," National Marriage Project, Rutgers University, 2004.
3. Rahel Musleah, "Finding a Village," *Hadassah Magazine* (March 2005): 18.

Recommended Resources

In addition to the sources cited in Notes, these books, articles, and websites may be of interest to readers. Note that the choicemoms.org website includes up-to-date recommendations as well as book reviews by Choice Moms.

SINGLE MOTHERHOOD

Engber, Andrea and Leah Klungness. *The Complete Single Mother.* Avon, MA: Adams Media, 2000.

Lamott, Anne. *Operating Instructions: A Journal of My Son's First Year.* New York: Pantheon, 1993.

Mattes, Jane. *Single Mothers by Choice.* New York: Three Rivers Press, 1994.

Sarah, Rachel. *Single Mom Seeking: Playdates, Blind Dates and Other Dispatches from the Dating World.* Emeryville, CA: Seal Press, 2006.

Sloan, Louise. *Knock Yourself Up: A Tell-All Guide to Becoming a Single Mom.* New York: Avery, 2007.

Websites

choicemoms.org — author's community of interactive tools and updated resources

choosingsinglemotherhood.com — details about this book and its author

groups.yahoo.com/group/choicemoms/ — author's online discussion site for Choice Moms, with an emphasis on in-depth conversation and resources

singlemothers.org — good resource by the author Andrea Engber singlemothersbychoice.com — support networks for Thinkers, Tryers, and Choice Moms

USING A DONOR

Aizley, Harlyn. *Author Buying Dad: One Woman's Search for the Perfect Sperm Donor.* New York: Alyson Publications, 2003. (Available at harlynaizley.com)

Brill, Stephanie and Preston Sacks. *New Essential Guide to Lesbian Conception, Pregnancy & Birth.* New York: Alyson Books, 2006.

Daniels, Ken. *Building a Family with the Assistance of Donor Insemination.* New Zealand: Dunmore Press, 2004. (Available at infertilitynetwork.org)

Domar, Alice D. *Conquering Infertility: Mind/Body Guide to Enhancing Fertility and Coping with Infertility.* New York: Penguin, 2002.

Ehrensaft, Diane. *Mommies, Daddies, Donors, Surrogates: Answering Tough Questions and Building Strong Families.* New York: Guilford Press, 2005.

Glazer, Ellen Sarasohn and Evelina Weidman. *Having Your Baby Through Egg Donation.* Indianapolis: Perspectives Press, 2005.

Lorbach, Caroline. *Experiences of Donor Conception Parents, Offspring and Donors Through the Years.* London: Jessica Kingsley Publishers, 2003. (Available at infertilitynetwork.org)

Montuschi, Olivia. Telling & Talking series. (dcnetwork.org, 2006)

Morrissette, Mikki. *Choice Mom Guide to Fertility.* Minneapolis: Be-Mondo Publishing, 2007.

Morrissette, Mikki, ed. Voices of Donor Conception series. Minneapolis: Be-Mondo Publishing, 2006.

Noble, Elizabeth. *Having Your Baby by Donor Insemination: A Complete Resource Guide.* Boston: Houghton Mifflin, 1988. (Old but thorough; used copies available at amazon.com)

Vercollone, Carol Frost and Heidi and Robert Moss. *Helping the Stork: The Choices and Challenges of Donor Insemination.* New York: MacMillan, 1997.

Weschler, Toni. *Taking Charge of Your Fertility: The Definitive Guide to Natural Birth Control, Pregnancy Achievement and Reproductive Health.* New York: HarperCollins, 2006.

For the Kids

Gordon, Elaine. *Mommy, Did I Grow in Your Tummy? Where Babies Come From.* E. M. Santa Monica: Greenberg Press, 1992. (Available at elainegordon.com)

Grimes, Janice. *Before You Were Born . . .* X, Y, and Me Books, 2003. Separate titles for single mothers who used donor insemination, egg donation, IVF, or embryo adoption. (Available at xyandme.com)

Our Story — Illustrated storybooks for young children. Separate books for children conceived through egg donation, through sperm donation into single-parent families, or through sperm donation into lesbian-parent families. (Available at dcnetwork.org)

Paul, J., ed. *How I Began: The Story of Donor Insemination.* Australia: Royal Woman's Hospital, 1988. Explanation for kids ages 5–8 about basic human anatomy, conception, insemination, and birth. (Available at infertilitynetwork.org)

Websites

dcnetwork.org — website of the UK-based Donor Conception Network

donorsiblingregistry.com — assists individuals in mutual consent contact with biological relatives conceived through sperm or egg donation

fertilityneighborhood.com — information on "how to choose a fertility clinic," and more

fertilityplus.org — good layman's source for sperm banks and fertility procedures, including home insemination

hrc.org — HRC (Human Rights Campaign) offers excellent information about politics, policy, and alternative family building, including sample agreements to use with known donors and valuable information about the process (find under "Family: Parenting" on hrc.org)

infertilitynetwork.org — offers an impressive library of information and support

maiamidwifery.com — offers phone consultations about donor negotiations and more

perspectivespress.com — books about fertility and adoption

spermcenter.com — helpful guide to banks and donors, created by a Choice Mom

surrogacy.com — good resource about legal and emotional issues related to egg donation, gestational carriers, and surrogates

Sperm Banks

Check the choicemoms.org website for up-to-date recommendations. Also check spermcenter.com for easy-to-use access to basic information about the roughly 1,500 donors any given month at one of the U.S.'s 20-plus sperm banks. Note that what follows is not an all-inclusive list, but is a guide to reliable sperm banks that are friendly to single women.

BioGenetics Corp. *(ethnically diverse)*, Mountainside, NJ. 908/654-8836, www.sperm1.com

California Cryobank Inc. *(large selection)*, Los Angeles, CA. 800/231-3373 or 310/443-5244, www.cryobank.com

New England Cryogenic Center, Brookline, MA. 800/991-4999 or 617/244-4447, www.necryogenic.com

Pacific Reproductive Services *(self-insemination and known-donor friendly)*, San Francisco, CA. 888/469-5800 or 415/487-2288, www.hellobaby.com

The Sperm Bank of California *(nonprofit, research-oriented, pioneering)*, Berkeley, CA. 510/841-1858, www.thespermbankofca.org

Xytex Corp. *(full service)*, Augusta, GA 30904, 800/277-3210, www.xytex.com

ADOPTION

Brodzinsky, David M., Marshall D. Schecter, and Robin Marantz Henig. *Being Adopted: The Lifelong Search for Self.* New York: First Anchor Books, 1993.

Eldridge, Sherrie. *Twenty Things Adopted Kids Wish Their Adoptive Parents Knew.* Ringoes, NJ: Tapestry Books, 1999.

Gilman, Lois. *The Adoption Resource Book.* New York: Harper Perennial, 1998.

Melina, Lois Ruskai. *Raising Adopted Children: Practical Reassuring Advice for Every Adoptive Parent.* New York: Harper Collins, 1998.

Morrissette, Mikki. *Choice Mom Guide to Adoption.* Minneapolis: Be-Mondo Publishing, 2008.

Pavao, Joyce Maguire. *The Family of Adoption.* Boston: Beacon Press, 2005.

Pertman, Adam. *Adoption Nation: How the Adoption Revolution Is Transforming America.* New York: Basic Books, 2001.

Varon, Lee. *Adopting on Your Own.* New York: Farrar, Strauss and Giroux, 2000.

Transracial

Register, Cheri. *Beyond Good Intentions: A Mother Reflects on Raising Internationally Adopted Children.* St. Paul, MN: Yeong & Yeong Books, 2005.

Wright, Marguerite. *I'm Chocolate, You're Vanilla: Raising Healthy Black*

and Biracial Children in a Race-Conscious World. San Francisco:
Jossey-Bass, 2000.
eeadopt.org — Eastern European Adoption Coalition
frua.org — Families for Russian Ukranian Adoption
fwcc.org — Families with Children from China
lapa.com — Latin American Parents Association
ocdf.org — Our Chinese Daughters Foundation
pactadopt.org — Pact offers great educational material for parents of
transracial families. Its program "Building Connections Across Cultures" is especially helpful.
simpleasthat.com — As Simple As That offers excellent resources that educate and entertain multicultural families, particularly those with children ages 3 to 8.

For the Kids

Lewis, Rose A. *I Love You Like Crazy Cakes.* New York: Little, Brown
Young Readers, 2000.
Shoettle, Marilyn. *W.I.S.E. Up Powerbook.* Ringoes, NJ: Tapestry Books,
2000. A 30-page workbook to give children ages 6 to 12 the tools to
choose how to respond to questions that come from benign curiosity,
ignorance, or intended insult.
Thomas, Eliza. *The Red Blanket.* New York: Scholastic, 2004. Sweet picture book for preschool children about a mother and her adopted
child.

General Websites

adopting.com — good guide to resources
adopting.org — good source for support
adoptionattorneys.org — source for finding lawyers specializing in
adoption
adoptivefamilies.com — excellent, comprehensive resource
adoptuskids.org — features photos of U.S. children awaiting adoption
angelfire.com/journal/adoptionhelp/adopthelp.html — excellent guide to
covering adoption expenses
childwelfare.gov/adoption/index.cfm — Child Welfare Information Gateway offers great information, including a U.S. directory of foster care
and adoption resources
davethomasfoundation.org — specializes in North America's foster care
system
everychildinc.org — specializes in special needs adoption and foster care

fwcc.org/financing.htm — useful 2003 article on financing Chinese adoptions, but applicable to anyone; includes other financing resources
irs.gov — search "adoption" for up-to-date tax benefit information and forms
nacac.org — education and advocacy
tapestrybooks.com — invaluable source of books about the entire adoptive process, including recommended books for young children

CHILDFREE LIVING

Carter, Jean and Michael. *Sweet Grapes: How to Stop Being Infertile and Start Living Again.* Indianapolis: Perspectives Press, 1998.
Defago, Nicki. *Childfree and Loving It!* London: Vision, 2005.
Engel, Beverly. *The Parenthood Decision: Discovering Whether You Are Ready and Willing to Become a Parent.* New York: Main Street Books, 1998.
Ireland, Mardy. *Reconceiving Women: Separating Motherhood from Female Identity.* New York: Guilford Press, 1993.
Safer, Jeanne. *Beyond Motherhood: Choosing a Life Without Children.* New York: Pocket, 1996.
nokidding.net — helps people form and join support groups with others who are childfree
resolve.org — includes a helpful childfree section

POLITICS

Coontz, Stephanie. *The Way We Never Were: American Families and the Nostalgia Trap.* New York: Basic Books, 2000.
Drexler, Peggy. *Raising Boys Without Men: How Maverick Moms Are Creating the Next Generation of Exceptional Men.* New York: Rodale, 2005.
Golombok, Susan. *Parenting: What Really Counts?* London: Routledge, 2000.
Hertz, Rosanna. *Single by Chance, Mothers by Choice: How Women Are Choosing Parenthood Without Marriage and Creating the New American Family.* New York: Oxford University Press, 2006.
Mapes, Diane, ed. *Single State of the Union: Single Women Speak Out On*

Life, Love, and the Pursuit of Happiness. Emeryville, CA: Seal Press, 2007.

Mintz, Stephen. *Domestic Revolutions: A Social History of American Family Life.* New York: Free Press, 1993.